Tourist Experience

To consume tourism is to consume experiences. An understanding of the ways in which tourists experience the places and people they visit is, therefore, fundamental to the study of the consumption of tourism. Consequently, it is not surprising that attention has long been paid in the tourism literature to particular perspectives on the tourist experience, including demand factors, tourist motivation, typologies of tourists and issues related to authenticity, commodification, image and perception. However, as tourism has continued to expand in both scale and scope, and as tourists' needs and expectations have become more diverse and complex in response to transformations in the dynamic socio-cultural world of tourism, so too have tourist experiences.

Tourist Experience provides a focused analysis into tourist experiences that reflect their ever-increasing diversity and complexity, and their significance and meaning to tourists themselves. Written by leading international scholars, it offers new insights into emergent behaviours, motivations and sought meanings on the part of tourists based on five contemporary themes determined by current research activity in tourism experience: dark tourism experiences, experiencing poor places, sport tourism experiences, writing the tourist experience and researching tourist experiences: methodological approaches.

The book critically explores these experiences from multidisciplinary perspectives and includes case studies from a wide range of geographical regions. By analysing these contemporary tourist experiences, the book will provide further understanding of the consumption of tourism.

Richard Sharpley is Professor of Tourism and Development at the University of Central Lancashire (UCLan), Preston, UK. He has previously held positions at a number of other institutions, including the University of Northumbria (Reader in Tourism) and the University of Lincoln, where he was Professor of Tourism and Head of Department, Tourism and Recreation Management. His principal research interests are within the fields of tourism and development, island tourism, rural tourism and the sociology of tourism.

Philip R. Stone is a former management consultant within the tourism and hospitality sector, and is presently employed as a Senior Lecturer with the University of Central Lancashire (UCLan), UK. He teaches tourism, hospitality and event management at undergraduate and postgraduate level. His primary research interests revolve around dark tourism consumption and its relationship with contemporary society.

Routledge Advances in Tourism
Edited by Stephen Page
London Metropolitan University, London

Tourist Experience
Contemporary perspectives

**Edited by Richard Sharpley and
Philip R. Stone**

Routledge
Taylor & Francis Group

LONDON AND NEW YORK

First published 2011
by Routledge
2 Park Square, Milton Park, Abingdon, Oxon OX14 4RN

Simultaneously published in the USA and Canada
by Routledge
270 Madison Avenue, New York, NY 10016

Routledge is an imprint of the Taylor & Francis Group, an Informa
business

Typeset in Sabon by
Sunrise Setting Ltd, Torquay, UK
Printed and bound in Great Britain by
CPI Antony Rowe, Chippenham, Wiltshire

British Library Cataloguing in Publication Data
A catalogue record for this book is available from the British Library

Library of Congress Cataloguing in Publication Data
   Tourist experience/edited by Richard Sharpley and Philip R. Stone.
      p. cm.
   Includes bibliographical references and index.
   1. Tourism.   2. Tourists. I. Sharpley, Richard, 1956 – II. Stone,
Philip R.
   G155.A1T5983 2010
   338.4'791–dc22   2010006257

ISBN: 978-0-415-57278-1 (hbk)
ISBN: 978-0-203-85594-2 (ebk)

Contents

List of figures

List of tables

Contributors

Barbara A. Carmichael is a Professor in the Department of Geography and Environmental Studies and the Director of NEXT Research Centre (Centre for the Study of Nascent Entrepreneurship and the Exploitation of Technology) in the School of Business and Economics at Wilfrid Laurier University, Waterloo, Ontario, Canada. She has an MBA from Durham University Business School, United Kingdom and a PhD from the University of Victoria, British Columbia. Her research interests are in tourism entrepreneurship, quality tourism experiences, special events, casino impacts, market segmentation and resident attitudes towards tourism.

Daniel R. Fesenmaier is a Professor in the School of Tourism & Hospitality Management at Temple University and Director of the National Laboratory for Tourism and eCommerce. He is also a Visiting Principal Research Fellow at the University of Wollongong. Daniel received his PhD in Geography from the University of Western Ontario, Canada. His research interests include destination marketing, advertising evaluation and information technology, and he is currently Managing Editor of the *Journal of Information Technology & Tourism*.

Sean Gammon is a Senior Lecturer at the University of Central Lancashire, Preston, UK, in the Department of Sport, Tourism and the Outdoors. He is currently undertaking research exploring the environmental psychological transactions that occur between sport places and individuals. Sean has written extensively in sport tourism, particularly in areas associated with motivation, heritage and nostalgia. Additionally, he continues to write and investigate the pedagogic strengths of incorporating leisure-related experiences into Higher Education teaching and learning.

Mary Beth Gouthro is Lecturer and Programme Leader at the School of Services Management at Bournemouth University, Dorset, UK. She currently leads the programme delivery of the BA (Honours) in Events Management programme, and lectures at the first and final year of the degree programme. Her research interests span the experience of consumption in areas that include tourism, events and leisure settings. She has published in the areas of event satisfaction in festivals, tourism consumption in heritage settings and perspectives on qualitative research approaches. Other research interests include festival and event volunteering, event motivation and qualitative research methodologies adopted in the scope of services management. Mary Beth's industry and consultancy experience spans the charity sector, corporate organisations, small business and government.

Ulrike Gretzel is an Assistant Professor in the Department of Recreation, Park & Tourism Sciences at Texas A&M University, USA and Director of the Laboratory for Intelligent Systems in Tourism. She is also a Visiting Principal Research Fellow at the University of Wollongong. She received her PhD in Communications from the University of Illinois at Urbana-Champaign, USA. Her research focuses on the representation of tourism experiences through digital media and on persuasion in human-computer interactions.

Tazim Jamal is an Associate Professor in the Department of Recreation, Park & Tourism Sciences, Texas A&M University, USA. Her research addresses theoretical and methodological issues in tourism, as well as collaborative tourism planning and sustainability in travel and tourism. She is especially interested in issues of dwelling and experience, climate change, community and eco-cultural sustainability. She teaches courses on tourism impacts, heritage tourism, sustainable tourism, international tourism and philosophy of social research. Tazim is the Co-Editor of *The SAGE Handbook of Tourism Studies* (2009). She has published widely in the tourism literature and is an editorial board member of several peer-reviewed journals.

Tony Johnston comes from Co. Donegal in the north-west of the Republic of Ireland and is completing a doctorate in Geography at the National University of Ireland, Galway (expected graduation 2010). His PhD focuses on the commodification of war space in the Balkans, particularly examining dark tourism in the post-war countries of ex-Yugoslavia. This PhD work is supervised by Professor Ulf Strohmayer. Tony's research is particularly focused on tourism geographies and has been presented at a variety of national and international geographical and tourism forums.

Naomi Kirkup is a postgraduate research student at Newcastle Business School, Northumbria University, Newcastle upon Tyne, UK. Her research interests lie in sport tourism with a particular focus on Olympic tourism and participant behaviour utilising qualitative methodologies. Her doctoral research focused on understanding Olympic tourist behaviour, especially those that undertake international travel to watch the Olympic Games. Although a relatively new researcher, Naomi has written an article published in the *Journal of Sport and Tourism* as well as presenting her research at two international conferences – one in Beijing and one in the UK.

Naomi also presented her research at a one-day conference funded by the ESRC on leveraging the benefits of the London 2012 Games. Naomi's research was featured in an article in the European edition of the *Wall Street Journal* in 2008.

Emma-Reetta Koivunen is a doctoral candidate in the Department of Information and Communications in Manchester Metropolitan University. Her research examines the social construction of the Shetland Islands in the context of tourism and the Internet. She has a master's degree in Social Anthropology from the University of Helsinki; her research analysed the impact of local community to the ways individuals use and conceptualise the Internet on the island of Fair Isle in Shetland. Her other research interests include the meaning of tourism for local communities and individuals taking part in it, the use of the Internet in everyday life, technology and gendered practices. She has presented in various conferences and co-authored an article on collaborative research practices in the *Journal of Research Practice*.

Yoon Jung Lee is a PhD candidate in the Department of Recreation, Park & Tourism Sciences, Texas A&M University, USA and a research assistant in the Laboratory for Intelligent Systems in Tourism. Yoon Jung's PhD thesis focuses on the experiences of short-term mission travellers. Her research interests also include volunteer tourism experiences as well as the formation of personal and social identity through blogs.

Linda Lelo is a doctoral student in the Department of Recreation, Park & Tourism Sciences, Texas A&M University, USA. Her research interests include dark tourism, tourism in Africa and African American tourists. Her dissertation topic is related to African American visitors to sites associated with slavery.

Mac McCarthy is a Senior Lecturer at the University of Central Lancashire, Preston, UK and also an Associate Lecturer with the Open University. He has developed and delivered professional development programmes for postgraduate students from a range of disciplines primarily in service sectors. He has been involved with researching the experiences of players in gay football teams in the UK, and its impact on personal development and community involvement. He is currently examining the responses of premier division football clubs to the FA strategy on homophobia. He has also worked as an independent management consultant, with a client base in the public and private sector throughout Western and Eastern Europe, as well as in Canada and Thailand.

Palloma Menezes is a PhD student in Sociology at the University Research Institute of Rio de Janeiro, Brazil. She has published articles on favela tourism in leading journals in Brazil and has written a thesis on the relationship between favela tourism, violence and heritage. At the moment, she is writing a dissertation on the experiences of The Pacifier Police Division (UPP), a new model of public security and policing that intends to bring police and population closer together, as well as to strengthen social policies inside favelas. By re-establishing control over areas that for decades were occupied by traffic and, recently, also by militias, the UPP is 'trying to bring peace' to favelas like Morro Santa Marta, Cidade de Deus, Jardim Batam and Morro da Babilônia e Chapéu Mangueira. Created by the current administration of Rio de Janeiro's Security Department, the UPP work with the principle of the Communitarian Police.

Martine C. Middleton is Senior Lecturer in Tourism and Leisure Management at the University of Central Lancashire School of Sport, Tourism and the Outdoors, with a PhD in Human Geography. Her research interests include environmental psychology, urban tourism, discourse analysis and cross-cultural behaviour. A central tenet to her applied research is the advocation and use of mixed methodologies: Q-sort techniques, NVivo and numerous contemporary research techniques. Publications include journal articles, book chapters and conference proceedings both within the UK and the wider academic community.

Sarah Quinlan Cutler is a PhD candidate in the Geography and Environmental Studies Department at Wilfrid Laurier University, Waterloo, Canada. Her research interests include tourist experiences, educational tourism, visitor management, travel guidebooks and responsible tourism practices.

Manfred Rolfes is Professor of Regional Science and Applied Human Geography at the University of Potsdam. Formerly he was a researcher at the Department of Geography, University of Osnabrück and at the Centre for Research on Higher Education and Work, University of Kassel. His research interests centre on interdisciplinary urban studies (socially integrative urban development; evaluation and steering of urban development; universities and urban development), uncertainties, risks and space (geography of crime and (un)certainties; mass media, risks and space semantics), and slumming in developing countries or emerging nations, especially the development and effects of touristic space semantics. His last book, co-authored with others, is *Townships as Attraction: An Empirical Study of Township Tourism in Cape Town* (2009).

Chris Ryan is the Foundation Professor of Tourism at the University of Waikato, Editor of the journal *Tourism Management* and the winner of a lifetime achievement award from the Taiwan Leisure and Recreation Association. Born in South Wales, Chris began teaching in Further Education in Nottingham and then joined the Nottingham Business School. He has since worked in Australia, Canada, the USA and now New Zealand, while his Visiting Professorships include those at Beijing International Studies University and the Emirates Academy, Dubai. His experience is international in nature, and he has worked in advisory capacities including at APEC Tourism Ministers level. In the last few years most of his research has been in China and Dubai, but his refereed journal publications (well over 100 in number) reveal past research with indigenous peoples of New Zealand and Australia, as well as studies of tourist behaviours and experiences in each of the countries in which he has worked. His books include *Tourism in China* (2008), *The Tourist Experience* (2002), *Recreational Tourism: Demand and Impacts* (2003), *Indigenous Tourism: The Commodification and Management of Culture* (2005 – with Michelle Aicken) and others.

Richard Sharpley is Professor of Tourism and Development at the University of Central Lancashire, Preston, UK. He has previously held positions at a number of other institutions, including the University of Northumbria (Reader in Tourism) and the University of Lincoln, where he was Professor of Tourism and Head of Department, Tourism and Recreation Management. His principal research interests are within the fields of tourism and development, island tourism, rural tourism and the sociology of tourism, and his books include *Tourism and Development in the Developing World* (2008), *Tourism, Tourists and Society*, 4th edn (2008) and *Tourism, Development and Environment: Beyond Sustainability* (2009).

Richard Shipway is Senior Lecturer in the School of Services Management, Bournemouth University, UK. His research interests lie in sport tourism, Olympic studies and the impacts of sport events. His recent work has focused on Olympic-related research themes connected with the 2012 Games, and he was previously awarded the prestigious Winston Churchill Fellowship to undertake an Olympic education project in Australia. Outside of the Olympic research arena, Richard has written several journal articles and book chapters which use ethnography to explore the lived experiences of long-distance runners. In 2008, he was instrumental in the organisation of the '1st Commonwealth Conference on Sport Tourism' in Sabah, Malaysia, attracting international industry practitioners and academic delegates with an interest in sport tourism. As a direct legacy of this conference and other international sport tourism initiatives, Richard was awarded a major ESRC (Economic and Social Research Council) project to develop future research linked to sport tourism and sport events.

Rochelle Spencer has a background working and teaching in international development and tourism having worked with the British Red Cross and Community Aid Abroad. She spent several years working in Cuba as an anthropologist conducting research for her PhD and coordinating study tours focusing on Cuba's unique social development model. Currently she is a postdoctoral research fellow on a large Australian Research Council Linkage grant with the Red Cross. The research investigates long-term community capacity building, exploring themes around active citizenship, social inclusion outcomes, and ways of working across Australian Red Cross community service programmes. Her chapter in this edited collection is drawn from her book *Development Tourism: Lessons from Cuba* (Ashgate, UK).

Davina Stanford currently works as a Research Associate for TEAM Tourism Consulting. Amongst many projects with TEAM Davina has recently coordinated, researched and contributed to a UNWTO publication *A Practical Guide to Tourism Destination Management*. The guide is an authoritative reference handbook concerning the full spectrum of activities involved in integrated destination management. Prior to joining TEAM Davina was a Commonwealth Scholar researching her PhD at the University of Wellington, New Zealand. Davina's research concentrated on understanding the role of the tourist in achieving responsible tourism in environmentally and culturally sensitive areas and she has published on this subject in the *Journal of Sustainable Tourism*.

Philip R. Stone is a former management consultant within the tourism and hospitality sector, and is presently employed as a Senior Lecturer with the University of Central Lancashire, Preston, UK. He teaches tourism, hospitality and event management at undergraduate and postgraduate level. Philip is also founder and editor of The Dark Tourism Forum, the premier online dark tourism subject resource facility and global alliance of scholars and industry practitioners (see http://www.dark-tourism.org.uk). His primary research interests revolve around dark tourism consumption and its relationship with contemporary society. He has published in a number of international academic journals, presented at a variety of international conferences and, with Richard Sharpley, is co-editor of *The Darker Side of Travel: The Theory and Practice of Dark Tourism* (2009).

Iis Tussyadiah is an Assistant Professor at the School of Tourism & Hospitality Management and affiliated with the National Laboratory for Tourism and eCommerce, Temple University, USA. Iis received her PhD degree in Human-Social Information Sciences from Tohoku University, Japan. Her current research interests include technology-assisted mediators for tourism experiences, narrative marketing in tourism and hospitality, tourists' spatiotemporal behaviour and tourist-activated networks, and urban tourism.

Introduction: thinking about the tourist experience

Richard Sharpley and
Philip R. Stone

In his now classic *Jupiter's Travels*, Ted Simon reflects upon

> the fascination with which I watch myself come closer and closer to
> merge with the world around me, dipping first a toe, then a foot, then a
> limb. Although I am made of the same stuff as the world, it used to
> seem that I might as well have been born on an asteroid, so awkward
> and unnatural was my place in the scheme of things... Then began a
> long apprenticeship, to become something certain in my own right, from
> which to see and be seen... to confirm that the world and I were, after
> all, made for each other.
>
> (Simon 1979: 176)

Like innumerable others before him and since, Simon is writing about a
journey. More specifically, he is writing about a four-year trip around the
world on a motorbike (named 'Jupiter'), vividly describing the places he visits
and passes through, the people he meets, and his adventures (and disasters)
related to his mode of transport. Significantly, he also reflects at length on his
personal experiences: his relationships with the people, places and cultures he
encounters, the purpose of his journey and, in particular, his own life and how
it has been transformed by his travels. Thus, his book is, in a sense, a story of
two journeys: the physical trip through time and space, with an identifiable
beginning and end; and a personal, spiritual journey of discovery and transformation extending beyond the temporal boundaries of the actual trip.

Interestingly, over 25 years later and at the age of 69, Ted Simon recreated
or, maybe, attempted to relive the original journey by embarking on another
global motorbike ride that was to last two years. Implicit in his subsequent
account (Simon 2007) is his disappointment that not only had many of the
places he originally travelled through changed dramatically, challenging his
remembered experiences of them, but also that he too had changed, that
perhaps the world and he were, in fact, no longer 'made for each other'.
Ironically, the meaning of his travels had in some way been transformed,
from a voyage of discovery into a nostalgic journey into the past, something
that he accepts in the title of that account: *Dreaming of Jupiter*.

Nevertheless, Simon's books together are, on the one hand, just one example of a genre of writing that has existed for almost as long as people have had the means or ability to engage in travel (Robinson and Andersen 2002). Since Herodotus, the fifth-century BC Greek historian, wrote about his extensive travels – and is thus widely considered to be the first 'travel writer' – innumerable travellers (or tourists?) have written about their experiences, in so doing undoubtedly inspiring countless others to follow in their footsteps or, in Simon's case, tyre-tracks (see, for example, McGregor and Boorman 2005).

On the other hand, they are also, along with much other travel writing, populist or journalistic evidence of what has long been recognised and considered within the academic study of tourism: that to consume tourism is to consume experiences; moreover, that tourist experiences are not uniform, even within specific contexts and places. Whether on extended overland adventures as described in much travel writing or on a more 'typical' one- or two-week holiday (though there is, perhaps, no longer a 'typical' holiday), the tourist experience is unique to the individual tourist. The personal significance of tourism or holidays is largely defined by an individual tourist's own socio-cultural world – as Urry (1990a: 23) observes, 'explaining the consumption of tourist services cannot be separated off from the social relations in which they are embedded' – and that social world is dynamic and continually evolving. Equally, the ways in which tourists interact with destination environments, cultures and communities is very much determined by their own 'cultural baggage'; their perceptions, values, experience, knowledge, attitudes, and so on. It is often said that, by going away on holiday, you can escape from those around you but you cannot escape from yourself. The implication is, therefore, that there are as many tourist experiences as there are tourists, each experience defined by the individual tourist, the 'social fabric that surrounds them' (Ryan 1997a: 1) and their consequential relationship with the destination. Hence, understanding the nature of the tourist experience would seem to be a difficult, if not impossible task.

Nevertheless, tourism as a social phenomenon, involving the movement of millions of people both across international borders and within their own countries, cannot be understood without knowledge and explanation of the meaning or significance of tourism to tourists themselves, of their interactions with the sites, attractions, events and people they encounter, and of the multitude of intrinsic and extrinsic factors that influence the nature and outcomes of those interactions. In short, fundamental to the study of tourism is the study of the tourist experience. It is not surprising, therefore, that attention has long been paid to it in the tourism literature from a variety of now well-known 'micro' perspectives familiar to anyone concerned with the study of tourism, such as tourism demand factors, tourist motivation, typologies of tourists and issues related to authenticity, commodification, image and perception. At the same time, equally well-known seminal works, such as those by Cohen (1979a), MacCannell (1976) and Urry (1990a; 2002), have proposed broader meta-theories of how tourist experiences are framed or constructed by the social world of the tourist.

We shall return to these shortly, suggesting in particular that the need exists for more focused research into tourist experiences that reflect their ever-increasing diversity and complexity and their significance and meaning to tourists, hence the collection of contemporary studies presented in this book. First, however, it is useful to consider two questions relevant to the study of tourist experiences: what do we actually mean by the term 'the tourist experience'; and, what influence, if any, has the increasing social institutionalisation and, in particular, what might be described as the 'consumerisation' of tourism had on the nature of that tourist experience?

The former is, at first sight, relatively easy to answer; the tourist experience is, by definition, what people experience as tourists. However, a distinction must immediately be made between the specific services (often referred to as experiences) consumed by tourists within the context of a temporally defined holiday or period away from home, and the broader experience (*the tourist experience*) that they collectively contribute to. Tourist services/experiences may be thought of as those that are produced or provided by the myriad businesses, organisations and individuals that comprise the tourism sector; they are, in a sense, commoditised experiences that meet an immediate need (a meal, a flight on an aeroplane, accommodation, entertainment, etc.) and hopefully bring immediate but short-term satisfaction or benefits. *The tourism experience*, conversely, is the experience of being a tourist, which results not only from a particular combination of provided experiences, but also from the meaning or significance accorded to it by the tourist in relation to his or her normal socio-cultural existence (most usually considered in terms of the experience of difference, novelty or the 'Other'), and which may be mediated by characteristics of the destination.

Implicitly, therefore, the tourism experience brings longer lasting benefits or rewards to the tourist, perhaps fulfilling socially determined needs or objectives; for if it does not, what logic would there be in continuing to seek the tourist experience? Of course, logic might not be a defining element of the consumption of tourism – tourism has long been described as irrational behaviour corresponding to a 'lemming effect' (Emery 1981) – but, nevertheless, the tourist experience is, in effect, the significance of engaging in tourism. However, this immediately begs the question, when is one a tourist and not a tourist? Particular forms of tourism, such as a short-break or a two-week holiday, are temporally defined, yet the meaning or benefits of these commence with anticipation and continue with memories, which subsequently feed back into anticipating the subsequent period of tourism consumption. Thus, the tourist experience may be continual (particularly if one agrees with Urry's (1994) assertion that, from a postmodern perspective, most people are tourists most of the time, though defined in relation to their dynamic social existence in general and by their maturation as tourists – or by their ascent of the 'travel career ladder' (Pearce 2005) – in particular. In this sense, the tourist experience then becomes not an experience determined by and distinct from the tourist's normal socio-cultural life but, rather, one element of it. Indeed, whilst this has undoubtedly long been the case for 'professional' tourists, such as Ted Simon, whose life, living and identity has been largely determined by his travel experiences, the same may now be said for tourists more generally.

This latter point relates to the second question above, namely, the extent to which the institutionalisation and consumerisation of tourism together have influenced the nature of the tourist experience. By institutionalisation, we mean that tourism has evolved, at least in western, developed nations, into a social institution; it has become an accepted, expected, 'democratised' (Urry 1990b), socially-sanctioned feature of contemporary social life, to the extent that to voluntarily exclude oneself from participation in tourism of any kind might be thought of as unusual behaviour. For example, a number of (non-academic) surveys in the UK have revealed that some tourists admit to not finding their annual summer-sun vacation a pleasurable experience, yet they continue to book their holidays year after year, perhaps finding it easier to endure the holiday than to explain why they would prefer to stay at home! Consumerisation, conversely, is used here as a term to describe the way in which tourism, along with other leisure activities, has come to be defined by commercial production and consumption; that is, where once leisure was active, simple and reflective, based upon an individual's intelligence, imagination and wit, there has been a move, according to Ramsay (2005: 31), 'towards fun and fashion, pampering rather than developing, lifestyle rather than living, buying into activities that are more isolating, though easily repeatable. In short, we have commodified leisure'.

Referring to tourism in particular, Ramsay goes on to cite John Carroll who, in his book *Ego and Soul: The Modern West in Search of Meaning* (Carroll 1998) describes contemporary tourism as the 'greatest and most successful lie of western, consumerist culture' (Ramsay 2005:102). By this, he suggests that tourists, through buying the annual summer holiday, believe they are purchasing a ticket to authentic encounters with people and places, to freedom from responsibility, from the consumerist realities of the everyday. In reality, according to Carroll, both tourists and the tourism industry are collaborating in a hoax where 'tourists persuade themselves that they are heroic and happy while in fact clinging to the few traces of the everyday which the holiday package allows them' (Ramsay 2005: 102). Far from escaping a consumerist routine, tourists are simply purchasing the opportunity to continue that routine elsewhere and, as a consequence, achieve instantaneous, short-lived consumption-based rewards, but are unlikely to benefit from reflective, developmental or meaningful experiences that are often claimed to be the purpose or outcomes of participating in tourism.

Taken together, the institutionalisation and consumerisation of tourism might suggest that tourists have largely become passive participants, encouraged by the belief that it is a socially sanctioned necessity and by the dreams promised by the tourism industry. By implication, the tourist experience has become shallow, short lived and, perhaps, meaningless. This is not, however, a new argument. Rather, it simply reflects a debate that commenced with the beginnings of mass transport systems (that is, the train) in the mid-nineteenth century and, in one form or another, has continued ever since. For example, ruing the advent of mass travel, in 1869 the novelist Henry James described the then new tourists as 'vulgar, vulgar, vulgar', epitomising the traveller–tourist dichotomy that continues to underpin arguments surrounding the 'lost art of travel'. Indeed, in a chapter of that name, Daniel Boorstin famously lamented the 'decline of the traveller and the rise of the tourist', with all that implied for the nature of the contemporary tourist experience:

> The traveller, then was working at something; the tourist was a pleasure seeker. The traveller was active; he went strenuously in search of people, of adventure, of experience. The tourist is passive; he expects interesting things to happen to him... he expects everything to be done to him and for him.
>
> (Boorstin 1964: 85)

Importantly, however, and as already noted above, the tourist experience is largely defined by the tourist's own socio-cultural world, a world that is constantly dynamic and evolving. Thus, whilst the rational, modernist culture of the first half of the twentieth century, characterised in the context of production-consumption by Fordist mass production, the dominance of the producer and the diluted, homogeneous cultural value of mass goods and services, (collectively referred to by Featherstone (1990) as the 'production of consumption'), was undoubtedly mirrored in the production, consumption and experience of tourism in particular, the subsequent emergence of a post-Fordist consumer culture, within which the consumer becomes dominant and the act of consumption has taken on wider socio-cultural significance (Lury 1996), has also undoubtedly been reflected in the practice and meaning of tourism. Not only do tourists enjoy a far wider choice of experiences (in the sense of experiences as products) – a vast array of new places, attractions, events and peoples have become commoditised as tourism products – but, as a result of technological advance, particularly the Internet, and innovation in the delivery of tourist services, they are able to actively exercise those choices according to the personal significance they attach to tourism in general, and to specific places, activities and experiences in particular. By implication, therefore, the nature of the tourist experience has itself become more complex; although tourism continues, perhaps, to play a functional role as a 'safety valve' that maintains society in good working order (Krippendorf 1986), the ways in which this role is fulfilled has also become more diverse, complex and personal to the individual tourist. For some, the hedonistic consumerist experience of the seaside may suffice; for others, it may be the experience of difference, danger or 'darkness' (Stone and Sharpley 2008) that is significant. Whatever the case, it is evident that the institutionalisation and consumerisation of tourism, far from diluting or simplifying the tourist experience, have rendered it increasingly diverse and complex.

Against this background, the tourist experience has long been the focus of tourism studies, particularly within a sociological framework. Indeed, with the exception of work on the economic benefits of tourism development, much of the early social scientific study of tourism was concerned with explaining and understanding the tourist and the tourist experience from both a micro-sociological/phenomenological and a structural perspective. For example, Cohen's early and still much-cited work on tourist typologies (Cohen 1972; 1974; 1979a) established a firm foundation for numerous subsequent models and typologies, whilst the study of tourism demand in general and tourist motivation in particular has remained a dominant theme in the study of tourism. Similarly, issues surrounding the concept of authenticity – a central theme in the study of the tourist experience – have long attracted academic attention (Cohen 1988a; Hughes 1995; Mehmetoglu and Olsen 2003; Wang 1999), whilst commodification, image and perception, the tourist–host relationship and so on have also proved to be popular and fruitful areas of research relevant to the understanding of the tourist experience.

At the same time, broader theories have attempted to locate and explain the tourist experience within the context of the tourist's socio-cultural world. Dean MacCannell's seminal work *The Tourist* (1976 and subsequent editions) proposes that, recognising that they inhabit an anomic, inauthentic socio-cultural world, 'modern' tourists are on a (ultimately unsuccessful or unfulfilling) quest for authenticity, although his specific concept of the tourist as a contemporary secular pilgrim has, perhaps, remained more relevant to the study of the tourist experience, inspiring more recent studies into the spiritual dimensions of tourism (Sharpley 2009). John Urry's *The Tourist Gaze* (1990a, 2002) has proved to be equally, if not more, influential in tourism studies, exploring both the evolution, democratisation and postmodern diffusion of tourism and the significance of the visual in the experience of place, although MacCannell and Urry's work is more recently criticised by the grandly self-proclaimed 'new wave' in tourism studies (Franklin 2009). Challenging the traditional 'dualisms' in tourism studies (familiarity/strangerhood; authentic/inauthentic; traditional/modern; sacred/profane; work/pleasure), this seeks to provide a more multidimensional explanation of tourism, focusing very much on the tourist but, at the same time, implying a new 'grand theory' of tourism. However, the fragmentation of work undertaken under the 'new wave' umbrella has prohibited its recognition or acceptance as a cohesive new body of knowledge.

It is not the purpose here to review the tourist experience as the focus of study within tourism; the volume of work is too great, the scope of topics and issues too broad. However, as a general observation, not only has the study of the tourist experience mostly been concerned with the relationship between tourists and 'their' world as opposed to how tourist experiences are defined by the places, events and peoples that tourists encounter but also, as tourism has continued to expand in both scale and scope, and as tourists' needs and expectations have become more diverse and complex in response to transformations in the dynamic socio-cultural world of tourism, so too have tourist experiences become more diverse and complex. As a consequence, neither earlier works on demand, motivation, and so on, nor broader 'meta-narratives' of tourist behaviour, are able to fully account for emergent motivations, behaviours and responses on the part of tourists. In other words, the need exists for more focused studies into tourist experiences that reflect their ever-increasing diversity and complexity, and their significance and meaning to tourists themselves; that, it, the tourist experience can only be understood by exploring specific contexts within which it occurs, albeit within the conceptual frameworks provided by the existing work referred to above.

The purpose of this book is to do just this. Based upon a number of papers presented at a recent international tourism conference: Tourist Experiences: Meanings, Motivations, Behaviours, hosted by the University of Central Lancashire, Preston, UK, it explores a number of contemporary themes, representative of current research activity, relevant to the understanding of tourist experiences. Following Ryan's literature-based review of different conceptualisations of the tourist experience, which reveals the complexity and diversity of the topic, the book is structured around five themes, as follows:

1 *Dark tourism experiences*: the concept of dark tourism has attracted increasing academic and media attention in recent years and is, arguably, one of the most popular contemporary issues within the area of tourist experiences. Of particular importance is the relationship between the experience of 'dark' places and the confrontation of death in contemporary societies.

2 *Experiencing poor places*: Townships, slums, favelas and other poor communities are increasingly becoming packaged and commoditised as tourist attractions, frequently by residents of these 'poor places'. Research into how and why such places are experienced by tourists enhances understanding of how tourism may mediate between poor communities and 'rich' tourists.

3 *Sport tourism experiences*: whilst sporting mega-events have long been associated with tourism, travelling to attend and participate in sports events, or visiting places where such events take place, may have significant meaning beyond the sport for those taking part.

4 *Writing the tourist experience*: information technology and new media have not only transformed how tourists communicate their experiences in time, content and style; they have also added an additional dimension to the tourism experience as 'travel writing' becomes 'travelling writing'.

5   *Researching tourist experiences: methodological approaches*: as tourist experiences become more diverse and complex, it is necessary to consider innovative and appropriate methodologies for revealing the depth and richness of tourist experiences.

This list is, of course, by no means exhaustive. As already suggested, the tourist experience is as diverse as tourists themselves whilst, given the continuing evolution and expansion of tourism in form, scope and scale, and the emergence of new tourist markets defined both geographically and socio-culturally, the nature and significance of tourist experiences will become yet more complex. Nevertheless, it is hoped that the chapters in this book will contribute to an enhanced understanding of a phenomenon that, in the early twenty-first century, continues to grow in social significance.

1 Ways of conceptualising the tourist experience: a review of literature[1]

Chris Ryan

Introduction

The purpose of this chapter is to offer a review of past literature and concepts of how tourists experience the holiday destinations they visit. However, in offering such a review, one needs to be mindful of the context within which the reviewer operates as this determines a number of key evaluations. First, it is to be assumed that the reviewer has a familiarity with the literature being reviewed but, in addition, any evaluation of such literature itself reflects the writer's own experiences as a researcher, and the context within which such research has been undertaken. Geographical context is thus important as, in part, it determines the nature of the destinations being examined and the cultural frameworks that dominate in those locations. Traditionally, the academic literature in tourist behaviour has been dominated by the North Atlantic English speaking world, which is also the home of many international business concerns. But in the twenty-first century other voices are coming much more frequently to the fore. The number of Chinese universities offering tourism is measured in the hundreds, and it might not be an exaggeration that the number of Chinese academics in our field may have alone doubled the number of academics teaching and undertaking research in tourism, even before one considers colleagues working in other Asian countries.

In many cases, an exposure to totally different ways of seeing the world would sensitise any researcher interested in human experiences to the role of culture and lead to a recognition that there are other ways of seeing the world apart from the North Atlantic post-positivistic empiricist tradition of research that, partly owing to the advent of computing power, began to frequent the academic tourism literature from the early 1990s. Taken together the work of Oceanic and Asian colleagues highlights the role of culture, language and interpretation when it comes to the question of tourism – why tourists travel, the experiences they seek, the way people of different cultures view the world, the role of difference and familiarity in travel, and the importance of acts of interpretation. To give but one example, and it is simplified, in the research conducted by Cathy Hsu, Liping Cai and Kevin Wong (2007) into the travel motives of Chinese senior citizens in Mainland

China, a series of emergent themes became evident. For many of their sample, the taking of holidays, especially any that might involve overseas travel, was an action of social irresponsibility. Such holidays were acts of frivolity not to be considered. The only possible exceptions might be holidays to visit extended family members, or perhaps holidays paid for by children who saw this as a means of discharging filial duties, again especially if it permitted visits to extended families. When one considers the changes that a 60-year-old person has experienced in China, that when they were 20 their adolescent views would have been shaped by the final decades of Maoist China, then such attitudes become more understandable. The desire to see extended family reflects a Confucian view of relationships and their importance. But of course generational differences in urban Chinese life mean different sets of expectations are emerging as a consumerist culture arises among the young.

In current research into visitor patterns at Mt Qiyun, one of the holy mountains of Taoism in China, many of the initial assumptions drawn on existing western research of visitor motives that led to initial items for a questionnaire had to be dropped as the nuances of meaning of mountain, place, temple, worship, burning incense and sunrise became clear (Ryan and Gu 2010). These factors, combined with the desire of village people for not only income enhancement but for contact with people from further afield, has given rise to a more nuanced and complex research pattern than that originally envisaged.

So, how do such observations shape research and understanding of the 'Tourist Experience'? At one level, it seems very simple. People wish to relax, learn, see new places, or see places made familiar to them by television and the Internet. It is obviously important to many people, as each year so many, but not all, spend significant sums of money on their holidays. Based on these apparently simple wishes has grown an industry of airlines, coach and bus companies, hotels, rental cars, attractions, resorts, theme parks and much else to form what some would have us believe is the world's largest industry, or to adopt Neil Leiper's (2008) terminology, an interconnected pattern of different industries. These desires are socially condoned and paradoxes emerge whereupon the reward for work is a period of non-work to be served by those working. Based on this observation, it can be argued that holidays can be important, cathartic and represent socially condoned patterns of alternative lifestyles. The parallels with the work of Bakhtin (1984, 1986) and concepts of the carnivalesque may be present when considering holiday taking behaviours. Yet the example of Chinese senior citizens has a lesson for us. If people were to view their holiday taking behaviour as involving antisocial actions, then the holiday and travel-related industries as we know them would be forced to change. Are concerns over airline carbon emissions and perceived linkages between carbon emissions and climate change sufficient to create a culture change where, like our Chinese senior citizens, travel will simply be seen as no longer socially acceptable? Social attitudes do not change overnight, but can and do change over a matter of a few decades. The general non-acceptance of smoking in a public place is today very different to what it was in the 1960s. Social consumption patterns can and do change. Or is it, as John Ap (1990, 1992) suggests, a question of social exchange theory of a basic sort, where stakeholders will engage in or accept an activity if the perceived utility is greater than the perceived cost? If it is, and he is right, then the nature of the tourist experience becomes a key to the future of the tourism industry.

Drawing on the prevailing literature of the nature of tourism experience, there are several concepts upon which to draw. These include the following:

Confirmation-disconfirmation theory of the ServQual type – a comparison between expectations and evaluations (e.g. Parasuraman *et al.* 1994).

Importance-evaluation approaches – the reasoned behaviour, multi-attribute approach. Yet these theories may not necessarily lead to high coefficients of determination when in quantitative models that postulate a given behaviour as the determined variable – perhaps because of the role of intervening or moderating variables that impinge upon the conative aspects of such models (e.g. Oh 2001). Such a comment, however, assumes that the researcher has incorporated such moderating variables into the proposed theory (for example, time constraints imposed by the simple fact of school holidays for families with young children), and a failure to introduce such variables may lead to potentially misleading high coefficients between frequency of given behaviours and suggested determinants. On the other hand, the researcher may argue that such models are not descriptions of reality, but abstractions that seek to permit predictions while being parsimonious. But, as researchers, are such caveats always made explicit in our literature?

Involvement theory – the degree to which the visitor becomes involved and the extent to which this involvement is enduring or situational. Holidays thus become extensions of life interests and not escapes from life. In the literature, examples may be found of serious recreation takers using holiday periods as major periods of meaning for their lives – meanings that are to them more important than the daily occupations in which they spend most of their year. One such example are some of the Civil War Re-enactors in the USA (see Ryan (2007a), on battlefield tourism, but also see Havitz and Dimanche (1990) on concepts of involvement in leisure).

The destination image – how it attracts, holds and establishes the criteria against which a visitor can evaluate their experience. While some of the concepts are derived from marketing theory, the subject links with all of the above perspectives. Destinations may be seen as packages of opportunity to fulfil perceived wants – and thus are not simply physical spaces but are also places of constructed meaning (e.g. Beerli and Martin 2004; Ryan and Gu 2008). Hence, as noted above, such meanings may be, at least in part, culturally determined as the visitor interacts with the place as experienced, the place as described by the tourist destination marketing organisations and, possibly, the place as a place of everyday residence.

Theories of liminality – the tourist is perceived as a person engaged in transitions from the ordinary to the extraordinary, and then back again to the ordinary – the stages marked by different formalities, ceremonies, and roles (Turner 1969, 1974, 1982). This theoretical construct has been used in explaining certain fantasies associated with tourism – for example, when analysing sex tourism (Ryan 2001) and backpacking (Cohen 1982a, 1982b).

Role play approaches – that is, the roles that tourists can adopt, and the degree to which these roles are motivated by a sense of role play. Urry (2002) has popularised the notion of the ludic playing tourists, who knowingly play 'a tourist role' because they perceive themselves as travellers and not tourists, but for the moment the tourist role bestows advantages. There is also the work of Yiannakis and Gibson (1992) and Gibson and Yiannakis (2002) where they show that a range of roles are open to tourists that reflect preferences on the dimensions of familiarity vs unfamiliarity, the structured vs the unstructured organisation and the desire for stimulating or tranquil environments. The concept of roles arguably underlies many of the market-oriented segmentation exercises found in the tourism academic literature, and while researchers have described these roles (e.g. Pearce 1982), what often remains unstated is the ease with which holidaymakers switch roles. Consequently a tourist may be today a 'hedonist', tomorrow an 'adventure tourist' and the day after, or the holiday after – a sun seeker! What do these roles possess in common? They are all the same tourist – or are they?

The Theory of the Gaze – the tourist's desire for the visually impressive (framed by the tourist's camera) means that the tourist industry shapes and directs the participant's gaze, that the gaze is framed within parameters that make sense to the gazer while others act roles as 'gazees' – or alternatively selective truths are presented that may not be truths as understood by people local to the visited place. Many citation studies have shown John Urry's (2002) concept to be much referred to – but authors like Hollinshead (1998a, 1998b, 1999) question whether researchers delve deeply enough. In this sense, Mike Hall's (1994) work on power relationships in tourism requires closer attention – for as Urry (1990a, 2002) himself notes, the gazes are specifically framed. Which raises the question – for whom and for what purpose? In different works, Ryan (e.g. Ryan and Aicken 2005; Ryan and Wang 2010) has suggested that questions of the authenticity of the gaze are misdirected, and the key issues are those of who authorises the gaze and to what purpose. This is particularly an issue when places are 'signed' as being of cultural and heritage interest and, in countries like China, specific voices and silences together form the articulations provided for the tourist that serve the interests of government as much as the preferences of the tourist.

The search for the back stage and authenticity – MacCannell (1999) argued that visitors do search for authenticity and want to penetrate the tourist veil – a view put forward to counter the earlier views of Boorstin (1964) who wrote of a death of travel and the emergence of a pastiche of experiences made ready for the hedonistic mind. As already commented, the question of authenticity has exercised the minds of many in our field, and there is a long history that includes the early work of Dann (1977), Valene Smith (1989), Cohen (1988a) and indeed Boorstin (1964) himself. These considerations link with the next category.

The theories of consumerism and the concept of the tourist as a collector of experiences. Many tourist experiences are constructed by profit-motivated organisations. However, if one accepts the arguments of Baudrillard (1975, 1981, 1983) in this regard, what of the issue of **authenticity**? Wang (1999, 2000) argues that while place may be constructed, there remains an existential authenticity – that is, while there may be little historic or cultural integrity to a place, tourists can still genuinely enjoy social interaction, have fun, reinforce social bonds including those of family, or indeed perhaps have a moment of catharsis. The studies of **well-being** undertaken by E. Diener (1992), E. Diener and M. Diener (1995) and E. Diener and C. Diener (1996) do not argue that a sense of well-being requires culturally authentic places. Again, to draw upon personal experience, my son and I had an authentic experience of fun when conducting our 'research' in the 'artificial' theme parks of Florida as to which was the best roller coaster ride. (For the record it was concluded that the Duelling Dragons was overrated and the Kragon undervalued!) While this may be seen as flippant, the point is that holidays provide opportunities for family bonding that arguably have social benefits that go beyond the economic measures of the benefits generated by tourism, and that these benefits occur in other than the culturally approved 'authentic places'. Satisfactory experiences arise from meeting not only needs, but also wants and fantasies, and the provision of such satisfaction is something that the tourism, recreation and leisure industries can do well.

Theories of mindlessness – Phil Pearce (1988) has written of how habitual so many of our actions can be, and there are many aspects of the holiday experience that are notable for their ordinariness. The times we check in for a flight or into a hotel, the lazing by the swimming pool, the turning on of a TV in a hotel room – considering all the times we have done this, how many times do these activities succeed in being memorable? Consequently, within the hospitality management literature the concept of **the critical incident** (Bitner *et al.* 1990) has attracted attention as has the search for the 'golden moment'. Therefore, many hotel chains deliberately seek means to better create the memorable experience – whether it be in more environmentally designed rooms, more comfortable beds, better blackouts or staff empowerment and carefully designed client loyalty programmes. Similar policies are being pursued by airlines as each tries to differentiate its service. Disney formalises the 'golden moment' by seemingly scheduling 'unscheduled' appearances by Mickey Mouse and his friends, so that encounters with the characters are the more 'treasured' for their very unexpectedness.

An alternative concept to mindlessness is suggested by the theory of **the career ladder** based on Maslow's hierarchy of needs. Again, Phil Pearce has initiated development of these ideas, initially in his books *The Social Psychology of Tourist Behaviour* (1982) and *The Ulysses Factor* (1988) and then subsequently, in the face of criticism, in amended versions in his work, *Tourist Behaviour* (2005).

A little-explored aspect of the holiday experience is the role of **how we experience time** on holiday. When writing the second edition of *The Tourist Experience*, Ryan (2002a) noted a comment made by John Urry in a review of the first edition of that book, and devoted a whole chapter to the subject drawing on the work of writers such as Featherstone and Lash (1999), Lash and Urry (1994) and Rojek (1993). There exist some studies that purport to show that as we grow older, so our experience of time changes – that as we age time seems to pass more quickly. Is this culturally or biologically determined? Certainly, in western business-oriented cultures people seek to manage time – and herein there exists an interesting aspect of the holiday. While the holiday is itself a constrained period of time marked by Turner's rituals of entry into and departure from the 'ordinary', one of the extraordinary aspects of the holiday is that time becomes more elastic. Arguably, it is this very elasticity of holiday time – these periods of socially condoned procrastination – that then contributes to the extraordinary experience of the holiday.

Another aspect of the holiday is the role of significant others on holiday and **theories of intimacy**. As Trauer and Ryan (2005) note, while the spatial and architectural aspects of a site or destination may remain unchanged, the experience of being there can differ significantly dependent upon with whom you share the place. Experiences of places change as one moves through life stages, and the place of one's youth can become a new place when being a parent with one's own children. It can also be observed that the previously visited place becomes a 'new' place because of the acquisition of past knowledge. A sense of exploration is possibly replaced by a search for the familiar and the hope of replicating past satisfactory experiences. Truly, if only from this aspect, destinations are multiple products, ready to be experienced in different ways.

Theories of flow and arousal – the latter pre-date the former going back to, at least, the work of Yerkes and Dodson in 1908 who found that levels of arousal could initially evoke better levels of performance, but that too high a level of arousal created feelings of anxiety that frustrated abilities to perform well. Modification of this approach indicates different sets of reactions, initially perhaps characterised by anger, but then declining to frustration and then apathy if the participant feels unable to manage a situation. Those who may have experienced flight delays by package holiday companies, being deserted by newly bankrupted airlines or frustrated by air traffic control delays or strikes may recognise this aspect of holiday experiences, and that they are better avoided. The work of M. Csikszentimihalyi (1975) and M. Csikszentimihalyi and I. S. Csikszentimihalyi (1988) has been used to explain the levels of satisfaction derived by adventure holidaymakers in countries such as Canada (Priest and Bunting 1993) and New Zealand

(Ryan 1997b). These theories are based on a construct that flow (and satisfactory experiences) exist when the participant's abilities are equal to the
level of challenge that exists within a given situation. If the task is too challenging, then the individual suffers frustration and possibly anger, but if the
reverse is true, then the situation is potentially boring. Like many simple
dichotomies, many caveats may be entered. Participants may self-create challenges in boring situations to deliberately avoid boredom, while frustration
may intensify a desire to learn. Both theories, however, reinforce concepts of
the tourist as an actor in the process of holiday making rather than simply
holiday taking and, thus, perhaps deserve more attention than they currently
appear to attract within the academic tourism literature.

Associated with these approaches is the consideration of **risk** (Ewart 1989;
Ryan 2003) – its perception by holidaymakers, the degree to which it is present, and its relationship with the levels of competency and skill possessed by
a holidaymaker. Additionally, for the industry itself, there is the means by
which operators, airlines and attraction owners manage risk and discharge
the duty of care. While dangers have been persistently present when undertaking travel (as studies into the relationship between tourism, terrorism
and crime have shown), and while holidays generally remain safe, for those
adversely affected the outcomes can be potentially fatal. These realities have
also meant that travel is today often associated with inconveniences as when,
for example, air travellers are subject to frisking at airports, can no longer
take liquids with them and, with reference to the United States, have to com-
ply with strict entry requirements, pre-registration of visas and baggage reg-
ulations. Lower levels of holiday risk-taking may also be associated with
digesting unfamiliar foods, engaging in unsafe sexual behaviour, or being the
victim of fraud or theft.

It is not claimed that the above list is exhaustive, but it is sufficiently long
to make one realise that any attempt to present definitive explanations of
the 'tourist experience' are fraught with difficulties. And certainly the above
list is deficient in one major sense, in that by concentrating to a large degree
on the tourist per se it largely omits mention of those working in the industry or resident at the destination with whom the tourist interacts – which
interactions are often thought to be potentially important as indicated in
Doxey's Irridex or more contemporary studies (e.g. Prayag and Ryan 2009).
Indeed, is a holiday destination a fixed, permanent entity to be experienced?
Butler's (1980, 2006a, 2006b) tourism area life cycle theory is predicated on
the notion of impermanence, but even if this notion is false, the holidaymakers themselves are not psychologically or physically static. Each layer of
past experience yields processes of learning and, however much one may
seek to replicate a past action or experience, past experiences shape future
expectations and wants, and in consequence tourists may wish for either
nostalgia or novelty. The late Richard Prentice examined the question as to
whether tourists seek 'difference' or familiarity – and often it can be a combination of both. Tourists may wish to visit a place new to them but made

familiar by media representations. It is suggested that this is particularly true of adventure tourism – where, for example, the actions of white water rafting are marked by ritual familiar to the tourist through television, even if previously never undertaken. Why might this be the case? One answer suggested by researchers such as Cater (2005), Ferguson and Todd (2005) and Ryan and Trauer (2005) is that the promoted image is congruent with a self-image and, while the experience may be 'uncomfortable', the subsequent telling of the story reconfirms a perceived self-status that perhaps, over time, becomes even more important than the actual hours spent on the river.

There remain still additional thoughts and questions unanswered by the above ideas. For example, how do tourists experience 'a holiday'? Is it a series of actions, connected only by a serial pattern of actions within a constrained period of time marked out by activities different from those of our normal life patterns? Or, is it an evaluation of a holistic experience where the serial pattern of actions only possesses meaning through a unification of motive and action? Alternatively, perhaps it is both?

Such questions only beget yet more questions – including the notion of whether these questions actually matter. And, if they do, how are we to research them? The former question is possibly easier to answer than the latter. The economic consequences of tourism identify that tourism is an important collection of associated industries (Leiper 2008) and that, however intangible the product, in contemporary western society the annual search for escape from the daily routine has generated very large flows of capital investment and built infrastructure. In doing so, tourism has significantly impacted upon the natural and social environment. It is also a cliché to note that tourism is as much a social phenomenon as an economic activity, and as such says much about the pattern of our lives, our society and the political structures that underlie our society. Politically, tourism may be a contested arena – certainly in Australasia one cannot be anything other than aware of how tourism uses and is used by native peoples in a wider political framework of addressing social, cultural and political marginalities. So too in China, tourism is a deliberate part of the policy of 'Socialism with Chinese Characteristics' and 'Social Harmony based on tenets of Good Science'. It is not, therefore, new to conclude that tourism experiences are important. They are important for individual holidaymakers – they help shape personalities and lives, and may be cathartic in their consequences if one takes into account the *Shirley Valentine* syndrome. Holidays are important for the communities and environments on which tourism impinges. But if destinations are subjected to a life cycle, so too might be the phenomenon of tourism itself – and, as noted earlier, one cannot automatically assume that current patterns of social activity will continue unchanged in the future.

But, given the current patterns of tourism, how do we envisage the constructs of the experience, and how do we research it?

At the first Tourism: the State of the Art conference, Ryan (1995) suggested the model shown in Figure 1.1. The antecedents lie in a combination of motives, past experiences, personality and socio-demographics along with marketing messages. Between these antecedents and actual behaviour at the destination lie the intervening variables of the actual travel experience, the accommodation and features of the destination. Behaviour is an adaptive outcome based on gaps between expectation and the perceived reality of the destination and the nature of social interaction with residents at the destination, tourism intermediaries and other tourists. Issues of perceived authenticity and the values attributed to those perceptions help shape subsequent behaviour, as do personality attributes, especially to my mind, the ability to engage in cognitive dissonance. Finally, an assessment of the experience occurs with varying degrees of satisfaction being the outcome.

This model is based upon earlier marketing models associated with researchers and commentators such as Kotler *et al.* (1993), and it is suggested that the framework retains some validity today, although one might now wish to amplify some characteristics of the model. These include: the role of a sense of belonging (or place attachment e.g. Gross and Brown 2006, 2008) in creating destination loyalty in terms of a willingness to undertake repeat visits; the role of word-of-mouth recommendations from valued sources; the economic decisions that permit patterns of trade-offs (e.g. trading accommodation up or down in standard to permit longer or shorter stays within budget constraints); and structural factors, such as levels of competition between tour operators, hotel chains, airlines and ancillary agents, not forgetting the role of the internet.

Models such as this begin to determine the patterns of research that may be undertaken. The model suggested in Figure 1.1 would permit one to quantify relationships through identifying different measures. Destination attributes and available activities could be listed and respondents asked to assess their

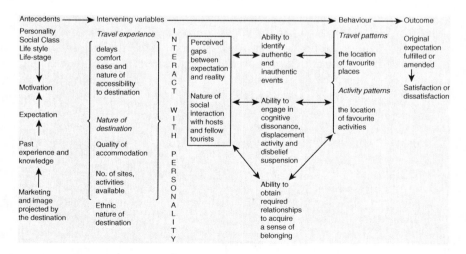

Figure 1.1 Antecedents, holidays and evaluation.

importance and evaluation of performance using the familiar Likert-type scales. Hotel features could similarly be assessed, and the nature of interactions between the variables would be quantified. Such research exercises are common, and increasingly such models are assessed through the use of structural equation modelling (SEM), especially given the growing ease of use of various software packages. Any examination of the tourism journals will show the popularity of this approach, especially perhaps in the last decade.

Nonetheless, in undertaking these research approaches, it is necessary to be reminded of the different paradigms of research that exist, and their underlying ontologies and epistemologies. This is not the place to repeat well-known characteristics of post-positivism, social constructionism, critical theory and variants thereof that include gender analysis, chaos and complexity theory, hermeneutics, etc. (e.g. see Guba 1990), but it is beneficial to recognise that the act of asking a question is not a neutral act – for in asking a question the researcher sets an agenda. A common problem associated with the use of questionnaires in research is that, all too often, the researcher has little or no knowledge of what is in the respondents' minds as they answer items established by the researcher's research process. For example, a respondent may agree with an item listed in a questionnaire and might even 'agree strongly' – but in the absence of the written prompt, is it an item of which the respondent would have even thought about? Certainly, in the hospitality literature there is concern about 'hygiene' factors in the sense that the absence of various services, such as a comfortable bed, will generate a lack of satisfaction with a hotel, but the presence of a comfortable bed is insufficient to create high levels of satisfaction (Gu and Ryan 2008). One response to this is to reiterate to the client that the comfortable bed is important – and this might be done in varying ways through the provision of information about bed design, the offering of pillow type options and various other modes of service familiarisation through which messages are conveyed to the client that a service of importance is being offered by the hotel. Satisfaction is thereby manipulated by the supplier to achieve the desired outcome. The customer becomes a conditioned client, by which it is meant that the guest's sense of what is important is shaped by being told that something is of importance. It is suggested here that the same thing can happen in responses to questionnaires. Often, perhaps, researchers fail to distinguish (in the use of questionnaires) between that which is salient to an issue, that which is important and that which is a determinant of behaviour, for all our use of statistical procedures.

Another problem about the type of model suggested in Figure 1.1 is that should one seek to create testable hypotheses and, say, test the whole model using SEM, though theoretically possible, the outcome would be a very long questionnaire that would probably quickly induce respondent fatigue. In short, there are many reasons to adopt more qualitative approaches to researching the nature of tourism experiences. This is not a new call. The debate about the role of emic and etic research has a long history in the tourism research literature with, perhaps, the obvious response being that there is a role for both. This generates subsequent debates. Do we adopt the pragmatic mixed methods approach espoused by writers like Creswell and Tashakkori (2007), who argue that research should be problem, not methodologically, driven, and adopt a form of triangulation whereby the researcher (subject to the constraints of budget, time and, dare one add, the exigencies of pressure to publish that arise from research assessments and career enhancement) uses more than one method to examine an issue? Such mixed methods approaches add, it is argued (Creswell and Tashakkori 2007), both credibility and reliability to the research. Certainly, it is generally accepted that the goals of research include the establishment of both credibility and reliability, for to cast these asunder may undermine abilities to forecast, manage, compare, plan, generalise and even perhaps understand. In the case of small samples and qualitative data derived from conversation, it is possible for the researcher to have recourse to the theories of Kelly (1955) and Allport (1937, 1955, 1961) to argue that generalisation is possible because the human condition requires some common understanding through language – for without that each individual is truly cast on stormy waters of loneliness. And it is also quite common for researchers to use such initial approaches to subsequently develop questionnaires designed for larger samples. But there are counterarguments against the mixed methods approach of which we must be cognisant even if they are uncomfortable.

First, different research methods are premised on different epistemologies and ontologies. The mixed methods approach retains, to my mind, the danger of the predominance of the post-positivistic model of research and the researcher-led agenda. Can the researcher as a critical analyst, who not only seeks to share in a construction of meaning with the respondent in the role of being a change agent, but who also seeks to aid respondents to challenge the status quo, necessarily adopt the stance implicit in post-positivism wherein the researcher has little role in influencing consensual, socially ordained 'truths' within a mixed methods approach to research? This example is possibly extreme, but variants of the argument persist whatever the mix of paradigms espoused in the mixed methods approach. There is also a second objection to the approach inherent in the mixed methods approach if its objective is to acquire reliability and credibility of research findings. Such goals reinforce the supremacy of rationality, and it is possible to question with reference to holiday experiences if rationality is to the forefront of a holidaymaker's mind. In the first edition of *Recreational Tourism*, Ryan (1991) noted the phenomenon of 18–35-year-old holidays, the drunken behaviour of the 'lager louts', and the need at the time for special tourism police forces to control the areas of bars and nightclubs. Is the want to drink to a stage of unconsciousness via a drunken sexual groping a form of rational behaviour – or an emotive response to a sense of emptiness in life? In 2009 in New Zealand, two tourists were killed by ice falls at a glacier, having ignored all the signs relating to safety and the conventional wisdom that one should not go to the ice face. Was their behaviour wholly rational? Are holidays as periods of con-doned escapes from responsibility ever entirely rational? From this perspec-tive one begins to question whether research methods based on assumptions of rational behaviour are ever wholly able to catch the richness of the tourist experience.

Tribe has written of the two different patterns of tourism research – the one oriented towards industry needs and the second based on other needs. For many reasons, and not simply those of the tourist-related industries, there is a need to generate data from which one can generalise, and hence there is a need for large-scale samples that permit prediction of human behaviours – but again to cite Ryan (2002a), behind observed behaviours can lie a multitude of different motivations. The same motive can give rise to different behav-iours (e.g. a need to relax may lead to both engagement in a physical activity or relaxation by a swimming pool), while the same activity can be motivated by different reasons (e.g. is the swimmer seeking a physical release from too many periods of sitting in front of a computer, or is that swimmer motivated by a wish to improve technique?). In these examples different respondents may well ascribe high levels of importance on a Likert-type scale to 'relaxation' and 'swimming' – thereby permitting a prediction of observable behaviour – but I wonder if readers are any the more knowledgeable about the nature of the experience. The tourist experience is shaped by many things: motive, past experience, knowledge of place, persons with whom that place is shared, patterns of change at the place, the images induced about place and activi-ties, individual personalities. So, it seems that to study the tourist experi-ence is of necessity a study of individual stories that, as researchers, one records, assesses and passes on, not as definitive assessments of truth, but as sources that inform evaluations of others' experiences. Tourism thus involves not only the study of organisations, and social, environmental and economic impacts, but a study of human behaviour at times of potential catharsis (the *Shirley Valentine* syndrome, e.g. Wickens, 1994; Ryan 2002a), and is possibly a metaphor for other forms of travel through life. Perhaps tourism academ-ics should also invite to the bodies of scholarship that examine tourism the philosophers with their concerns of meaning, truth and beauty, for tourism is not only an industry, not only a social phenomenon, not only a building block in the formation of personal psychology, but it is also a means by which a philosophical wonderment about people can illustrate truths of the human condition.

Note

1 This chapter has previously been published as a paper in *Tourism Recreation Research* 35(1). The author is grateful for permission to reproduce it here.

Section 1

Dark tourism experiences: mediating between life and death

Philip R. Stone

> Cheap holiday in other peoples misery
> I don't wanna holiday in the sun
> I wanna go to the new Belsen
> I wanna see some history
> Cause now I got a reasonable economy
> (Sex Pistols, 1977)

On 14 October 1977, the British punk rock band the Sex Pistols, famous for their anarchist views on social conformity, released their fourth single 'Holidays in the Sun'. The band's vacation to the Channel Island of Jersey inspired the lyrics of the song, with John Lydon (also known as Johnny Rotten) saying:

> We tried our holiday in the sun on the Isle of Jersey and it didn't work. They threw us out. Being in London at the time made us feel like we were trapped in a prison camp environment. There was hatred and constant threats of violence. The best thing we could do was to go set up in a prison camp somewhere else. Berlin and its decadence was a good idea. The song came about from that. I loved Berlin. I loved the Wall and the insanity of the place. (cited in Savage 2005)

Whilst hedonistic and pleasure-seeking experiences in the sun are considered staple ingredients of (mass) tourism, for the Sex Pistols at least, the search for a non-conformist tourist experience took them to 1970s Berlin. Divided by the Berlin Wall into liminal places, the juxtaposition of profligacy in capitalist West Berlin with the asceticism of Communist-controlled East Berlin, together with remnants of Nazi Germany's attempt to exterminate Jews during the Holocaust – hence, the song's reference to Belsen – provided the Sex Pistols with an 'alternative tourism experience'. Of course, the Holocaust, as a period of history that still symbolically haunts contemporary imagination for the scale of atrocity committed against Jews and others, and the concept of tourism may appear an anomalous conjunction. However, a combination of memorial narratives, political imperatives and touristic (re)presentations and infrastructure have ensured the Holocaust and its dead are now mediated through heritage tourism experiences where murder and mortality are unique selling points. Consequently, John Lennon and Malcom Foley in 2000 published their theoretically fragile yet inspiring book of 'death-related' tourism cases, including but not limited to the Holocaust, bringing their previously defined concept of 'dark tourism' (Foley and Lennon 1996) to mainstream academic and media attention. Yet, in fact, the Sex Pistols were singing about the nihilism of modern touristic travel to sites of death almost two decades before.

Hence, the purpose of this introductory essay is to reveal, albeit briefly, dark tourism within the context of contemporary approaches to mortality and to signpost empirical research that examines dark tourism as a (new) mediating institution between the dead and the living. The section also introduces subsequent chapters that address both the conceptual framing of dark tourism, as well as the commodification of 'death spaces'. First, however, the concept of dark tourism – that is, 'the act of travel to sites associated with death, suffering and the seemingly macabre' (Stone 2006: 146) – has a long historical pedigree. Even before the Sex Pistols' musicological immortalisation of 'cheap holidays in other people's misery', visitors have long travelled to places or events associated one way or another with death, disaster and suffering (Sharpley and Stone 2009). Whilst Lennon and Foley (2000) suggest dark tourism is an intimation of postmodernity, they draw upon Rojek's (1993) earlier work of 'Black Spots' tourism – death sites which are commercialised postmodern spectacles dependent upon (re)constructed simulacrum (after Baudrillard: see Poster 1988). Meanwhile, Seaton (2009) offers an alternative view of dark tourism development. He suggests the origins and transformation of dark tourism, or what he terms 'thanatourism', was traditional travel that has evolved and been shaped by profound shifts in the history of European culture – and which still impacts today. Consequently, Seaton argues three key historical epochs have defined thanatourism in its current Western tradition. In particular:

- *Christianity*, as it evolved between the fourth and sixteenth centuries, and its unique doctrinal emphasis on fatality – specifically, Seaton points out with reference to the Cross as Christianity's identifying symbol, 'Christianity was the first, and only, world religion to make an instrument of torture and death its corporate logo' (ibid.: 527);
- *Antiquarianism* and its related *secular-sacred* ideology of national heritage that first emerged in sixteenth-century Europe, and which included the recording and subsequent promotion of significant deaths of cultural

figures, politicians, artists, and so on, as well as memorials, epitaphs, effigies and ancient burial grounds;

• and, *Romanticism* and its complex nexus of literary, artistic and philo-sophical ideas that were founded in Britain, France and Germany in the last half of the eighteenth century and through the nineteenth century, and which added to the propensity for secular, death-related travel and which continues today.

A full critique of Seaton's developmental sketch of thanatourism is beyond the scope of this essay. However, Seaton's synthesis of Romanticism with dark tourism evolution may shine light on the construction of meaning of present-day dark tourism experiences. In particular, it is the Romantic por-trayal of mortality that is important, as well as its influences upon perceptions of death today. Mortality was a major subject of Romantic art, literature and travel which 'turned death into sensibility – not so much a religious and moral mediation in the medieval, *memento mori* tradition, [but] as an imaginative dwelling on fatality for aesthetic gratification' (Seaton 2009: 531). Hence, the *Romantic death* of the nineteenth century, termed by Aries (1981[2008]) as 'Thy Death' (or 'The Death of the Other'), evolved through a waning of eternal damnation messages prescribed by priests with advancements in med-icines prescribed by doctors. Moreover, with the emergence of the modern family and its new structures of feeling (Porter 1999a), attention became fixed not on the decedent, but on those who continued to live. Influenced through Romanticism, including the quixotic depiction of death in art, literature and poetry, the rituals of death became much more sentimental (if not morbid), and mourning became a family concern which perpetuated the memory of the deceased. The Romantic death became a death-with-dignity, a *good death* where calmness prevailed in readiness for a dignified departure from the mortal world. The good death was an illustration of how man paid respect-ful deference to the laws of nature, and how the time of passing became an opportunity to put 'things in order'. Indeed, the Romantic death was signified by the writing of wills with final bequests bestowed, sanctimonious instruc-tions given to survivors, forgiveness sought both from companions and God, promises of reunions made, and final words spoken. As Tercier (2005: 12) notes, 'the business of the [Romantic] deathbed became just that: the tidy-ing and tying up of unfinished business'. Thus, the Romantic reconstruction of the deathbed was nothing more distressing than a final, peaceful sleep. With a darkened room, family and loved ones at the bedside, affairs in order, peace made with both survivors and God, and with a few gentle and quiet farewells, the decedent would dignifiedly drift off into an eternal slumber. Of course, this Romantic death was an ideal, in the mindscape of a Victorian society who came to think of death as simply a way of 'expiring consumption' (Jalland 1996). In its ideal form, the Romantic good death appeared to be a perfect coincidence of both social and biological death, which did not rely (solely) upon ontological continuity. However, whilst spiritual aspects were still important to the *good death* and religious forms of the death-with-dignity still embraced the hope of an eternal existence, deathbeds that were increasingly secular found solace in relief from pain and discomfort. In short, Romanticism (re)created death and the dead for (re)evaluation and contemplation for the living. In turn, tourism of the day reflected these contemplative aspects and thus involved visits to sites of fatality depicted in Romantic art and literature, and included trips to graveyards, mausoleums, historical battlefields, as well as traumas and disaster sites (e.g. Howitt 1840; Hall 1853).

However, the deathbed has undergone a metamorphosis during the twentieth century which continues to the present day. According to Aries (1981[2008]), in his seminal historical overview of death, the period saw the emergence of the *invisible death* or *forbidden death*. It is within this phase that Aries reveals his revulsion for modern developments and suggests modernity is marked by a waning of faith, especially for an (eternal) afterlife. Kellehear (2007) later characterised the invisible death as the *shameful death* for the lack of overt social exchanges between dying individuals and those who (institutionally) care for them. Hence, with the full onset of secularisation, the invisible death is signified by the role of institutions, especially the medical establishment where increasing bureaucratisation and hospitalisation, as Aries alleges, 'robbed the dead and dying of all dignity' (1981: 559). Therefore, the invisible or forbidden death, where deaths 'disappeared' from the community gaze, is largely as a result of the process of medicalisation. Certainly, the position of the physician at the nineteenth century (Romantic) deathbed became entrenched and consolidated through advancements in therapeutic techniques and pathophysiology, as well as an expanding pharmacopoeia (Porter, 1999b). Augmenting the position of the physician as an 'authority over death' were technical advances and acceleration of the bureaucratic superstructure that became the foundation of the modern state. With increasing hospitals (and later hospices) and dispensaries, combined with the professionalisation of disposal of the dying through regularisation of death certificates, post-mortems and the storage of dead bodies, the invisible death became almost just that: concealed and obscured behind the facade and machinery of the (new) death, dying and disposal industry. Consequently, with increasingly industrialisation being applied to the deathbed, in terms of both processes and procedures, Porter (1999a: 84) notes, 'rather as the *philosophes* rationalised death, modern man has in effect denied his own mortality, and death has become taboo' [original emphasis]. Hence, as the twentieth century progressed, the physicians' control over the process of dying increased, and death was moved out of the familiar environs of the family and community to become institutionalised under a medical gaze. Thus, the shift of power and emphasis from priest to doctor is now almost complete, as secularising processes have made the world (post)modern. Notwithstanding, the care of the soul and body has moved realms from post-mortem religious ritual to ante-mortem medical protocol. As Tercier (2005: 13) notes: 'In the ideal modern death, biological, social and ontological death not only coincide but are meant to occur in such an instant that, perhaps, the whole business [of mortality] can be ignored, allowed to slip past unnoticed. Hence the invisibility of death.'

However, to suggest that death is invisible within contemporary society ignores the popular cultural and media depictions of death; including those represented by dark tourism. Thus, it is here where an absent/present death paradox lies. Indeed, *real death* of the Self has been sequestered from the public gaze during the past 60 years or so (e.g. Mellor 1993; Mellor and Shilling 1993; Willmott 2000). However, in its place is *(re)created death*, where the Significant Other dead cohabit the living world through a plethora of mediating channels, including literature, architecture, monuments, the media and popular culture images (e.g. Harrison 2003). Stone and Sharpley (2008) augment this sequestration thesis, advocating real death has been relocated to a back region of medics and death industry professionals, and where modern-day mortality, or at least its depiction, is revived through a substitute of recreated situations and memorialisation, including those found within dark tourism (re)presentations (also see Stone 2009a, 2009b). It is these representations and their consequent meanings that potentially provide dark tourism as a mediating experience that links the dead with the living (also see Walter 2009). Harrison (2003: 158) notes this linkage and outlines the role of the Significant Other dead:

> The contract between the living and the dead has traditionally been one of indebtedness... The dead depend on the living to preserve their authority, heed their concerns, and keep them going in their afterlives. In return, they help us to know ourselves, give form to our lives, organise our social relations, and restrain our destructive impulses. They provide us with the counsel needed to maintain the institutional order, of which they remain authors...

Furthermore, Stone (2010) empirically illustrates this linkage through research at a range of dark tourism sites, attractions and exhibitions. Particularly, Stone demonstrates, albeit to varying degrees, that dark tourism provides an opportunity to contemplate death of the Self through gazing upon the Significant Other dead. Consequently, he suggests visitors to a range of dark tourism sites hope for a good *Romantic* death for themselves yet, in a paradoxical age of death sequestration dominated by medicalisation, the likelihood is for a 'hi-tech' death stage-managed by medics and professionals. Hence, where the *invisible* deathbed has been recreated, rather than denied, dark tourism experiences provide a contemporary mediating channel of mortality reflection for the Self through the Other dead. Ultimately, therefore, dark tourism is a (new) mediating institution, which not only provides a physical place of mediation but, also, allows the Self to construct ontological meaning and to reflect and contemplate both life and death through a mortality lens.

Drawing upon the work of Walter (2008), Stone (2010) suggests four key reasons why dark tourism is a mediating institution:

- Dark tourism mediates mortality by representing and communicating death.
- Dark tourism mediates mortality by providing the visitor with an opportunity to accumulate 'death capital' upon which individuals may draw to aid reflection and contemplation.
- Dark tourism mediates the complexity of death whereby contemporary mortality is reconfigured and revitalised through dark tourism spaces.
- Dark tourism mediates rapid social change through symbolically displaying the Significant Other dead.

Of course, the relationship between dark tourism sites and dark tourist experiences is one of continued research inquiry. As Walter (2009: 52) notes, 'dark tourism confronts us not with human suffering and mortality, but with *certain kinds* of human suffering and mortality' [emphasis added]. Therefore, future research agendas need to address the type, level and consequent of dark tourism as a mediating institution. Particular questions need asking as to the nature of dark tourism experiences, including, what is the meaning/perception of 'dark' in relation to dark tourism? How intentional are dark tourists in their consumption of sites of death? What is the role of dark tourists as semioticians? Moreover, how is suffering and death commodified for contemporary consumption? The task of interrogating these questions begins in subsequent chapters. Indeed, Tazim Jamal and Linda Lelo in Chapter 2 explore the conceptual and analytical framing of dark tourism. In particular, they scrutinise African American slavery heritage, under the guise of performative experiences and intentionality, and evaluate what constitutes 'dark' in dark tourism. They ultimately suggest the notion of *darkness* is a socially constructed one rather than objective fact. Meanwhile, Tony Johnston in Chapter 3 explores the social and commercial construction of death space, particularly within the context of post-war Croatia and Bosnia. Specifically, he notes the blurring of memory and imagination of post-war Sarajevo and the inherent tensions of public war space commemoration with place of private (tourist) enterprise.

Generally, however, the theme of dark tourism, under various pretexts, is growing within the tourism literature. Indeed, the subject was the most popular at the Tourist Experiences: Meanings, Motivations, Behaviours International Conference at the University of Central Lancashire in April 2009, from which this book derives its content – a reflection, perhaps, that research spotlights are now beginning to shine upon the complexities of dark tourism. Thus, regardless of whether dark tourism is an imitation of postmodernity; or has its origins in the fatality that was central to the development of Christianity; or developed through Antiquarianism and the discovery of heritage; or whether Romantic ideals still pervade a contemporary consciousness of death – at the philosophical core of dark tourism is the concept of mortality. In a contemporary age where real, ordinary and normal death is hidden behind medical and professional facades, yet abnormal, extraordinary death is recreated for popular consumption, dark tourism plays a potential mediating role between life and death, linking the living with the dead. As such, the dead have always been guardians of the living, either through religious rituals or by secular myth making. Therefore, through dark tourism mediation we give the dead a future in order that they may give us a past. Ultimately, dark tourism helps the dead to live on in memory so that they may help the living go forward.

2 Exploring the conceptual and analytical framing of dark tourism: from darkness to intentionality

Tazim Jamal and Linda Lelo

Introduction

The inter-disciplinary domain of 'tourism studies' and paradigmatic divisions between theoretical, critical and functional research (applied foci like planning, marketing, management) present significant barriers to the theory-building task in culture, heritage and tourism research. Consider, for instance, the persistent problem of the micro-level (individual tourist/resident) aspects ending up being treated separately from macro-level (social/political/economic) issues. Micro-level visitor motivation studies may be undertaken using social psychology theories, for instance, while the exoticising and marketing of people and their pasts to tempt visitors to distant 'remote' lands (by an array of cultural and marketing intermediaries) come under the critical gaze of macro-theorists studying political economy and institutional structures. One consequence of this disciplinary fragmentation is that the local–global interrelationships of tourism, culture and heritage are under-studied, under-stated and under-theorised, affecting understandings of tourism as a social and cultural phenomenon, and as an economic and political tool for vested interests.

Furthermore, the rise and globalisation of the culture industries has blurred the boundaries between travel, tourism and everyday life, leading public culture and tourism scholars like Keith Hollinshead (1998c) to argue that, if at one time tourism derived its meanings from the sliding interpretation of culture, today, perhaps culture derives its meaning from the sliding interpretation of tourism. Notions of 'tourism', 'tourist', identity and belonging are problematised in this globalised domain of transnational migrations and socio-economic flows, and inter-disciplinary scholarship to address the theoretical and methodological challenges of studying culture, heritage and tourism becomes an urgent priority (Franklin and Crang 2001).

This chapter addresses the concept of 'dark tourism', including the meaning of 'dark' in this term. The discussion, aided by examples of African American cultural heritage in the US, offers insights into developing an analytical framework for the study of dark tourism as a performative and *intentional* engagement.

Categorising and labelling challenges

Is dark tourism a sub-set of heritage tourism? Is a curious American visitor touring battlefield sites in Normandy, Holocaust memorials in Poland and the Ann Frank House in Holland (in between visiting marijuana-enhanced bars and Amsterdam's infamous red light district) a heritage tourist? Or a dark tourist? A secular pilgrim? What constitutes an 'authentic' experience? Older discussions on this topic tried to separate the sightseeing 'tourist' from the 'traveller' (for example, the package mass tourist versus the solitary traveller seeking genuinely to experience local life and culture, or engaging in remembrance of a loved one's death). Other scholars invite comparison with pilgrimage, as the tourist experience is seen to embody the tension between secular and transcendental, the sacred and the profane (Graburn 1989; Smith 1998). Bruner's (1996) study of African American visitors to Elmina Castle in Ghana offers a glimpse of sliding meanings of travel to this 'dark' site whose visitors range from roots-seeking travellers to curious 'heritage' tourists.

Research on tourist motivations (which spans a rich spectrum from recreation, rest and relaxation to searching for existential meaning and belonging) has also incited protracted debates (see Jamal and Hill 2002 for one perspective), which invariably spill over into questions of motivations in heritage tourism and dark tourism. Cultural and heritage studies in academic concentrations outside of traditional, business-oriented tourism programmes reveal a far more complex terrain of identity politics and socio-economic survival at play. *Experience* in heritage tourism is about life, existence, belonging and change – from the past into the present and future. It involves a performative act of appropriating, interpreting and communicating aspects of the past through performance, storied texts, physical sites and material artefacts. On the *production* side, representations, enactments and displays of heritage are influenced by a network of mechanisms, industries and stakeholders. Marketing intermediaries (for example, tour operators, packagers, advertisers) and the culture industries (including the production of film, literature, art, music, etc.) play an influential role in the production as well as *consumption* of cultural and heritage goods (Jamal and Kim 2005). Post-structuralist and postmodern critiques added further fuel to the proverbial fire by challenging clear-cut categories, labels and divisions (like production-consumption) as well as essentialist claims to authenticity such as portrayed by MacCannell (1989) in *The Tourist*. Matters such as agency, voice, ethics and authenticity are of little concern to the 'post-tourist', as tourism in the postmodern world is a superficial, hedonistic, pleasure-driven activity accompanied by commodification, staging and spectacle (Rojek 1993; Urry 1995).

So, is a pilgrim travelling to Mecca on a Hajj also a cultural or heritage tourist? Is a daughter travelling to her mother's memorial service a heritage tourist, 'dark tourist' or a traveller? Motivation and interpretation are seen to be of primary importance in addressing these questions – heritage 'resources' are demand-driven, argue some. Graham, Ashworth and Tunbridge (2000: 153) state that 'heritage cannot be considered in terms other than the demand for it...'. Numerous studies (and marketers) have attempted to tackle 'motivations' in tourism and heritage tourism. For example, one thread that has been identified is that of the heritage tourist seeking identity and belonging: roots-seeking travel is seen almost as a spiritual journey to arrive 'home'. Consider the 'OE' experience (the Overseas Experience) described by Bell (2002). For decades, young New Zealand adults (called Pakeha) have left their homes with a backpack on a voyage that also represents a 'spiritual journey of discovery of the world and of the self', into being a New Zealander (Bell 2002: 144). Many travel 'home' intending to experience their British roots, and experience places learned about in childhood, such as Big Ben or Westminster Abbey (Bell 2002). They are secular pilgrims, Bell argues. Their experience bears some resemblance to the experience of religious pilgrims as they encounter sacred objects and architecture. The OE experience results similarly in a rite of passage, albeit a secular one. Young Pakeha transition to a different phase of adulthood upon their return home; in a secular parallel, their symbolic journey reinforces their cultural identity and cultural heritage as New Zealanders.

Striking similarities may be seen in Bruner's (1996) description of African American visitors to what appears to be a 'dark' site: Elmina Castle in Ghana (one of many holding/shipping points for an active slave trade). For many, their visit was akin to secular pilgrimage, involving travel to a 'centre' away from home (to which some returned regularly, others visited once only); it was a quest for roots, 'to experience one of the very sites from which their ancestors may have begun the torturous journey to the New World' (Bruner 1996: 291). Some visitors from the African diaspora experienced a spiritual connection; as Bruner observed: 'one woman is reported to have fasted in the dungeon for three weeks and afterward stated that she achieved a spiritual reunion with her ancestors (ibid.: 291)'. But are visitors to Elmina Castle dark tourists, heritage tourists, or both? An examination of some of the literature accumulating around this topic area raises important issues for studying travel to sites of 'darkness'.

Dark Tourism

A closer look at the question that is currently preoccupying a number of tourism scholars is clearly merited: What is Dark Tourism? Are visits to ghettos and slum areas like those portrayed in the Oscar-winning film *Slum Dog Millionaire* in the same category of 'dark' as Holocaust Tourism, Thanatourism, Slavery Tourism, Atrocity Heritage (Ashworth and Hartmann 2005) or other apparently dark forms such as War Tourism (Smith 1998; Dann and Seaton 2001)? Despite several critical reviews and attempts to develop typologies, the term continues to remain poorly conceptualised, both with respect to the concept of 'darkness', and with respect to visitor motivations and experiences. Some researchers focus on the economics or politics of heritage, for instance, Tunbridge and Ashworth's book *Dissonant Heritage* (1996). Others aim at the 'dark side of tourism' (Dann 1998), developing typologies (for example, Sharpley 2005), introducing new concepts and terms like 'Black Spots' (Rojek 1993) and studying visitor motivation to heritage sites (Poria *et al.* 2006). Characteristic of an emerging field of study (a 'pre-paradigmatic' phase in disciplinary evolution, to use Thomas Kuhn's 1970 characterisation) and exacerbated by inter-disciplinary fragmentation as noted at the beginning of this chapter, conceptual challenges abound for researchers of dark tourism.

The term dark tourism as used by Malcolm Foley and John Lennon (1996: 198) described a 'phenomenon which encompasses the presentation and consumption (by visitors) of real and commodified death and disaster sites'. Tony Seaton's 1996 article provided another defining term, thanatourism, which refers to 'travel to a location wholly, or partially, motivated by the desire for actual or symbolic encounters with death, particularly, but not exclusively, violent death, which may, to a varying degree be activated by the person-specific features of those whose deaths are its focal objects' (Seaton 1996: 240; also see Seaton 2009). Seaton (1999) subsequently developed five thanatouristic categories:

1   travel to watch death: for example, public hangings or executions;
2   travel to sites after death has occurred, such as Auschwitz;
3   travel to internment sites and memorials, for example, graves and monuments;
4   travel to re-enactments, such as US Civil War re-enactors; and
5   travel to synthetic sites at which evidence of the dead has been assembled, for instance, museums.

Dark tourism sites come into the productive spheres of capitalism and consumption through *tourism*, where the *production*, presentation and re-presentation of these sites occur via a range of actors, for *consumption* by visitors. Yuill (2003) provides several examples showing that, each year, visitors around the world flock to an ever-increasing number of sites associated with death and disaster: 1998 statistics at the Anne Frank House in Amsterdam showed 822,700 people passing through the swinging bookshelf into the annex that once hid eight Jewish refugees during World War II. In 1999, the Alamo in San Antonio saw 2.5 million visitors at the site where 179 men died defending their vision of an independent Texas. In 2000, the Auschwitz-Birkenau Memorial and Museum reported 434,000 visitors at the camp that exterminated approximately 1.5 million people during World War II (Auschwitz-Birkenau Memorial and Museum 2002).

The literature provides numerous studies and examples of sites where friends and relatives journey to actual or associated sites of death; reasons range from partaking in commemoration and (collective) memory, to seeking catharsis or dealing with survivor guilt. Private memorialisation forms an important distinction from public memorialisation, for instance, of public entities (see various chapters in Mitchell 2007, including Chapter 13 on Dark Tourism, by Lennon and Mitchell). Memorialisation and interpretation are two ways of assuaging feelings (guilt, fear of forgetting, remembrance, reconciliation, and so on). A substantial number of visitors to Auschwitz may think of their visit as a pilgrimage, 'as a journey of commemoration and witness', especially visitors who are survivors and families of survivors and victims (Keil 2005: 483). But, numerous authors argue that pilgrim-like expectations of liminality, expectations of solemnity, 'atonement', and even education motivations are strongly mediated by visitor expectations and mimetic forms and processes of representation and framing (Young 1993; Keil 2005). Even where a desire for historic education may be a strong motivator, the tools employed by the tourism 'industry' to frame, interpret and symbolise the past generally serve up a socially constructed 'Distory' – Disney history – as Hollinshead (1998c) put it.[1]

Lennon and Foley (2000) argue that such significant sites often become both famous and notorious, thus inducing staging and spectacle for the curious: 'Horror and death have become established commodities, on sale to tourists who have an enduring appetite for the darkest elements of human history' (p. 58). These authors do not include friends and relatives visiting sites of death, disaster and atrocity heritage in their definition of 'dark tourists'. They reserve this label for curiosity seekers, incidental visitors seeking superficial amusement, novelty and fun. 'It is those who visit due to serendipity, the itinerary of tourism companies or the merely curious who happen to be in the vicinity who are, for us, the basis of dark tourism' (Lennon and Foley 2000: 23).[2]

Seaton's (1999) study of the Battle of Waterloo attempts to explain how such dark tourism sites are 'constructed' and memorialised in public consciousness. He analyses the battlefield as a major destination and attraction, using MacCannell's (1989) five-step sacralisation process. These include naming (naming of the battle Waterloo), framing and elevation (for example, via numerous monuments related to the battle), enshrinement (for example, the Waterloo church), mechanical reproduction (such as in literary and touristic media) and social reproduction (for example, naming streets and towns after Waterloo). Study of the assassination of JFK (Foley and Lennon 1996) and the unsuccessful attempt to develop a thematic Dracula Park in Transylvania, Romania (Shandley *et al.* 2006) similarly illustrates the important mediating role of visual and print media, literary and film influences, plus tourism marketing intermediaries.

Dark tourism sites can be seen as ranging from actual event locations to off-site locales that are connected to such an event (such as museums commemorating a disaster). Heeding claims that on-site experiences constitute 'darker' (more 'authentic') experiences than off-site memorials of the same dark event has led some scholars to propose a 'Dark Tourism Spectrum' showing a 'darkest' (at the on-site end) to 'lightest' (at the associated sites end) set of 'products' (Stone 2006). This type of framing offers useful discussion of place meanings and authenticity, and merits closer examination, particularly if the mediating role of marketing and cultural intermediaries is as significant as projected. Issues of representation prevail in both on-site and off-site locations (as well as in virtual sites), as shown by Hall (1997) and Kirshenblatt-Gimblett (1998).

A thanatological perspective on dark tourism consumption has also been recently proposed (Stone and Sharpley 2008). Like every attempt to theorise this sociological phenomenon, much remains to be done to bridge the micro–macro divide in dark tourism studies and engage in a closer scrutiny of what constitutes 'dark' in dark tourism. A look at some sites of African American heritage offers some insights into this discussion.

Example: Dark sites of African American cultural heritage in the US

African Americans are the second largest ethnic minority in USA, representing 12.3 per cent of the total population (U.S. Census Bureau 2000), and have played a major role in the establishment and development of the United States as a nation (National Park Service, n.d.). First brought to the New World as indentured labour, many generations of enslaved Africans arrived subsequently during the transatlantic slave trade between the fifteenth and nineteenth centuries, facilitated by nations like Great Britain, Portugal, Spain and France (Berlin 2003). Although the transatlantic trade was declared illegal after 1803, domestic slavery in the United States continued until 1863, just before the end of the Civil War.

African American cultural heritage is displayed in a wide diversity of sites, such as ones related to the lives of the enslaved Africans (for example, the Cane River Creole National Historical Park described below), sites related to African American participation in World War II, such as Tuskegee Airmen National Historic Site, or sites devoted to the life and achievements of African American personalities, such as the Martin Luther King, Jr. National Historic Site. Today, many former plantations are visited by tourists or used for events like retreats and weddings. They are a part of the heritage of enslaved Africans who toiled in cotton, indigo, rice and sugar cane fields for numerous decades. Researchers studying plantation or slavery tourism often associate this phenomenon with the term dark tourism (Buzinde 2007).

A large number of sites associated with the African American experience in the United States are managed by the National Park Service (NPS), a federal agency within the Department of the Interior. The NPS administers 391 Park System Units (parks, national monuments, seashore sites, battlefields and other recreational and cultural sites), including about 42 directly related to the African American heritage. For the purpose of discussion in this chapter, we have selected two NPS sites related to past African American enslavement (Table 2.1): the African Burial Ground National Monument was chosen for its history, the richness of documentation available about the site, and observations made by one of this chapter's co-authors during a site visit in October 2008. This visit occurred on both 10 and 11 October 2008 and coincided with the closing of the special week-long event 'Passing the Torch – Youth Week 2008' that had been organised by the African Burial Ground National Monument. Cane River Creole National Historical Park (part of the Cane River National Heritage Area (NHA)) was also selected for its historical focus on enslavement, and also because of its popularity in the public and research domain. Brochures from the office of the Cane River National Heritage Area located in Natchitoches, Louisiana, describe the Magnolia Plantation Complex, which surrounds the Magnolia Plantation Home located in the NHA, as 'the agricultural and industrial portion of an extensive Creole cotton plantation' (see Table 2.1). It includes 18 acres of out-buildings, a blacksmith's shop, a plantation store, a gin barn, eight cabins and a former slave hospital (Cane River Creole National Historical Park, n.d.).

The National Park Service presents extensive information about the African presence in early New York at the site of the African Burial Ground National Monument, in brochures and videos, plus the site's website. Passing the Torch – Youth Week (5–11 October 2008), Kwanzaa (December 2008), and Black History Month (February 2009) were some of the recent events organised on site. Celebratory of African culture, they are educational and progressive. Included were African dances presentation, African puppet making and waist beading workshops. Also showcased were a video and artefacts to help understand the life conditions of both freed and enslaved Africans on the African Burial Ground National Monument site. The event of Passing the Torch to younger generations complemented Black History Month, which is celebrated annually nationwide and includes teaching young black children the history and stories of their ancestors. School tours, children's story time and media projects are some of the venues where older and younger generations interact in sharing knowledge that might not be available in conventional school programmes.

Various interactive opportunities and interpretive stories of the enslaved Africans living in New Amsterdam (today's New York) are provided at the African Burial Ground National Monument, and are a recognition of the important role they played in the political, economic and cultural development of the nation-state (America) (The African Burial Ground, n.d.). The historical, archaeological and cultural findings on site also clearly portray a 'dark' side of New York history. Interpretive programmes and markers remind visitors that about 15,000 enslaved African bodies were buried under what became the financial heart of the city, the nation and the world (National Park Service 2008). In 1991, excavations for the construction of a federal building uncovered the 'largest colonial-era cemetery for enslaved Africans in America', estimated at 6.6 acres (The African Burial Ground, n.d.). The site is committed to honouring the memories of those African children,

Table 2.1 Two National Park Service sites related to African American
enslavement history

Site	History	Visitation	Stories presented
African Burial Ground National Monument New York, NY	From the 1690s until the 1790s, both free and enslaved Africans were buried in a 6.6-acre burial ground in Lower Manhattan, outside the boundaries of the settlement of New Amsterdam, later known as New York. Lost to history due to landfill and development, the grounds were rediscovered in 1991 as a consequence of the planned construction of a Federal office building.[a]	Site does not collect visitor demographics. Personal observation during site visit (10–11 October 2008) suggests significant presence of black visitors.	The Memorial commemorates the lives of about 15,000 enslaved Africans who were buried in the area. The visitor centre displays artefacts and exhibits, offers workshops and other educational programmes for youth and adults related to African culture (for example, burial art).
Cane River Creole National Historical Park (Magnolia Plantation) Natchitoches, Louisiana	Magnolia Plantation was the main plantation house of Ambrose LeComte. It was most likely constructed by slaves in the 1830s. Magnolia Plantation is set along Cane River Lake amid 10 acres of open flat farmland. The plantation includes ... an overseer's house, slave quarters cabins, a plantation store, a corn crib, a blacksmith shop, a pigeonnier, and a cotton press-gin building. Ethnicity and class tended to overlap so 'black' usually equated with agricultural laborers who occupied the quarters in the 19th and 20th centuries.[b]	Mostly Caucasians (94 per cent), a few African Americans (2 per cent). Mostly out-of-state visitors (65 per cent).[c]	The house tour offered by a private owner tells the story of the past owners. The tour offered by the NPS tells the story of the lives of the enslaved, and includes visiting slave cabins and the cotton press-gin. Also, visitors are engaged in singing.[d]

Notes
a   Directly cited from http://www.nps.gov/afbg (Accessed 10 February 2009).
b   Directly cited from http://www.nps.gov/cari/historyculture/upload/significanceofmagnolia-
    plantationwpictures.pdf and http://www.nps.gov/cari/historyculture/upload/
    summaryethnographyofmagnolia. pdf (Accessed 22 December 2008).
c   This information is related to the general Cane River National Heritage Area, not just
    Magnolia Plantation (Stynes and Sun 2004).
d   A video on the *New York Times* website shows Park Ranger Carla Cowles engaging
    visitors in a singalong (http://partners.nytimes.com/library/national/race/magnolia/
    indexnav.htm (Accessed 16 February 2009)).

women and men who lived and died around there in the seventeenth and eighteenth centuries, as described on the on-site memorial:

> We commemorate this African Burial Ground with an "Ancestral Libation Chamber." Through Seven Elements, The Ancestral Chamber will serve to physically, spiritually, ritualistically and psychologically define the location where the historic re-interment of remains and artefacts of 419 Africans has taken place. It will also serve to acknowledge the site as a "Sacred Place" where thousands of Africans are currently buried.
>
> (The African Burial Ground, n.d.)

Although the atmosphere at the site's memorial (outdoor structure) appeared to be somewhat solemn, the atmosphere at the visitor centre, inside the Ted Weiss Federal building, was more lively as visitors appreciated the different artefacts, engaged in conversations with the park rangers and other personnel, collected a variety of brochures, watched a documentary video and participated in workshops.

Magnolia Plantation at Cane River Creole National Historical Park differs considerably from the above example. Magnolia Plantation was first built during the 1830s by slaves, occupied by the Frenchman Ambrose LeComte, and was then reconstructed in 1899 after it was burned down by the Union army in 1864 (National Park Service, n.d.). The property includes multiple buildings such as the main house, slaves' cabins, corn crib, overseer's house, plantation store, blacksmith's shop, pigeonnier and cotton press-gin building. These structures, although some are quite deteriorated and others have collapsed, allow for a visual, place-based understanding of the life conditions on the plantation, for owners and enslaved inhabitants (ibid.). Before part of it was sold to the National Park Service in 1994, the Magnolia Complex was owned by Betty Hertzog, whose family lived on the property more than 200 years ago (Thompson 2000). She owns the larger part of the plantation which includes the main house (that Mrs Hertzog resided in) as well as thousands of acres of arable flat lands, an alley of 150-year-old live oak, and magnolia trees (Crespi 2004). An alley separated her side from that owned by the National Park Service. She hoped that the NPS would use the land to 'preserve her family's stories and teach future generations about the agricultural practices that made Magnolia the Goliath of Cane River when cotton was king' (Thompson 2000). According to Thompson (2000), many African American visitors complained about the content of the house tours offered by Mrs Hertzog, and claimed that the stories of the enslaved had been whitewashed (ibid.). By contrast, tours provided by Park Ranger Carla Cowles on the other side of the park attempted to expose the realities of the lives of the enslaved and challenged her audience as 'she makes it personal, makes the tourists become slaves, if only for one mental moment' (ibid.).

The 'production' of heritage at sites related to US enslavement history is clearly a highly sensitive and contested issue, and interpretations of this slice of history have political and personal implications. In *Representations of Slavery: Race and Ideology in Southern Plantation Museums*, Eichstedt and Small (2002) examined 122 interpretive museums at former plantations in Georgia, Virginia and Louisiana that they toured (also see Hadley and Hall 2004). On-site museums were organised into categories based on the way slavery was interpreted. The category 'symbolic annihilation', for instance, denoted plantation museums that removed the traces of the African American presence from their narratives (Modlin 2008: 266); this category came into effect where slavery was mentioned three times or less during the tour narrative, as represented by words like 'slave', 'slavery', 'enslaved' (Modlin 2008: 275). Similarly, Butler's (2001) study led him to conclude that most plantation sites 'whitewashed' the stories of slavery and mainly focused on the histories of the original owners, the architecture, the current owners, the landscapes and gardens, as well as the US Civil War. His findings were based on a textual analysis of documentation (brochures) obtained from more than 100 plantations in twelve Southern US states including Louisiana, Virginia and North Carolina.

While further research is clearly needed, one might speculate that a closer analysis of the narratives on the Hertzog Magnolia Plantation may indicate a similar form of 'symbolic annihilation' may be taking place on the privately owned section of the plantation (Thompson 2000, described black visitors who felt the stories were being whitewashed), while the African American Burial Ground National Monument portrays a diverse mix of celebratory, cultural and more sombre historic narratives to illustrate the multiple facets of enslavement on that site.

African American visitor profiles

The 'consumption' of enslavement heritage offers further insight into the performative engagement of visitors with the site. A survey of African American tourists conducted by the Strom Thurmond Institute of Government and Public Affairs at Clemson University (1998) showed that they were between 45 and 54 years of age, earned middle to upper class incomes, had at least some college education, were employed in professional/technical positions, and lived in suburban and urban areas. On the topic of destination choice and reasons for visiting (motivations), 36.4 per cent of the travellers surveyed disagreed with the statement 'visiting former slave plantations in the South does not interest me' (25.4 per cent agreed), 36.8 per cent disagreed with the statement 'the history of slavery in the South is best left forgotten' (35 per cent strongly disagreed). It was found that 44.4 per cent disagreed with the statement 'I don't like the feeling of being around things that remind me of the hardships imposed on Blacks in the past' (20.5 per cent strongly disagreed), and 38.5 per cent strongly agreed with the statement 'by learning more about their heritage, Black Americans develop a stronger ethnic identity' (35.9 per cent agreed). These results indicated that African Americans *are* interested in visiting sites related to enslavement history. Overseas, African Americans are a major market segment for international destinations such as Ghana; they are motivated by curiosity, root-seeking experiences or hope for redemption (Bruner 1996; MacGonagle 2006; Reed 2004).

A recent study by Butler *et al.* (2008: 289), aimed at identifying 'the typical visitor to tourist plantations and his/her relative desire to learn about aspects of slavery', offers a more nuanced insight into plantation tourism. Their results revealed that the typical visitor to the Laura Creole Plantation in Vacherie, Louisiana earned more than the average American household and was more educated than the average American. Only 3.5 per cent of the 1,266 surveyed visitors self-identified as black or African Americans compared to the 85 per cent who typed themselves as white/Caucasians. Foreign-born visitors (21.9 per cent of the respondents) showed a higher interest in slave narratives than other narratives like architecture, landscape or the US Civil War (Butler *et al.* 2008). African Americans were not the group with the highest interest in slave narratives; they are less likely to visit plantations – which are perceived to present negative (darker?) images of slavery – and more likely to visit sites such as the Civil Rights museums which show a more positive image of African American experience in the US (Butler *et al.* 2008; Shipler 1997). How such visitors might perceive the shades of darkness (to lightness?) at the African Burial Ground National Monument may be a useful study, especially in comparison with the two types of stories seen to be presented at Magnolia Plantation above.

Towards an analytical framework for Dark Tourism

The discussion in the first part of the chapter shows that the inter-disciplinary domain of tourism and heritage-related studies, as well as the paradigmatic divisions between theoretical, critical and applied forms of research, present significant barriers to theory-building. Micro–macro dualisms are evident in characterisations of 'tourism', 'heritage tourism', and the 'tourist' or 'heritage tourist'. In those instances where dark tourism appears to fit synergistically with heritage tourism, similar dualisms may be identified. Jamal and Kim (2005), amongst others, have argued that research must be oriented towards the non-binary, productive dynamism of culture and heritage – they are not simply 'represented', displayed or enacted in touristic spaces but, rather, involve contestation, reification, negotiation and performativity (involving networks of relationships and acts of relational power). It can be similarly argued that definitions and descriptions of 'dark tourism' must be revisited to better express its *performative* dimensions. Rather than focusing exclusively on its 'production' or 'consumption', the relationship between individual and the space (including personal relationship to the heritage represented) and the meaning-making that is part of the embodied experience at the site are important research agendas.

The discussion and examples provided in the previous section also indicate that a broader characterisation of dark tourism seems to be needed, one that encompasses not only death but other 'dark events', such as historically and socially significant events: segregation, crime, war, death, murder, atrocity and disaster, for instance. Sites of 'darkness' would range broadly from plantation sites, sites of atrocity, battlefield sites, to ghettos and slums. And discussions on dark tourists' motivations and experiences would similarly span an eclectic range. The discussion of African American heritage above supports this important research agenda: identifying what is meant by 'dark', how such sites of contested heritage are experienced by visitors (agents) – their relationship to the site, their intentions, the acts undertaken, and the physical as well as symbolic aspects (representations) of the site (the productive aspects, presented, enacted, interpreted, resisted by various stakeholders). Is the African Burial Ground National Monument a site of dark tourism? If the degree of emphasis on dark, sombre enslavement stories (including deaths) is the relevant criterion for gauging 'darkness', it can be argued that the park ranger's storytelling on one side of Magnolia Plantation make that site much darker – those narratives appear to raise feelings of discomfort as well as rage (Montes and Butler 2008). It should be also noted that black and white tourists in the US do not have the same perception of plantation sites – the former tend to see them as 'sites of repression, brutality and death' and the latter are likely to perceive 'beauty shrouding the shame' (Montes and Butler 2008). While future research is needed to explore this further, it could be hypothesised that sites like the African Burial Ground National Monument, that present a more uplifting story of enslavement, may be viewed less 'darkly' by African American visitors than sites like Magnolia Plantation at the Cane River Creole National Historical Park, where the harsher realities of slavery are one type of experience offered (contrast this to what some visitors perceived as 'whitewashed' narrative on a different part of the plantation).

This discussion also suggests that the notion of *darkness* is a socially constructed one, rather than an objective fact – there is no 'essence' of darkness that imbues the site. Racial/ethnic background as well as intentions and motivations of the visitors influence how they perceive and relate to sites like Magnolia Plantation and the African Burial Ground National Monument. Poria *et al.* (2003) suggest that the motivations of visitors who perceive a personal relationship to the site will differ from those who do not feel such a connection (also see Poria *et al.* 2006, where the authors argue that tourist perception is key to understanding visitation patterns – the meanings attached to the objects rather than the objects themselves will influence their decision to visit or not). Eichstedt and Small's (2002) study of plantation museums supports the above claim. Their study indicated that African American visitors neither wanted to visit plantations that water down slave narratives, nor did they wish 'to be understood or defined as a people by their experience of enslavement' (ibid.: 256).

The notion of 'intentionality' is clearly an important research agenda. The tourism literature is replete with research on tourist motivation, but the link to intention is rarely defined or discussed well. It appears as if researchers either consider intentions and motivations to be synonymous, or are unaware of the need to differentiate the two (see Phillips and Jang 2007, for a rare exception). In the case of dark tourism, for instance, one might ask: What is the 'intention' of the African American or Anglo-American tourist in relation to a black civil rights heritage site, or a plantation tourism site? Intention is related to motivation, in that while intentionality denotes a general directedness towards an object (for example, intending to visit the Magnolia Plantation while in Louisiana), motivation relates to the reason that spurs action (that is, to actually visit the site). Is there a relationship between what type of experience the visitor intends to obtain, such as educational versus wanting to connect psychologically to one's enslavement past, and the perception of a plantation site's 'darkness'? Drawing upon relevant literature in philosophy, tourism studies and the social sciences, an important future goal is to explore the nature of the intentions and actions that must be brought to an event for it to count as a genuine case of Dark Tourism, and the visitor (agent) as a Dark Tourist.

A preliminary analytical framework ('RAISA') has been proposed by Dr Michael Hand, Dr Tazim Jamal and Dr Christopher Menzel (Glasscock Working Group, TAMU; Jamal, 2007) that will be further elaborated upon and modified as investigation continues. RAISA addresses what can be identified as key dimensions of tourism and of other forms such as heritage tourism and dark tourism: Relationship, Agent, Intention, Site and Act. Using this approach, the phenomenon of dark tourism can be characterised as involving a relationship between a particular site and an agent with a certain intention, engaging in a certain act at that site. For instance, a genuine event of dark tourism must involve more than a mere site visitation by an agent. If, say, a construction engineer goes to Dachau intending only to investigate the material out of which the barracks were built, one could not characterise this as dark tourism, nor the engineer a dark tourist – the *intention* of the agent towards the site is simply not of the right type, nor do her plans there involve a relevant act.

But what is a 'right type' of intention of the agent towards the site? This relates directly to the issue of what constitutes a genuine case of 'dark tourism', or a genuine 'dark tourist'; one might wish to use the problematic notion of authenticity here, and ask what might be an authentic example of dark tourism, or what makes for an authentic dark tourist. What is the right type of intention of an agent towards a 'dark' (heritage) tourism site? A distraught African American son travelling to a memorial service for his mother does not have the intention to be a 'tourist' and learn about or experience the site/place; he intends to mourn his mother.

The RAISA framework may be helpful to address such questions as it attempts to approach the production and presentation of the *site* performatively. It is an analytical approach that attempts to bridge the micro–macro divide that has tended to fragment theory and research in 'tourism studies'. Future investigation might fruitfully focus on 'dark' as an experiential mode in itself, and examine this in relation to the types of sites noted in Table 2.1. This might help us to develop a better description of dark tourism and the dark tourist, while clarifying relationships to other relevant modes such as heritage tourism.

Acknowledgement

Dr Michael Hand, Dr Tazim Jamal and Dr Chris Menzel proposed the RAISA framework based on a series of working group meetings in 2005–6 on dark tourism. Our thanks also to the Melbern G. Glasscock Center for Humanities Research for financial support (Glasscock Stipendiary Fellowship and travel to conference support) to present the paper on which this chapter is based at the Tourism Experiences: Meanings, Motivations, Behaviours conference in Preston, England, on 2 April 2009.

Notes

1 Authors like Hollinshead (1998c) have addressed the 'tourism production' aspect very well; bringing the supply-side and demand-side together is an important future agenda – see Sharpley (2005) for one such perspective.
2 Cohen (1979a) found that novelty is an essential element of tourism experiences; however, he also noted that many tourists preferred a bubble of familiarity in order to appreciate the novelty of their experiences. By contrast, Yuill (2003) discusses a number of public sites where commemoration and remembrance are supposed to be primary objectives. In part, sites of atrocity are intended to warn against repeating such events. Butler (2001) notes the dangers to society of not remembering slavery.

3 Thanatourism and the commodification of space in post-war Croatia and Bosnia

Tony Johnston

Introduction

> The battlefield, an otherwise undifferentiated terrain, becomes an ideologically encoded landscape through the commemorative function of the 'marker'. As a marker inscribes war onto material soil, *it* becomes the sight. Without the marker, a battlefield might be indistinguishable from a golf course or a beach. Guided by a system of markers and maps, the tourist/strategist re-enacts the battle by tracing the tragic space of conflict by foot or by car.
>
> (Diller and Scofidio 1994: 48)

Dark tourism, or thanatourism, is defined as travel to a site primarily or partially motivated by a desire to encounter death (Seaton 1996), and much fascination with the topic has emerged over the past decade. Research has been carried out into many facets of dark tourism, and it has quickly become accepted as one of the most striking themes in the literature on post-mass tourism.

Dark tourism was a term first coined by Foley and Lennon (1996) in an article discussing visitors to the site of JFK's assassination. This article, and another from Seaton (1996) on Waterloo, became two of the earlier major pieces associated with research in the field, although previous work by Rojek (1993) on so-called 'black spots' had introduced the concept of dark tourism in all but name. A follow-up book from Lennon and Foley (2000), comprising a number of case studies of 'dark' sites, brought together a multi-site exploration of instances of dark tourism for the first time. Other work carried out on dark tourism has included case study-style research on a variety of locations, including: Althorp, where Princess Diana was laid to rest (Blom 2000); the Scottish battlefield of Glencoe (Knox 2006); World War II associated sites, such as Auschwitz and the Holocaust Museum (Cole 1999); Hiroshima and Nagasaki (Siegenthaler 2002); the penal institutions of Alcatraz and Robben Island (Strange and Kempa 2003); communism heritage tourism in Romania (Light 2000); and, of course, the site of JFK's assassination (Foley and Lennon 1996). Theoretical work in the area has also emerged, including Wight's (2006) exploration of methodological issues in thanatourism research, Stone's (2006) model proposing a dark tourism spectrum, and Stone and Sharpley's (2008) thanatological perspective on the consumption of dark tourism.

This diverse, yet incomplete, list is evidence of the broad horizons of what has become one of the most covered themes in the tourism literature, as well as demonstrating how tourism research continues to develop new boundaries. Moreover, dark tourism has also grasped the attention of the media and numerous articles have been written on its sub-topics, including: the ethical dilemmas of dark tourism, interpretation at sites, visitor motivations, memorialising and more. Research groups and websites, such as the Dark Tourism Forum (http://www.dark-tourism.org.uk) and Grief Tourism (http://www.grief-tourism.com), are further evidence of the increased attention this phenomenon has attracted in recent times. In summary, the commodification of suffering for the consumption of the tourist continues to generate much debate.

In the same year as Foley and Lennon's (1996) paper on dark tourism, Seaton coined the term *Thanatourism*, which he defined as: 'travel to a location wholly, or partially, motivated by the desire for actual or symbolic encounters with death, particularly, but not exclusively, violent death, which may, to a varying degree be activated by the person-specific features of those whose deaths are its focal objects' (Seaton 1996: 240).

This definition is interesting as it expands somewhat on Foley and Lennon's work on dark tourism, which primarily adopts a site-based, supply perspective, by placing more emphasis on the motivation of the visitor, particularly if the scale of death or destruction is especially intense or violent. This shift towards the visitor's motivation begins to open a debate on shades of dark tourism, from both the perspective of the visitor and of the site. Seaton continues by proposing a continuum of thanatourism, and his observation that the dark tourist wishes to understand or encounter the tragedy associated with the site is especially important. Expanding on Seaton's continuum of intensity above, Stone (2006) and the Lonely Planet Bluelist (Pickard 2007) propose scales by which to gauge the 'darkness' of the tourist or site. Lonely Planet's special section on dark tourism suggests a five point 'darkometer', ranging from 'opaque' to 'too dark'. The creation of the scale posits the argument that there are fundamental differences between 'dark' destinations and the motivations for visiting them. For example, point 1 on the scale, the 'opaque tourist', likes to visit museums where 'evidence of death has been assembled... By definition you're just about a dark tourist, but then so are most people.' (Pickard 2007: 124). Point 3 on the scale, however, is perhaps more aligned with some of the sites written about in recent academic papers. The 'die-hard dark tourist' in the middle of the scale goes to 'memorials and internment sites – monuments to death and graveyards like Rwanda's Gisozi Genocide Memorial'. They take their 'dark seriously'. At point 5 on Lonely Planet's scale is the tourist who is 'too dark'. These people visit places which have not yet recovered from catastrophe. They also visit public executions and torture. In Lonely Planet's view 'neither of them has any justification'. (Pickard 2007: 124).

Stone (2006: 151) further develops the ideas on scale of darkness by proposing a dark tourism spectrum which sets out both the perceived product features of dark tourism and the tourist's motivation(s) for visiting them. The paper discusses the range of dark tourism sites, starting with the darkest, which Stone writes are generally sites of suffering and death. Usually only a short time has passed since the tragic event and tourists to the site perceive it to be authentic. Commodification of the site may be education-oriented and will probably involve a high political ideology. Thus, the site is history-centric and more about education, conservation and commemoration. The visiting tourist wishes to be at the site when history happens, which gives it 'the ultimate test and seal of authenticity' (Keenan, in Diller and Scofidio 1994: 137).

At the other end of the scale is the lightest type of dark tourist. Stone (2006) argues that there is a crucial difference in the sites visited by these people – the sites are associated with death rather than being actual sites of death. At these sites, a longer period of time has passed since the events which they commemorate. A stronger emphasis is placed on the entertainment value of the site and, thus, visitors may perceive it to be inauthentic. Sites at this end of the spectrum usually also have a higher tourism infrastructure than the darkest sites, which may not cater to the everyday needs of the tourist. The site, therefore, becomes of entertainment value, with a focus on earning tourist cash and providing romanticism. Miles (2002) also touches on this idea, writing that the Holocaust Museum in Washington DC provides historical contextualisation for the Holocaust. In contrast, places like the Oświęcim Museum of Auschwitz 1 and Auschwitz-Birkenau focus on death itself, placing emphasis on the scale and horrific methods of mass murder. This places Auschwitz-Birkenau near the darkest end of the spectrum, whilst the Holocaust Museum in Washington focuses more on interpretation, audio-visuals and historical contextualisation. Cole (1999) also discusses this idea, presenting Auschwitz 1 as the 'Tourist Auschwitz' where, owing to the redesign of space, the tourist has entered 'Auschwitzland' before they know it. Auschwitz 2, where the majority of the executions took place attracts significantly less tourism and, as Cole suggests, suffers from a blurring of memory and imagination. Similar arguments can be discussed in relation to Sarajevo and are presented below.

Background to tourism in ex-Yugoslavia

Yugoslavia's tourist industry was one of the strongest in the Balkan peninsula before the country disintegrated. Pre-war, in 1983, total tourism receipts for Yugoslavia as a whole totalled $929 million and it was recognised by the government as a key area for development. In the early 1980s, tourism was underdeveloped in Eastern Europe, although in terms of tourist arrivals and receipts, Yugoslavia vastly outstripped competitors like Poland, Czechoslovakia (as it was then) and Hungary and was not far behind the Greek market (Buckley and Witt 1987: 96). In 1984, Sarajevo hosted the XIV Winter Olympic Games. At the time, these were the largest ever Winter Olympics in terms of both the number of athletes and media attention (Visit Bosnia-Herzegovina 2009) and were also the first and only Winter Olympics to be held in a socialist state. The city earned over $100 million in TV revenue and sponsorship (International Olympic Committee 2008) and attracted huge numbers of tourists.

Moving forward to the war period, Sarajevo was placed under siege by Bosnian Serb forces, whilst Dubrovnik and Vukovar were shelled relentlessly. Lasting almost four years, from April 1992 to February 1996, the siege of Sarajevo was the longest siege of a capital in the modern history of warfare. Approximately 10,000 people were killed in Sarajevo, many more thousands were injured, and the cost of damage to the city from shells and other siege incidents was estimated to be $25 billion (Kaufman 2002: 88; also Amanpour 1996). In 1996, the city's airport reopened for commercial flights and, subsequently, the tourism bureau began welcoming tourists back to the city. One of the initial tours involved visiting some of the sites associated with the conflict. In 1997, 1998 and 1999 the city's tourist numbers totalled 40,565, 47,565 and 68,520 respectively (Dzeko 2001: 9). Despite the growth each year, however, numbers were still small. By the year 2000, some 3,814 beds were available in the city, approximately half the number from the immediate pre-war period. In 2007, research amongst 56 travel operators around Europe shows there are still concerns about safety despite the war ending over ten years earlier and no operators run package tours to Bosnia-Herzegovina (Koumelis 2007).

From late 2006, efforts were made to enhance the marketing of Sarajevo as a tourist destination, with the city aiming to achieve five per cent growth per year for the following ten years. In 2007, the national tourism authorities also launched a large marketing campaign entitled 'Enjoy Life', which featured a four-minute-long commercial shown on feature TV shows around the world (Zuvela 2007). That same year, the country also attended the World Travel Market in London for the first time, describing itself as 'Europe's Hidden Secret'. Additionally, in 2007 visitor numbers for the first four months of the year showed a twenty per cent higher growth rate than the previous year (Zuvela 2007) and Sarajevo was named as the 43rd Best City in the World by Lonely Planet travel guides.

Methodology

With some notable exceptions (for example, Wight 2006), little has been written about methodologies for dark tourism research. Typically, research in the field usually employs strong qualitative methods, utilising ethnographic techniques to decode the construction of a site or, for those looking at visitor motivations, the deconstruction of a gaze. This qualitative work can include participant observation, interviews with tourists, interviews with tour guides and policy makers, and discourse analysis of the interpretation and presentation of sites for consumption. The research described in this chapter similarly uses a mixture of qualitative techniques to establish how space is commodified for the dark tourism industry. Logically, when the case study is a city with sites of greatly differing variables, mixed methods must be employed to generate an appropriate position. The research here comprised interviews with tour guides, participant observation on war tours throughout ex-Yugoslavia and discourse analysis of newspaper articles.

Public bodies and war space commodification

Evidence from news reports over the past decade indicates that public institutions, non-profit organisations, and the government and its officials are beginning to transform some of the spaces associated with the war in Yugoslavia and, specifically, the siege of Sarajevo. These spaces mainly present memorialisation of the events of the 1992–5 conflict, and include: The Canned Beef Memorial (a memorial designed by artists to sarcastically acknowledge the European Union's aid work during the war), Sarajevo Roses (red cement memorials where shells exploded) and The Tunnel Museum (a museum at the beginning of the tunnel which breached the siege lines). The Tunnel Museum is, in particular, an example of commodification, for although it is owned and managed by a private enterprise, evidence has emerged illustrating the desire of public institutions to play a role in its future development.

The erection of these memorials illustrates that, to some extent, Sarajevo is beginning to approach the stage where interpretation is appropriate and desired by tourists and locals alike. These memorials contribute somewhat to official interpretation of the events of the early 1990s, something which until recently has largely been in the hands of the international community and private stakeholders. While there is, perhaps, less commemoration in Dubrovnik, Vukovar in north-eastern Croatia has fully embraced the process of memorialisation, particularly by preserving the town's water tower in its war-damaged state. This preservation of war scars in itself becomes part of the memorialisation process (see Figure 3.1).

In addition to memorialisation, it appears that various governments are beginning to realise the potential value in economic terms of war tourism. Lennon and Foley (2000) note at the start of their book *Dark Tourism* that one of the first things that happens in a museum is the exchange of cash. While memorialisation and interpretation may be the key aims of the government in the commodification of war spaces in Sarajevo, the revenue-generating potential is most certainly not being ignored. In February 2008, Semiha Borovac, the mayor of Sarajevo, spoke to *Condé Nast Traveller* (Hammer 2008) about attempting to purchase the Tunnel Museum from

Figure 3.1 Vukovar Water Tower, March 2009.

the Kolar family who own the house and land where it is located. Despite their attempts, however, the tunnel is still in private hands, for now. 'It could be like Anne Frank's apartment,' the mayor of Sarajevo told the reporter, 'but this one family is preventing it from happening.'

In August 2008, the tunnel was again in the news (Tanner 2008), this time as the major political parties in Sarajevo had agreed to rebuild it. Damir Hadzic, mayor of the Novi Grad district of Sarajevo, said, 'We have political agreement from all parties. We are going to start rebuilding next year.' The same article later quotes Hajrudin Ibrahimovic, the Sarajevo region's minister for war veterans' affairs, who also wishes to restore some of the original tunnel. 'The tunnel needs to be reactivated. It could be a joint venture with a foreign firm.' (Tanner 2008).

Private enterprise and war space commodification

For several years, a number of private entrepreneurs have been operating relatively successful dark tourism businesses in Sarajevo. Two of these tour operators have, in particular, been bringing tourists to the war sites since the end of hostilities. Zijo Jusufovic, a private tour guide licensed by the state, operates a variety of war tours. In terms of this chapter the most important of these is his 'Mission Impossible Tour', a five- to six-hour tour of the city which takes in sites ranging from cemeteries and the destroyed Winter Olympic Village to the Tunnel Museum. At the time of writing, his tour costs €80 per person which, in terms of the tourism industry in Bosnia, would indicate that it is aimed at the more affluent end of the market. Other tours offered by Zijo Jusufovic include a shorter version of the 'Mission Impossible Tour' and day trips to Srebrenica in Eastern Bosnia. At the other

Figure 3.2 Sarajevo Tunnel Tour, July 2008.

end of the market, hostel owner Haris Panchuk runs daily tours to the Tunnel Museum, which cover transport, admission to the museum and a drive to the top of the city for panoramic views. These tours are operated by one of the city's hostel agencies.

The war tours operated by Mr Jusufovic and Mr Panchuk take in many sites which are no longer used for their original purpose but now instead serve the dark tourism market. One example is the abandoned Olympic bobsleigh tunnel in the city's outskirts. The chute crosses between the Federation of Bosnia-Herzegovina and the Republika Srpska, and this crossing has created difficulties in implementing potential new uses. Instead of operating for winter games or other purposes, the tunnel now serves as a stop on the 'Mission Impossible' itinerary as a point for tourists to reflect on the difficulties of post-war economic and cultural rebuilding. A second site on the tour is a Jewish cemetery nearer the city centre, representative of the once flourishing Jewish population in the city. The cemetery, now no longer in use and badly damaged from mortars and shells, is visited by dark tourists and pilgrims, both to remember the dead of the cemetery and also to view the unmitigated damage of war. Another site commoditised by dark tourism is the restaurant Panorama. Formerly a beautiful restaurant over-looking the city from the top of the mountain, it now stands abandoned, allowing visitors to visualise the siege and sniper positions.

Past work in the literature indicates that tourists often have a desire to experience first hand the graphic images which they have become familiar with from news reports, film and other media.

Figure 3.3 Abandoned Olympic bobsled chute, Sarajevo,
March 2009.

Dark tourism is positioned at the cross-roads of the recent history of
inhuman acts and the representation of these in news and film media.
Interpretations of such events and their commercial development or
exploitation are central to consideration of this area. Dark Tourism is the
term adopted by the authors for these phenomena (Holocaust museum
and J.F.K. assassination location visits) which encompass the presentation and consumption (by visitors) of real and commoditised death and
disaster sites.

(Foley and Lennon 1996:198)

Thanatourism trips to the former countries of Yugoslavia focused on the
Balkan conflict are not solely a post-war phenomenon. Evidence suggests
that dark tourism 'products' were available for consumers as early as ten
months into the war. In October 1992, reports emerged that an Italian travel
agent, Massimo Beyerle, was offering war tours to the edge zones of conflict
(Fedarko 1993; Marín 1993). A group of 12 people, at $25,000 per person,
could visit regions such as Sarajevo, Vukovar or Dubrovnik to see, first hand,
history in the making. Other trips on the agent's itinerary planned for visits
to the Lebanon, Somalia and the former Soviet Union. These trips promised
to bring tourists into dangerous situations which put the violence and horrors
of war into touching distance. Considering Lennon and Foley's work on dark
tourism (2000), the Lonely Planet Bluelist (Lonely Planet 2006) or Seaton's
continuum of intensity (1996), it is easy to position this type of trip as the
darkest type of thanatourism; the purest form which desires close encounters with death first hand based primarily on the sheer scale or methods of
killing involved.

Other evidence from the siege period includes the 1993 *Sarajevo Survival Guide*, published by the independent Bosnian production company, FAMA (meaning *Rumours*). This guidebook opens with the pretext that it is intended to:

> be a version of Michelin, taking visitors through the city and instructing them on how to survive without transportation, hotels, taxis, telephones, shops, heating water, information, electricity. It is a chronicle, a guide for survival, a part of a future archive where wit can still achieve victory over terror.
>
> (Prstojević 1993)

Further sections in the guidebook detail how to make one USA lunch aid pack feed five people, how to keep fit by running past sniper positions, where to buy petrol (from UNPROFOR or the black market) and how to get a letter out of the Former Yugoslavia to the rest of the world. The guidebook was published in English and the publisher has been quoted as saying that the idea of this ironical guide occurred to him because, at the time, he began to grow very irritated with journalists who flew to Sarajevo from all over the world in order to subsequently present their 'experience of the war' (Hötzl 2006).

Two maps of the city's war zones are also available: in Sarajevo's Tunnel Museum, online and in at least one of the city's bookshops. Similar guidebooks presenting the war are available throughout Dubrovnik. The more detailed of the two Sarajevo maps was again produced by FAMA and is a hand-drawn map of the city and the surrounding outskirts and hills. The map comes with a full legend which tells users of the UN-controlled airport, the destroyed railway station, the siege tunnel, UNPROFOR headquarters, sniper and tank positions, and shell marks. The other map, produced by the Tunnel Museum, again focuses mainly on the siege positions and is available for purchase at the museum.

Examining other war-damaged areas of the Balkans provides further contextualisation of war tourism in Sarajevo. The Croatian coastal city of Dubrovnik, now almost fully physically recovered from the war, also offers war tours. Dubrovnik attracts mass tourism to its beaches, nearby islands, famous walls, local cuisine and many other 'modern' selling points. However, for those looking for something a little different, a short walking tour or a half-day excursion telling the story of the Dubrovnik siege is available. These tours, like the Sarajevo counterparts, operate at both the high and low ends of the market. The half-day excursion cost €140 for a group of two, while the one-hour-long walking tour in the city costs €10 per person. The tour takes in the city centre sites which show the damaged rooftops and pavements of the old town. Although mostly repaired, several city centre scars remain which the visitor may miss without a tour. Additionally, the tour provides historical context to the war, and visitors learn an interpretation of the conflict in Croatia.

In mid-2008, one of the world's most wanted war criminals, Radovan Karadzic was captured in Belgrade. Karadzic was indicted by the International Criminal Tribunal for the Former Yugoslavia in 1995. After 11 years on the run, the former leader of the Bosnian Serbs was captured in Belgrade city centre on a bus. For some time, Karadzic had been living in Belgrade disguised as a doctor of alternative medicine. He lived publicly in disguise and lived a very different life to what one would imagine as a wanted fugitive. In 2008, after his capture, a Serbian travel agent began offering tours of the locations linked to the doctor. Vekol Tours in Belgrade run a half-day tour round the locations Karadzic frequented daily. 'I hope this program will serve as a trigger for our other tours designed to show Serbia in a beautiful light,' Tanja Bogdanovic told *Balkan Insight* (Balkan Insight, Author Unknown, 2008). Vekol's tour involves a visit to New Belgrade block, where Radovan Karadzic lived, and to a bakery shop and grocery shop where he was a regular customer. Tourists also visit his local pub, Luda Kuca, where they can have a sip of his favourite drink. *Balkan Insight* also writes that tourists can purchase a pancake in the Pinocchio pancake shop, where a speciality awaits – a Karadzic pancake. The tour concludes with a panorama viewing of the Special Court where, after he was captured, Karadzic was detained before being extradited to The Hague (Balkan Insight, Author Unknown, 2008). The company also runs two other tours related to the 1990s conflict, including a tour of sites linked to late war criminal Zeljko Raznjatovic 'Arkan', as well as sites that were bombarded during the NATO bombing campaign in 1999.

The final example comes from the north-eastern town of Vukovar, on the banks of the Danube. Vukovar suffered extensive damage during the conflict and became one of the landmark sites associated with the disintegration of Yugoslavia. The town is now host to one tourist agency called Danubium, which takes visitors on private guided tours associated with the conflict. These include a visit to the water tower (see Figure 3.1), a large cemetery with a garden of remembrance, the hospital which was used in the siege and, finally, the site of a mass grave and execution spot with a museum located close to the town at Ovcara. Like Mr Jusufovic's tours in Sarajevo, the Vukovar tour is aimed at dedicated dark tourists, costing approximately €50 for a three-hour walking or bicycle tour.

Again, the Vukovar and Ovcara tour illustrates that a range of sites associated with a conflict or death can be commodified for tourist purposes. The town of Vukovar contains the water tower, which preserved in its war-damaged state has become commodified as a scar. The hospital in the town contains a museum for tourists who wish to learn about the war, and, although not a synthetic site, features reconstructions of the conditions endured by the victims of the conflict. The mass grave and site of a large execution in the town illustrate another type of commodification again, acting primarily as memorials to the dead, but also acting as signage and facilitating war tourists who wish to visit the key locations of the conflict. Finally,

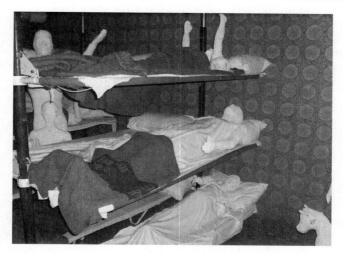

Figure 3.4 Vukovar hospitial.

as observed by the author on all tours in Vukovar, Sarajevo and Dubrovnik, the opportunity to speak with tourist guides who lived in their cities during the conflict again provides an opportunity to analyse the commodification of the war.

Conclusion/discussion

> Look, still Holocaust is popular. Genocide against Jews from the Second World War. Still concentration camps are popular. I saw in this Dark Tourism movie made by Canadian TV that millions and millions of people are visiting these bloody destinations still. In Cambodia, in Vietnam, in Poland, in Latvia. In Sarajevo it will be more and more. Actually I'm not afraid of the future. People will come. People will spend money. People will buy property here.
>
> (Zijo Jusufovic, Mission Impossible Tour Guide, Sarajevo, 2008)

Like past research on thanatourism, this chapter aims to further the existing body of work, promoting the notion that the field has a complex and chaotic nature. There are many ambiguities in thanatourism research: the field is still relatively new, research is exploratory, methodological frameworks are only in early stages of development and much of the work has employed largely empirical techniques. This chapter seeks to further the body of early work in dark tourism research by proposing that both the experiential and production sides of thanatourism sites should be examined in conjunction to provide a more holistic understanding of this phenomenon. Research into thanatourism must also involve an examination of the production of signs, the role of tourists as semioticians and the resulting consumption of culture which occurs with any kind of tourism. If one considers an example desti-nation, especially a complex region like the Balkans, the context of the above notion begins to clarify a little. For example, Sarajevo has since Ottoman times been a destination for travellers and, as a major Balkan transit point, it is immediately clear that the city's past has always been concerned with 'tourists' of some description. This creates difficulties in establishing a 'starting' point from which to research. For example, the shooting of Archduke Franz Ferdinand in the city in 1914, often attributed with triggering World War 1, placed Sarajevo firmly in the eye of the western media in the early twentieth century. The bridge beside which the Archduke was assassinated later became a dark tourism location itself and many visited the site over the last century. This history of dark tourism in Sarajevo creates an extra layer with which to consider the commodification of thanatourism space.

The commodification of these sites throughout the Balkans illustrates a desire to commemorate the war. While memorialisation might take place at a number of sites for reasons other than tourism, the commodification of sites certainly facilitates the dark tourist. MacCannell's seminal work on authen-ticity in tourism (1973) suggests that the modern tourist seeks authentic experiences. This chapter proposes that it is this demand for authenticity among dark tourists which helps to commoditise battlefields and other spaces of war. However, MacCannell also writes, of course, that this search for authenticity often proves fruitless, as tourists encounter 'staged authenticity'. In the creation of dark tourist gazes by public and private institutions, this staged authenticity comes later in the dark tourism spectrum. Destinations thus become focused more on profit and entertainment as opposed to politi-cal ideologies and education.

Although Lennon and Foley (2000) position dark tourism as a feature of postmodern tourism, they also correctly state that travel to gaze on death is certainly nothing new. Indeed, to contextualise this in the case of Sarajevo, tourists to the city pre-war often took in the site of the assassination of Archduke Franz Ferdinand, the starting point for World War I. If these dark tourism gazes can be considered a rise in spectacle, it is necessary to consider Virilio's work on The Museum of Accidents to help contextualise their exis-tence. His paper (2006) tells us that since the 1990s, approximately seventy per cent of large disasters (> $35 m) are man-made as opposed to natural catastrophies, and that our industrialised societies have, far from promoting quietude, 'developed disquiet and major risk, and this even so if we leave out of account the recent proliferation of weapons of mass destruction' (ibid.: 1). These disasters often become dark tourist sites themselves and this commodification process must be explored further. Virilio (2006: 3) hints that television and the media is to blame (or thank?) for this increase in the rise in spectacle, suggesting that 'Where the broadcasting of horror is con-cerned, television has, since the end of the last century, been the (live) site of a constant raising of the stakes ... we are now seeing the sudden synchronisa-tion of emotions.' This showcasing of death and mortality, and the resulting rise in thanatopsis, writes Virilio, has replaced the media's previous obsession with sexual liberation and it now reflects and entices more on 'repulsion than on seduction'; 'death will have replaced sex and the serial killer the Latin lover' (ibid.: 4).

This changing shift in voyeurism saw Virilio's idea of creating a museum of accidents come to fruition in 2002, and replications of this voyeuristic notion are visible in the dark tourism market in Sarajevo. Virilio's 'museum' involved a photographic display of hundreds of images which showcased international accidents at the Fondation Cartier Pour l'Art Contemporain, Paris. Similar instances occur in Bosnia: the variety of museums exploring the war, the privately available tours and the abundance of memorialisation in the city appear to have a relentlessly demanding market for consuming the siege. Virilio's overall premise is that, if the accident is a result of the speed of progress in the twentieth century, we have reached a point where a need has emerged to present and analyse these incidents. Do those entrepreneurs in the tourism industry in Sarajevo feel the need to present the incidents of 1992–6? And do visitors to the city also feel the need to connect with and understand these events? Further exploration on the nexus between memorialisation, consumption and commodification of death is needed to present a holistic understanding of this complex tourism phenomenon.

Section 2

Experiencing poor places

Tourism has long been concerned with the experience of the 'Other'. Whether, in MacCannell's (1989) terms, seeking authenticity, driven by a thirst for adventure or, just simply perhaps, wanting to 'get away from it all' – in order to survive modern society, people feel the need to escape periodically from it – tourists have been attracted by novelty, difference, a change from the normal. Typically, however, the 'difference' that has been packaged, commodified and sold by the tourism industry has largely been a selective, sanitised difference. Although Boorstin's (1964) notion of the tourist as a cultural dope satisfied with 'pseudo-events' is, in all likelihood, little more than a caricature of contemporary tourism, there is no doubt that tourists have long sought out places, events and experiences that verify a 'rose-tinted' preconception of the 'Other', 'packaged for consumption into easily digestible and, preferably, photogenic chunks' (Simpson 1993).

More recently, opportunities have been provided for tourists to experience the harsher side of tourist destinations, the places traditionally omitted from the glossy tourist brochures. Variously described as, for example, reality tourism, poverty tourism, slum tourism or, the case of proactive involvement on the part of tourists, volunteer tourism, such opportunities enable tourists to experience or witness places and communities that suffer the very socio-economic challenges that tourism, as an agent of development, is alleged to address. Despite the increasing popularity of such tourism, however, little academic attention has been paid to the ways in which it is experienced by tourists; questions with respect to what motivates tourists to participate in 'reality tours' and how they make sense of and respond to the experience remain largely unanswered.

In this section, Manfred Rolfes 'sets the scene' in Chapter 4 by exploring poverty tourism in the townships of South Africa, the favelas of Rio de Janeiro and the slums of Mumbai, India. Drawing upon his own research and the work of others, he reviews the development of tourism to these destinations, explores the nature of these experiences for tourists, and concludes with some overall 'observational-theoretical' conclusions. In the following chapter, Rochelle Spencer focuses her attention on rights-based tourism, a proactive attempt to not only highlight or educate tourists in the socio-economic challenges faced by poor or disenfranchised communities, but also to encourage them to support efforts to alleviate such challenges. Based upon her work in Cuba, she identifies the benefits associated with NGO-organised study tours for both participants/tourists and the ways in which the longer-term socio-cultural environment of local communities may be enhanced through tourism. Finally, in Chapter 6, Palloma Menezes provides a personalised account of her research into the tourists' experience of the Rocinha favela in Rio de Janeiro. Drawing on her analysis of photographic images that tourists use to illustrate narratives of their experiences, she explores the manner in which interaction between tourists and the local community occurs primarily through the practice of photography.

4 Slumming – empirical results and observational-theoretical considerations on the backgrounds of township, favela and slum tourism

Manfred Rolfes

Poorism, poverty tours, cultural tours, slumming... What are we talking about?

The phenomenon discussed in this chapter cannot be summarised in only one sentence. It is a relatively new form of tourism in the globalising cities of several so-called developing countries or emerging nations; namely, visits to the most disadvantaged parts of the respective city. These are mainly composed of guided tours through disadvantaged areas, often inappropriately called slums. These tours are offered on a relatively large scale in South African cities, Brazil's Rio de Janeiro or Sao Paulo, Mexico City, Cairo, as well as in Indian metropolises, to name some examples. International tourists are the primary target group of such tours.

The terms used to describe this tourism phenomenon are very disparate. In some articles, authors refer to these tours as 'social tours' or 'reality tours' because a number of them are explicitly presented or advertised as being 'authentic' or 'realistic' and expressed as touristic experiences 'off the beaten path'. Moreover, it is claimed that tourists participating in these social or reality tours specifically seek authentic or real experiences (Freire-Medeiros 2009a: 581; MacCannell 1999: 105). Other authors tag the tours as a form of cultural or ethnic tourism (Ramchander 2004; Jaguaribe and Hetherington 2004), generally emphasising their educational aspects. Both cultural and ethnic authenticities are placed at the centre of these experiences and, in this context, the opportunity for cultural exchange is important.

Then again, terms like poorism or poverty tourism are used to describe these tours. These terms express morally dubious socio-voyeuristic aspects. In particular, media reports (daily press and touristic trade journals) utilise these expressions, frequently criticising the economic valorisation and marketing of informal or marginal settlements, slums, favelas or townships – and particularly the sordidness and poverty there – as tourist attractions (Weiner 2008; Gentleman 2006; Danielzik and Khan 2006).

Furthermore, the term 'slumming' occurs in tourism research. In 1993, Welz examined the phenomenon of slumming or 'negative sightseeing' using the example of tourism in Harlem (New York City), where she located the culture-historical roots of the term.[1] Koven (2006), however, cites the term being used as early as the nineteenth century, in Victorian England. He describes the practice of slumming as a leisure activity pursued at the time by the upper and upper-middle classes of London society. Pott and Steinbrink (2010) show that today's slum, favela or township tours can be ranked within this slumming tradition. The focus of their approach is the consideration that a town's poor, other or dark side is set at the centre of leisure or touristic activities. Their assessment is that this again expresses the desired experience of reality and authenticity. Therefore, slumming will be used in this chapter as the most appropriate term for this form of tourism. Already introduced to scientific discussion by Welz (1993), Dowling (2007), Koven (2006) and Pott and Steinbrink (2009), slumming considers even earlier forms of this touristic phenomenon.

This conceptual ambiguity may also reflect the difficulty in attributing a specific goal or objective to participation in this form of tourism. What actually poses as the attraction visited during the tours through slums, favelas or townships? Certainly, the descriptions slumming, poverty tourism and poorism would suggest that sordidness and poverty seem to be the touristic attraction. However, the presumption that providers of these tours primarily show human wretchedness, illness and infirmity or unworthy living conditions is not borne out in practice. Generally, such tours do not focus on visiting sordidness and poverty; it is not an explicit part of the guided tours' agenda. Nevertheless, sordidness and destitution do, inevitably perhaps, play an important part in this tourism phenomenon. Tourists, as well as tour guides and scientific sources, associate sordidness and poverty, along with violence and crime, with the terms township, favela or slum. If it can be assumed that participants of these tours want to see what they expect to see in these places, which means they anticipate their experiences (Urry 2002), then sordidness, poverty, crime and violence are the core element of this form of tourism. In this respect, the terms slumming, poverty tourism or poorism are appropriate, as they correspond to the tourists' anticipations. However, tourists certainly cannot or would not state an interest or curiosity in poverty as a motive for participating in a favela, slum or township tour; this triggers moral indignation and criticism of voyeurism. Nevertheless, these introductory comments emphasise that poverty is a significant element of these tours; poverty turns out to be one appealing part of this kind of tour. Thus, this aspect can be considered as a significant, linking element of township, favela and slum tours. However, the tours are not explicitly aimed at showing or visiting poor living and housing conditions, but poverty does form the background of this tourism phenomenon.

To date, relatively few empirical studies of this specific phenomenon within the tourism industry have been undertaken (for Brazil: Freire-Medeiros 2007, 2009a; Menezes 2007a; Jaguaribe and Hetherington 2004; for South Africa: Rolfes *et al.* 2009; Ludvigsen 2002; Ramchander 2004, 2007;

Rogerson 2003, 2004; Margraf 2006). These studies focus primarily on the tourists' motivation for visiting such districts and, typically, a basic interest in a country's culture and the residents' living conditions is revealed as the tourists' main motive. For example, cultural and political-historical dimensions also present an interesting part of township tourism (Ramchander 2004; 2007). Favela tourism also attracts customers by marketing exoticism and samba (Freire-Medeiros 2007, 2009a; Jaguaribe and Hetherington 2004). Tourists are interested in experiencing the complexity and diversity of the visited destination. Therefore, poverty is not the sole motive to participate in such tours. However, why and to what extent sordidness, poverty or socioeconomic disadvantages seem appropriate to satisfy these motivations poses a highly interesting question from an epistemological point of view.

The following sections of this chapter refer to and comment on these developments and insights regarding slumming based on research and experiences in South Africa, Brazil and India. Specific questions that are addressed include: What do tourists want to see? What is shown? Why is it shown? Subsequently, the phenomenon is explored from an observational-theoretical perspective and, in the context of slumming, existing and produced differentiations, and the specific forms they take, are highlighted.

Slumming – three case studies

Methodology

In order to approach this form of tourism for the purpose of the abovementioned research questions, extensive empirical research was conducted in Cape Town (South Africa) in 2007 and 2008. Additionally, more limited empirical field studies took place in the course of shorter visits to Rio de Janeiro (Brazil) in 2008 and to Mumbai (India) in 2009. These three cities were chosen as they offer a notable number of commercial slumming tours. Moreover, all three cities feature strong socio-spatial polarisation which manifests itself in the form of informal or marginalised settlements as well as, to a sizeable extent, in the form of socially disadvantaged districts. Within all three metropolises, these marginalised settlements are part of everyday life. Furthermore, these cities are comparable with respect to their tourism-related attributes although whilst a widespread mass-touristic offer already exists in Cape Town and Rio de Janeiro, this only applies in part to Mumbai.

An insight into these research trips is presented in the following sections within the framework of short case studies. The findings of the empirical research in the three investigation areas are drawn upon in extracts in order to emphasise parallels and differences within this form of tourism.

Key data about the three case study areas

Cape Town is the main destination for international tourists to South Africa and attracts over one million international visitors each year. Township tours, that is, guided touristic tours through residential areas of the black population that used to serve as politically motivated propaganda tours for the Apartheid regime (Ludvigsen 2002: 17), have turned into a mass phenomenon. It is estimated that 300,000 such tourists visit the townships in Cape Town each year (AP 2007; for details, see Table 4.1).

In Rio de Janeiro, professionally conducted favela tourism is a growing market segment, albeit much less significant in terms of quantity than in Cape Town. For Rocinha, the most frequently visited favela in Rio, the annual number of visitors is estimated to be around 40,000 (Freire-Medeiros 2009a: 580; Menezes 2007a: 12). For the city as a whole, the number can be assumed to be only slightly larger. Thus, favela tourism in Rio Janeiro remains at a significantly lower volume than township tourism in Cape Town (see Table 4.1).

In Mumbai (formerly Bombay), slum tourism[2] is a very recent phenomenon. To date, no scientific studies into this form of tourism have, to the author's knowledge, been undertaken, although there are a number of experiential tourist reports of those who participated in these tours. Furthermore, only a few individual tour operators have internet presentations providing statements about the contents of the tours[3] (see Table 4.1).

Township tourism in Cape Town (South Africa)[4]

The tours and the observed sights

The 20 analysed tours were carried out by 12 different operators. The number of participants varied significantly, ranging from two persons in a minibus to 30 tourists travelling in a coach. All tours were led by black or coloured tour guides, most of whom claimed to live in a township themselves. Every tour exclusively had so-called black townships as its destination. However, for safety reasons, it was advised not to participate in tours to coloured townships. The tours proceeded from the inner city to the townships.

Table 4.1 Information about slumming in the three case study areas

	Cape Town	Rio de Janeiro	Mumbai
Tourists per year	>300,000	>40,000	>5,000
Main destinations	tours to almost all townships	Rocinha and some other favelas	Dharavi
Tours since...	1990/94	1992	2003
Number of tour operators	40–50	7–8	1–2
Offers	half day, day trips, B&B	half day, day trips, B&B	half day, day trips
Costs half day trip($)	20 US	20–30 US	8 US

Source: compiled by the author.

Most of the tours visited the townships of Langa, Gugulethu and Khayelitsha (cf. Figure 4.1). Irrespective of the township visited, the tours usually combined very similar elements:

- historical or cultural sights,
- visit to pre-school institutions (sometimes including singing or dancing performances by children),
- visit to various residential areas and different types of housing,
- visit to a *sangoma* (traditional healer), including the optional consultation,
- visit to a *shebeen* (informal pub) with *umqombothi* (traditional beer) usually served to the tourists,
- visits to private homes.

During the township tours, the tourists were offered various opportunities to buy souvenirs or (local) arts and crafts. Moreover, they were able to make donations during visits to social institutions. Though contact with residents was possible at every stop, such encounters were observed almost exclusively during the visits to the *shebeens*.

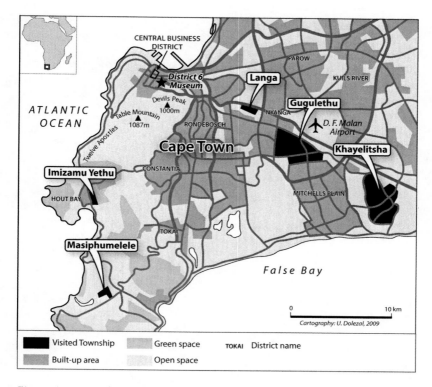

Figure 4.1 Visited townships in Cape Town.

Perspectives and views of the tour operators

Nine tour operators were asked about their motives for offering township tours. As expected, commercial motives were ranked highest. The tour companies have to work profitably in order to compete in the market. In this context, the interviewees highlighted the increasing demand for township tours, and the larger companies in particular referred to the fact that township tours were an important extension to their product range. In addition to economic motives, a number of other – rather idealistic – reasons were stressed by the tour operators. Some emphasised that their tours were meant to show what life is like in the communities, conveying knowledge about African culture, history, and giving an authentic insight into what they themselves called the 'real life' in South Africa. These goals were primarily mentioned by the owners of small companies who lived in townships themselves. Furthermore, all of the interviewees stressed the developmental relevance of township tourism and expressed their intention to initiate positive social and economic processes in the townships. Some of the operators also remarked that they wished to use a share of their profit to support particular projects in the communities.

Tour operators were also asked about their conception of what the tourists expect from the tours. A large proportion of the interviewees emphasised that the tourists were mainly interested in getting to know township residents and in interacting with the locals. Apart from this, the operators assumed that tourists were curious about poverty and developmental processes and that, generally, they had an interest in South African daily life and culture. In the opinion of the operators, many tourists wanted to see the far side of Cape Town and search for a complete or real picture of the city or the country.

This view was also shared by the local agents in the townships themselves, who were in direct contact with the tourists during the tours (for example, the owners of *shebeens*, restaurants and shops as well as artists and souvenir traders). They believed that tourists were especially attracted by the different way of life in South African townships. They stated that tourists wanted to see how people lived in the townships and get to know phenomena like locales or institutions that do not exist in their own countries (for example, *shebeens*, *sangomas*, local arts and crafts, music and dances, exotic food and beverages).

The township tours are arranged according to these assumed motives of and beliefs about the target group. The tour programmes include specific stops, particularly at places that are assumed to exemplify typical properties of black townships and the black community. Some operators choose their stops in order to explicitly present the residents' poverty to the tourists and to offer possibilities to improve the situation by, for example, donating to projects. Thus, the tour operators intentionally present both the poverty and the developmental potentials of the townships. Their point of view is that the tours have to show the bad living conditions in the townships as well as the positive changes. Others place the focus mainly on the positive sides of the townships and consciously omit badly developed areas so that the tourists' picture of the townships will be as positive as possible. These operators tend to focus on cultural heritage.

Observations of the tourists

The perspective of the tourists is analysed on the basis of responses by 179 tourists obtained through the use of a standardised questionnaire handed out before entering the townships. The questionnaires were filled in shortly before the beginning of the tour. Only 79 tourists also completed a standardised questionnaire immediately after the tour. Consequently, 79 statements about the tourists' expectations prior to the tour and their assessments afterwards are available.

After the township tour, the tourists were asked what observations they had made during the course of the trip and what had impressed them the most. Eighty-five responses were received to this question by 62 of the 79 persons (cf. Figure 4.2). Many of the visitors were particularly impressed by the friendliness of the township residents, this point being mentioned by more than 30 per cent of respondents. In addition, 20 per cent noted the comparatively high standard of public and commercial infrastructure as a surprising feature. The fact that these two aspects were striking to so many of the tourists can obviously be ascribed to the fact that they did not expect such high standards. After all, two-thirds of the visitors associated the township with poverty before the beginning of the tour. Given such expectations, it is no surprise that happy people and developed infrastructure (and technology) are particularly unexpected to the visitors.

These results are a first strong indication that the tourists' perception of the townships changed during the tour. To allow for a refined description of the tourists' images of townships, the tourists were asked to complete a semantic

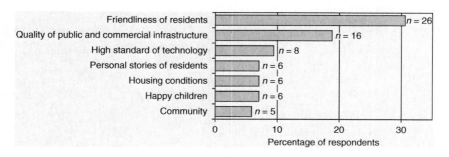

Figure 4.2 Tourists' impressions after the tour.[a]

Note

a 'Please write down words describing your impressions about your township tour.'

profile before the beginning and after the end of the tour. In the questionnaire, opposing word pairs were presented, conceived as scales for assessing the tourists' perception of townships. The tourists were asked to decide which of the respective two words corresponded best with their own ideas of a township. In this way, a specification of the tourists' expectations (images) was rendered possible. Figure 4.3 illustrates how the responses before the tour (black line) differ from those after the tour (grey line). It is evident that the ratings had changed remarkably. Interestingly, there is a tendency to give more positive evaluations after the tour in the case of all word pairs.

From the analyses, it becomes apparent that the visit has brought about significant changes in the tourists' perception of the townships. The choice of sights and sceneries presented by the tour operators and the agents within the townships had apparently not missed the intended goal (that is, to improve the image of the townships). An image of dreariness and greyness has become more variegated and at times even veers towards bright and rosy. Further analysis of the inquiries after the tour supported by interviews with individual tourists shows that cultural categories gain in importance for the majority of the tourists.

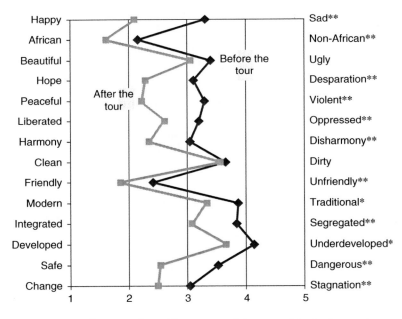

Figure 4.3 Evaluation of specific aspects of the townships before and after the tour.[b]

Note

b 'Here is a list of pairs of contradicting words. Tick spontaneously which of the following words better describe the township.' In order to test the significance of the differences, the U-Test was applied (* = 5%-level, ** = 1%-level).

Favela tourism in Rio de Janeiro (Brazil)[5]

The tours and the observed sights

In Rio de Janeiro, minibuses, open-top jeeps, or motorbikes were used as means of transportation, although walking tours were offered as well. The number of participants varied between 2 and 15 persons. Three such tours were analysed. These focused on Rio's most frequently visited favelas, Rocinha (unofficially estimated to have over 150,000 inhabitants), as well as the two smaller favelas of Vila Canoas and Tavares Bastos with 3,000 to 5,000 inhabitants each. All three favelas are located in the south of the city and are, thus, easily accessible for tourists. Moreover, touristic sights and the city centre are relatively nearby (cf. Figure 4.4).

Although the tours were arranged by substantially different operators, their courses were very similar. The core feature of each attended tour was a walk through the alleys and trails of the favelas. In terms of particular locations visited and specific aspects explained, the tour guides emphasised the following:

- explanations regarding the mechanisms of socio-geographic differentiation and spatial disparities within a favela (especially rent and property market, and unemployment),
- information regarding modern infrastructural equipment (wireless LAN, health services) and up-to-date shopping and services infrastructure, such as fashion stores, banks and cafés,
- opportunities to acquire local products and souvenirs, especially of an artistic or cultural nature,
- meetings with voluntary workers on social or cultural projects and/or visits to such projects,
- visits to or tours of schools, kindergartens or other institutions serving children and adolescents,
- impressions of private residences, communication with their inhabitants,
- visit to a restaurant or café.

However, a further aspect played a major role in all tours: weapons, violence and the drug trade. The statements of the tour guides in this regard were often contradictory and ambiguous. Sometimes during the tour, the drug trade and crime were described as everyday phenomena in a favela and, moreover, visitors were warned not to photograph certain groups of people. At other times, life in a favela was described as absolutely safe, where violence and drug problems are merely media-hype characterisations.

Perspectives and views of the tour operators and tour guides

Only seven or eight agencies offering favela tours were found in Rio de Janeiro. Their degree of professionalism and their product range varied greatly. Some

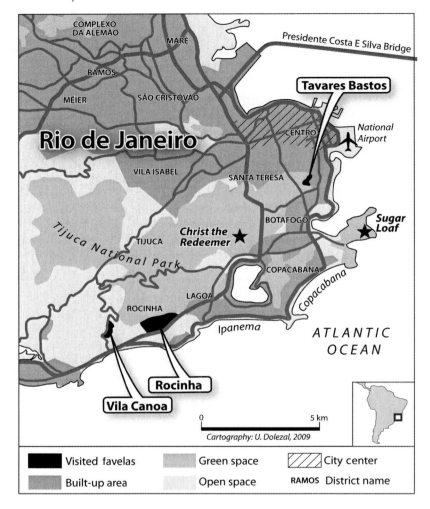

Figure 4.4 Visited favelas in Rio de Janeiro.

operators stated that part of the money earned through favela tours was returned to those areas in the form of social or cultural projects. Nevertheless, the main goal of the operators was to secure and broaden the financial basis of their enterprises.

According to this research, which is supported and complemented by the results of Freire-Medeiros (2009a), the majority of operators intend to present an authentic image of the favelas to show real life. However, they do not aim to do so by explicitly showing the life of the favela inhabitants as being precarious or poor. In fact, by stressing the relatively high standard of living, the advanced infrastructural equipment, the modern range of services and the varied shopping opportunities, they strive to demonstrate the living conditions in favelas as being absolutely normal and attractive. An illustration of this focus can be seen in the tour guides' repeated references to the traditional Brazilian cheerfulness which is associated, for example, with carnival and the numerous samba schools. According to Freire-Medeiros's research, some tour operators have already expressed concern that the image of the favela presented in Rocinha does not sufficiently match the tourists' expectations because it's not poor enough (Freire-Medeiros 2009a: 584).

Furthermore, the tour operators explicitly aim to correct the public image of the favelas, which is dominated by violence, crime and the drug trade. They consider these images to be primarily conveyed by national and international media, which they accuse of grossly exaggerating the situation in the favelas and of consistently returning to such negative aspects as the central focus of their reports. However, especially in this regard, the tour operators' arguments are self-contradictory and inconsistent. Many of them described violence, drugs and crime as a rather marginal problem in the favelas. Life in a favela was presented as normal, non-violent and safe. Nonetheless, during favela tours the tourists were repeatedly confronted with potential crime and the drug trade. However, in these situations, armed patrols were described as normal, certain streets were avoided because of the open drug trade and the photographing of certain situations was discouraged (Freire-Medeiros 2009a: 584). According to this, the tour operators were indeed concerned with safety and crime, but at the same time, not wanting this to disturb the tourists, they are downplayed.[6]

Motivations and observations of the tourists

Since no relevant empirical information is available as yet, valid statements about the motives of tourists who participate in favela tours cannot be made. Nevertheless, some authors suggest that the tourists want to see those phenomena in the favelas which they expect to encounter there: poverty and violence/crime (Machado 2007: 72; Menezes 2007a: 18–20). This can be supported in part with statements of the interviewed tour guides. The image of favelas assumed to be present in the minds of all international tourists is dominated by poverty, violence, as well as crime, which is disseminated by the international mass media. Several authors ascribe a major role in the construction of that image to the film *City of God* (Freire-Medeiros 2009a: 582–83; Machado 2007: 72). The tour operators also assume that tourists are concerned with poverty and violence/crime which is why they usually aim to break down that image.

The few statements by tourists as to their motives about attending favela tours indicate a somewhat different picture. They claim to be interested especially in the living conditions of the inhabitants, in real life, or in a different, hitherto unfamiliar aspect of tourism in Rio de Janeiro. They expect the tour to help them gain a more comprehensive impression of Brazil. Freire-Medeiros assumes that the favelas, their specific architecture and their inhabitants are being exoticised in various ways and, thus, constructed as a tourist destination. Favelas are increasingly marketed as tourist destinations which leads to an emphasis on culture and lifestyle (Freire-Medeiros 2009a: 582–84). According to this perspective, it is striking that flyers, brochures and posters in tourist accommodations, especially youth and backpacker hostels, advertise visits to overnight stays at favelas through favela parties, Brazilian funk music and favela hype.[7]

Slum tourism in Mumbai (India)[8]

The tours and the observed sights

Dharavi is *the* destination of slum tours in Mumbai; with approximately one million inhabitants it is the biggest slum in Asia (cf. Figure 4.5). Figures to indicate the quantitative scale of Dharavi slum tourism can only be estimated. According to media reports (Weiner 2008; Kendle 2008; Viggiano 2008; Schröder 2007) and tour operator statements, slum tours are provided to any extent by only one agency, Reality Tours & Travel, which has been offering tours to Dharavi since 2006. Another company does exist but it organises only very few slum tours.

Similar to the tours offered in Cape Town and Rio de Janeiro, the Dharavi tours are designed as reality tours. In summary, the available information on the course of a slum tour in Dharavi indicates the following stops or points of interest:

- notes on the socio-spatial and ethnic differentiation in Dharavi and information about cultural variety and the coexistence of different population groups,
- visit to recycling activities and a variety of small-scale industries, such as tannery, embroidery, pottery, and so on,
- detailed information and explanation regarding the economic significance of Dharavi for the national and global economy,
- visit to the market and commercial and cultural centre of Dharavi,
- information on the partly provisional and insufficient infrastructure of Dharavi (especially waste-water disposal and electricity),
- living and domestic conditions of the inhabitants, visits to the homes of the inhabitants,
- visit to social and cultural projects.

Perspectives and views of the tour operators and tour guides

The goals of the tour were pointed out frequently during the tour by the guides and during the interview with the Reality Tours & Travel tour operator. Thus, the agency sees a major goal of its work in breaking down the negative

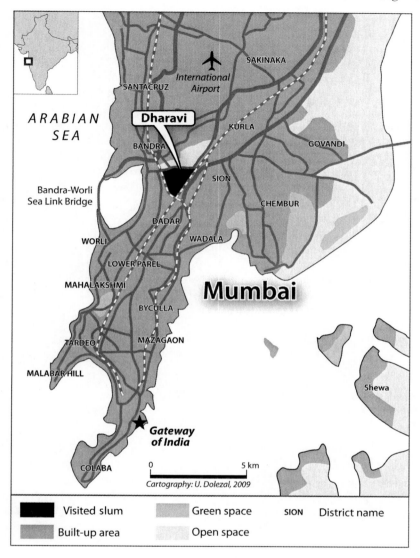

Figure 4.5 Visited slum in Mumbai.

image of Dharavi and its residents. For this purpose and in order to increase their understanding and empathy, the tourists of different countries, races and social classes are presented with everyday life in the slums. Therefore, the central issue is to deliver an authentic or realistic image of the slum. The hard-working slum population and their living and working conditions are presented. This does not just aim at revising the negative image of the slum but also at enhancing and enabling intercultural learning and understanding.

Apparently, the focus is particularly on the multiple economic activities. According to the tour operator, a major part of the earnings (80 per cent) go towards educational projects and language courses for the inhabitants of Dharavi.

The tourist view

Regarding slum tourists in Mumbai, no valid indications on their participation motives are available. Undoubtedly, international visitors to India are familiar with the media images of Indian slums, as indicated by the results of the qualitative interviews. It cannot be asserted to what extent curiosity about poverty may motivate their taking part in tours. However, poverty or misery certainly is one expected factor. According to the qualitative interviews with tour participants conducted during the field stay and also the findings of Meschkank (2009), it is apparent that participants claim to be interested especially in real life and the living conditions of the inhabitants. Moreover, they state that poverty, poor living or hygiene conditions are or were expected to be seen. After the tour, they were positively surprised about how active and committed the slum residents are in mastering the hard living conditions. They were astonished at the large spectrum of economic activities.[9] Like the tourists in the townships of Cape Town and the favelas of Rio de Janeiro, the slum tourists of Mumbai were also motivated by the expectation of seeing another side to the 'glistening metropolis' and mainstream tourism.

Slumming from an observational-theoretical point of view[10]

Guided tours in South African townships, Brazilian favelas and Indian slums are a very complex tourism phenomenon. They are extraordinary as tourists are confronted with the phenomenon of 'poverty' in very different ways depending on the specific touristic destination. Before, during and after the tours, poverty is made the subject of discussion. It is implicitly marketed as a supposed attraction, presented as reality or authenticity, and efforts are even made to conceal it. Poverty as a phenomenon and setting is omnipresent during every tour, even if tour providers aim at specifically not making poverty the focal point of the touristic observation. The three case studies have shown what alternative observation patterns of poverty are served as viewing points during the tours and how the tour providers attempt to construct an alternative picture to poverty.

However, poverty is a significant difference or distinction within the phenomenon of slumming. It is evident that a major portion of international tourists visiting the settlements view these places as areas of urban poverty. These districts are excessively laden with features like misery, hopelessness, unemployment, exposure, disease and, sometimes, hunger and poverty. A very similar observation and connotation of urban poverty is also evident in the mass media. For Davis (2006), slum is primarily connected with the expression of urban poverty as misery or distress as described above. This perspective of urban poverty should be labelled here as a *first-order observation*. It indicates what poverty is. When observing poverty by primarily focusing on the misery and suffering of humans as its borders and differentiation, slums and informal settlements are, in particular, presented.

From an ethical point of view, it now seems morally objectionable to observe this kind of poverty within a framework of touristic activities (Freire-Medeiros 2009a: 582). Thus, this moralising view observes, judges and evaluates the manner in which the above described poverty is marketed as a tourist attraction. Townships, favela or slum tours are observed as 'poorism' or 'poverty tourism'. Therefore, from a moralising perspective, this kind of tourism is usually criticised and condemned as voyeuristic and undignified. Thus, the observation of poverty tourism should also be classified as a *first-order observation*.

It has been revealed how these two first-order observations – the observation of poverty in informal settlements and that of poorism/poverty tourism – are being observed by tour operators or agents within the communities, who do after all benefit from this kind of tourism. Tour operators' descriptions and their relevant statements have pointed out that the choice of emphasis on the tours is justified as they refer to such first-order observations. The following is evident:

- The tour operators, too, regard such voyeuristic first-order observations of poverty with scepticism and are critical of such views on urban poverty. The tours aim at relativising poverty as the primary association with townships, favelas or slums. The goal is to correct the observation according to which poverty is the primary factor dominating living conditions in these areas. From their point of view, life in informal settlements is not exclusively characterised by poverty, misery and suffering. Rather, the inhabitants' creative engagement with the precarious living and working conditions is presented. The aim is to display the so-called 'poor quarters' as not being ruled by apathy, fatalistic lack of perspective and socio-economic exclusion. Even though life there is presented as hard, positive impulses of development, success and the normality of the situations of those living there are focused upon. Thus, one could describe this as a *second-order observation* commenting on the charged contents of the first-order observation.
- The tour operators further refer to the moral-ethical observations and evaluations of poverty tourism. Tours in the marginal settlements that primarily aim towards a voyeuristic viewing of poverty, misery and suffering are also vehemently opposed by the majority of tour operators. They define the tours they offer explicitly and clearly, distinguishing them from such 'zoo visits' or 'safaris'. In order to profile their own tours as authentic, real or community-based, tour operators intentionally use those

constructed negative examples and nourish them deliberately. While their own tours are emphasised and presented as unique, competitors' tours are discredited as voyeuristic. This differentiation is used deliberately by the tour operators to distinguish themselves from the competition.

As an initial summary, it can be stated that, on the one hand, the discourses around slumming are concerned with the discussion about the touristic viewing of poverty and whether this view is morally supportable. On the other, the discussion is directly connected with the specific notion of poverty as proposed by those who criticise the tours. This stems from the inflammation of ethically motivated criticism of tours, especially from the idea that during the tours, a type of poverty is presented that is almost exclusively defined by the suffering, misery and distress of the people. However, the tours aim precisely at not promoting this view of poverty.

The tour operators oppose the negative observation of the tours as 'zoo visits' or 'safaris' with a positive alternative. Key terms and core concepts in tour construction are authenticity and reality. Here, authenticity and reality cannot be understood as essentialist or ontological entities. They must rather be perceived as social constructions or as observations by the tour operators. During the tours, the operators show what they consider to be authentic, real or everyday. It was demonstrated which strategies and means the tour operators utilise to be able to present or market their tours as authentic and realistic. This should be specified once more.

In the specifications of township tourism, historical, political and cultural categories were stressed in a specific way. This is certainly primarily a result of the ethnically segregated development of South African cities under Apartheid. The historical development of the townships and the political struggle against Apartheid as well as Black African culture (handcraft, *sangoma*, *shebeen*) are the trademarks of township tours. Culture has hereby been introduced as a relevant category in slumming in Cape Town. According to Pott (2007: 107), culture is a dominant mode of city tourism. Culture is said to be 'a mode of observation for the observance of differences as cultural differences' (Pott 2005: 92). Culture is conceived of as a social construct by the observer. Thus, in township tours, the observation of poor quarters also takes place in the context of culturalisation. South African culture, its tradition and history take centre stage. Thus, poverty is semantically equated to a cultural tour (Ramchander 2007: 40). This cultural connotation goes along with ethnicisation. It is not about South African culture and tradition but primarily about the culture and tradition of the black population. Ethnicisation and ethnic diversity have already been shown as an important scheme of touristic observation elsewhere (Rath 2007).

With respect to the favela tours in Rio de Janeiro, two elements are particularly conspicuous: first, the explicit references to the very good provision in terms of infrastructure, services and shopping and, second, the considerable focus on themes of violence, crime and the drug trade is a special feature of favela tourism. The latter are, on the one hand, highly repellent for tourism but, on the other, they belong to a repeatedly activated observational scheme – particularly in favela tourism but also to a smaller extent in township tourism. Tourism research has revealed a variety of examples where tourist destinations are, amongst other reasons, particularly attractive because they play on an ambivalence of security and insecurity or of life and death.[11] However, whereas township tours aim to dissolve the association of townships with violence and crime, some favela tours more or less openly stress and market these risks of crime, drugs and violence (Freire-Medeiros in Chagas 2006). Crime and violence thus become a mode of observation activated in favela tours, characterising the everyday life situation in the poor quarters.

An observational scheme not discussed thus far takes centre stage in Indian slum tourism: the pronounced economic and innovative power in the poor quarters. The high economic energy and extreme industriousness of the slum inhabitants are stressed as an important distinction during the tours. Even under very precarious living conditions, a high potential for economic activity rather than apathetic inactivity or helplessness prevails – that is the message of the tour operators and the dominating scheme of observation.

Finally, it is to be noted that all observed tours laid special emphasis on the production of an authentic and realistic perspective. The tours were constructed in such a way that the observation of the living conditions in the visited quarters could be presented to the tourists as authentic and realistic. The fact that poverty can be or is observed during the tours is thus pushed into the background. The reduction of the importance of poverty as an observational scheme is also achieved by offering and using alternative observational schemes, such as culture, ethnicity, drug crime or economisation. Even if poverty does not always present the tourists' and tour operators' predominant observation perspective, every now and then it still comes to light in places. Poverty is an important category which structures and interweaves this form of tourism in numerous ways. However, poverty tourism or poorism are not the appropriate terms for this touristic phenomenon. They suggest that the aims of these tours are the deliberate sightseeing and the explicit demonstration of poverty. It has been shown, however, that this simple observational perspective does not do justice to the complex phenomenon discussed in this chapter.

Notes

1 See the considerations about slumming in New York in Dowling (2007).
2 The term slum tourism is used in numerous sources referring to touristic tours to informal settlements in Indian megacities. The operators of such tours also describe them as slum tours.
3 See http://realitytoursandtravel.com/slumtours.html (accessed 6 August 2009).
4 A major part of the empirical evaluation was conducted within a research project in Cape Town, led by the author in February/March 2007. Furthermore, during another field stay in February/March 2008, further empirical follow-up surveys

took place. Different township tours were attended. The routes, stops, special observations and notable occurrences were recorded. Qualitative interviews with tour operators, as well as with agents within the townships were conducted. Tourists were interviewed by using semi-standardised questionnaires. All results are available in detail in Rolfes *et al.* (2009).

5 The empirical analyses were conducted during the author's favela visit in July/August 2008. Different tours were accompanied and the essential contents and stops of the tours were recorded. Furthermore, qualitative interviews with tour guides and several tourists were conducted.

6 'The truth is that drug dealers make the peace...Peace means no robbery, and that law is very well respected.' Statement by a tour operator in Rio de Janeiro, quoted in Yurchyshyn (2008).

7 See http://www.jazzrio.com.

8 Professional and regular slum tours in Mumbai are only offered by one tour operator. Consequently, the empirical findings presented in this chapter refer solely to one attended slum tour, one expert discussion with the tour operator and qualitative interviews with the tour guides and tourists. Initial results of an empirical research conducted in the context of a master thesis are incorporated within the following explanations (Meschkank 2009). The empirical research was conducted by the author during a field stay in Mumbai in March 2009 and an extensive survey in the course of a master thesis between February and April 2009.

9 Qualitative interviews with 19 tour participants were conducted (Meschkank 2009: 55–57).

10 For further details about the background of the observational-theoretical approach see Egner (2006) and Rolfes (2009).

11 Cf. on dark tourism: Stone and Sharpley 2008; See reports in the mass media about war or terror tourism.

5 Rights-based tourism – tourist engagement in social change, globalised social movements and endogenous development in Cuba

Rochelle Spencer

Introduction

Using a theoretical framework of solidarity and new social movements, this chapter articulates a critical theoretical development of rights-based tourism. The research is based on my association with the former Oxfam Community Aid Abroad Tours (OCAAT) and Global Exchange's Reality Tours (GERT) in Cuba. These are subsidiaries of development and human rights organisations that are devoted to 'responsible' tourism in developing countries. A central focus of their operations is to educate tourists about the development issues that people are faced with and what local and international efforts are being made to alleviate and improve these issues. The hope is that by educating tourists and providing them with opportunities to meet and discuss these issues with local people, they will a) minimise the negative impacts typically associated with tourism, b) disseminate what they have learnt to their peers, and c) work towards supporting efforts to help these countries.

The Cuban Institute for Friendship of the People (ICAP) works with the tour operators to arrange meetings with a combination of non-government grassroots organisations, government agencies, academics, doctors, artists and the like, combined with visits to community projects to provide insights into contemporary Cuban life. The idea is that Cuba has a national programme of social development that can be identified through these (and other) institutions. Hence through art, schools, health clinics, organic agriculture and so forth, we learn the story of Cuba.

The undertaking of cultural research into tourism and social development in Cuba provided a situated understanding of tourist experiences as forms of cultural exchange and transformation. It appears that through experiential learning, NGO study tours transform tourists. The anthropology of tourism perspective has often addressed transformation from one state to another. However, in order to capture the complexity of transformation, I reframe it in terms of social and cultural change. Notions of personal transition within tourism are not straightforward shifts but are nuanced and complex. One important dimension is the ways in which tourists and their engagements facilitate the networking of new social movements. Accordingly, education provides the platform for subsequent action where the notion of 'meaningful' experiences has instrumental outcomes, such as solidarity with Cuba. These experiences highlight that there is resonance beyond the tour itself. This is of interest for what it says about tourist identities and necessarily so if particular styles of tourism make people feel morally superior.[1] To understand this broader picture, we need to consider levels of agency that go beyond self-interest within the tourism-development nexus and its application in the streets of Havana today through a rights-based development framework.

Rights-based development

Rights talk stops people being perceived as 'needy', as 'victims' and as 'beneficiaries'. Instead, it enables these same people to know and present themselves as rightful and dignified people who can make just demands of power and spell out the duties of power in terms of moral and political goods (Slim 2002: 3). Rights-based approaches to development provide a framework and give weight to what is taking place in Cuba with NGO study tours. Rights talk gives development a moral vision (Slim 2002: 3). It is pious and makes people feel virtuous. It is this framework that I draw on to make an argument for ways in which tourism can be utilised by development. In this respect tourism moves beyond simply boosting the economy to having wider implications for local people.

In the last decade, rights-based approaches have gained more attention in development discourse. There appears to be some agreement upon basic elements, but there is no single, universally agreed rights-based approach (Ljumgman 2005). Rather, 'there are plural rights-based approaches, with different starting points and rather different implications for development practice' (Cornwall and Nyamu-Musembi 2004: 1415). Essentially, human rights are cited as both the moral and legal entitlements to basic well-being and dignity (Ljumgman 2005). They are the 'social and political guarantees necessary to protect individuals from the standard threats to human dignity posed by the modern state and modern markets' (Donnelly 1989). This brings us to consider dignity as an inalienable aspect of human existence and raises interesting questions for how development either improves or diminishes human dignity. The human rights framework is unique in its ability to intersect with various aspects of development (Van Tuijl 2000) and, as such, it provides a paradigmatic foundation for global communication at both the human and institutional levels because as Van Tuijl (2000: 619) argues, 'people need structures and language to relate to each other, to frame what they want to identify as progress or development in their lives'.

The value of incorporating rights into development practices lies broadly in its normative and ethical aspects. A human rights approach to development sets out a vision of what *should* be, thereby providing a normative framework, and it makes an ethical and moral dimension imperative to development assistance. Hamm (2001) recognises that a rights-based approach does not necessarily guarantee success, but it does bring about important changes for the ongoing sustainability of a relationship between development and human rights in this era of neoliberal globalisation and 'empire'.

Many would concede that this approach is not new.[2] Examples of elements central to a rights-based approach that have been taking place for decades include development work that engages local people in a more active process of social transformation, and advocacy and empowerment projects towards capacity-building. Demands by disadvantaged social groups for participation in decision-making in order to promote bottom-up and people-centred development have been at the core of development literature since the late 1970s. Often, development organisations, international financial institutions and sometimes even NGOs have a somewhat formal notion of participation, which can mean informing local people of development projects rather than including them at inception (Gardner and Lewis 1996). But the shift in focus, where internationally agreed legislation supports these practices, *does* 'change the way in which they come to be viewed by development agencies and national governments' (Cornwall and Nyamu-Musembi 2004: 1418), because a rights approach implies that participation is a right and, thus, includes control of planning, process, outcome, and evaluation of the path of development (Hamm 2001: 1018–19).

The tour groups to Cuba at both agency and state level are, for a number of reasons, heavily participatory, giving tourists a close sense of precisely what it means to see this level of engagement in development as a 'right'. The reframing of participation as rights is about assisting people to claim their rights *and* strengthening the capacity of those responsible to fulfil their duties; thereby, it shifts the development framework from assessing only the needs of beneficiaries. The Cuban organisations that take part in the tours can be considered to also be strengthening their ability to 'do' development in Cuba.

The failure of many national governments and international institutions to ensure human rights leads to the perennial question concerning rights-based approaches to development: who is responsible for providing 'rights' – community, NGOs, national governments, or international bodies? Indeed, even though rights-based discourse is employed within international aid, far too often donor countries do not see themselves as bearing any responsibility in the realisation of these rights (Cornwall and Nyamu-Musembi 2004: 1423–25). Thus, we have seen a rise in new social movements which represent the subaltern voice and demand human rights. It is clear that to think about alternatives to development requires redefining theoretical and programmatic notions of development itself. This possibility relies largely on the actions of social movements and can, thus, best be achieved by building upon their practices. It is essential to link proposals of alternative visions of society with the ongoing work of social movements (Escobar 2005: 344).

Conceivably, social movements, as symbols of resistance to the prevailing politics of knowledge and power, provide avenues for the re-imagining of the Third World. A mosaic of new social movements, supported by NGOs, is emerging to actively mobilise around issues of human rights, and to resist and contest the orthodoxy of economic globalisation. This is because many consider that the failure of development, combined with the nature of current global neoliberal tendencies, undermines human well-being and dignity. The NGO campaign for a rights-based approach to development that spear-headed the World Summit for Social Development in Copenhagen supports this. Indeed, a rights perspective is helping NGOs to respond to some of the challenges they face to become more relevant in the development arena (Van Tuijl 2000: 617). It is largely NGOs that take the initiative in guiding the grassroots development activities (McMichael 2004).

New social movements have responded to the failure of development and the social exclusion exacerbated by globalisation through attempts to reframe development as a question of rights. Human sustainability requires conservation of community in inclusive terms rather than the exclusive terms of economic globalisation (McMichael 2004: 281, 307). Many of the people negatively impacted by the processes of development and globalisation look to NGOs to represent their needs. Thus, many NGOs support new social movements, whose focus is to defend the rights of the oppressed or to create local and sectoral sites of resistance – ecological, feminist, ethnic, human rights. Other forms of resistance to the globalisation project include growing consumer advocacy, for example, against sweatshops and child labour. As I will demonstrate, part of that growing consumer advocacy includes new types of tourism selected for their 'educational', 'responsible' and 'political' overtones and tourists' 'moral' inclination to do something 'good'. What we see happening with new social movements is a political interconnectedness, globally and nationally, that at its core has a human rights focus on development. This wave of concern can also be discerned in the rise of the types of tourism I focus on here and in the types of networks they propagate.

Despite criticism of rights-based approaches to development, we need to consider human rights because processes of neoliberal economic globalisation threaten the social standards of those in developing countries who are often powerless. Human rights offers a cogent agenda with which to consider tourism as a means to sustainable development. A rights-based approach to development provides both the conceptual and practical framework for empowering the subaltern voice. NGOs, such as GERT and OCAAT, assisting local people to get involved in tourism have the capacity to support people to claim their right to participation and thereby strengthen their sense of human well-being and dignity. This aspect of the NGO tours gives them a moral underpinning because not only are they seen as educational, but also as rights-based and thus sustainable. In this sense, we might reframe our typologies and imagine the emergence of 'rights-based' tourism. Global conjunctions, historical perspectives of development, and moral imperatives of recent development trends inform tourism and what is taking place in Cuba.

Social movements and tourism

The role of social movements is to challenge hegemonic ideas in society about development, democracy and human rights. New social movements were developed in the 1960s and 1970s in Europe to explain emerging new movements that did not fit the previous social movement model of Marxian class conflict. They place a greater emphasis on collective identity, values and lifestyles and a tendency to emerge more from middle than working class constituencies (Friedman and McAdam 1992; Johnston and Klandermans 1995; Melucci 1996).

The term social movements 'covers various forms of collective action aimed at social reorganisation. In general, social movements are not highly institutionalised, but arise from spontaneous social protest directed at specific or widespread grievances' (Abercrombie, Hill and Turner 1994: 389). 'Social movements are defined precisely in terms of what they supposedly bring about: new forms of politics and sociality' (Escobar 2005: 345). GERT and OCAAT are agents of network building by virtue of the intense social experiences they provide to tourists. Their tours may serve as a catalyst for increased social movement participation. As facilitators of new social movements, these NGOs hope to harness the power and influence of educational development-oriented tourism for its ability to facilitate motivation and mobilisation efforts.

Throughout the 1980s, social movements established themselves through NGOs, moving beyond the boundaries of nation states by producing transnational avenues of financial and political support and uniting people globally on issues such as environment, human rights and refugees (Tsing 2000). Indeed, many post-development scholars have embraced new social movements as a means of directing alternatives to conventional development (cf. Esteva 1988; Escobar 1995; Rahnema 1997; Sachs 1992; Illich 2001a, 2001b; Hall 2002). New social movements are distinguished by an expressive politics, and their resistances to the 'developed society' model as the institutions of the welfare state have receded. They challenge the declining legitimacy of development in its national and global incarnations in an effort to internationalise the realities of the indigenous actors of resistance (cf. Guha 1983, 1988, 1996; McMichael 2004; Parajuli 2001; Spivak 1988, 1996).

As my research from Cuba reveals, emerging tourism niches forecast an increasing interest between globalised social movements, tourist engagement in social change and endogenous development. Identifying these conjunctions entails exploring beyond new social movement membership (Barkan, Cohn and Whitaker 1995). Belonging to an organisation is manifested in a variety of distinctive ways. NGO study tourists demonstrate a high involvement in new social movement participation. Their level of support in such movements through charities, development agencies or conservation groups indicates their commitment to and involvement with global development issues. One member may make regular financial contributions and receive a newsletter while another participates in activism and campaigning. Additionally, many participants are motivated to join an NGO study tour as a means to financially support projects and facilitate connections with other like-minded people and local people in developing countries. In analysing social movements, Knoke (1988) tells us that it is necessary to include *external* and *internal* forms of participation. Typically, studies of social movement participation analyse internal forms, such as volunteering, involvement in administrative procedures, voting or running in elections, and the provision of resources. External forms of participation include lobbying to politicians, writing letters to them, attending rallies and, as I argue, participating in NGO study tours. These tours are a form of *external participation* in new social movements that evidence a 'movement of movements' (Klein 2004: 220) precisely because of their international reach, because the people that participate in them represent a mosaic of groups and campaigns that make up new social movements, and because of the networks created during the tours.

The creation of networks is an important aspect of new social movements and this is key to NGO study tours in Cuba. 'New social movements are rhizomic (assuming diverse forms, establishing unexpected connections, adopting flexible structures, moving in various dimensions – the family, the neighbourhood, the region) (see Deleuze and Guattari 1988). Social movements are fluid and emergent, not fixed states, structures, and programs' (Escobar 2005: 347). Individuals and organisations that are linked together through one or more social relationships become networks, which are an important element of social movement participation and potentially reinforce activism support (c.f. Klandermans and Oegema 1987; McAdam and Rucht 1993; Knoke 1988; McGehee 2002). For example, our ties to family and friends or work colleagues can influence our worldview and our support for political and social issues. These informal ties that form our social networks are important reference points that are vital to network development, participation and commitment to social movements (Lichterman 1996: 24). This is fundamental to the success of NGO study tours in mobilising support, because the people who participate in a tour each have their own social networks to which they disseminate information about their experiences in Cuba.

The ability to make a commitment emanates from important and valued connections among individuals (Boyte 1980), like the connections forged on NGO study tours when people feel a sense of communitas (Turner 1969) with other participants sharing the same experiences. These informal connections attest that networks can be a vital source to inspire participation. Again, this corresponds with the goals of GERT and OCAAT as they hope that participation in their tours will lead to the dissemination of information about the NGO's work and social development in Cuba, thereby encouraging people to get involved. GERT and OCAAT utilise tourism as a means of educating tourists to become more active in campaigning on issues of international concern. McGehee's (2002) study of Earthwatch expeditions found that participation encouraged social movement engagement. Her research indicates, as does mine, the effect of networks on individuals – developed during intense educational tourism experiences – to increase participants' motivation and intention for future activism.

Cultivating solidarity

Sometime after coordinating my last study tour in Cuba, I received a long email from tour participant, William. He was writing to update me on the past year and a half, revealing that on his return from Cuba he joined the Australia Cuba Friendship Society, largely owing to the persistent efforts of Georgia, one of the other tour participants who had also become a member of the Friendship Society. He has since worked his way through the ranks to become President and informed me that another tour participant, Inez, has also since joined and become the Secretary. In his email, he wrote:

> The Cuban odyssey was the best trip I have ever been on and I have decided to return with the Southern Cross Brigade in late December. As I'm returning to Cuba you may be able to advise me on new issues and people to meet with while I am over there; last week we met with the Cuban Consul.

William's experience exemplifies a common outcome from the study tours – a strong commitment to Cuba's ongoing development. This is one example of post-tour solidarity and I cite others throughout the chapter. In this example, three people who had met on an NGO study tour in Cuba subsequently joined a branch of the Australia Cuba Friendship Society, actively participating in advocacy and political solidarity efforts towards Cuba. William's email reinforces the opinions of people I talked with about the personal benefits of NGO study tours, and demonstrates that people consider these tours to have enduring implications:

> The advantage of this travel is a view of the socio-political system and life as it is lived by the people, warts and all!
>
> (Stan)
>
> Access to local people, learning about the country, travelling in a way that supports local interests, not multinational corporations.
>
> (Gertrude)
>
> Access to organisations, people, and smart interesting group members who ask questions I might not have thought of.
>
> (Henrietta)

If we are to effectively engage the intersection of tourism and development, then we need to know what these opinions tell us – and why they matter. First, they highlight what participants see as the main personal benefits of this form of tourism; access to the supposedly authentic 'backstage' of the local community (MacCannell 1973, 1992), like-minded fellow travellers and an accompanying educational component. Such statements highlight the politicised commitment of tour participants and the opportunities provided by the tours to exchange information about networks and to develop ties. Second, they feed into arguments about tourism experiences and personal transformation. Some theorists have argued that tourism can offer a chance for learning and subsequently produce a personal transition through a sense of renewal or recreation (Crompton 1979; Krippendorf 1984; Weiler 1991). Others argue that tourists do not experience personal transformation owing to the limits of their interaction; their trips are typically of short duration and thus provide little opportunity to interact with locals, and tourists typically do not speak the local language (Bruner 1991; Laxson 1991). Many studies examine tourist experiences in terms of the impact on hosts and, more recently, tourists (Cohen 1974; Cohen 1979a, b; Dann 1999; MacCannell 1976; Masberg and Silverman 1996; Urry 1990a, b). Nash (1996), however, points out there has been little research into the persistence of attitude change owing to tourism, and that there is a need for more research into whether tourism has significant and enduring consequences for the tourist and their society. Thus, while changes to the host have been long examined, changes to the tourist have been explored much less.

For NGO study tour participants, their experiences of Cuban culture differ from mainstream tourism precisely because of the nature of the interaction with local people. Their experiences include entering the perceived 'backstage' of Cuban culture and ways of life precisely because they met with grassroots organisations and discussed local development problems. The participants I talked with consider such interactions in positive terms. This showed clearly that 'the experiences of tourists can be enhanced through the provision of opportunities to interact with local people and experience different cultural settings' (Ross and Wall 1999: 677). These findings substantiate claims that 'intense' rather than 'superficial' social interactions between cultures are associated with positive attitude change (Amir and Ben-Ari 1985; Ahmed *et al.* 1994; Pizam *et al.* 2000). The people I questioned emphatically talked about the educational aspects of their experiences. A learning objective was fundamental to selecting this type of tour, and it is the educational element that fosters solidarity with Cuba. NGO study tours offer tourists an intense learning experience – people return home with a more comprehensive understanding of development. Moreover, these NGOs hope that participation in their study tours might permanently change people's commitment to supporting development initiatives once back home.

Talking to tourists about their experiences reinforced my impressions of the viability of this form of tourism. For example, Oscar, an American horticulturist in his forties, emphasised the importance of expanding these tourism initiatives. In his opinion:

> Getting the general public on this mode of visiting another country is critical. I think many people would shy away from Global Exchange's 'radical activist' side. Those who are less likely to sign up for a cultural awakening are certainly not going to if the tour company is also perceived as 'radical' or 'threatening'. The challenge is to maintain the activist aspect without coming across as anti anyone.

Oscar's opinion on the importance of this form of tourism sheds some light on why it is worth investigating tourist encounters with development. A crucial method by which we can understand the ongoing viability of the intersection between tourism and development is to examine what happens to the people who are part of this touristic process. Typically, studies of development and anthropological studies of tourism look at the hosts and the impact on local communities, but this misses a key part of the picture – the impact on tourists and how this in turn transforms their broader cultural traits.[3]

Do development-oriented tours lead to exchanges beyond immediate financial support that affect the social and cultural environment of local people in positive ways? Hodge (2004: 17) argued that through the sharing of ideas both with local people and with people back home, volunteer participants can promote a greater understanding of some of the issues regarding systems of aid and development, thereby increasing the contributions they make to development initiatives. This leads us to further a central tenet of my argument: if tourism and development are becoming entwined in various ways, then more attention should be paid to the tourist experience in specific ways. The question more importantly becomes: does a meaningful engagement, which embodies a particularly powerful experience for tourists, lead to a process whereby tourists become actual agents of development?

Participants in NGO tours in Cuba gain a nuanced understanding of Cuba and development. This could be because they have always been interested in interculturality, international issues and development. This type of tour feeds into their lifestyle and is a reflection of their identity as educated, politically active, environmentally concerned advocates of human rights, thus indicating an already extensive understanding and interest in Cuban affairs. This form of experiential learning enhances personal identity for many NGO tour participants. If their experiences lead to a more informed understanding of Cuba and the role of development processes, then we can argue that this facilitates a transformation from tour participant to agent of development, which occurs both within their exchanges with local people and on their return home as they disseminate information about Cuba and its social development. Therefore, it is necessary for us to look at the terms of transformation and the ways that tourists acquire agency through experiential learning.

The point in addressing tourist experience is to gain an insight into whether and in what ways tour participants perceive their 'culture contact' as meaningful. Referring to volunteering experiences, Hodge tells us that a principal achievement is 'the cultural exchanges that take place between volunteers and locals, and the heightened level of understanding which impacts on both cultures. Such exchanges have become critical in the current global-political climate – their value cannot be underestimated' (ibid.: 15). This perspective applies to NGO study tours too because they perpetuate links between countries by creating networks that foster solidarity. In these ways, participants consider that their culture contact is more meaningful than any such contacts experienced within mainstream forms of tourism. For example, Ingaberg says of her NGO tour that it was 'one of the best trips ever and intellectually started me thinking and acting in a different direction'.

One benefit of NGOs operating study tours is the promotion by participants of the NGOs' philosophies and objectives on their return home. This too applied to the Cuban organisations involved with the study tours, as they see the tours as a means of promoting Cuban solidarity once the tourists have returned home. A transformation takes place because there is an increased commitment specifically to Cuban issues by many participants. NGO tour participants are politicised people (either already or become so) and many of them return home and write letters to their politicians, write articles in their local newspapers and community newsletters, give presentations, talk to friends, family and colleagues disseminating what they have learnt about Cuba, and they even join their national Cuba Friendship Society. For example:

> I believe the Cuba at the Crossroads tour introduced us to important movements in Cuban culture and politics. The tour made us aware of the difficulties facing the Cuban people and government and sent us home determined to help in their struggle. The Global Exchange tours are helping to educate Americans about Cuba.
>
> (Henrietta)

It is in these ways that we can conceive of NGO study tourists as agents, even to a minor degree, of development. There is a shift that takes place when tourists return home and boost either the development efforts of the NGO they travelled with or the solidarity efforts with Cuba. Prior to their Cuban NGO tour, they were not directly involved in supporting Cuba, but on their return they become relatively active in their support for Cuba, even if they were already involved in other charitable efforts.

This suggests that this form of tourism achieves an exchange beyond just a material and immediate social level. The elements most participants cite as significantly impacting on their experiences, and indeed, as highlights of their tours, were the seminars and project visits, the time they had to meet local people and make deep connections, and the opportunities to undergo these experiences with like-minded travellers. 'The exchange of ideas and thoughts and friendships with local persons and with each other are extremely satisfying to the tourists and I think the local people' (Innes – Oxfam Tour). Thus, it was the educational, the intellectual, and the affective exchanges with other participants and local people that were significant.

Tourists arrive with aspirations to learn about development in Cuba from local people and they leave with knowledge about development and a relative commitment to Cuban solidarity. The seminars and project visits represent opportunities to engage with local people on an intellectual and emotional level. Exchanges occurring in a tourism development context are arguably improving the social and cultural environment for the local people because they are empowered to create global networks through these touristic exchanges that celebrate their cultural, agricultural and political diversity compared to the hegemonic neoliberal capitalist model. The impact of such experiences could be seen to transform tourists into nascent agents of rights-based development because of the overall sense of fleeting well-being for local people that such exchanges facilitate and the solidarity links it cultivates.

Discussions with people on the tours revealed that learning about Cuba's development issues possibly led to a more reflexive and critical interpretive tourist in terms of their awareness of the government's attempt to improve its geopolitical position through international tourism initiatives. As I have been suggesting, it is through NGOs such as Oxfam and Global Exchange and associated tourist experiences that tourists promulgate messages of solidarity with Cuba.

In discussing what she has mostly learnt about and felt impacted by, Henrietta, an elderly American on the Cuba at the Crossroads tour, says:

> I have a much more concrete sense now of how, and how much, the embargo hurts Cubans, the mechanics by which it does so, and what the Cuban government and people have done in response. I will be writing to my political reps about ending the embargo and I do hope to work something of the Cuban experience into my healthcare talks. Meanwhile I've been mainly talking to friends and even clients about the insanity and destructiveness of the embargo.

Her account of how her tour impacted her is a striking example of the power of this form of tourism to positively affect external participation in new social movements (Knoke 1988). Not only is she intending to write to her politicians, but she intends to incorporate information about Cuba in a professional capacity and has already been sharing information within her social network.

Furthermore, having learnt how the Cuban government is utilising tourism as a developmental tool as part of its response to the embargo, Henrietta goes on to discuss some important issues relating to the embargo and tourism, demonstrating her considered response to information gleaned through the seminars and project visits:

> My main observations concern how the embargo is directly and indirectly dragging down the Cuban economy and how the answer they're seeking in tourism may be putting the entire culture at risk. I also observed what appears to be an interesting and potentially dangerous generational divide. Many of the people who were there for the revolution still seem to have great enthusiasm for it and great appreciation for what it accomplished. Younger people however who have no memory of pre-Castro days long for a better material life; not unlike the pre- and post-Depression generations in the US I guess. Tourism and the dual economy are introducing into Cuban life new economic and social disparities that could undermine the real, functional egalitarianism that has I believe made the revolution's successes possible.
>
> (Henrietta)

It has not been my intention to analyse the host experience, such as the well-being and dignity of local Cuban people as a result of these tours. But in my endeavour to investigate this form of tourism, let me make some claims for its contribution to rights-based development. What we can see taking place is a form of development that is more than just about structural adjustment leading to economic development so prevalent throughout Latin America. It is a form of rights-based tourism where local Cuban people who are actively engaged in the development process also create networks with international tourists in an effort to foster solidarity. Creating solidarity through networks is linked to the capacity of tourism to bring about subjective changes in the conditions of Cuban people. Arguably, this form of tourism promotes increased self-realisation of local people and tourists alike through a programme of educational and affective exchanges that enhance notions of empowerment and independent agency. The weight of these social contacts cannot be dismissed, and thus what follows is an exposition of the transformative nature of NGO study tours through experiential learning that leads to these productive outcomes.

Transformative experiences and endogenous development in Cuba

A critical question that underpins research into the conjunction of tourism and development is how tourist experiences are integral to the macro factors that influence tourism. For example, has this form of tourism emerged out of larger tropes of development, or is it being driven by the tourism decisions of a more discerning, Western, new middle class? If aspects of development are intersecting with tourism, then its ongoing sustainability will depend greatly on tourists' experiences. Consequently, development specialists need to consider what people are gaining from their tours.

As previously mentioned, tourism studies typically focus on the 'hosts' with fewer studies examining what happens with the tourists themselves. Of those studies that have centred on the tourist experience, Turner's 'rites of passage' theory provides a popular framework for analysing the process of transformation from one state to another (Turner 1969, 1977). An important theme in my research is whether the tourists perceive that their experiences reinforce their lifestyle and thereby reaffirm chosen aspects of their identity, or whether their experiences are in fact more profound and bring about a transformation evidenced by an increased commitment to supporting development efforts.

Participants in NGO study tours, who are typically middle class, make short visits to communities in developing countries. As they are introduced to the development issues of a particular country, the organising NGO expects that they will learn from their exchanges with local people. Through a busy schedule of meetings and project visits, the study tours offer tourists intense experiences and there is no doubt tourists return home with a more nuanced view of development. But notions of transformation are complex and cannot be understood merely as a direct transition from one state to another. For the majority of tour participants, the tours *reinforced* existing attitudes and behaviour precisely because most claimed to already contribute to development efforts through financial support, activism, fundraising and so on. Furthermore, most of them consider participating in an NGO study tour as part of a broader inclination to support development work. My research shows that greater commitments were made and that transformation is, therefore, not a black-and-white process. It can be shown by a number of practices, some not always self-consciously evident to the tourist.

Arguably, these tourists are not just interested in meeting the exotic 'Other' as objects to be viewed, but rather they are engaged in what they perceive to be meaningful contact with local people in order to exchange ideas and information about development issues. They can disseminate this information on their return home in an act of solidarity and contribute to the development efforts of the organising NGO. The respondents indicated that their tour did change their previous ideas and affected their prior knowledge of Cuba. Wilhemena discovered through the seminars and projects many contradictions in Cuban society:

> Urban agriculture seems to be communism at its best. In that sense I grew to appreciate how communism can care and provide for its people (for example, the agriculture project we visited that was growing for the elderly). In a similar light, I understood how it was the introduction of capitalistic ways (like selling produce at the markets) that was spurring the economy into a state of recovery. So many contradictions!

The tour definitely changed my prior understanding of Cuba. I didn't know much of Cuba except the anti-Castro propaganda the US government spouts.

Oliver felt that since his tour he had 'a much broader base of knowledge about the country especially compared to the average American'. The tours offered people enriched experiences of Cuba through the lens of development. For these participants, the tour provided educational and intellectual experiences that transformed their prior perceptions of Cuba. Ruben exclaimed, 'It is such a great experience because it affects you and you have to change.' Their statements illustrate the tour's power to affect participation in new social movements through supporting development. Sebastian said to me, 'I want to be involved in development and community development issues and become more of an activist now,' and for Wilhemena:

> the lasting effect on me is that I will be engaged in Cuban politics and human rights from now on. I think Cuba/US relations are a fascinating story and I think that from now on Cuban news/culture/politics will be a hobby of mine. The trip has inspired me to grow my own vegetables – this is certainly a lifestyle change. I am inspired to spread the word about urban agriculture in Cuba and to encourage people to visit. I recently held a slide show on Cuba and will present another one next month at the University of Michigan. I also hope to write an article to further disseminate information of Cuba's unique model of relieving food crises through urban agriculture.

The personal transformation expressed by Oliver resulted from seeing how materially poor Cuban people are but how happy they appear:

> I become more and more humble about materialism. I have learned to be happy with what I have, because it is still much more than many people in the world. I try not to let small things get to me anymore, because now it just seems stupid to stress over minor inconveniences in life. I have food, clean water, healthcare, and a roof over my head. What more could I really ask for?

Oliver's idealism reflects images of utopian community and simplicity that many people in the West feel alienated from as evidenced by the increasing mobilisation of new social movements. For Valmia: 'My tour has certainly increased my understanding and appreciation of the hardships Cuba is having as a result of the embargo and natural disasters'.

As we can see through participant accounts, horizons were extended for some tourists, the individual dignity of local Cuban people they met with was valued, and the trust and solidarity that the groups created through sharing histories, difficulties or goals potentially fed into giving local Cuban people some degree of support in their attempts to reinvent themselves as more active subjects in their communities. For the tourists, the high levels of inter-action with other tour participants, local officials and local residents facili-tated the establishment of network ties that are so important to the success of new social movements (McGehee 2002).

What we observe with these tours in terms of transformation is that there is actually a strong emphasis on increased learning and a strong sense of reinforcement of identity. Nearly all respondents discussed ways they shared and made use of their knowledge of Cuba once back home. Older participants indicated that they already led what they depicted as 'simple' lifestyles and support good causes. For many participants, their experiences in Cuba have reinforced their commitment to supporting causes both at home and abroad. Ingaberg has experienced 'an awakened interest in garden-ing and a reinforced notion that organic agriculture is something that the West could embrace more fully. As a whole the trip solidified ideas that were brewing already in my head.' Likewise, Valmia says her tour rein-forced her 'will to continue supporting as many environmental, family plan-ning, and civil rights organisations that I can afford. I've always been an activist and will continue to contribute and disseminate pertinent informa-tion and lobby congressional members.' Josephine confirms that 'the tour has revived my commitment to my conservation approach to living and being vocal about issues of social justice and environment… I have since written articles in our newsletter and sent emails to staff and friends about my learning experiences in Cuba.' For Stan, the tour 'has served to support my prior resolve to lead a relatively simple, environmentally responsible lifestyle, sensitive to the plight of others around the globe and the social injustices they suffer'. James said, 'The tour has confirmed that I do need to continue being vigilant about not only Cuban, but Australian matters such as detention of asylum seekers, Aboriginal reconciliation, racism, unemploy-ment, and foreign affairs.' These statements highlight the politicised com-mitment of tour participants and the opportunities provided by the tours to exchange information about networks and to develop ties.

Following Hollander (1981: 29), 'the utopian susceptibilities of contem-porary Western [tourists] are part of a long-standing tradition'. Many of the tourists involved in NGO study tours demonstrate very strong similarities to Western intellectuals who travelled to the Soviet Union during the 1930s. For example, Tom who joined an OCAAT tour is typical of the burgeoning middle classes and their lifestyle choices. He works in renewable energy design, his wife grows organic vegetables, they have travelled to former Soviet countries and they are active members of the Nottingham Refugee Forum. Francesca also joined an OCAAT tour; she actively supports chari-ties and human rights groups with fundraising, lobbying, organising and public speaking along with paying financial contributions and memberships to various welfare and conservation agencies. She has also participated in a number of NGO study tours and travels independently.

While we cannot generalise that all NGO tourists going to Cuba have these experiences, I suggest that by and large the majority do share these positive responses. The experiences tourists have engage them at a particular level of action that enables them to feel they are doing something positive; there is a level of change in the participants' behaviour in the form of increased solidarity efforts on their return home. At the very least, new relationships are established that allow for the creation of networks between the tourists and local people they meet and also between the tourists themselves. Thus, tourism and development are creating new kinds of solidarity and transnational connections. It is a form of interaction that is didactic and provides experiences with local Cuban people that is productive because of the creation of networks. McAdam and Rucht's (1993) model of information exchange within social movements demonstrates that the dissemination of ideas and activities on a global scale occurs through such networks.

Conclusion: Rights-based tourism

The exchanges between tourists and local Cubans give Cuba an increased presence within a wider geopolitical and social world in which it has been subject to a decades-long embargo. The engagement of tourists and locals is an integral part of the development process as they share their knowledge and expertise with each other. Subjective micro-transformations of this kind lead to potential multiplier effects beyond the tours themselves in the form of new networks being built, role models being created and positive social change being promoted. Such experiences, combined with the goals of the NGOs and the intentions of the Cuban government, indicate several positive outcomes. First, aside from material support for the Cuban organisations meeting with the study tours and discussing development issues specific to Cuba, the positive outcomes consist of imparting knowledge about Cuban realities, thereby facilitating solidarity between countries and potentially empowering Cuban people. This can subsequently impact on future international relations for Cuba by assisting in their future development (i.e. through tourists returning home to lobby their politicians about trade relations), which has been threatened by the US trade embargo.

Second, for the NGOs who organise study tours to Cuba, the positive outcomes consist of participants learning about development efforts and disseminating this knowledge on their return home and, perhaps, becoming more committed to supporting development efforts. Third, for the participants, the positive outcomes include partaking in a study tour that contributes money and possibly a sense of well-being to local communities, gaining 'backstage' access not otherwise available to tourists, being educated while travelling and meeting like-minded people. But most importantly, they become actively engaged in activities linked to social solidarity and change. While the tours are not 'new social movements' per se, they lend themselves to particular outcomes associated with the power of new social movements. The level of impact on the tourists themselves through transformation leads to agency that in turn enhances social capital in Cuba. I have indicated there is an increasing tourism niche developing, which focuses on an exchange of knowledge and which undoubtedly has positive implications for a host country, leading as it does to the creation of global networks and solidarity.

Development-oriented tours aim to move beyond typical touristic presentations of Cuba and counter the anti-Cuba rhetoric stemming from the US government and the Cuban diasporas. Cuba is all too often represented by discourses that shift between diverse idealistic visionary representations of a bastion of socialism fighting against consumerism and capitalism to dystopic representations of a socialist country frozen in the 1950s and a victim of the Cold War. The NGO study tours do more than feed into discourses of representation by providing Western tourists with opportunities to experience Cuba through a series of meetings that allow people to gain nuanced insights of Cuban realities, both positive and negative. Solidarity through tourism, in whatever form this emerges, can be considered an important tool for development agencies, social movements and NGOs in terms of explicit ways of promulgating issues of rights, social justice and good governance.

In this way, solidarity connects directly with rights-based development. Solidarity becomes important in the tourism context, because it is implicitly expressed as an objective of NGOs and explicitly expressed by tourists as a key motivation for participating in NGO study tours. Likewise it is expressly a political and developmental goal of the Cuban government. We can effectively envisage solidarity as a means for tourists to participate and act as agents of change in the development process. Indeed, it is a novel means through which Cuba has developed a way to partially resist the economic and social constraints of the blockade. It acts as a new form of global coalition and interconnectedness that builds on previous alliances that have since dissolved, as was the case with the Soviet Union where Cuba engaged in cultural exchanges with nations who were politically sympathetic.

Participants in development study tours are, through their solidarity efforts, agents of a rights-based form of development. The tours have the power to affect participants in positive ways that encourage people to be more active in a growing social movement of foreigners supporting Cuba. Tourists become agents of development by supporting the development projects of the NGO they travelled with to Cuba and supporting Cuban solidarity. What is produced here is rights-based tourism.

This tourism-development nexus is not just about material and financial exchanges but also about intellectual and affective elements that are exchanged and developed. This fits within a rights-based development framework where the notion of well-being is achieved by broadly conceived notions of political and moral support that is not just about money. Tours contribute (on different scales) to the development of dignity and well-being because

NGO tourists leave Cuba with a sense of connection and the commitment to support development in Cuba.

The sharing of ideas with local people, fellow tour members and with people back home can promote greater understanding of issues regarding systems of aid and thereby increase the contributions they make to development. It is this impact that leads to the 'transformation' from tourist to agent of development because tour participants are engaged in more long-term intellectual and instrumental ways that transcend the tour itself.

To what extent and how consistently such tours improve the social and cultural environment of local people by enhancing their sense of well-being and dignity remains unclear. But my argument that international networks and solidarity are created leads us to ask such questions. This chapter demonstrates that if a development tour is found to encourage or intensify solidarity with Cuba or social movement participation in some form, then the results could be used to promote rights-based tourism as a means of encouraging organised social action and rights-based development.

Notes

1 See Butcher (2003) for critique about the increasing trend of a moralisation of tourism and see Smith and Duffy (2003) who focus more broadly on issues of ethics and tourism.
2 Organisations such as the ILO, UNICEF, Save the Children, UNDP, OXFAM and Care have adopted and trialled aspects of a rights-based approach. Indeed their experiences have contributed to the evolution of human rights approaches to development with perhaps the most extensive advancement of international human rights being their integration into all UN activities – thus making the conceptual link between human rights, democracy and development. In the last decade bilateral donor agencies such as Sida and DFID have also begun promoting rights perspectives within their agendas.
3 See Frey, N. (1998) *Pilgrim Stories: On and Off the Road to Santiago*, University of California Press, California; Graburn, N. (2002) The Ethnographic Tourist in Dann, Graham (ed.) *The Tourist as a Metaphor of the Social World*, Wallingford: CABI.

6   Tourists' photographic gaze: the case of Rio de Janeiro favelas

Palloma Menezes

Introduction

In his reflection about contemporary society, John Urry (1990c) says that being a tourist is one of the distinctive characteristics of modern life. Tourism is the complementary opposite to the work logic: vacations are a sort of qualified idleness. Not travelling is like not having a nice enough car or a less than beautiful home, because tourism in modern societies confers status and is thought to be a necessity of the body and mind.

Many authors claim a profound change has happened, or is somehow still happening, in contemporary societies; Fordism has given way to post-Fordism. This means a change in typical production modes, which are shifting from mass consumption towards a more individual pattern. According to some thinkers this change is also seen in contemporary tourism's mutant qualities. According to Poon (1989), this process entails a passage from 'old tourism', based on pre-formed packages and patterns to 'new tourism', which is much more flexible and commercial. According to this author, segmentation is the most significant trait of post-Fordist tourism.

Because of this continuous segmentation process in tourism, we cannot nowadays speak about it as a single experience, but only as a set of increasingly diversified travel practices. Among these readily available diversified and segmented practices we find a new tendency called *reality tours*. Urry (1990c) affirms one of the hallmarks of this so-called 'new tourism' is that practically every aspect of social life may be sold as a product. Reality tours take Urry's considerations to the extreme by transforming disasters, atrocities and poverty, for example, into products no different from any others.

Freire-Medeiros (2006) explains that modes of tourism such as reality tours find motivation and legitimacy in a 'craving for reality', in Richard Sennett's definition, and through the 'passion for what is real' of which Alain Badiou speaks. To help understand this new form of tourism, it may be divided into two types: 'dark tours' and 'social tours'.

This first form of reality tour, known as 'dark tourism' (Lennon and Foley 2000), deals with the tourist's growing interest in places connected with disasters and tragedies. Examples of this sort of tour embrace a spectrum of intensities of darkness, from 'dark fun factories' at the lighter end of the spectrum through to camps of genocide at the darkest (Stone 2006), and include an enormous diversity of sites, from the place where President Kennedy was assassinated in Dallas, Texas, to Polish extermination camps and even to radioactive areas surrounding Chernobyl (Sharpley and Stone 2009).

The second form of reality tour, known as 'awareness tourism', is frequently sponsored by NGOs as a sort of political activism, and is intended to raise tourists' awareness of the problems and challenges facing disadvantaged societies and communities, and to contribute to or support programmes designed to improve the lives of such people. Sometimes referred to as volunteer tourism, this form of tourism may include taking tourists to dig a well near the US–Mexican border, to sow and harvest in rural Guatemala, or even spending a week or so in Middle East land occupation settlements.

In this chapter, I consider a kind of tour experience that combines elements from both types of reality tour, specifically, tourism in the Rocinha favela (slum) in Rio de Janeiro. This experience which makes poverty an item for consumption – also known as *poverty tourism* or *pity tourism* – is not exclusively Brazilian. Similar examples are to be found in several other parts of the world, such as the townships of Soweto in South Africa, the slums of Kolkata (Calcutta) in India and Villa 20, a slum area in Buenos Aires, Argentina. The particular case of tourism in Rocinha[1] was selected here because, according to Freire-Medeiros (2006):

> The favela which is invented and sold as a tourist attraction stretches the canon of reality tours to its limits: it provides both altruistic, politically correct commitment in view of the local social landscape and a sense of adventure and amazement in view of the physical landscape. It is the experience of *authenticity*, of *exotic* and of *risk*, all in one spot.
>
> (Freire-Medeiros 2006)

First contact with favela tourism

The Rocinha favela became an official tourism landmark in the city of Rio de Janeiro in September 2006, as a result of a law[2] passed by Mayor César Maia. Four months later, the newly instated State Governor Sérgio Cabral Filho announced that nearly 72 million Reais, co-funded by the Federal Government, were to be invested in Rocinha's infrastructure, including new streets, new daycare centres, housing units and even a small hotel set atop the favela. The purpose of this was not only to enhance the quality of life for favela dwellers and to restrict further growth of the favela, but also to encourage tourism to this area.

Most cariocas (natives or inhabitants of Rio de Janeiro) are unaware that such tours exist, although favela tourism has come to be known worldwide both through the Internet and as a result of the relative notoriety granted to the favelas by a number of articles that have appeared in national

(Brazilian) and international newspapers in recent years. I was one of those people who, until relatively recently, overlooked the fact that favelas have nowadays become one of the main tourist attractions sold in the 'cidade maravilhosa'. Indeed, prior to 2004, when I began to research Travel Culture in Rio de Janeiro,[3] I had never set foot in a favela.

After a few months of research, however, I boarded a moss-green jeep belonging to a tour agency in order to observe guides, tourists[4] and favela dwellers. One of the principal issues I was concerned with was 'how do tourists put together their representation of favelas based upon their impressions during the Rocinha tour?' What sort of relationships are there between guides, tourists and locals during tours? What are the boundaries and extent of this experience which transforms poverty into a tourism commodity? Who really benefits from these favela tours?

Although at that point I had not yet found the answers to these questions, I had already realised that, although visting the favela was new for me, favela tourism is by no means a recent phenomenon. There are reports of travellers who visited Rio de Janeiro in the first half of the twentieth century, such as the Spanish Ambassador José Casais, which reveal that visiting favelas has long been an established element of tours of the city:

> Y yo quise conocer el Morro. Hay cerros en la capital que gozan de mala fama, pero cuando uno los visita se convence de que de malo solo tienen eso: la fama… Yo fui a los morros de día y de noche y solo tuve que cruzarme con gentes educadas que al pasar me saludaron amablemente.
>
> (Casais 1940: 25–26)

Roughly translated, the Ambassador wanted to visit the Morro; there are hills in the city that suffer a poor reputation, but it is only their reputation that is bad. Visiting at night, the Amabassador met only educated, amiable people.

Nevertheless, it is only more recently that significant numbers of tourists have become interested in visiting favelas. In the last few years, Rocinha has been visited by around 3,500 people per month, led by independent guides and by eight agencies[5] which cover the local market. Rocinha[6] is already so well established as a tourist destination that agencies have been offering increasingly diversified services to cater to different demands. Tourists may, for instance, choose whether to take a tour on foot, by van, by jeep or by motorcycle; by day or night; with or without meals and guided by locals or by foreigners. Moreover, during the tour the visitors, who are mostly foreigners, may even acquire products made 'by Rocinha', such as T-shirts and comic books, or make financial donations to the favela's 'social projects'.

According to Freire-Medeiros, 'the touristic product known as favela' may be interpreted as a 'contact zone'. These zones, a concept attributable to Mary Louise Pratt, would be somewhere between the idea of public space as 'an area of free critical thinking removed from constraints of Church and Court', as described by Habermas, and complete, brutal oppression of the oppressed.

> Contact zones are 'social spaces where different cultures meet, clash and mesh, frequently in markedly asymmetrical relationships of domination and subordination', from which paradoxically emerge other possibilities of representation of Self and of Others. Considering the favela which tourism invented as a contact zone allows us to understand it as both physical and symbolic landscape in which layers of discourse settle in multiple representations: tourist representations of the favela and its inhabitants, representations of the tourists by locals, representations of the favela made by locals for the tourists, and so forth – a continuous spiral of representations.
>
> (Freire-Medeiros 2006)

While developing the methodology to investigate this 'spiral of representations', it became evident that, in addition to the planned fieldwork involving interviewing agency owners, tour guides, favela residents and tourists, I could also use the photographs taken by tourists during their tour as an important data source. Consequently, I analysed 710 pictures posted in 50 photologs created by tourists who had visited Rocinha.

When analysing the photologs, I endeavoured to understand the world view expressed through the photographs taken by tourists during their Rocinha tours. My intent was to identify the representations of the favela in these pictures, so I began by screening which elements of the favela were portrayed as the focus element.

The main elements portrayed by tourists were sorted into main groups, as follows: homes (205 pictures); local inhabitants (150); streets (84); favela infrastructure (61); views from Rocinha (43); plants and animals (43); commerce (38); tourism-related aspects (38); favela walls (37); and cultural and leisure activities (11).

As is evident from these figures, local people are the second most photographed aspect of Rocinha. Thus, because a deeper analysis of all the above aspects which the study of these pictures would entail is beyond the scope of this chapter, here I focus only on the pictures tourists take of favela dwellers. I do so because the taking of pictures of people requires a detailed and careful analysis, for it involves social relations, ethical issues and several controversies.

Images of Rocinha locals

Many authors consider the photograph to be an arbitrary construction (Sontag 1981; Ball 1992; Basin 1982; Berger 1982; Banta 1986; Tagg 1988; Kossoy 1999). The act of taking a photograph begins when somebody recognises the content of a scene and then selects the aspect of this scene that deserves to be highlighted. In the photographic moment, tourists include and exclude certain visual elements – the excluded elements also represent data or information – in order to highlight the essence of the scene from the point of view chosen.

The choice of which element deserves to be seen or not seen varies according to the cultural filter that is behind the camera. A tourist from the 'First World' who is visiting a favela probably would not focus his camera on the same elements that a tourist from Africa would focus on. However, regardless of gender, nationality or age, it is important to consider that all tourists, before embarking on their travels, are exposed to imaginative repertoires – movies, travel guides, photos – that not only anticipate what will be seen and experienced in the places visited but also direct the beholder's eyes to the new landscapes that will be encountered.

In his reflection about tourism and photography, Ramamurthy (2004) suggests that tourists, having already consumed an array of exotic and glamorised photographs of the place before arrival, search out these very images and sites to visit and photograph in order to feel that their trip is complete, so that their experience is, in a sense, verified. Thus, while many of the experiences revolve around architectural monuments, the desire to consume exotic/ anthropological images of people is also something very important during the travel.

The first trend identified in my field studies and later confirmed when analysing the pictures was that children are much more photographed than adults. In the 50 blogs I analysed, there are 150 pictures of children as compared to only 25 pictures of adults or senior citizens. In other words, tourists who posted their pictures on these sites took six times more pictures of children than of adults.[7]

Image 1 and Image 2

Most people portrayed in these pictures are black, like the man and the children in Figures 6.1 and 6.2 below. This may reflect the fact that the greater proportion of the favela population are black; however, it may also imply that tourists prefer to take pictures of people who fit the stereotype of 'favelados' as people who are 'black and poor'.

> The dominant photographic language of the tourist brochure has also affected how tourists construct their own photographs. These snapshots tend to reinforce the constructed and commodified experience of travel: what is photographed is that which is different and out of ordinary. Most tourist snapshots also use a vocabulary of photographic practice which is embedded in power relations.
>
> (Ramamurthy 2004: 227)

Nowadays, much commercial photography exploits exoticism and 'Otherness', along with the ingredient of glamour, to entice viewers and

Figure 6.1 Image 1.

Figure 6.2 Image 2.

consumers. As a result, some ideological constructions of colonial domination have become so naturalised that we hardly notice them (Ramamurthy 2004). Certainly, in the context of the tourist experience of Rio de Janeiro, images of exoticised 'black and poor' children are used to encourage favela tours through tourist brochures, travel agencies' websites,[8] and so on.

The very choice of a particular destination by the tourist is based on an 'anticipation of the experience' which consists of a dialogue with the images of a given place carried by the media, images which create an interpretative and behavioural frame for the tourist (Urry 1990c). Such images circulate through news agencies, films – national and foreign, fictional[9] and documental – photographs, magazines, travel guides, advertising campaigns, and so on, helping build expectations and desirabilities that are an intrinsic part of the so-called travel culture (Freire-Medeiros 2009b).

I experienced how such images affect the way that tourists construct their own photographs, when one local told me about an episode in which tourists didn't want to take pictures of her son because he is white:

Once when my son was younger they wanted to take his picture, but when I got there with him they refused because they wanted a black kid. Sometimes they don't, but they have to realise it's a mixture of everything. My father is from the north-east and so is my mother, but I don't look at all like him. My dad is dark skinned with frizzly hair and I am blonde and green eyed.[10]

Another characteristic of the pictures that tourists take of locals is that a large number of them are portraits.[11] The social identity which tourist pictures showcase is that of the happy, always smiling poor. There are almost no pictures of frowning or angry people in the photologs depicting Rocinha.

Promoting the circulation of portraits of this population which, so far, has not been frequently depicted is also a manner of exposing images in which the locals may identify and recognise themselves. This is because a significant portion of the favela population do not associate themselves in the media representation of 'favelados' as social actors frequently linked with guns and violence. Now, several locals have started to recognise themselves in these new images produced by tourists. A number of local favela people told me that they have received pictures tourists took of them, which were sent through the agencies. They all felt appreciated by way of the creation and circulation of these photographs which, far from reflecting a 'traditional' image of favela communities, show them as happy, smiling individuals.

The smiles of the population of Rocinha that appear in many photographs in the tourists' blogs are also commented on in the photos' subtitles that highlight how people are seen to be 'genuinely happy in the favela'. When I asked them what they remembered of their favela tour, many tourists said the same thing to me: 'The smiley, friendly faces ... the simplicity of their lives'; 'The smiles of the children we met!'. Moreover, many foreign visitors were surprised by how the inhabitants of Rocinha face poverty and the difficult situation in which they live:

> I found many of the people genuinely happy considering how little they had. I also saw the social problems with drugs, teenage pregnancy, lack of employment, terrible living conditions and general poverty. It was amazing though how many people smile and how so many in the community help each other.

> I was expecting to see what you see in documentaries and press articles: poverty, violence and sad faces. No, it did not match these expectations – for which I am glad. They seemed very happy and much friendlier than we thought. They smiled a lot. We interacted with some of them briefly, but unfortunately the language barrier was a problem.

When one speaks about taking pictures of people, one cannot ignore the ethical issues this practice entails. Many intellectuals label favela tourism as a 'zoo of poor people', in which locals are photographed as cowering and defenceless animals. However, this was not the perception I had in the field. Locals do not seem to be indignant at being photographed. Indeed, most locals with whom I spoke indicated that they do not have a problem with being photographed; the few who did say they had an issue justified it by alleging shyness or shame related to being photographed in any situation, but not because these are pictures taken by tourists from another country.

A few community 'leaders', such as representatives of neighbourhood associations, claim that tourists should ask for permission before taking pictures of people. They also claim that it is the tour agencies' fault for not orienting their clients as to what can and cannot be photographed. Others question the use tourists will make of these images, fearing that pictures of young girls – for example, dressed in shorts – might be used for inappropriate purposes.

In short, I have come to realise through my fieldwork that the ethical limits of favela tourism, specially the issue of pictures, are still being built and negotiated. Let us picture the following scenario: if a tourist donates money to a daycare centre and wishes to take pictures of bathing kids, for example, should he be able to do so? According to some locals there seems to be no problem, the most important thing being the donation[12] itself. According to others, however, this is unacceptable and should be resisted. For example, there is one daycare centre which is visited daily by people on a tour with an agency called 'Exotic Tour' in which the coordinator has expressly forbidden the taking of pictures of the children, because the mothers allegedly do not like having their children photographed by strangers.

Now let us picture another scenario: can a tourist take pictures inside a home if he or she wishes to? Once I was interviewing people at Rua 1 and witnessed the following situation: while a group of tourists was buying souvenirs, one of their number crossed the street and started going up the stairs that led to a home. The homeowner, who works at a nearby bar, saw him and followed to see what he wanted. As soon as she got there he started pointing up and trying to explain he wanted to enter the house. When he got there he turned the doorknob and found the door was locked. He then pressed a 10-Real bill into her hand so she would let him in.

After a few minutes, the lady happily crossed the street and told her friend – who by sheer luck I was interviewing – that the tourist had given her 10 Reais to take pictures of her home. Her friend said 'sure they have to pay, if they want to come in our homes they have to pay'. And the bar owner declared: 'goodness, if a gringo like this showed up every day my life would be made, I'd let him take pictures of my kid and all!' However, another local who was with us said that her home can be photographed for free: 'it's all right if a tourist wants to take pictures of my home, but he mustn't notice the mess because we are renovating. I wouldn't feel invaded or bothered – as long as they let me dress up for the pictures everything would be fine!'

Image 3 and Image 4

Although these statements contradict the notion that locals are concerned or bothered by the presence of tourists and are helpless victims of

Figure 6.3 Image 3.

Figure 6.4 Image 4.

pictures, we cannot help but ask a few questions, such as: if someone visited these tourists' country of origin and decided to take pictures of the inside of their homes, would they allow it? If someone offered them money to take pictures of their home, would they accept it or would they feel offended and invaded? These are questions to which I do not have answers. However, I believe that we must think about these issues to be able to understand the complex interconnections between pictures and favela tourism.

Representations of the favela: what changes after the Rocinha tour?

To provide a simple answer to the question of what impression tourists have of the favela would be a difficult, if not impossible, task. Nevertheless, from the results of my research it is evident that the impression of the favela that tourists have after the tour is vastly more complex and multifaceted than the one they had before.

I interviewed 30 tourists before their visit and found that most of them equated the image of favelas to poverty and violence. When I asked them about what they had expected to find in Rocinha and whether they had really found what they were expecting, I typically received the same response:

> No, it didn't match my expectations. It was not as poor as I was expecting, people were well dressed with MP3 players, mobile phones and so on and I certainly didn't imagine this would be the case. The houses were also far sturdier than I was expecting – I thought that people would live in places which were really makeshift but they seemed like proper, well built houses.

I was expecting the crowded streets and the various levels of poverty but I didn't foresee the 'normalness' of it all, the way in which the people of the favela get on with life with smiles on their faces. Everyone was so welcoming, and there was a lot of respect, it was a pleasant surprise.

Many tourists said they expected to find poverty, violence and unhappy people but, after the tour, they say living conditions in the favela aren't as bad as they thought. Here we find evident dialogue between media references and personal contact experience: some pointed out that their expectations prior to the tour were based on documentaries and newspaper articles. Moreover, it is important to note that many tourists expressed the view that the 'reality' of

Rocinha is far more interesting than what is represented in the media. I tried to keep an open mind. I expected to see poverty and evidence of crime and drug gangs. Maybe I expected the inhabitants to show curiosity in the tourists but they didn't. I suppose it didn't match my expectations because I had seen similar poverty or worse in other parts of South America. If anything, I was impressed by the favelas and the resilience of the inhabitants. It confronts the stereotypes and myths of the favela that people believe in. It shows the reality of life in the favela. It is not always like the film *City of God*. It is not all guns, drugs and violence, although that is partly true. It shows the favelas in the context of Brazilian society. For example, the possibility of rich and poor living side-by-side, the corruption of the police, the failures of Brazilian governments to tackle the housing problems of the favela dwellers and the importance of the favelas as a source of cheap labour that fuels the continuous expansion of Brazilian cities.

As can be clearly seen in the response above, there is a change in the tourists' perceptions about what is a favela. Such a transformation in tourists' impressions of favelas is also evident in their representations of them in the images posted in photologs and in the captions and texts they post on these sites. When asked directly whether their views of the favela had changed they answered in the affirmative:

I see the favela as multi-dimensional, not something I only associate with news reports or movies. I see actual faces and homes and real lives. This is not to say that I feel like I am an expert on favelas now, but it is now more 'real'.

Totally, it changed from being a sad, scary place to be, to an incredible community that has its serious problems but that survives in the way it knows how, with laughter and friendships, music and painting.

Yes – in a positive way. Everyone on the tour was surprised at how 'normal' the Favela was. People were just getting on with their everyday lives and seemed to enjoy living there.

Nevertheless, it is important to remember that these new perceptions do not come from subjective, individual views alone. The tours are organised in such a manner that a collective tourist impression of the favela is created. This is an impression that is influenced by the agencies even before tourists leave their homes – when people visit the agency website to have an idea of what they are about to see in Rio de Janeiro – and which is influenced throughout the tour by the guides who say which places to linger in and for how long, what should and should not be captured by camera, and so on.

As the perception tourists have of favelas changes during the tour, so does their representation of Rocinha inhabitants. Both the interviews and the analysis of photologs images that I have carried out seem to point to a *humanisation* of locals through favela tourism; they are no longer associated solely with marginality and criminality but, rather, come to be seen as 'normal people'.

Western media tends to depict favelas as nothing more than havens for drug dealers, gun crime and gang warfare. These tours enable people like us to see that there is so much more to these places including normal honest people just struggling to live.

Final considerations

A large number of pictures taken by tourists during their tour, such as in Figures 6.5 and 6.6 below,[13] focus on smiling faces, people who seem happy and content with their lives. I believe this type of image no doubt contributes towards consolidating a more complex representation of favelas than that prevalent in the media, which show Rocinha locals, for example, only as actors or victims in violent actions.

Image 5 and Image 6

Nonetheless, I feel it is important to question up to what point this sort of social construct – which some tour agencies[14] sell to tourists – of the favela dweller as someone who lives his life in 'merriment and samba' in spite of adversities they face is just as stereotypical as the construct, typically depicted by the media, in which favelas are filled with suffering poor or with outlaws. In other words, it could be argued that saying that favelas are beautiful and that everyone in them is happy and smiling is as reductive as saying they are a ghetto of poverty and criminality.

It is also important to consider who benefits from this new representation of favelas created after the tours. Is it the locals, the agencies or the tourists? Some locals believe that, by visiting Rocinha, tourists would be sensitised by seeing that it is not only a place on the margins, of criminal activity, and therefore would be willing to help the 'community' more. Tourists, in their turn, seem to believe that they are somehow helping the community simply by visiting the place, a belief based upon the erroneous impression that the tour money would directly aid favela dwellers.[15]

Figure 6.5 Image 5.

Figure 6.6 Image 6.

Agencies, for their part, suggest that they are contributing by helping to boost the population's self-esteem – which would be achieved by the presence of tourists in the favela[16] – by encouraging them to donate and by eventually aiding some daycare centres or schools.[17] I did not, however, find any evidence of negotiation between local inhabitants and agencies about what each party can and/or should earn from tourism. According to Freire-Medeiros (2006), 'most of the time the favelas do not profit in equal standing from benefits created by tourism'. Therefore, it would be necessary to 'define new strategies to reinvest revenues brought by tourism in the favela itself, not as a type of charity, like it is nowadays, but as a result of the local inhabitant's participation' (Friere-Medeiros 2006).

Furthermore, it might be necessary to ask ourselves to what extent certain choices are part of these agencies' strategy, such as the choice of taking the tourists to visit only the prettiest and most urbanised part of Rocinha – only one agency takes tourists to visit Roupa Suja (*Dirty Laundry*), the part thought to be the poorest and most precarious of the favelas – and finishing off on a rooftop to admire the view of the sea. This strategy might be directed towards tourists completing the tour feeling happy and relieved, with a clear conscience that those poor people do not live in such terrible squalor and moreover that they, as good citizens, have done all they can to help these people – which would be simply paying for the tour (in their minds the funds would be sent to the favela), visiting a daycare centre and at most buying some souvenirs or making a donation.

I believe the success of Rocinha as a tour destination may be a result of the guides' skill in transforming the impressions that foreign visitors have of the favelas, by means of their discourse and of the route they choose to show the favela. Making Rocinha appear to be prettier – because several other aspects of favela life are shown during the tour – less poor and less violent than may have been imagined prior to the tour might be a strategy which pleases both its inhabitants – who are tired of seeing only a negative image of the favela and the 'favelados' in the media – as well as the tourists, who end up feeling they have seen the 'real' favela and not only its dark side as shown in movies and news. As stated by one of the owners of an agency, Jeep Tour:[18]

> The main goal of the favela tour is finding out whether the images which reach the foreigners are true to the image we know to be real; because the images which go out to foreign countries only show violence, and that isn't real … violence happens anywhere in the world, there is violence everywhere. Favelas are societies within societies, that's what we want to show. The idea behind this tour is showing tourists that this isn't the real image of the favela; it's people, the local inhabitants, workers, well, there's a whole structure… My view is: they [the tourists] must check out whether the image they have is like this … the main goal in selling favelas is profiting the most from its bad side.

Furthermore, for tourists it might be less disturbing to think that people in the favela are not as poor and do not lead such miserable lives as initially perceived. It may also be argued that it is more comfortable for tourists to keep pretty pictures of an exotic place in their memories and scrapbooks – whether physical or virtual – than pictures which show the downside of living in favelas.

Image 7 and Image 8

Figures 6.7 and 6.8 present syntheses of life in the favela. Figure 6.7[19] was taken by a tourist during a tour and summarises the joy of a local with a smile on her face. Figure 6.8 was taken by photographer Marcos Tristão and depicts a mother's pain at losing her daughter to a stray bullet amidst a conflict between drug dealers and police in Morro dos Macacos. By making this comparison, I do not intend to show these images as opposite nor present them in a simplistic manner – as the good side which must be shown and the

Figure 6.7 Image 7.

Figure 6.8 Image 8.

bad side which must be hidden or vice versa[20] – but only to say these are two sides of the same coin, or two aspects of daily life in the favela.

Will both be shown during favela tours? Will both infiltrate the perception tourists build as to what constitutes life in Rocinha? Is showing the marks of violence upon the walls in the favela – as do practically all guides – enough to make tourists understand the marks violence imprints on people, on the locals who are targets for both police and criminals?

Although answers to many of these issues do not come easily, I believe that recognising them is important to comprehend not only the benefits of favela tours, but also the limitations of such experiences. Contrary to contemporary arguments, I do not believe that tours to Rocinha are constructed only to enable tourists to gaze at the poor and reinforce their stereotypical images of the 'favelados'.

Rather, I would suggest that, as I have endeavoured to demonstrate in this chapter, when tourists visit Rocinha they build a much more complex and multidimensional representation of the favela than the one they had before. However, this does not mean that other stereotypes, such as that of the 'happy poor' or that of the favela as 'community', result from the visit, for two principal reasons. First, the inherent time constraint of favela tours does not permit foreigner visitors to develop a deeper understanding of life in the favela whilst, second, the language barrier does not enable them to interact without the intervention of tour guides. As a result, the tour experience frequently ends up being purely visual. And contact between tourists and locals ends up occurring almost exclusively though the camera lens. Thus, the act of taking pictures is, in most cases, one of the few moments in which tourists and locals somehow interact.

Image 9 and Image 10

Figure 6.9 Image 9.

Figure 6.10 Image 10.

Notes

1 According to Freire-Medeiros (2006), in order to understand favela tourism you must set it in a double context. It must be seen firstly in the scope of the world-wide expansion of the abovementioned so-called reality tours, and secondly, in the 'phenomenon of worldwide circulation and consumption of favela as a trademark, a sign to which ambivalent meanings are associated, placing it as both violent territory and cradle of preserved authenticity.

2 Law # 779/2006 by burgess Liliam Sá, PL.

3 Under Professor Dr Bianca Freire-Medeiros. From February 2005, this research started specifically investigating the 'construction of the favela as tour destination'.

4 Here I use the term *tourists* to refer specifically to those who have visited or intend to visit favelas. It is important to state this clearly because, as previously mentioned, 'we cannot nowadays speak about it as a block experience, but only as increasingly diversified travel practices'. (Carneiro and Freire-Medeiros 2005)

5 All eight travel agencies selling Rocinha tours have their own website, which typically contains descriptions of the tours, tourist comments and tips on good behaviour during the tour. Almost all motivate the tourist to bring a camera, saying for example: 'Don't worry and bring your camera!!!' or 'You're welcome to bring your camera or VCR'.

6 After Rocinha entered the official tour site listing for 'Cidade Maravilhosa', locals from other favelas like Babilônia, Prazeres and Providência have been trying to get together and organise in order to exploit the tour 'potential' of the places thay live in in different ways. In 2005 'Pousada Favelinha' was established in Morro do Pereirão. The Projeto Favela Receptiva, in Vila Canoas – which proposes that tourists be housed in local favela dwellers' homes – also began in 2005. And in May 2006, 'the Vidigal favela was opened for tourists' (Freire-Medeiros 2006).

7 According to Marcelo Armstrong, owner of the Favela Tour agency 'the restriction on taking pictures of people other than children at school is a condition imposed to the clients of FAVELA TOUR – a fact which might partly justify the larger number of pictures of children in relation to adults – or eventually to some of the artists which showcase their work in the first tour stop at Rocinha.'

8 In regard to favela tourism, one of the most significant references is the sites of agencies that sell packages to tourists. Very often people pick out and prioritise the elements that will be photographed based mainly on the sites visited before travelling (Menezes 2007b).

9 All tourist operators and guides working in Rocinha I interviewed mentioned the international success of *City of God* as largely responsible for the increased interest in the favela as a tourist destination.

10 Part of an interview with a Rocinha inhabitant, July 2007.

11 Even though the picture above is black and white, most pictures tourists take are in colour.

12 Agencies routinely encourage tourists to donate to daycare centres or schools they visit in the favela. In their website, Jeep Tour agency, for example, warns tourists that 'in order to visit daycare centres, schools or neighbourhood associations, you must donate directly to the place you visit' (http://www.jeeptour.com.br/roteiros5.htm).

13 http://www.flickr.com/photos/simontrancart/185434004; http://www.flickr.com/photos/94211922@N00/322673600.

14 I bear in mind that it is not possible to speak either of favela tours or of agencies as if they were all the same. Each agency sells a different tour – uses different means of transportation, has different ideas of what to show and what not to show tourists – which in turn begets a different perception of what Rocinha is. Although I did not detail each agency's singularities in this chapter – for I think the study of these singularities alone would warrant a new chapter – I would like to clarify that I do not ignore their existence and the important role they play in the tourists' views of what is a favela.

15 'The downside was that the money spent on the tour did not chiefly go towards the people who live in the favela – I was not given an answer when asked how much of the profits are used to benefit the people, but was told that the awareness of tourists via the tour provides more donations to the causes of the people. If I had known this before the trip I would have investigated other companies that donate some of their profits.'

16 For further information on the issue of self-esteem see Freire-Medeiros (2006).

17 Favela Tour agency, for example, makes regular donations which help maintain the NGO Para Ti, in Vila Canoas. On the agency website it is said that: 'Arriving in Vila Canoas, visiting the "Para Ti" community school. This social project is partly financed by the tour. Besides regular classes, the school teaches local kids initial computer skills and the art of making handcrafts that can also be purchased by the visitor.' (http://www.favelatour.com.br/program_ing.htm).
Exotic Tour agency helps a daycare centre and has its own social project called 'Oficina de Turismo da Rocinha'. On the agency website you see the following information: 'Rejane Reis is the coordinator of the workshop which trains local youngsters as guides to take you on this unique tour. Your visit will help a local school as well as create work opportunities within the community.' (http://www.favelatourismworkshop.com).

18 Interview by Bianca Freire-Medeiros in 2005 at Jeep Tour headquarters.

19 http://www.flickr.com/photos/fabiovenni/320554154/in/set-72057594105393344.

20 It is worthwhile to note that there is ample literature dealing specifically with the impact images may have on observers. Some say these might have shock-therapy value, making people react to the depicted reality. Others say that in the same measure they create a feeling of solidarity; they also atrophy that feeling. This atrophy would be caused by the overabundance of images which numb people to their impact. For more on this issue see Sontag (1981, 2003).

Section 3

Sport tourism experiences

Over the last decade, increasing attention has been paid to the phenomenon of sport tourism, or the interrelationship between two major contemporary socio-economic phenomena, namely, sport and tourism. Sport tourism is typically and simply defined as travel related to participation in or observing sport (Standeven and De Knop 1999: 12), yet falling within this brief definition is a vast array of events and activities that may be described as such. Indeed, the parameters of what is or isn't sport tourism are somewhat fuzzy. For example, does the concept necessarily only include sport as it happens or, as considered here in Chapter 7, can tourism to places where sporting events occur, such as football stadia, be considered as a form of sport tourism? Tours of the city of Barcelona, for instance, include a visit to the famous Nou Camp, yet many visitors would not describe themselves as 'sport tourists'. Similarly, events such as the Olympic Games are often, and legitimately, studied in the context of 'mega-events' in general as opposed to sport tourism in particular. Inevitably, therefore, much of the sport tourism literature has, until recently, been primarily concerned with issues of definition and measurement: what is sport tourism, who are sport tourists, what do they do, how much do they spend, and so on? Conversely, relatively little attention has been paid to how sport tourism is experienced.

The chapters in this section begin to contribute to this gap in the literature. As already noted, Chapter 7 by Sean Gammon explores the role and meaning of the sports stadium itself, rather than the events it hosts, as a tourism attraction. Referring to the notion of the 'sleeping stadium', he considers the way in which visits to 'empty' stadia may provide powerful and meaningful experiences for visitors. In Chapter 8, Richard Shipway and Naomi Kirkup focus more explicitly on the experiences of participants in and spectators at sporting events. Drawing on research undertaken amongst active sport tourists at long-distance running events and passive spectators at the Beijing Olympics, they compare and contrast experiences as well as arguing for qualitative approaches to research in order to uncover the depth of meaning inherent in both active and passive participation in sport tourism. The section then concludes with Mac McCarthy's chapter (Chapter 9) which, based upon a case study of the Gay Football World Championships held in London in 2008, explores the inherent meaning and potentials for participant tourists/players in this event.

7 'Sporting' new attractions? The commodification of the sleeping stadium

Sean Gammon

Introduction

The literature relating to the many relationships that sport has with tourism has been steadily increasing over the last five years. Undoubtedly, the overwhelming theme in the majority of such studies has principally focused on the economic impacts generated by major/mega sports events (Weed 2006). However, more recently there has been a growing interest in understanding sports structures and sites as significant tourism attractions in their own right (Gammon and Ramshaw 2007; Stevens 2005). Whether it be the home of a hallmark team or stadia associated with particular events, there is clear evidence that many sports structures are becoming an integral part of many destinations' tourism portfolios (Fairley and Gammon 2005; Gibson 1998; Weed 2008). Whilst the trend for both tourists and excursionists alike to visit such attractions is increasing, there has been little discussion relating to the management of them – along with any deep understanding of the motives and experiences of those that attend.

This chapter returns to Standeven and De Knop's (1999: 58) premise that the nature of sport tourism is an 'experience of physical activity tied to an experience of place'. It will draw primarily on two studies carried out at the Millennium Stadium in Cardiff (Gammon and Fear 2007) and Twickenham Stadium in London (Ramshaw and Gammon 2010), and aims, first, to explore the reasons for this recent visitor trend, and, second, to determine in what ways the experience of a stadium outside of event conditions contributes to visitors' perception of place.

Stadia and tourism

Unsurprisingly, staging events has long been linked with generating significant tourism, especially when associated with hosting major/mega sports events (Hughes 1993; Kasimati 2003; Pruess 2005; Ritchie 1984; Weed 2008). Indeed, it is often explicitly cited by organisers as being one of the primary reasons for bidding for events in the first place. However, the sports event landscape is a complex one, including hallmark events, special events, mega and major events, and festivals, all of which generate an array of economic, social and environmental impacts.

Undoubtedly, the overwhelming literature related to hosting major sports events has tended to focus upon the measurement of economic impacts, as well as upon the legacy issues related to the sustainable usage of the facilities once the event has ended. But regular and/or hallmark events rarely generate such concerns relating to future stadium usage, though many have to adapt their stadia as venues for non-sporting events in order to supplement income when out of season. In addition, those responsible for sports stadia and other sites of sporting significance (Gammon 2004) have over the last 20 years recognised the importance, both in terms of extra revenue and positive public relations, of opening up their facilities to the public outside of when events are normally held – and thus, to treat their venues as traditional visitor attractions. This has led stadia to be described as the sleeping giants of tourism (John 2002), owing to their potential of appealing to a wide range of customers, though arguably those who have an interest in sport are more likely to be drawn to such structures:

> The inherent appeal of stadia as special places where heroes play and legends are made gives them the type of attributes on which more recognized visitor attractions are based – atmosphere, sense of occasion, evocation and emotion… It is apparent that an important part of the appeal of the stadium as a visitor attraction is its potential to give visitors a real experience of 'sport as heritage… '
>
> (Stevens 2005: 213)

So sports sites are now perceived as more than just places in which events take place; they are now places to visit, to stand near to, to touch, to record an image of or, perhaps, to experience more intimately through a tour. They have become what MacCannell (1999) might refer to as famous for being famous, much like many other attractions. In short, the stadium has grown in importance, from an often aesthetically indifferent utilitarian structure into an iconic symbol of a place, team, sport and/or event. Its elevation to tourist attraction has much to do with the global appeal of sport and the manner in which it is promoted and reported via the media. However, that is clearly only part of the reason, for sport holds great meaning and personal significance to those that follow and participate, a point not lost on Mangan (2006: 1):

> Sport seduces the teeming 'global village'; it is the new opiate of the masses; it is one of the great modern experiences; its attraction astonishes only the recluse; its appeal spans the globe. … Sport for many has replaced religion as a source of emotional catharsis and spiritual passion, and for many it is among the earliest of memorable childhood experiences – so it infiltrates memory, shapes enthusiasms, serves fantasies.

Predictably, sport tourist attractions generate similar complex issues relating to representation, customer motivation and authenticity as their non-sporting counterparts. Intriguingly, the sports attraction market (Hinch and Higham 2004) has become far more competitive in recent times, which has meant that those responsible for marketing and promoting their sports sites have had to become more creative in distinguishing themselves from possible competitors. This has led to a number of sports stadia becoming popular venues for numerous non-sporting conferences and events. Such market-led competition has irrefutably contributed to the commodification debated in both in sport and tourism.

The commodification of sports stadia

Disputes concerning the commodification of both sport and tourism have been covered extensively within the literature, and have been dealt with in very similar ways (Coakley 2009; Cohen 1988b; Stewart 1987). For example, the concerns over destinations (and the sites found within) being commodified for the delectation of the visiting tourist is commonplace. The primary concern is often grounded in the notion that such economic exchange results in places morphing into sites and sights that tourists desire to see and pay for – rather than offering more honest culturally based representations. Of course, the dilemma is that economic exchange is the oxygen of tourism, and it would be difficult to envisage it existing without it. Clearly, the debates are not whether tourist places should be commodified, but rather to limit, where possible, the negative impacts to people and places that such commodification can cause. Such debates are extremely complex and are at the nub of tourism studies and, therefore, beyond the scope of this paper (for further coverage see Cohen 1988b; Greenwood 1989). However, in the context of this chapter it is the growing cultural and economic exchange and interdependence between tourism and sport that will be the primary focus.

Sport, too, has experienced similar debates regarding commodification; that in some way it has lost its soul and its integrity to the marketplace. Such disquiet is based upon the idea that decisions to participate, watch and follow a sport are largely dependent upon cost rather than some intrinsically driven interest or curiosity. There is little doubt that the commercial expansion of sport is not new, though the global appeal of many sports (fuelled by the media) have substantially accelerated such developments and have, in turn, excluded many from direct participation. However, much as in tourism, sport's ability to grow evermore popular is inextricably linked to its capacity in appealing to a widening spectrum of interested parties. It is worth acknowledging that many have argued (as have those commentating on tourism) that without commodification sport would not be the omnipotent force it is today (Coakley 2009).

There is little doubt that sports events have been treated as commodities for many years, but there now seems to be a double commodification going on: one associated with the event, the other with the place in which the event or events take place. The stadium is sold as the authentic place for a particular sport, team or event. For example, Manchester United's Old Trafford markets itself as the authentic theatre of dreams, while Twickenham Stadium promotes itself as the spiritual home of rugby, and the Millennium Stadium in Cardiff boasts that it is the home of Welsh rugby. In addition to the museums and halls of fame that may lie within these stadia, an increasingly popular offering is the stadium tour. The major selling point of the tour is that:

> it offers visitors an opportunity to experience a deeper connection with a stadium (and as a consequence, a team player or sport) by accessing areas otherwise preserved for the very privileged. Moreover, they offer a chance to walk in the shadows of the legends and heroes, and by doing so experience an authentic insight into their exclusive world(s).
>
> (Gammon 2004: 38)

To what degree the experience is authentic is unclear and will be discussed later in the chapter and, although the drive to see the unseen may be significant in the customer decision process, it is unclear in what ways the experience of the stadium empty (when asleep) differs from when an event takes place (when awake). Moreover, it is unclear how these experiences collectively contribute to visitors' perception of place.

Experiencing the stadium

The manner in which a stadium is experienced is dependent upon a myriad of factors, such as an individual's history with the place, whether they are local or a fan, and whether they have experienced the stadium during event conditions. Gaffney and Bale (2004: 26) offer an interesting perspective on how individuals experience stadia:

> Our sensual experience of the stadium, rooted within place (seats, sections, sides, ends, boxes, etc.), rooted within space (the stadium), within a larger place (the city), within ever larger spaces (region, state, nation, hemisphere, globe, solar system) contributes to the idea that all the senses are geographical; each contributes to one's orientation in space, to an awareness of spatial relationships, and to the appreciation of the qualities of particular places, which include those currently (through residence or visiting) and those removed from time.

They not only highlight the personal antecedent factors that affect experience but also the many ways a stadium can be experienced, or sensed when visiting. By taking a phenomenological perspective, Gaffney and Bale (2004) explore how a stadium is sensed and experienced, primarily focusing upon somatic (bodily) receptors. They also offer additional perspectives linked to sensing history and belonging, which collectively illustrate the complex and individualistic nature of a stadium or, indeed, any structure that can be felt and experienced. However, their discussion is framed around event conditions; when the stadium is inhabited by the sights, smells, sounds and atmosphere that would normally be expected in such situations. Consequently, it is important to explore to what extent the experience of an 'empty' (or asleep) stadium differs from event conditions – and how such experiences may potentially contribute to a deeper understanding of both sport and tourism places. As a result, the following discussion principally refers to the stadium tour as an appropriate context in which to explore experiences outside event conditions.

As detailed above, Gaffney and Bale (2004) offer eight senses in which the stadium can be felt (for simplicity they predominantly focus upon football stadia), which will be a helpful place to revisit when comparing and contrasting how the empty stadium is experienced.

Sight

Given the often grand and rather imposing scale of many stadia, it is little wonder that they are first experienced from afar as salient features of many cityscapes. In the UK, such unapologetic posturing within the built environment is accentuated further by placing new stadia on the urban periphery, or by clearing the surrounding developments of more centrally positioned structures, and by doing so promoting their size and domination more. Once closer, the stadium facade becomes visible, perhaps more so outside the many distractions that take place during events. Indeed, many stadium tours will take customers outside the ground in order to draw attention to particular architectural features that would be otherwise missed or ignored. Undoubtedly, more recently constructed stadia are no longer the drab, utilitarian structures they once were, for today time, thought and a great deal of expense is invested on the external design. However, it is arguably once inside the stadium that the biggest contrast takes place; for the 'empty' venue can feel a very different space outside event conditions. Of course, the manner in which it is experienced will depend upon the existing relationship and history (if any) an individual has with a stadium. Clearly, for the ardent fan the empty stadium can seem a strange place where what was once familiar becomes different or strange, rather like a child entering their school after normal teaching hours. Seats have replaced bodies and, if on a stadium tour, different visual perspectives will very often be experienced for the first time. Research carried out at the Millennium Stadium (Gammon and Fear 2007) found that it is not unusual for those on such tours to announce that it's like seeing the stadium for the first time. Tours also offer different, more intimate sights to the individual, sights usually reserved for the privileged few such as players' locker rooms, media centres and executive boxes. It is unclear to what extent such access affects an individual's sense of place, though previous studies suggest that such experiences can be very powerful and memorable (Gammon and Fear 2007).

Gaze

Drawing on the work of Foucault (1977) and Urry (1990a), Gaffney and Bale (2004) suggest that the stadium, as well as the paying fans, can be gazed upon, primarily by those occupying executive boxes:

> The one-way reflective glass prevents the crowd from knowing whether or not any one is in the luxury boxes, looking out at them. They are thus under continual surveillance by the corporations and upper classes who purchase the rights to this panoptic gaze.
>
> (Gaffney and Bale 2004: 28)

In this sense, the spectators at events are in effect part of the spectacle; they are to be gazed down upon from positions of power and authority, for to fully appreciate the full entirety of a sports stadium not only must the competitive action be taken in but also the reactions of the fans. Such collective gazing (Urry 1990a) is solely associated with experiencing the stadium when full and/or during event conditions and obviously differs when the stadium is empty. Sports stadia could be compared to grand country houses which are, according to Urry (1990a: 45), ' ... designed as public places: they would look strange if they were empty. It is other people that make such places. The collective gaze thus necessitates the presence of large members of other people ... '. Sports stadia are no different, but it is their strangeness when empty that is arguably the primary appeal to visit them and, consequently, will involve a different form of gaze. Also, unlike the relatively composed behaviour of country house visitors, the potentially rowdy and intimidating environment of a sports stadium during event conditions can be quite off-putting. Consequently, there are tourists who are happy to collect gazes, where a tour represents no more than a ticked-off box of places to visit and things to do. In this case, there is little attachment with place: the tour represents an opportunity to experience a stadium safely and comfortably, without the 'unpleasantness' of the crowds. The hidden sights encountered on the tour will still be of interest as they represent a symbolic hierarchy 'between the hallowed and/or hidden space(s) of the great and privileged and the ordinary, everyday space(s) of the visitor' (Gammon and Fear 2007: 27). In contrast, those who have stronger links to a stadium, such as fans and/or members of the local community, will experience such sights more intimately where the gaze is far more romantic (Urry 1990a). Privileged viewpoints are no longer reserved for those that can afford it, for in many cases tours will take visitors up to the executive boxes where the panoptic gaze will now be experienced by proxy. Indeed, tour guides when accessing such places will encourage visitors to imagine what it must feel like to inhabit such areas on match days. Similarly, when other sites are visited, such as players' locker rooms, the entrance to the pitch and the dugouts, the gaze is an imagined one; in this case from the players' perspective.

Sound

Undeniably, the experience of sound contributes powerfully to an individual's sense of place, and no more so than in and around a stadium during an event. It is, perhaps, the dynamic and extreme nature of the noise that leaves such a lasting impression to those who have not experienced it before. The sanctioned screaming, shouting, cheering, chanting and singing are positively encouraged, and is acceptable behaviour almost unique to many sporting venues (though the intensity and regularity of noise is of course dependent upon the sport and the action). Sound defines a stadium – it gives it life – a point not lost on Gaffney and Bale (2004: 31) who go as far as to suggest that 'without sound the stadium is empty'. So, what of the auditory experience of a stadium when empty? For visitors on the tours at Twickenham Stadium and the Millennium Stadium (see Gammon and Fear 2007; Ramshaw and Gammon, forthcoming), the quietness promoted a hushed reverence similar to visiting places of worship. The voices which would normally be lost amongst the cacophony of the crowd now stood out, generating a stronger sense of self-awareness.

Of course, there is rarely complete silence during a tour as there is usually some form of maintenance going on in preparation for the next event. Seats are cleaned, rubbish cleared and grass mown. However, the noises these everyday activities generate are enormously amplified by the emptiness of the stadium, rendering them almost important backstage features of the tour experience.

Touch

Gaffney and Bale's (2004) analysis of touch focuses chiefly upon the experience of being in a crowd on match day rather than any direct interaction with the structure itself. They point out that the restrictive movement of being in a crowd is part of the stadium experience; that the normal rules of personal space and individualism is given up to the amorphous power of the horde, for: 'the individuals create the crowd, and the crowd consumes them' (Gaffney and Bale 2004: 32). Touching the stadium when empty offers a very different and literal interpretation of this sense, and illustrates the potent symbolic nature of *stadium as place* (Ramshaw and Gammon 2010). Crowds act very much like garments, they hide much – and during match days their mere presence equates to certain areas being strictly out of bounds. A key feature of the tour is that many of these areas are revealed and/or made accessible:

> The attraction of the stadium tour is that it offers more than an opportunity to experience the superficial features of the structure, for these

can be experienced during an event. The tour offers a deeper familiarity with the stadium. In many cases the route of a tour will stop and enter quite ordinary spaces like the changing rooms or the dug-outs, but the importance of these spaces is elevated by the extraordinary place in which they are set and the fact they are, or have been, used and experienced by heroes and legends.

(Gammon and Fear 2007: 27)

As visitors enter these areas there is (where permitted) much direct physical interaction; locker room benches are quickly occupied in an attempt to get somehow closer to the heroes; numerous pictures of visitors are taken next to the shirt (jersey) of their favourite players; and hands are placed upon any object or structure that may be considered worthy or important enough to touch and feel. Through touch a deeper connection with place is sought, as if to channel the great deeds of the past or to somehow get closer to the spirit of the place.

Smell and taste

Similarly to the above examples smell and taste are explored by Gaffney and Bale (2004) within the context of an event. They point out that the smell of a stadium has some very powerful nostalgic triggers that affect both spectator and player alike, much in the same way it does in tourism (Dann and Jacobsen 2002). Smell during a tour plays a lesser part in sensing the stadium, primarily because the odours associated with the event have been replaced by the antiseptic smells left by the cleaners and maintenance staff. Locker rooms are no longer the hot sweaty cauldrons they are when occupied by the players, and the seating areas do not emit the smells of food and drink that would be normal during a match. Pitch side may be the only time during a tour that visitors experience an advantaged perspective as they are close to the grass, but to what extent this differs from occupying nearby seating areas is uncertain.

In terms of taste, Gaffney and Bale (2004) concentrate on the food and drink that is traditionally consumed before, during and after matches. The suggestion made is that each stadium has potentially its own identifiable cuisine that has a ritualistic connection to the match day experience. Clearly, it is doubtful that a stadium tour could evoke equally notable practices.

History, belonging to a crowd

In addition to the more traditional somatic senses, there are many other ways a stadium can be experienced, such as ambience and atmosphere, as well as history, place and space. Sensing the history of a place can be a memorable event, a point not lost on Gaffney and Bale (2004). However, the experience may be linked more firmly to heritage rather than history as those visiting stadia may be drawn not so much by the chronological age of a place but more by the social and cultural meanings that such places evoke. As discussed earlier, the extent to which someone will feel an attachment with place is dependent upon their previous experiences of it. For some, there is little doubt that an opportunity to experience a stadium outside an event is related to their need to somehow get closer to it; to recognise and appreciate the stadium as an important place, both personally and collectively. By occupying and experiencing the inaccessible and the unseen, a stronger connection is made, for 'to be inside a place is to belong to it and identify with it, and the more profoundly you are the stronger is the identity with place.' (Relph 1976: 49). Therefore, in some cases sensing a place's history and heritage will in turn accentuate feelings of attachment and belonging. But feelings connected to belonging are not so obviously allied with being part of a crowd, at least not in the same way as spectatorship and participation at an event. Sports stadia can be potent symbols of home, not just for those that reside nearby but for those whose associations may at first appear to be less obvious (Bale 1994). The global appeal of sport means that many teams and places associated with particular sports or events hold meaning for fans and aficionados across the world (Higham and Hinch 2009; Maguire 1993). As a result, sports places can act as powerful symbols of home, not only as representations of the home of a particular sport (for example, Lord's Cricket Ground) or a symbol of a team, but more generally as being part of the real and imagined national identity of an entire nation (Ramshaw and Gammon 2010). Sports stadia emit powerful spiritual connections that, for many, represent what Cohen (1992) has described as the centre out there. These centres unsurprisingly become places of secular pilgrimage, where tour visitors are promised memorable experiences firmly linked to authenticity.

Authentic experiences of stadia?

Attending sports events can, for the curious visitor, offer opportunities to experience authentic cultural insights of a community or an entire nation. To see a people at play is an opportunity to experience the many cultural nuances and heritage-related practices that define them, whether they be good, bad or indifferent (Jarvie 2006; Nauright 1996). For ' ... visitors who attend local sporting events, participate in local activities, or visit local sites to venerate sports/people are afforded a unique opportunity to access the backstage of a destination' (Hinch and Higham 2005: 246). In a later publication, Higham and Hinch (2009) make a compelling case that the manifestations of sport spectatorship are firmly entrenched in the search for authentic sport experiences, where outcomes of competition are genuinely unknown. It could be argued that the venues where the competitions are held are, by association, delivering simpler authentic experiences linked to the actual sport that takes place within them. But to suggest that sports events represent a more encompassing authentic experience of place may be problematic; after all events are staged and, by definition, there must be an element of performance. The enormous global appeal of sport and the consequent media coverage has meant that fans and spectators are aware of the cameras and will understandably behave self-consciously in front of them. For the visitor to such events, performances are probably unimportant, for they too will perform but in a more playful way, as a *flaneur*:

> The contemporary sporting *flaneur* likes to guide, in semi detached fashion, through a cornucopia of experiences. During sporting mega-events, *flaneurs* can float among different spectator groups outside stadia or in city centres, absorbing the international interplay of different national dress, colours, tongues and intoxicating substances within a single public space.
>
> (Giulianotti 2005: 132)

The extent to which fans and visitors will perform will undoubtedly be determined by the size and coverage of the event, though it would be wrong to conclude that such experiences are inauthentic as a degree of performance may well be expected at such events. Hinch and Higham (2005, 2009) suggest that Wang's (1999) typology, which explores authenticity in tourism, is a helpful starting point in understanding what part sport plays in people's lives. Wang (1999) outlines three ways in which authenticity can be understood; objective authenticity which concerns the expert verification of an object as genuine; constructive authenticity which focuses upon the perceptions of such objects by the onlooker (tourist) and the symbolic meaning attached to them; and existential authenticity which represents a sense of true being, of feeling and behaving in a way that is true to ourselves.

As a result, it has been argued that sports attractions offer all elements of the authenticity framework; they offer rare opportunities to engage in, and experience, legitimate cultural activities (Hinch and Higham 2005). Plainly, the discussion above concerning the complex manner in which a sports stadium can be felt underpins this notion of authenticity validation. Nevertheless, much of the debate concerning authenticity is framed around the context of an event, where the structure in which the event takes place is largely sidelined. It must not be forgotten that stadia are the vessels that house these experiences and, therefore, have important social and cultural meanings in their own right. To ignore or dismiss them is equivalent to solely focusing on the wine whilst neglecting the significance of the container in which it is drunk.

Higham and Hinch (2009) maintain that to attend a sports event offers visitors an opportunity to immerse themselves in the backstage of any given community; to witness the drama of a match amongst those who normally watch, provides the visitor a unique insight of a place and people. There is much merit in this proposal, though it has to be acknowledged that their presence will to a greater or lesser degree affect the authenticity of the occasion. Similarly, it had been suggested that stadium tours convert what is considered backstage to frontstage (Higham and Hinch 2009), which may be the case but perhaps this misses the point. In terms of authenticity, tours are marketed as providing access to authentic areas usually out of bounds to the 'regular' spectator. Managers of tours commodify sports stadia as important places in and of themselves, such as the home of a team or of a particular sport, whilst also selling the promise of accessing special places that lie within. In basic terms, that is the *raison d'être* of the stadium tour. Certainly, what this illustrates is the many meanings attributed to the word 'place'. It may be appropriate for the purposes of this chapter to adopt Cresswell's (2004: 7) definition of places as, ' ... all spaces which people have made meaningful. They are all spaces people are attached to in one way or another.' (For a more detailed discussion of place, see Cresswell (2004)). So, in this sense the tour offers what Wang (1999) would refer to as objective authenticity, where features along the way are authenticated as real or genuine. Also, tours will emphasise the symbolic features (constructive authenticity) of a stadium, which will be promoted by both media and tour guides alike. For example, Twickenham promotes itself as the spiritual home of rugby, in the same way Wimbledon does of tennis. Furthermore, stadia may act as a symbol of place, such as St James' Park in Newcastle or Old Trafford in Manchester (Ramshaw and Gammon 2010). But it is the existential authenticity that should be highlighted here, for sports places hold for many a profound meaning that transcends the draw of many other attractions. For the committed fan, these places represent not only a sense of home but a spirit of place that evokes feelings of awe, wonderment and personal reflection. A stadium or sport venue encountered outside event conditions may not offer the same connection with the people of the place it represents, but it does generate a different type of bond, associated with history memory, nostalgia and heritage. Paradoxically, it is the quietness linked to tour visits which seems to amplify the personal and collective recollections that hold such deep meaning for those that visit. It is little wonder that visiting sports stadia has been equated to a secular pilgrimage, an opportunity perhaps for visitors to pay their respects to a place that has become an important part of their personal and social identities (Gammon 2004; Mosher 1991; Springwood 1996). Tours cannot promise an absolute authentic backstage experience, as the areas they access have understandably been prepared for visitors, but they can pledge an opportunity to feel an intimacy that would not always be possible during an event.

Conclusion

The empty or asleep stadium, then, offers a very different experience to that encountered during an event. Unsurprisingly, the management and marketing of sports sites are framed around the commodification of place, linked to authenticity and home. However, the rich variety of visitor profiles suggests that customer motives are both multifaceted and potentially conflicting, much in the same way as more traditional sacred sites. For example, stadia tours will often comprise of highly identified fans, who display a degree of veneration towards many of the tour highlights, as well as the less-attached visitors whose interests are far more casual, and ephemeral at best.

What appears to bind the array of customer drives is the desire to see the unseen, not only to experience sports sites when not in use but also to gain an insight of what lies behind the scenes; to get a glimpse into 'authentic' backstage. To what extent a stadium is truly asleep during such visits is of course a moot point, as backstage areas are often prepared for visitors and usually there is much activity and planning for future events. Perhaps it would be safer to conclude that, at least when the visitor is present, one eye always remains half open. But stadium tours offer more than just the prospect of satisfying the curious visitor, for they also present a more intimate setting in which to reflect and experience place. The impact of such experiences may well be both moving and memorable, an outcome of which is not to be ignored by other non-sporting attractions.

8 Understanding sport tourism experiences: exploring the participant–spectator nexus

Richard Shipway and
Naomi Kirkup

Introduction: Understanding sport tourism experiences

This chapter explores the experiences of sport tourists by looking at the dual concepts of passive and active involvement in sport-related travel, passive involvement usually referring to watching sport and active referring to participation in sport (Hinch and Higham 2001). As more research focuses on the sport consumer and their behaviour, it is becoming increasingly clear that the sport consumption experience is a complex one (Crawford 2004). Therefore, research embracing this complexity is paramount to driving the academic area forward.

Specifically, the purpose of this chapter is to examine the experiences of different types of sport tourists and to offer some explanations that may contribute to an understanding of these experiences. From a practitioner's perspective, a better understanding of the experiences of sport tourists' behaviour and experiences will allow sport tourism stakeholders to gain further knowledge of, and to cater to, the needs and wants of their clients. In particular, there is a need to move beyond simply profiling sport tourism participants to further understand and explain these profiles (Gibson 2004). The findings of many studies have arisen out of practitioners' desires to illustrate that sport tourism can bring positive benefits to participants. The need to understand, as well as describe, sporting behaviour was addressed to some extent by Shipway and Jones (2007) who explored distance runners' perspectives when competing in a four-day international event in Cyprus, and similarly in a subsequent study at the 2007 Flora London Marathon (Shipway and Jones 2008). These studies identified the need to focus upon the social identities of participants in order to develop an understanding of their subsequent behaviours. This chapter further explores this central role of identity and its relationship with sporting activity, and the resultant experiences of both the active and passive sport tourist, as well as introducing the concept of the sport tourism locality as a 'third place' outside of the home and work environment. It suggests that it is both the event and tourism experience that is central to both groups of sport tourists; however, these distinct experiences are greatly enhanced by the sense of identity that sport tourists attach to their chosen activity in the respective tourism localities.

An exploration of the sport tourism identity

As noted above, this chapter seeks to add to the body of knowledge in the area of sport tourism, where there remains a relative paucity of qualitative research into the experience of both active and passive sport tourists. On the one hand, in the context of distance running, there have been several quantitative, but few qualitative, studies exploring recreational and marathon running (Masters and Ogles 1995; Masters *et al.* 1993; Ogles and Masters 2000, Ogles and Masters 2003). On the other hand, specifically in the context of Olympic tourists, there exists a lack of research into the reasons for travel to watch the Olympic Games. The literature on the more passive sport spectators reveals that the majority of studies focusing on motivations to attend sports events place an overreliance on the use of college students as participants, as well as focusing on travel to watch regularly competing teams, which represent only one small proportion of the increasingly diverse world of sport spectators.

Social identity theory has gained increasing prominence in terms of its ability to explain group behaviour in a variety of contexts, ranging from terrorism to sports fandom (Jones 2006), focusing its analysis upon the group, rather than the individual or interpersonal level (Thoits and Virshup 1997). Social identity theory focuses upon the importance of individuals defining themselves in terms of the groups to which they belong ('we'), rather than their own personal characteristics ('I'). Social identities are important for a number of reasons. They provide the individual with a sense of belonging, a valued place within their social environment, a means to connect to others, and the opportunity to use valued identities to enhance self-worth and self-esteem. 'Casual' leisure (such as taking part in a casual sporting activity) is unlikely to provide a significant social identity (Stebbins 2001); however, serious leisure activities, such as competing in a sporting event, for example the New York City Marathon, have the potential to do so (Green and Jones 2005), with travel to take part in sporting activities likely to make the sporting identity more salient (Shipway and Jones 2007).

Within the sport spectator literature, identity is particularly pertinent and is cited as being a common motivator for sport spectators. However, much of the literature in this area is dominated by research highlighting the correlation between sports teams and spectator identification (see, for example, Wann and Dolan 1994; Wann *et al.* 1996). For example, James and Ross (2004) suggest that fans may attend games regularly to feel like part of the team, and associated with this team identification are feelings of euphoria the fan would experience as part of a team success and the isolation of oneself from others during times of failures (Correia and Esteves 2007). However, the Olympic Games in particular offer a sense of identification unique to the event, the athletes or a particular sport rather than a particular regional team. Therefore, the sense of identification provided by attending the Games requires further research in order to understand and cater for these unique identities. Bhattacharya *et al.* (1995) determine that, as identification has desirable consequences, the key for practitioners is to create identification.

In order to delve into the social world of the sports spectator, this study draws on literature from the consumer behaviour field by utilising Means-End (ME) Theory. According to Marsh (2007), ME theory is a way to understand consumer decision making in purchasing products by determining which product attributes meet or satisfy which particular consumer goals and the reasons the consumer values those goals. McIntosh and Thyne (2005) argue that, in the context of tourism, ME theory provides a deeper understanding of tourist behaviour by linking specific service attributes to personal values. Wansink (2003) describes how, when consumers are first asked why they purchase a product, they typically describe attributes of the product, such as price, quality and so on. However, he notes that these are seldom the reasons for people purchasing the products. Rather, it is the consequences that begin to show us the underlying reasons for consumption and that reveal the values that give us the real reasons for people purchasing the product. According to Klenosky (2002), within tourism the theory provides a framework for relating the attributes of a particular tourism product to the important factors that influence travel behaviour.

Gibson (2004) suggests that, in the domain of sport tourism, there is a need to move knowledge forward beyond the 'what' and towards the 'why', examining some conceptual tools that could be applied to understanding and explaining sport tourism behaviour. Similarly, Weed (2005) suggests that, in the field of sport tourism, work on experiences is primarily descriptive and, as a consequence, what this research overlooks is *why* such experiences are enjoyable and *why* participants would like to repeat them. He argues that sport tourism is an area of study that lacks methodological diversity, rarely asking the 'why' questions, and in approximately 50 per cent of cases does not employ clear theoretical perspectives to underpin what is largely descriptive research. Therefore, elaborating on the ideas of Gibson (2005a) and Weed (2005), this chapter develops a clearer understanding of sport tourism experiences and suggests reasons why 'sport tourists do what they do', through two contrasting research methods.

Research methods

In exploring the experiences of both active and passive sport tourism participants, this chapter utilises two contrasting qualitative methodological approaches in order to establish how they can help us to better understand sport tourism. It is acknowledged by Gibson (2004) that a distinction exists between active and passive sport tourists and, as such, this chapter addresses both groups of sport tourists through the use of contrasting methods of enquiry. More specifically, it investigates whether the actors ('active' distance runners and 'passive' Olympic tourists) involved have different social constructions of outcomes than many positivist studies might predict. The chapter, therefore, aims to move beyond the domain of sport tourism studies, adopting a focus that is clearly within core social science disciplines. For example, it looks at relevant concepts that originate from sociology and social anthropology, as well as cultural studies. Telling stories is important in terms of belonging and identity, in terms of creating a sense of kinship/togetherness, and establishing myths of sport tourism groups. The chapter draws from marketing and consumer behaviour literature to help explain the behaviours of Olympic tourists, and examines how meaning (i.e. identity) is created through engagement within the sport tourism world.

A qualitative approach was employed, exploring the way people make sense of their social worlds, and to understand social reality from the point of view of participants engaging in sport tourism activity (Shipway and Jones 2008). It was important to study both active and passive sport tourists in their natural settings, attempting to make sense of, or interpret, this phenomenon in terms of the meanings people bring to them (Denzin and Lincoln 1998a: 3). This approach was taken through an analysis of the lived experiences of human actors – sport tourists. This methodological approach leads to a personal, first-hand enquiry into the lived experience of the sports participant and, as such, represents an interpretivist approach, rather than a more scientific or positivist stance.

The first part of the study adopts a style of research – ethnography – which is distinguished by its objectives; namely, to understand the social meanings and activities of people in a given 'field' (Brewer 2000) and to explore the participant behaviour through first-hand experience (Holloway and Todres 2003). In this case, this approach emerged through an exploration of the distance runner as a sport participant. Ethnography is the description and interpretation of a culture or social group, and its aim is to understand another way of life by focusing on ordinary, everyday behaviour. Ethnography is literally the description (graphy) of cultures (ethno), and the objective of an ethnographic study is to provide an in-depth study of a culture that includes behaviour, interactions and language. This chosen approach involves close association with, and 'active' participation in, this sport tourism setting. Immersion within the social world of the distance runner provides an insight into the unique identity of the distance runner.

In relation to sport specifically, ethnographic research holds much potential for the sociology of sport (Silk 2005). This chapter employs ethnography as a more suitable research tool to study human beings within their natural social world, in this case, the social world of the sport tourist. It has been used previously in sport studies for detailing sporting communities (for example, see work by Atkinson (2000) on ticket scalping; Sands (2000) on the surfing subculture; Tsang (2000) looking at elite rowing;

or by Wheaton (2000) on windsurfing). These are all good examples of how ethnography has been used to describe and understand sporting cultures. Data collection for the distance running events studied involved engaging in semi-structured interviews, participant observation and observational studies. Morgan (2007) suggests that tourism meanings can best be unlocked through methods that analyse how people talk about and interpret their experiences, such as narrative analysis of interviews or ethnography. Data were not quantified at any stage, as the intention was to explore the issues of 'why' and 'how'.

The second part of this study, within the Olympic tourism setting, utilises a qualitative research method known as laddering. Laddering is a semi-structured, in-depth interviewing technique which aims to uncover the meaning of certain behaviour linked to the product attributes and personal values of the consumer. It was deemed important within this study to research the Olympic spectator at the time of the Games in order to gain a clear understanding of the meaning attached to the consumption. Therefore, interviewing Olympic tourists during their trip meant that there was no reliance on post-trip recall or pre-trip intentions which may differ from the actual trip occurrence.

The laddering technique has been frequently employed within the consumer behaviour milieu (see, for example, Grunert and Grunert 1995; Nielsen *et al.* 1998; Vannoppen *et al.* 2001). The technique uses a series of interactive and probing questions that allows the researcher to link the reasons for consumption to the attributes of the product, the benefits of consumption and, ultimately, the reasons why such consequences are valued. The researcher begins by asking the respondent why they have travelled to watch the Olympic Games. The answer given then forms the basis of the next question. For example, the researcher may ask the respondent 'why have you travelled to Beijing to watch the Olympic Games?' to which the respondent may then reply 'to see the event live'. The researcher would then continue asking 'why' questions in response to the previous answer until the reasons for spectating have been exhausted, whereby the more personal reasons for consumption will have been revealed. The respondent will move up a ladder that links consumption to the attributes of the product, to the consequences of consumption, and to the personal reasons linked to those consequences. Wansink (2003) notes that laddering assesses deeper reasons why consumers do what they do and that, once aggregated, these perceptions allow for more profound insights to be uncovered. Thus, this study responds to the critiques of both Gibson (2004) and Weed (2005), who argue for the need for deeper understanding of the reasons sport consumers do what they do.

The following section now highlights how the application of the two methodological approaches outlined above were used to elicit a range of themes that subsequently emerged from the data within a selection of sport tourism settings. In doing so, these themes provide a deeper insight into the experiences of both active and passive sport tourists.

Results: The journey towards a deeper understanding of sport tourism experiences

In relation to both the distance running sport tourist and the Olympic tourist, this study focuses on the sense of identity that participants receive from engaging in sport tourism activity and how this impacts on the tourist experience. In the context of the distance running sport tourist, five key themes emerged from the data. This first and most dominant emerging theme is linked to the search for a running identity. This theme has several sub-themes, including the expansion of the concept of 'serious sport tourism' which was first developed by Shipway and Jones (2007). The second dominant distance running theme was the importance of the 'event experience' as an active sport tourist, whilst the third emerging key theme was the runner's need to train and prepare, often months in advance, for sport tourism activities and events. The fourth emerging theme was the role of sport tourism and distance running as a 'third place' outside of the home and work environment, whilst the fifth and final key emerging theme was linked to the sport tourist participant's desire for a healthy lifestyle. This series of linked themes and sub-themes offers the opportunity for a detailed insight into the 'social world' of the distance running sport tourist and, in so doing, for developing a greater understanding of their tourism experiences.

As previously outlined, the dominant theme of this chapter is that of identification with the activity of both distance running as a sport tourism activity and the consumption of the Olympic tourism experience within the tourist setting. In the distance running environment, an underlying theme which constantly emerged during fieldwork was the serious, almost professional approach towards the activity adopted by all sport tourist participants towards their racing, preparation, training and overall attitude towards distance running. A key aspect of the experience was that the sport tourism event provided access to a social environment of like-minded people, especially within the tourist setting. This sense of identity was equally pertinent for Olympic tourists in Beijing for the 2008 Games. Running participants were exhibited as serious, committed and activity driven. This is referred to as 'serious sport tourism' in previous studies by Shipway and Jones (2007, 2008), developing the concept of 'Serious Leisure' (Stebbins 2007). There now follows an exploration of two of the key emerging themes from data collected in the distance running environment, which will then be followed by an exploration of the behaviour patterns and experiences of Olympic tourists.

The first theme investigates the extent to which distance runners develop a strong feeling of identity from participating in sport tourism activity, followed by an exploration of the role of distance running and the sport tourism setting as a 'third place' outside of the home and work environment. The results illustrate that there is a degree of synergy between both the social world of the distance running sport tourist and the Olympic tourist in terms of the importance of both sport tourism identity and the concept of the sport tourism 'third place'.

A sense of sport tourism identity

All active participants clearly identified themselves with the activity of distance running, thus confirming the idea that certain forms of active sport tourism activity could provide a valued social identity. Distance running sporting events provide a setting whereby participants were able to undergo an 'identity transformation', in reality, a shift in identity salience from work or family-based identities to the leisure identity (see Shamir 1992) and become 'serious', almost professional runners in a social context within an event or tourism setting. Thus, the very act of attending running events allowed the running identity to become more salient, and more enduring (at least for the duration of the sport tourism holiday) than other identities, that became less salient as participants were distanced from them. This in itself seems to provide an attraction for such events, in that most of the other events for these runners, even for those at a relatively skilled level, were often short lived, whilst a prolonged visit to a sport tourism running event provided a unique opportunity for a period of extended enactment of a particular identity.

Observational data supported the suggestion that at times when sport tourism participants were not directly competing at the events, the majority of participants wore clothing identifying them as runners, most notably in terms of T-shirts containing logos or insignia demonstrating participation in past distance running events, many of which were overseas. A number of runners also wore running apparel throughout the duration of their sport tourism trips, including during social activities. The adoption of these 'signs and symbols' of a running identity, illustrated largely through running clothing, proved to be an important part of the tourism experience. Interviews confirmed that much of this clothing held nostalgic or sentimental value, while acting as a 'badge of honour', providing an indication of the possession of subcultural capital (Thornton 1995) in the form of completed races, which was clearly the capital valued by the group. The sense of social identity as a runner was reinforced by the special meaning and association attached to the vest, T-shirt, rain jacket or sweatshirt that many of the participants wore throughout the duration of the sport tourism period (cf. Shipway and Jones 2007), as evidenced through the stories associated with each garment told by some of the runners.

Runners talked continually about past performances and past events that they had taken part in, and the discussion of previous experiences was by far the most dominant topic of discussion in the days leading up to and after all the sport tourism events studied. Interestingly, however, sport tourism participants demonstrated less commitment to their running identity after the event finished, focusing partly upon other identities, such as work or family, although still predominantly focusing upon the running identity. This supported Green and Jones' (2005) suggestion that participants were able to escape their enduring identities associated with their home lives (which was not the case when simply training, or competing close to home), but that overseas destinations or domestic weekend running breaks provided a setting whereby participants were able to undergo an 'identity transformation' and become 'serious', almost professional runners. The importance and 'serious' approach to participating in both overseas and domestic events was illustrated by Emma G., a 56-year-old female runner from London, England whose comments were typical of many runners:

> My husband and I will be going to America in January to do the Marathon, and then we will train for Paris in April. We plan to compete in the Davos Challenge in Switzerland in July, and then the New Forest Half Marathon in September. Our final event of the year will be the Athens Classic Marathon in early November. Oh yes, we also have a plan for next year too – I really fancy the Two Oceans Ultra Marathon in Cape Town.

Discussion between participants emphasised the importance of travel, in that races that were held in distant or unusual locations held greater perceived social capital within the running community than those within their home countries. Thus, conversation focused upon races in Boston, New York or Sydney, for example. This storytelling seems to have a dual function. First, it is a key aspect of establishing the credentials of individuals within the group and, second, it serves the function of reinforcing the individual's own sense of identity (Clark and Salaman 1998). Through such means, identities were affirmed. A more in-depth analysis of sport tourism identity within the distance running social world can be found in Shipway and Jones (2008).

Aligned with the strong feelings of identity for the activity of distance running, additional key themes emerged from the data collection settings, including the role of distance running and the sport tourism setting as a 'third place' outside of the home and work environment. This theme of a sport tourism 'third place' will now be identified, both within the distance running and Olympic tourist social worlds, as an area that would benefit from further investigation, to assist with a deeper understanding of sport tourism experiences.

The sport tourism 'third place'

The 'Third Place' was a term introduced by Oldenburg (1989) to describe places where people could meet for social interaction, most notably in the form of conversation, to consolidate or develop a sense of identity, and contribute strongly to social capital and citizenship. They are located away from the first (home) and second (work or school) places. According to

Oldenburg (1989), the loss of such third places has been a key factor in changing leisure behaviour away from being socially based and towards a culture of home-centred consumption of TV, video and the Internet. Although nearly all of the limited literature on 'third places' refers to their apparent decline, this chapter investigates the growth in one particular leisure activity, sport tourism, and investigates the extent to which the growth in the popularity of sport-related travel, could be seen as fulfilling the need for a third place for sport tourism participants.

The contention here, therefore, is not that generally third places are necessarily in decline, but rather it is the traditional third places, such as pubs, or cafes, that are in decline. Conversely, it is suggested that sport-related travel and activities, such as distance running or attending mega sporting events like the Olympic Games, provide alternative new third places that reflect the changing demands of modern twenty-first-century society. This section of the chapter argues that sport tourism activity fulfils some of the criteria of the traditional third places. It also suggests that the emergence of third places is proving to be an increasingly important and attractive way to experience sport within tourism or event-related settings, be it within either a distance running or Olympic-related environment. The comments of Anthony P., a 45-year-old runner from the North of England, were typical:

> I usually go to Portugal in the spring for a Marathon Training camp. There's a regular group of people who go every year. As a group, we run in the morning, relax by the pool during the day, have another group run in the late afternoon and then have a meal in the evening. It's great to escape from the cold weather at home, and to socialise and train with different people. It's an annual event in my running calendar.

Thus, it is evident that the wider social context of the third place would be an important motivation for people embarking on sports-related travel. If such sport tourism holidays and breaks are fulfilling the needs of the third place, then the implications are important both in terms of the wider social benefits that occur from third places in terms of increased social capital and citizenship. During a conversation at a central Beijing hotel, the comments from John, a 25-year-old elite athlete from Nottingham in England, were typical of many Olympic tourists:

> I have been saving for this trip since watching the 2004 Olympics in Athens four years ago. My sport is athletics and I have tickets for every evening session at the track. A few of my friends are actually competing over the next three days. I have come here on my own, and I'm sharing a room with two other runners. I hadn't met them until I arrived two days ago, but they are nice guys, and we have been travelling together to the events each night. This trip is expensive, but the Olympics are only once every four years.

It is proposed that sport tourism third places are a common meeting ground for people with diverse backgrounds and experiences. Today's society is highly scheduled and structured, and we often forget that the most enjoyable and memorable moments of our lives are never really planned, for example, the opportunity to observe Olympic athletes set world records at the 2008 Beijing Games, or to complete an overseas marathon in a personal best time.

Olympic tourism experiences

Within the context of the passive sport tourist, the dominant themes emerging from the data were that the experience of spectating at the Olympic Games creates and reinforces a sense of belonging. Further, many respondents noted the building of identities from their experience – whether identification with a sport, an athlete or as a nation. Escapism from the pressures of normal life into a third place, such as the 'Bird's Nest' Olympic stadium in Beijing, the 'Live Sites' developed across host cities, or other alternative Olympic venues across a host destination, served to reinforce social relationships, identities and belonging. These themes are outlined below.

In the context of the Olympic tourist, the first dominant theme within the data is that spectating at the Games offers the Olympic tourist a sense of belonging. The dominant ladder leading to this value led from social interaction, to group affiliation, and to a sense of belonging. This is consistent with the work of many of the major motivational models of sport consumption (see, for example, Wann 1995; Milne and McDonald 1999; Trail and James 2001; Funk *et al.* 2002) that detail group/social interaction as a major motivator for sport consumption. However, as ME theory progresses to the deeper reasons for consumption, this motivation is linked to a need for social belonging which is rarely mentioned within the sport consumption models which themselves are largely formulated through quantitative research. Therefore, this chapter argues that it is only with further qualitative enquiry that the deeper reasons for consumption can be uncovered. In their qualitative study of World Wrestling Entertainment (WWE) fans, Deeter-Schmelz and Sojka (2004) noted that a sense of belonging was one of the most frequently cited values by consumers of WWE. They reveal that the experience facilitates a bond amongst consumers by providing a focal point for conversation and activities. Smith and Stewart (2007) observe that sport consumption enables spectators to share a common interest in the 'Game', whilst the need to foster relationships with like-minded people can cement feelings of belonging (Fink *et al.* 2002). What these results signify is that previous quantitative studies only reveal the surface reasons, such as social interaction, for attendance rather than probing for deeper reasons, which, as demonstrated here, reveals deeper significance.

The second dominant theme within the Olympic spectator results highlights identity as a major motivator for attending the Games. The findings suggest that, owing to the relative investment in time and money, travel to watch the Olympic Games would represent a strand of serious leisure which, as suggested by Green and Jones (2005), has the potential to create significant social identity. The dominant ladder leading to this value led from a particular sport/athlete, to self-esteem, and then to identification. Once again, the consequence of self-esteem is consistent with the sport consumption models (see, for example, Wann 1995; Milne and McDonald 1999), as is the deeper reason of identification. However, within the sport consumption literature, team identification is commonly cited (see, for example, Wann and Dolan 1994; Wann *et al.* 1996). Conversely, there is little exploration within the existing literature on identification with particular sports or athletes. Drawing on the work of Bhattacharya *et al.* (1995), this study supports the view that belonging to a group results in a person identifying with that group (i.e. I am a member). The results indicate that this could be membership of a group of fans particular to specific sports, or fans of particular athletes, rather than a team which has dominated the existing spectator literature on identification. Olympic spectators identify themselves in different ways unique to the sport or athlete, for example, with an identity of a 'boxing' fan or perhaps with an identity of a 'Usain Bolt' fan (the triple gold medal winning Jamaican sprinter).

Linked to this theme was the opportunity to celebrate national pride and create national identities. This sense of national pride was illustrated in a conversation with Robert S., a 35-year-old Olympic tourist from the South of England:

> Three of us bought the official 'Team GB' T-shirts and we also managed to buy some mini Union Jack Flags and temporary face stickers. When we got into the Bird's Nest Stadium, we were sat amongst another group of Brits, which was fun. Unfortunately, we didn't get to hear them play 'God Save the Queen' during the medal ceremonies, but we did have a wonderful time cheering and supporting our athletes.

The dominant ladder leading to this value led from following a national team, to a sense of belonging, and then to national pride. However, previously little has been written in the sport consumption literature about the notion of national pride although, more recently, researchers have begun to identify national pride as a reason for attending sports events (Funk *et al.* 2001; Funk *et al.* 2002). Barrer's (2007) study demonstrates that international spectator sports are of central importance to contemporary constructions of national identity. He further notes that stadia often become celebratory spaces where spectators bond with each other and demonstrate a symbolisation of their nation as much as the competing athletes do. As globalisation intensifies, sport is increasingly used as a vehicle for the reaffirmation of national identities (Mariovet 2006); in the face of globalisation and allegedly increasingly homogenous societies, individuals are searching for new experiences that allow them to differentiate and identify themselves with individual nations, for example, 'I am Irish'. Attending the Olympic Games undoubtedly caters for this need.

This study also supports the argument of sport consumption as a 'third place' and suggests that the stadium/sporting arena acts as a contemporary third place in the context of sport spectating. The stadium allows for escapism from the norm, allowing for the development of social identities, whilst developing social relationships and affirming the sense of belonging. Within the tourism literature, escapism is widely cited as a motivator for travel (Dann 1981; Iso-Ahola 1982; Leiper 1983) and is paralleled within the sport motivation literature (Wann 1995; Trail and James 2001). This chapter supports the notion of sport tourism consumption as a form of escape and argues that the third place, in this instance the Olympic Games, acts as a location for this escapism whereby sport tourists can reinforce the functions associated with the third place. As Oldenburg and Brissett (1982) suggest, the third place provides opportunities for experiences and relationships that are otherwise unavailable.

In summary, this chapter argues that continuous involvement in the sport tourism social world (either as an active participant or passive spectator) does provide individuals with social experiences and relationships that are increasingly unavailable in today's modern society. This has a close alignment with the underlying key theme, identity and sport tourism. Increasingly, experience is pre-planned, scheduled, organised, goal oriented, rationally defended, overly controlled and commercially packaged (Oldenburg and Brissett 1982). The third place in sport tourism (be it on the finish line of the Boston Marathon or the atmosphere in the Beijing Water Cube swimming pool) is often a forum for high intensity and excitement. Too often, we ignore the vital area of human experience, an active involvement in a third place. In this case, it is demonstrated through both active and passive involvement in the social world of the sport tourist. Further, the existing research in sport consumption is overreliant on existing scales which do little to add to our understanding of other emotions that may be specific to particular sports or events.

Conclusion

The intention of this chapter was to describe, not prescribe, how the social world of sport tourists might be written about and known differently, which remains important if we are to develop a deeper understanding of sport tourism experiences (Gibson 2005b). The key emerging theme is the sense of identity that sport tourists receive whilst immersed in the sport tourism setting. The experience of both active and passive sport tourists remains an area that has received limited scholarly coverage and existing sport studies remain largely rooted in the positivist tradition. This exploration of both distance runners as active sport participants and Olympic tourists as passive sports fans contributes towards filling this research gap. This research challenges the dominant forms of quantitative sport representations and, in using qualitative methodological approaches, contributes towards a deeper understanding of sport tourism. The findings also highlight opportunities for future research in sport-related travel and introduce the concept of the 'sport tourism third place'.

Similarly, the findings indicate that, within the passive sport tourist experience, future research ought to be qualitative in nature to allow for deeper explorations of this complex world. As Fairley (2006) suggests, travelling to watch a sport event is not merely about viewing the event, as the many forms of media available allow us to do so without travelling to the event. Future research is needed in the areas of Olympic spectating to further understand the identities consumers seek by travelling to watch the Games, as well as the sense of belonging they are searching for amongst their compatriots within a third place.

Outcomes from both fieldwork studies suggest that the dominant positivist, scientific model of research in sport studies fails to understand or capture the real nature of social settings (Atkinson and Hammersley 1994). While the existing typologies of sport tourism are extremely useful (Weed and Bull 2004), limitations lie in their inability to account for sport tourists who cut across typology classifications based on the unique aspects of their chosen activity, be it rugby, football, tennis, swimming, golf, skiing, distance running, or any other form of sport tourism activity. James and Ross (2004) admittedly note that, to date, research on sport consumption has focused on testing and refining scales that assess motives of sport consumers. These findings argue that these existing scales do little to help understand those deeper reasons for consumption. This chapter argues that in order to understand the social world of both active distance running sport tourists and Olympic tourists, future research needs to be qualitative in its nature rather than conceptualising sport tourism activities in terms of variables and the relationship between them. In the wider context, this chapter also attempts to illustrate the extensive potential for qualitative research on both 'active' and 'passive' sport tourists.

9 We are family: IGLFA World Championships, London 2008

Mac McCarthy

Introduction

In this chapter, I seek to explore the meanings and motivations associated with attendance, both as participant and as audience, at the International Gay and Lesbian Football World Championships in London, 2008.

Gay tourism has been the subject of a number of studies in recent years, largely focused on the marketing opportunities offered by lesbians and gay men, but also exploring motivations. These studies have led to an inherent bias towards defining the gay market through the concept of the Pink Pound and an emphasis on hedonistic and, to a lesser extent, cultural motivations. Numerous commentators have referred to this bias not only from a gender perspective but also from a socio-economic one. Within this context, desire has been appropriated as a motive that is predominantly sexual. This narrow definition has, to some extent, marginalised other explorations of gay tourism and contributed, albeit inadvertently, to the stereotypes that are prevalent, notably around gay men.

Sports tourism has been concerned with identifying categories of demand and, more recently, of participation that allow for the development of marketing strategies and, at the same time, provide a means of exploring the perceived importance of sports events for visitors. In turn, this has led to a recognition of the importance of subcultures, previously identified within sports activities, and their continuation into the realm of sports tourism. Self-identity becomes an important factor here, for participants and spectators alike; affiliation with one's club or one's favoured player, or simply the sport itself, provides the basis for developing social interaction with others. This activity within the field of sports tourism has special resonance, as retelling of stories of the past unites individuals and allows them to participate in the making of stories for the future. Such stories encompass triumph, loss, glory and even, on occasion, ignominy, yet serve primarily to unite participants and supporters in shared meanings. Indeed, loyalty and commitment to team and sport figure large in the discourse of participants and spectators which, in turn, lead to a sense of belonging and provide a history and meaning that can be shared.

In this chapter, there is an exploration of these ideas and how they combine in the construction and examination of the phenomenon of gay sports tourism. Concurrent with this is an exploration of the role of desire as it links to psychological freedom and an implicit politicisation in the process of staging the World Championships. Both constructs cannot be divorced from the world of gay sports tourism and, indeed, I shall argue are implicitly linked.

Background

The Leftfooters football club hosted the World Championships in London, in August 2008, an event promoted annually by the International Gay and Lesbian Football Association (IGLFA).[1] Alongside being the largest gay sports event held in the UK since 2001, when London last hosted the championship, this event was particularly memorable for having the support of the Football Association (FA). The FA had not only hosted the announcement of the Leftfooters' success in winning the bid a year earlier at a high-profile event, it also invited representatives from the 40 teams participating in the Championships to a reception held in Soho Square, the FA's headquarters during the week of cultural and social activities associated with the tournament.

Gay and lesbian teams competed from 14 different countries, including Australia, Argentina, South Africa, Iceland, Mexico, USA and Japan. The attendance of teams from some African countries was particularly significant because these teams were often denied the political freedom to express their sexuality openly at home. Whilst some teams from other countries generally faced less overt oppression, a number were, nevertheless, discreet and avoided publicity as far as possible. Those from more open societies had less of a problem with publicity and appearing in photographs of the event. Some individual team members had concerns because of perceived pressures from their jobs.

As well as players, there were a large number of supporters, mostly from the UK, where the majority of teams came from, but many from the competing countries came too. Together, they constituted a significant group of people intent on enjoying football, London and the range of experiences that such an event might offer as tourists in an international capital. At the same time, for some the experience was a brief taste of freedom in terms of sexuality and sexual expression within a safe space, whilst for others it provided an opportunity for spontaneous political expression. Members of the African lesbian teams were frequently seen and heard, as they chanted songs on the sidelines between games.

The event is significant from the perspective of both sports tourism and gay tourism, both of which have been explored in the literature and are reviewed later in the chapter.

The event

The event is allocated to a club and to a venue by means of a bidding process, with the bidders playing host to the IGLFA committee, consisting of members from numerous countries. Leftfooters FC, who are based in London, won the bid to host the 2008 event and a formal launch was held at the Football Association's Headquarters in Soho Square in the summer of 2007. The launch was a high-profile event, attended by several well-known personalities as well as senior FA staff.

One year later, when the World Championships took place, they were marked, not only by the obvious occurrence of the tournament, but also by a series of predominantly social events around London as part of the celebration that the games marked for members of the gay amateur football world. For the FA, this was also clearly an opportunity to signal its commitment to inclusivity in association football and to its initiatives to stamp out homophobia. This commitment has been noted in the production of the FA's strategy for handling homophobia in the professional game (Football Association, n.d.) and supporting events, such as the World Championships, provide opportunities to demonstrate it further, not only in the amateur game but within the arena of gay football itself. This step not only signals the FA's stance against homophobia but additionally signals its support for gay football and for greater inclusivity.

For players and supporters alike, the tournament provided a touristic experience that can be examined in terms of both sport and sexuality.

Gay tourism

Guaracino (2007) has identified the key reasons underpinning gay tourism, though largely from the perspective of the market. He suggests that Lesbian, Gay, Bisexual and Transgender (LGBT) tourism is largely focused on a number of key features. First, people wanting to travel to LGBT-friendly destinations seek out those destinations that are perceived to have liberal or permissive attitudes, a well-established gay infrastructure and places that offer safe spaces. The gay press provides plenty of coverage of such destinations, together with details of the range of offerings, from cultural spaces to beaches and nightclubs. Second, people seek out gay destinations as a result of wanting opportunities to engage with other LGBT people when travelling, regardless of the destination itself, allowing them to socialise with others and to feel safe and relaxed within a subculture of shared understanding. Third, many people have particular desires associated with cultural space and which can also encompass safety issues – the combination is crucial, for many gay travellers. Finally, LGBT tourism provides opportunities to explore a gay lifestyle. For many, these opportunities may be few and far between at home. Thus, additionally, for gay men and women who are in the closet, travel provides opportunities for a degree of liberation, albeit temporary.

The nature of the tourist space is also significant; a reputation for violence will lead to discretion on the part of visitors and local members of the LGBT community. On the other hand, where a place has a reputation for greater freedom, visibility and even hedonism, there is likely to be more active participation in the activities available and in the local lifestyle.

Hughes, commenting on the gay and lesbian tourism market, suggests that 'buying a distinguishing way of life' may well be a motivation, driven possibly by 'discrimination, exclusion and rejection by society and a consequent desire to formulate alternative identities that are self-affirming' (Hughes 2004: 58–59). Visiting a supportive destination with opportunities for exploring this, albeit for a limited time, provides many gay men and lesbians with a short but liberating experience. This may be considered an escape from the everyday reality; alternatively, it may result in an affirming experience that contributes to longer-term personal development and confidence. Alongside that, he suggests that motivations are largely the same as for straight tourists, namely rest, relaxation, culture and good food. He further cites Badgett (1997), Fugate (1993) and Field (1995) in support of the growing realisation that the gay market is by no means homogeneous and that the 'high spend, high hedonism' view of gay men, in particular, on holiday is something of a myth. Gay men are likely to earn less than their straight counterparts though, on the other hand, they may well have higher disposable income. Many gay men are still reluctant to be identified in the workplace and, as part of their strategies for preserving a level of anonymity, may well opt to avoid higher-profile jobs.

A study by Clift and Forrest (1999) indicated that the motivations for visiting a gay-friendly holiday destination are also linked with potential opportunities to be socially and sexually active with other gay men. Given that gay space is seen as important, it is hardly surprising that a holiday is viewed as an extended temporal opportunity to be gay and an expression of sexuality openly is highly likely to be social and possibly, ultimately, sexual (Hughes 1997). Hughes further suggests that since the existence of gay space is limited and because of continuing social disapproval of homosexuality (despite a growing acceptance in recent years which is by no means universal), travel provides a means of establishing and confirming sexuality:

> Given that the fulfilment or achievement of gay identity often involves travel and is thus, in practice, a variation of tourism, it may also be argued that the search for gay identity is itself conceptually a form of tourism.
>
> (Hughes 1997: 5)

Cass (1979) developed a six-stage model to explain the developmental process through which lesbians and gay men progress in order to consider, and then develop, their sexual and ultimately social identity that gives relevance to their sense of self. She emphasised the importance of the link between self and society in providing a basis for change and stability in individuals. Her assumption that individuals experience discomfort as a result of dissonance between personal and societal perceptions of self led to the conclusion that individuals will seek to rectify this inner conflict and their success will be gauged in terms of personal growth.

The emergence of gay space is often cited, also, as evidence of a climate of greater social acceptance (Wood 1999; Hughes 1997) and the increasing commercialisation of gay spaces provides further compelling evidence in support of this. The lesbian and gay traveller can now readily identify and access gay villages in destinations around the world. Equally, lesbian and gay travellers can locate LGBT events that attract significant numbers of visitors, from Gay Pride events to sports events, such as the World Championships. However, the limiting of that space to specific areas and events suggests the existence of gay ghettos, both in terms of physical space and psycho-social space. The notion of the gay ghetto is problematised within discussions of gay sport generally and team sports, in particular. This will be considered in more detail later in the chapter.

This brief review makes the case for the prevailing view of the gay tourist market and travel motivations, but it poses some questions with regard to attendance at, or participation in, a significant sporting event. These questions expand and enrich existing perceptions of motivations and lead to an understanding of the interaction between the personal and the political in the enactment of lesbian and gay presence at significant sporting, cultural and social events.

Parrinello (1993) considered the notion of the holiday as part of a psychic journey that begins with planning and anticipation and ends with recollection and elaboration. This process contributes to the creation of meanings from personal viewpoints and locates them in the social milieu of the tourist. The sharing of meanings is significant for personal development, for the development of gay identity and for decreasing, at least for a short time, individual feelings of isolation. They add, too, to a sense of celebration of self and community. Woodside *et al.* (2000) concluded that tourism creates tourist experiences in the negotiation between the extraordinary and the mundane (Daskalaki 2003). This can encompass approaching a significant event or place with a sense of awe and anticipated meaning, alongside becoming involved in the daily transactions of life that are managed quite differently from one's experience at home. For the lesbian and gay traveller, the event is the main attraction and being part of that is a cause for celebration; at the same time, there is the disturbance of one's reality in eating and drinking in openly gay venues which may not be available in daily life throughout the rest of the year. Allied to this, Swarbrooke and Horner's (1999) consideration of psychographic segmentation suggests that lifestyle, attitudes, opinions, personality and, crucially, values determine consumer behaviour. Thus, knowing that one is gay may be enhanced by one's rare and crucial venture into a space where one can be gay. One's values as a lesbian or gay man may find new dimensions of meaning in opportunities to explore one's sense of being.

Heath and Wall (1992) refer to the importance of benefit segmentation, where the benefits derived from a tourism experience are the basic reasons for choice of destination. If values and benefits form the drivers, the creation of meaning and the positioning of the extraordinary against the mundanity of everyday life provide important goals, as we shall see when considering the findings from the tournament.

Gay men's football

Writers on other major gay sports events, most notably the Gay Games, have pointed out the importance of the event for gay and lesbian participants. Deane Young (1994: 11), cited in Jones and McCarthy (2010), comments on the experience of participating in the Gay Games as being transformative, with participants acknowledging 'the joy of being wholly who they are and joining hands with a circle of comrades'. Davidson (2006) explored the intense focus on inclusion, on achieving a personal best as a motivation and the proclamation of gay pride at the Gay Games. She suggests that overt pride in participation supersedes the shame that gay men and lesbians have previously been forced to endure both on and off playing fields and disallows its expression. This is evident too in gay football teams in the UK (Jones and McCarthy 2010), and was a factor in the responses from some of the international teams at the World Championships. Many of those interviewed in a study of gay football teams in the UK commented on the difficulties they experienced playing sports at school, and of the oppressive pressure to live up to masculine images reinforced by a heterosexual hegemony. For those who did not, there were taunts that focused on their failure and attracted the label of being gay, presented in pejorative terms. Thus, many were presented with a strong sense of shame at their failure to be a 'real boy'. Since many of those in such situations were still unsure about their sexuality, growing awareness was invariably accompanied by an internalised sense of shame. The representation of professional football in the media supports a heterosexist view of players, reinforcing masculine hegemony, and occasional reports of the possibility of gay players in the professional game are couched in terms that suggest scandal and, implicitly, shame. Those interviewed in the initial study spoke of finding support and a stronger sense of self by joining a gay team, the gradual loss of this sense of shame and a sense of belonging. This was very evident also in interviews with international players at the World Championship. In gay football, dealing with this cloak of shame positively suggests a psychological space where the personal and the political are united.

For others, a hidden gay identity continues to be the norm in everyday life away from the event. Thus, the notion of community is important within the sphere of gay sport as it provides a psychological space which is less terrifying than the realities of the straight world, particularly if one is in the closet. Consequently, there is opportunity for increased self-esteem, for accepting one's own homosexual identity and for developing bonds between each other through 'activity and involvement in a shared interest' (Siegal and Lowe

1995: 127). In previous research into gay men's football teams, Jones and McCarthy (2010) noted the importance of a sense of belonging within the teams that, for many players, presented a sense of family. As Halberstam (2003: 313–14) noted, community groups that support and embrace queer culture provide alternatives to 'kinship-based notions of community ... such as family, heterosexuality and reproduction'. Players talked of their team as a second family, providing support that often real families did not, especially if the players were still in the closet. Living a double life is still very much the reality for a significant number of lesbians and gay men, so locating a source of support is important for dealing with the consequent sense of isolation. For those who were out to families and friends, their football exploits in a gay team became part of family discussions, providing them with one means of integrating family and gay community life. Alongside helping them to feel more integrated, it was a means by which families could understand better both the sexuality of their gay family member and the realities of the gay community.

Allied to this notion of second family is another key finding from the earlier research, namely, the opportunity for personal growth that playing in the team afforded. Alongside a sense of belonging through sharing a common interest, the increase in self-esteem and developing a second family, many players found self-acceptance and a way of developing their identity as gay men. This led to increased confidence and an improvement in psychological health, alongside the physical health gains associated with playing sport. It has to be said that these may well have been mitigated somewhat by the accompanying social activities, which largely figured around nights out in pubs.

A final point from the earlier research that is relevant for the present discussion concerns the public nature of playing in tournaments, and of reaching beyond the established enclaves of gay space and gay presence in places such as Old Compton Street in London, Canal Street in Manchester, the Marais in Paris or the Castro area in San Francisco, to name but a few. Sanderson (1999) suggests that the ability to be public in such places has led to the confidence to step beyond the gay scene in search of alternative social activities, including a growing interest and participation in sport. It is important to emphasise that team sports, such as football, provide such opportunities for socialising away from the gay scene; this allows those who lack the confidence to visit gay venues or those who have become disenchanted with its limited range of opportunities for socialising to find an alternative that allows them to find friends and affiliation within a safe space amongst people with a common interest. Many players, however, will visit a gay venue as a group, after a game. Thus, the gay scene is not abandoned but rather is realigned as part of the team experience.

The acquisition of non-traditional spaces and claiming them for the gay community is noted by Wellard (2002), Pronger (1990), Deane Young (1994) and Hekma (1994). In claiming football as part of that space, there has been an inevitable challenge to hegemonic masculinity. This is further challenged by the embracing of a different set of values that focused on inclusion, participation, fairness and rejection of violence and aggression. Many gay teams play in their own league and tournaments, but some join other amateur leagues and thus play against perceived straight teams, drawing a range of comments from their opponents, from the highly disparaging to gradual acceptance. By making the presence of gay football more public, the challenges to masculinity and the claiming of larger arenas as a gay space raises the profile of gays and lesbians in the public eye. The FA gave support to the IGLFA World Championships, thus providing legitimisation to space acquisition and using the tournament as a signal of its own commitment to kicking homophobia out of football.

Inevitably, growing visibility has led to increased political activism, and this proved to be a contentious point in the earlier research. The vast majority said there was no sense of politicisation in their choice to play for gay teams. However, as Sanderson (1999), Krane *et al.* (2002) and Crocker and Major (1989) have suggested, stigmatised individuals are likely to engage in social change activity, particularly where opportunities for increased confidence and a sense of community are evident. Thus, many teams participate in Gay Pride parades, for example. Amongst the international players at the World Championships, political activism was a recurring theme, whether it be through seeking publicity in their own country through participation or (in the case of the South African women's team) through singing and chanting.

The creation of gay teams, leagues and tournaments is implicitly political and a reaction to discrimination (Deane Young 1994). Skeggs (1999) acknowledges the contribution these changes make to identity politics.

Sports tourism

Sport has long been recognised as a focal point for tourism; the physical aspect of activities act as a draw for both participants and spectators, with location acting as a further draw, especially where it offers opportunities to engage in touristic experiences (Kurtzman 2005).

Weed (1999) points out that a range of studies have identified a Sports Tourism Demand Continuum with both participants and spectators categorised as 'sporadic, occasional, regular, committed and driven'. He posits a strong relationship between participation and the importance placed upon both the activities and the trips, participation being interpreted as both a player and a spectator. Being there takes on a special significance, strongly linked to self-identity, borne of the experience which is enhanced through the retelling of significant moments at points in the future.

Thus, the sporting event takes on an element of folklore which is, arguably, enhanced by being enacted in a designated space that has involved travel; Graburn (1983, cited in Weed and Bull (2004)) expands upon this, referring to ritual inversion where home life is contrasted with the tourist experience.

The sense of escape from normality and the opportunities to live out one's hopes and dreams through being part of an experience carries with it the hope of being significant and becoming part of the folk memory of the sport itself. Certainly, at the World Championships there were elements that were considered to be an escape from normality, namely the chance to be in London and thus far from home, and to be present at an event that carried both sporting and social significance. All of the players and spectators who were interviewed referred to the opportunity to be part of an extended family and to be present at an event that was contributing to the growing visibility of gay men and lesbians in sport and, thus, in spaces not normally associated with the gay and lesbian community. It is this, in particular, that contributes to Weed's (1999) notion of self-identity, for here it is both the sporting self and the sexual self. The importance of the experience in sports and socio-cultural terms rendered participation highly significant for attendees. Thus, the notion of interacting within one's subculture with 'familiar stranger[s]' (Nixon and Frey 1995, cited in Weed and Bull (2004)) was important for players and spectators alike; many spoke of the bond that existed with participants they had met at previous events but which was also believed to exist potentially in meetings with new people.

The cultural phenomenon that Standeven and De Knop (1999, cited in Weed and Bull (2004)) refer to where activity and space combine is enhanced here by psychological and emotional bonds, not only associated with the game but with a sense of unity amongst a minority that still feels itself oppressed. This gained greater credence with the interviews held with players from countries where being gay was still problematic. Kretchmarr's (1994, cited in Weed and Bull (2004)) philosophical rationale – the desire for the 'good life' that encompasses sport and achievement – here encompasses a sense of freedom also.

Findings

Research at the IGLFA World Championships, London 2008, was conducted largely through a series of video diaries, eliciting responses from players to a preset range of questions.[2] This was augmented by additional dialogue, informal conversation and observation. This approach was taken because of the limitations imposed by the time constraints and demands of the tournament itself, and because of inevitable language difficulties as it was decided to focus on responses from overseas players. An added limitation was the fact that some players did not want to risk being public in any way because of the nature of their situation at home. Thus, being at the tournament was a group effort at finding gay space, escaping heteronormative constraints and embracing, for a short time at least, gay liminality. By contrast, others saw their contribution to the research as an opportunity to make statements that were overtly political and rooted in gay rights activities in their homeland. Still others positioned the research within the context of the social and cultural activities associated with the Championships and viewed the interviews as part of the fun and celebration of participating.

Broadly speaking, responses divided more or less equally into two kinds: those associated with participation in the sporting event (whether as player or spectator) and those that focused on the opportunities afforded by the tournament to explore London, the gay scene and interactions with other participants.

An important element that emerged from informal conversations was storytelling of past events and experiences, which ranged from accounts of victories in previous tournaments to the opportunity to be at the London tournament, to participate and to have contributed to a presence. This sense of presence was in terms of giving meaning simultaneously to the event and to oneself as a gay man being part of something significant.

It became apparent that the Championships provided an opportunity to be in a gay space but that gay space is redefined, in terms of London itself and in terms of the football pitch, an established space for heteronormativity and hegemonic masculinity. All of the international players were aware that London offered a gay space, in terms of Old Compton Street and the Earl's Court area. Additionally, some had heard of Kudos, a bar frequented by gay Asians, and The Quebec, a venue frequented by older gay men. It was clear that many had made good use of the Internet as a guide to Gay London. London also offered opportunities for sightseeing beyond gay venues and culture; it is a cultural centre and a major tourist attraction. Visiting the established sights was thus a motivation, but added to this was the opportunity to visit these whilst experiencing the freedom of being gay. This was important for those players who came from countries where being gay was unacceptable and even dangerous.

Establishing new friendships, rekindling old ones and even exploring the possibility of the holiday romance were clearly important also. The tournament offered possibilities for adventure that, for some, was an exciting possibility that echoed notions of desire. Collins (2007) explored the relations between gay hosts and travellers in the Philippines, identifying the importance of '"connections" that require an emotional bond rather than as exchanges that pivot exclusively on the negotiation of money for sex'. The notion of connection is not confined to sex workers, nor is it confined to the hosts, if one takes account of the comments of players, particularly from countries where homosexuality is viewed negatively. The importance of desire was evident on the part of travellers, whether as a temporary element of the holiday experience or as a rather more fundamental longing associated with ideas of escape. The travellers in this case were international and visiting London, a place that offered a greater sense of freedom and with it the possibility of something more permanent than the holiday romance.

Collins (2007) has made studies of gay travellers and their interactions with host communities, particularly in relation to sexual activity. She commented on the way hosts characterised their 'connections' in terms of emotional bonds rather than simply sexual encounters and the strong emphasis on the importance of desire. A number of participants spoke of meeting socially with other participants from other countries and none made specific reference to sexual encounters, although conversation was marked by occasional light-hearted innuendo. A number, on the other hand, were observed in establishing relationships that involved handholding and occasional kissing, suggesting that desire was important. Others were observed in gay pubs in the evenings establishing contacts, not always with other participants but with locals, again with an implicit motive of desire.

It was clear from the interviews that part of the adventure of the visit was the ability to walk around quite openly in a gay space and in a tolerant city being a gay man. Whilst this may have had no discernible impact upon behaviour, it was a significant aspect of self-awareness. There were players who took advantage of the opportunity to strike up liaisons with others and to take the bold step of holding hands. One or two established holiday romances. In spite of this, for a number there was a certain reticence in taking part in the video diary sessions. Allied to this was, for some, the discovery of a gay lifestyle and opportunities for openness simply in terms of a feeling of freedom. Very few players from countries where being gay was problematic were willing to talk, but those that did expressed a strong sense of liberation – for a short period of time, they could feel free and be free.

The tournament offered opportunities to make a political statement in ways that accorded very much with the conditions that prevailed in their homeland. Thus, for Americans it was part of a continuing process of being openly gay and maintaining one's rights and one's sense of self, whilst for the female team from South Africa the statement was one of defiance. Some of their team had, in the preceding four years, been murdered for their sexuality. Their expression took the form of protest songs in the sidelines as the tournament progressed. For others, simply being there was a means of participating in gay politics and, despite their reticence at being interviewed, was nevertheless important. The Mexicans loudly proclaimed that they were the only out gay team in Mexico, that they actively sought publicity at home and abroad, and that they were making a public statement for gay rights at home by playing nationally and internationally. At home they played against straight teams. Part of the statement extended to an on-pitch chant and dance, together with wearing pink kit.

Conclusion

A number of players spoke of the significance of the event in experiential terms – as an event that made a political statement, that allowed opportunities both to play sport and to make a claim to an arena that continues to be seen in heterosexist terms, rife with the values of hegemonic masculinity, and that offered a safe space where communities could meet. As one player put it, 'at home I play with my team and they are my second family; I came here and saw that my family is here too'. Some, as a result, spoke of solidarity and expressed their commitment in terms of a movement for gay rights.

The World Championships give support for Franklin and Crang's (2001) criticisms of tourist studies as 'a series of discrete, enumerated occurrences of travel, arrival, activity, purchase, departure, ... an expanding field through ever finer subdivisions and more elaborate typologies as though these might eventually form a classificatory grid in which tourism could be defined and regulated.' (ibid.: 6). The overlaying of sporting interest, of touristic experience, of family togetherness and of expression of gay rights are inextricably entwined in this complex reading of the World Championships.

Undoubtedly, the minutiae of travelling were part of the experience, and were the necessary activities required to enable the event to happen. But the experience for players and spectators reached beyond this to reflect their view, quoting Löfgren (1999: 6–7), of 'a cultural laboratory where people have been able to experiment with new aspects of identities, their social relations ... and also to use the important cultural skills of daydreaming and mindtravelling'. In this context, daydreaming encompassed the dreams of winning, hopes for many of a more liberal and, indeed, liberated future and the possibility, for a while at least, of being part of a community where identity was a source of pride and inclusiveness was a right. In particular, for those who remain in the closet at home, the World Championships provide a brief opportunity to experience this sense of liberation amongst friends who see themselves as a worldwide family.

Collins' (2007) comments concerning more nuanced senses of relationships, in her discussion of sexuality and tourism, are no less relevant here where, in this context, the sexual consumer is less focused on sexual activity than on observing and feeling part of a sexual freedom that has its roots in gay politics. Participants from oppressive societies were reversing the role of the western gay traveller and consuming the spectacle of this freedom (Jackson and Sullivan 1999, cited in Collins (2007)) in their own terms. Those terms are couched partly in the fantasy reported by Löfgren (1999) in relation to sport and partly in political struggle and personal freedom. Part, of course, was a simple combination of freedom and curiosity; many did, indeed, visit gay venues in London that they perhaps had heard of through the Internet.

Franklin and Crang (2001) cite MacCannell (1992) as suggesting 'a more reflexive tourist, with a sceptical second gaze, interested in the minutiae of everyday life ... tourism may be far more rooted in the culture of the everyday than we have hitherto acknowledged' (ibid.: 12). The mood of those interviewed was closer to euphoria than scepticism; certainly, hope was mentioned frequently, alongside a sense of belonging. Much of this came from contrasting home and touristic experiences but at the level of the everyday, such as the freedom to walk down the street, to be together with relatively open acts of affection and to participate in a game that nevertheless remains rooted in hegemonic masculinity. Time and time again, people spoke of the football and their sense of family within it.

Notes

1 The International Gay and Lesbian Football Association (IGLFA) was 'founded in 1992 with the intention of promoting Association Football ... in the gay and lesbian community and to promote gay and lesbian football to the world at large' (from http://www.iglfa.org).
2 Primary data collected by M. McCarthy and L. Jones at the IGLFA World Championships, August 2008.

Section 4

Writing the tourist experience

Travel writing has existed for as long as people have travelled. Not only were early travellers driven to explore beyond the boundaries of their known world but, as Herodotus (*c.* 485–425 BC) first demonstrated, they were compelled to record their travels for others to read. Indeed, travel writing was one of the earliest genres of writing and, to this day, remains popular amongst authors and readers and, undoubtedly, a profitable product for publishers. Travel writing is also, however, of significance for reasons beyond its longevity and the large number of books and other travelogues that have been written. It represents a continuing socio-cultural history, both of the places visited and described and of the places where the traveller comes from, for it has long been recognised that the majority of travel writing is as much about the author as it is about his or her travel experiences. In fact, in much contemporary travel writing (or, in the case of travel blogs, what may be described as 'travelling writing'), place has become largely irrelevant, the focus being on the emotions and experiences of the writer. At the same time, there is no doubt that travel writing has proved to be inspirational to its readers, whether encouraging them to travel themselves or simply to dream of places afar.

Not surprisingly, therefore, travel writing has been widely considered as a form of literature. Less attention, however, has been paid to it within the context of tourism studies in general and as a vehicle for enhancing our knowledge and understanding of the tourist experience in particular. The three chapters in this section focus, therefore, on how the analysis of travel writing, in various forms, may contribute to the study of tourist experiences. First, in Chapter 10, Emma-Reetta Koivunen compares two travelogues, written two centuries apart, based upon travels to the Shetland Islands in northern Britain. Confirming that much travel writing is concerned with the construction of a personal social reality, she identifies similarities between the two examples, particularly the self-identification by each author as 'heroic traveller'. In the following chapter (Chapter 11), Ulrike Gretzel and colleagues explore a contemporary form of travel writing (so-called consumer generated media (GCM), such as online travel blogs), and its construction, meaning and consumption by others. Though identifying rapid growth in the incidence

GCM travel writing, they suggest that more research is necessary to identify the full impact and significance of this recent form of travel narration. Chapter 12 concludes this section with a study into how the analysis of travel journals written by participants on study visits may indicate the level and extent of their reflective thinking and, hence, learning. That is, Sarah Quinlan Cutler and Barbara Carmichael propose a system for evaluating travel journals, their research suggesting that, subject to a number of caveats, considerable reflective thinking and experiential learning may occur during, or as a result of, travel experiences.

10 Creating your own Shetland: tourist narratives from travelogues to blogs

Emma-Reetta Koivunen

Introduction

The focus of this chapter is on two texts describing travel experiences in the Shetland Islands. The first narrative is a travel diary of a trip undertaken in 1832 by a young man (Charlton 2007), the second is an online blog of a trip undertaken by a woman in 2002 (Cherny 2006). By analysing these texts, the chapter aims to enhance our understanding of how tourists make their experiences in Shetland meaningful. In addition, I argue that these stories are, in the end, more about the tourists and tourism as a phenomenon than about Shetland per se. While the stories tell about the place the tourists visit, the Shetland landscape and culture only set the scene for the stories. Instead, the stories reflect a genre of travel writing in which the tourists use their travel destination to reflect their own culture and their personality.

In analysing these stories, the chapter draws on the theory of Social Construction of Reality (Berger and Luckmann 1971 [1966]) and the ethnographic analysis of texts; these two theoretical frameworks are reviewed in relation to tourism and tourist narratives in the next section. The chapter then explores how meanings derived from experiences not only reflect reality, but also are cultural constructions. They are described through such language and symbols that make them understandable to others sharing the culture (Urban 1996: 5–6). Following an introduction to tourism in Shetland and its development and transformation from early nineteenth century to the beginning of the twenty-first century, the analysis of the two narratives focuses on three themes central in travelling as well as in the construction of the differences between the tourist experience and the everyday life of the writer. These are the travel to the destination, experiencing the place and the scenery, and interaction with other people. The conclusion explores the implications of the research for our understanding of the cultural construction of narratives as well as commenting on the relationship between tourist experience and the destination.

Literature: texts and reality construction

This chapter utilises the theory of Social Construction of Reality (SCOR) (Berger and Luckmann 1971). According to this theory, phenomena as various as objects, identities and places are not naturally given; rather, the meanings attributed to them are constructed through social interactions. Two theoretical concepts developed from SCOR that are central to this chapter are the notion of everyday life as a paramount reality and the role of language in constructing reality. Berger and Luckmann (1971: 15) explore how subjective meanings become objective facts. They see that the social world is developed, transmitted and maintained in social situations. These constant negotiations lead in time to the development of institutions, such as kinship and social class – as well as the idea of tourism being necessary for one's well-being (Urry 1990a: 5). This creates a sense of an objective reality which exists independent of individuals (Berger and Luckmann 1971: 78). They define reality as 'a quality appertaining to phenomena that we recognize as having a being independent of our own volition (we can not "wish them away")' (ibid.: 13).

Research on tourism and Social Construction of Reality has focused on how tourist destinations have been constructed (Hughes 1998; Saarinen 1998), experienced (Selby 2004) and marketed (Iwashita 2003). This chapter utilises SCOR in the context of tourism interactions, looking not only at how the destination is (re)constructed, but also at how the experience of being a tourist is reproduced through tourist narratives. The chapter starts from the point of view that, even though tourist narratives appear to be about a destination, the reality that they are reconstructing is that of the tourists. As reality is socially constructed and influenced by the situation in which it is created and maintained, the reality of one society differs from that of another. In addition, Berger and Luckmann suggest that people are conscious 'of the world as consisting of multiple realities' (1971: 35). The way in which Berger and Luckmann understand the 'multiple realities' of different societies is related to the anthropological understanding of 'culture'. The classical anthropological definition of culture offered by Tylor (1920, cited in Burns (1999: 56)) is that 'Culture ... is that complex whole which includes knowledge, belief, art, moral law, custom, and any other capabilities and habits acquired by man as a member of society'. Central to Tylor's definition is the notion that culture is acquired as a member of society and, thus, Burns (ibid.) points out and continues, ' ... in this definition culture is about the interaction of people and how they learn from each other'.

The idea of multiple realities is interesting for analysing tourism as it provides a means of conceptualising the different social settings that the tourist experiences both at home and in the destination. Berger and Luckmann (1971: 35) point out that among these different realities, the everyday is a 'paramount reality' which, owing to its significant nature, is impossible to ignore. The everyday reality appears as already objective, an ordered reality that seems to exist without our input. The reality of everyday life 'is taken for granted *as* reality' (Berger and Luckmann 1971: 37, italics in original), it is something that is not questioned. For tourists, the change from one reality to another is often seen as a central motivation for travel. Being a tourist, travelling away from home means distancing oneself from the everyday reality (Urry 1990a: 2–3; Boissevain 1996: 4). As Graburn (2001: 42–43) observes, 'tourists leave home because there is something that they want to get away from'.

Use of language in constructing reality

Berger and Luckmann (1971: 49) point out that, for individuals to be able to transmit and create knowledge of the social reality through interaction, they need meaningful symbols. The most important of these is language. However, Berger and Luckmann also maintain that while language is used in the construction of everyday life, it also sets limits to that process. Language has rules and structures that one has to follow and it provides individuals 'with a ready-made possibility for the ongoing objectification of my unfolding experience' (ibid.: 53). Language also provides categories for typical experiences, such as 'a holiday', or 'an island tourism destination'. While language typifies experiences, it also anonymises them, 'for the typified experience can, in principle, be duplicated by anyone falling into the category in question' (ibid.: 53).

Another significant characteristic of language is that, even though it has origins in face-to-face interaction, it can be detached from it (Berger and Luckmann 1971: 52). Language also has a capacity to 'communicate meanings that are not direct expressions of the subjectivity of "here and now"' (ibid.). This is relevant for tourist narratives. During their travel, tourists are looking for stories, not only to tell about their experiences but also to help them to explain their life and define themselves in relation to others. The stories tourists write and tell about their travels, like all narratives, make their experiences intelligible in a form that can be publicly shared and distributed (Urban 1996: 5). These narratives are not neutral descriptions of experiences but cultural constructions.

In tourist narratives, cultural knowledge can be seen in the constant opposition between 'home' and 'away', as well as the 'Otherness' of the people in the destination (Galani-Moutafi 2000: 2). Through comparisons with 'home', the writer makes the experiences understandable to their presumed audience, who are more familiar with the home environment than with the travel destination (Galani-Moutafi 2000: 20). While tourists come from various cultural backgrounds, the majority of them share the western cultural ideal of holidays as an indicator of status and a near 'human right'. The fact that the tourists share the western cultural idea of holidays does not mean that Shetlanders would not share this as well. However, the fact that Shetlanders travel widely does not matter for tourist narratives. What is important about Shetland is the difference from the familiar environment, rather than the similarities.

Analysing texts

Social Construction of Reality is a theoretical framework; Berger and Luckmann did not suggest methods for empirical research. For this chapter, I utilise tools from the ethnographic analysis of communication. Within anthropology, the analysis of communication has largely focused on analysing spoken forms of communication (for example, Hymes 1962; Briggs 1986; Urban 1996). However, the majority of the methods can also be applied to the analysis of textual materials.

Within anthropology, the well-known, but at times contested, Sapir-Whorf hypothesis shares the same basic assumption as Berger and Luckmann of the relationship between language and social reality. Sapir-Whorf hypothesis argues that the 'categories and structure of a language' have a close relationship to 'the ways humans are able to experience the world' (Eriksen 2001: 227). Putting this another way, the narratives of one's experiences are cultural constructions, described through the language and symbols that make them understandable to others sharing the culture (Urban 1996: 5–6). Moreover, Charles Briggs (1986: 39) suggests that each speech community teaches its members the 'rules that relate to form, context and meaning'. These rules are central for analysing speech and texts. In the following analysis of the two tourist narratives, the texts are placed in the context that they were created in. The narratives are then deconstructed into relevant thematic categories for detailed analysis of their content.

The case: tourism in Shetland

The main tourist attractions of the Shetland Islands have not changed much during 200 years: beautiful scenery, nature and wildlife. Home to a population of about 22,000, Shetland is the most northern part of the United Kingdom. The remoteness of the islands means that social and cultural life has evolved at its own pace. In the terminology of Social Construction of Reality, the everyday life reality of Shetland is different from the mainland United Kingdom. Many visitors view Shetland as a relic from past times, a place where they can get in touch with the exotic and authentic which is missing from their modern urban lives.

However geographically remote the Shetland Islands might seem, over the centuries they have nevertheless been a meeting point of cultures and ideas, with visits from the Vikings, and merchants, fishermen and whalers from Norway, Germany, Holland and Greenland (Brown 1998: 63–64). Similarly, whilst for many Shetlanders daily life is based around the village (Cohen 1987), Shetland men working on navy, fishing and merchant boats are among the most travelled Britons (Butler and Fennell 1994: 350). The twenty-first century Shetland is now connected to the world with a high level of Internet use (Koivunen 2006: 45).

Shetland tourism in the early 1800s

One of the reasons for Shetland's relative remoteness was that slow and arduous travel long meant that visitor numbers remained low. Until the nineteenth century, travellers primarily came for work purposes: government officials, military, ministers and fishermen. However, the development of steamboats made Shetland a little more accessible for leisure travellers (Butler 1998: 129).

At this time, the majority of these leisure visitors were independent travellers on 'voyages of discovery, literary figures, or members of the aristocracy on extended vacations, often on their own transport' (Butler and Fennell 1994: 349). These included the author Robert Louis Stevenson, whose family were involved in the planning and construction of several of the Shetland lighthouses. He also invited Sir Walter Scott for a visit in the early 1800s, and he later set the classic novel *The Pirate* in Shetland. This novel played a part in inspiring visits to the islands, including the travel diary writer Edward Charlton. He (Charlton) describes excitedly of their passing these scenes: 'But before breakfast was announced, another and far more important object occupied our attention. Sumburgh and Fitfield [Fitfull] heads, the scenes of *The Pirate*, rose in blue and rounded masses before us' (Charlton 2007: 4–5).

Shetland tourism in the early 2000s

Two hundred years later, transport to Shetland has, of course, become faster and more regular, with an overnight ferry daily from Aberdeen and several flights from Scotland. However, for the modern tourist this can still seem an arduous – and expensive – journey to take. At the same time, while tourism has become a common activity, travel to Shetland has remained of more limited interest to tourists with the wealth from the North Sea oil industry meaning that tourism in Shetland has not evolved as intensely as in many other remote areas. During the construction period in the 1970s, the oil industry often block-booked all transport and accommodation in Shetland, slowing down the tourism market. Subsequently, it took some time for tourism businesses to convince the outside world that Shetland was not a paradise that had been spoilt by the oil (Butler and Fennell 1994: 353).

However, in the twenty-first century tourism has become a key element in Shetland's economy and everyday life, with annual visitor numbers of around 47,000. Indeed, it is now a growth industry, and many locals view it as an activity of increasing importance as the oil industry decreases. Within Shetland, the road and ferry networks have improved immensely, making travel within the islands a relatively easy task (Cohen 1987: 10). Most tourist visits occur during the summer season, and mainly by independent travellers. Shetland culture also attracts visitors at other times, however, for events such as the Shetland Folk Festival and the winter fire festival 'Up-helly-aa'.

Analysis of the narratives

As noted in the introduction, this chapter compares the narratives of two different tourists visiting Shetland in different eras. The first is the travel diary of a young man who visited the islands in the early nineteenth century (Charlton 2007), the second the travel blog detailing a young woman's more recent visit (Cherny 2006). The analysis of these narratives focuses on three themes central to the tourist experience: travel to the destination; experiencing the place; and interaction with other people, both with travellers and locals. The first theme frames the travel experience by creating the physical distance from the home environment, while the two following ones are central in creating the social distinction between the familiar home environment and the different reality experienced in the destination.

Travel to Shetland

Travel and, subsequently, the travel writings of the nineteenth century were framed to replicate imperialist adventures (Abrams 2005: 3). One of the things that made these travels worth telling about was the difficulty of travel, implying that not everyone could venture there. Shetland was perfect for this; while travel had become easier with the advent of steamboats (Butler 1998: 129), it still took several days. Charlton begins his story with his 1832 travel to Shetland from Leith on the schooner *Magnus Troil*. He describes that the ship, 'certainly could not boast either of imposing size or inviting cleanliness, but it was well manned for the coasting trade, having as many hands on board as the collier brigs between London and Newcastle' (Charlton 2007: 1).

He also tells of how, even though he was at sea for the first time, and many of the other travellers were seasick on the travel, he was not; 'such, however, did not prove to be the case with me. I was never better in my whole life' (ibid.: 2). The only trouble the journey by sea caused him was boredom when so many of the other 'ladies and gentlemen' would not venture on deck and keep him company. From very early on in the narrative, Charlton creates the distinction between himself and the other travellers. Even though these are, as himself, reputable people, he seems to be the only leisure traveller (or the only adventurer) on the boat, the others mainly being Shetland merchants returning home with their families.

Whilst Charlton describes his travel from Scotland to mainland Shetland, Cherny, in describing her 2002 travels, tells of the boat trip from mainland Shetland to the island of Fair Isle. In the twenty-first century, the travel from mainland Scotland to Shetland is, of course, easier than in Charlton's time, even though still expensive and slow compared to many other destinations. However, travel to Fair Isle, in contrast, is still a journey that excites the independent traveller looking for something out of the ordinary.

Cherny (2006) starts by stating, 'Fair Isle is a small dot in the North Sea between the Orkney Islands and Shetland, all of which are north of Scotland'.

This is a very typical way of setting the scene when describing Shetland, not only telling the physical location, but also painting the picture of the remoteness. She continues by describing her travel to Fair Isle; a boat, the *Good Shepherd IV*, goes out from Shetland three times a week in the summer; it takes two and a half hours and, 'is famous as a rough ride … even in good weather, this boat pitches around quite a lot'. Although on her boat trip to Fair Isle nobody was seasick, she nevertheless quotes stories she has heard of people being sick over the rail into the sea. She also tells of the alternative; 'If this is discouraging, one can fly for about 70 pounds, but the flights are much less likely to go as scheduled, because of fog. The statistics for on-time flights is very, very low' (Cherny 2006).

Both these narratives bring out the difficulty of the travel, the relative remoteness of the place. All the troubles they had to go through to arrive at this place give the travel extra significance and separates them from regular tourists, or, as Abrams, describing historical travellers (2005: 3) states, the writers 'trumpeted their own bravery in choosing to travel to such a place'. Travel from home to the destination provides the transition from the reality of everyday life to the reality of being on holiday. This physical change of scenery also inflicts an emotional change from one reality to another.

Experiencing the place – and the weather

Tourism is often seen in opposition to home; people travel to see and to experience something different from their home experiences. The two following sections are about creating a difference between the destination and home by contrasting the unfamiliar with the familiar. The first section is framed by Urry's (1990a) concept of the tourist gaze, specifically taking in the scenery and being an outside observer. The second section draws on Veijola and Jokinen's (1994) critique of Urry's work to look at the physical, bodily engagement with the place through the intense Shetland weather and the dangers it poses.

Tourist gaze and Shetland scenery

Urry presents tourism as a highly visual experience; a principal characteristic of tourism is a greater sensitivity to visual elements of landscape than in the everyday life, 'the tourist gaze' (1990a: 3). This idea can be related to Berger and Luckmann's understanding of different realities, in that they define one characteristic of everyday life as that it is not questioned (Berger and Luckmann 1971: 33). Conversely, when we are travelling, everything is new and exciting, and even 'normal' events and sights gain our attention. Charlton describes his enthusiasm in observing every detail: 'I remember well with what intense curiosity I gazed upon every bird and rock and house and field, and how I wondered that all on board were not equally astonished with myself' (Charlton 2007: 7). His observation also brings out clearly how this enthusiastic interest in the scenery involved only him; the other travellers were mainly merchants and family members returning to Shetland for whom this was a normal reality. He later continues his excited observations of Shetland: 'How foreign is everything around me. Fields without hedges, a fort without soldiers, a town a sea port without wharves of piers, and a country all without a tree: how different, how wild and yet to my eyes how strangely beautiful' (ibid.).

Charlton's romantic ideas about Shetland also guide his descriptions of encounters with wildlife. Seeing a storm petrel fly by the boat, he describes this as follows; 'suddenly a small shadow as of a spirit of the deep flitted under the bowsprit, passed and repassed, and at times hovered with a fluttering, uneasy motion on the surface of the ocean' (ibid.: 4). In the darkening night he could barely see what it was but assumed it to be 'the terror of sailors, the wandering, persecuted Stormy Petrel' (ibid). Storm petrels are frequently seen during or at the approach of storms and are, therefore, as Charlton describes, a 'terror of sailors' considered a bad omen. However, he saw the storm petrel in a different light: 'to us it betokened no ill, and I hailed its appearance as a native of the isles I was about to visit' (ibid.: 4).

Cherny does not provide as enthusiastic a description of the scenery; in fact, she hardly mentions it. Rather than description, she defines Fair Isle through tangible topics, such as defining the size of the place; 'The island itself is just three miles long and a mile and a half wide.' After that she focuses on what there is not on the island: 'There are no cash machines, no pubs or restaurants, no hotels, few cars, and only a couple roads connecting the handful of houses and churches.' There are a few things though: 'There's a North lighthouse and a South lighthouse, a tiny local history museum, and a shop with post office' (Cherny 2006). Describing the nature of Fair Isle she mentions: 'For some reason lots of rare Northern birds stop over on this tiny rock for a breather while flying around the North Atlantic. Perhaps they like the locals and the quiet scenery' (ibid).

The differences in these two narratives bring out the changes in tourist experiences. Charlton is one of the privileged few who get to travel to such places. He is a romantic explorer in search of authentic experiences in rural communities that contrasted with the urban life he was familiar with (compare Abrams 2005: 3; Blaikie 2001). Cherny instead is a cynical postmodern traveller who has experienced many things and 'knows' there are no authentic experiences, there is no exploring left to be done. This difference in views is also apparent in their relationship with Shetland. Charlton spent several months in Shetland and afterwards came back to visit Shetland again. Cherny instead says: 'Three days was sufficient for me on Fair Isle', although she is not totally indifferent to the experience, continuing; 'I would happily go back any year during puffin nesting season though!'

Going beyond the gaze

Veijola and Jokinen (1994) criticise Urry's focus on (sight)seeing at the expense of other senses. Veijola and Jokinen instead (1994: 133) argue that tourism is a bodily issue, something in which we immerse ourselves fully. They critique Urry's notion of the tourist 'gaze' by pointing out that it is 'rather the tourist *body* that breaks with the established routines and practices' (ibid.: 133, italics in original.). When tourists travel, they not only gaze at new sites around them, but get involved with many practices they would not at home – like singing and dancing together. Thus, Veijola and Jokinen emphasise the distinction between gazing at experiences and being a part of them physically, noting that tourist rituals create roles, 'and through them individual sentiments become collective experiences' (1994: 134). In these situations, people find 'a common language, a shared situational grammar' (ibid.). They point out that whilst watching a tourist ritual leaves one out of context, being a tourist does not.

In Shetland, the intense weather conditions, from rain and strong winds to intense fogs, ensure that every tourist is physically, bodily involved in the experience. Encounters with the weather appear regularly in both narratives. Charlton had the unfortunate privilege to experience one of the most destructive storms in Shetland's history. In the storm of 1832, several fishing boats went missing with over a hundred casualties. While Charlton later refers to the loss of life and is sympathetic for the devastation caused to the community, at the time he just enjoyed the elemental nature of the storm:

> … Certainly, I at the time enjoyed thoroughly the tumult and roar of wind and sea, and as I saw no immediate danger likely to result to the inhabitants of the islands from the hurricane, the wild war of elements, the screams of the sea fowl and the white foam of the seething billows relived against the dark heather hills to the North was, to my imagination at least, a most soul-strinning scene.
>
> (Charlton 2007: 13–14)

Cherny's experience of the quickly changing Shetland weather came during a hill walk to find puffins, the comical looking birds that attract even non-birdwatchers. Despite the fact that the overall numbers of puffins have been falling drastically, during the summer months there are still tens of thousands on the island. Unfortunately (for her), Cherny arrived about a week after the birds had left the island for the winter, so spotting a puffin required some effort. Another girl staying in the Bird Observatory, Violet, came to look for them with her. Cherny describes how they walk across the island with little luck of finding puffins. Eventually they decide to walk across the hills to get to the northern cliffs.

> It was very hot. We plodded generally northwestward across miles and miles of dried up heather, pretty bad walking because you had to keep an eye where you stepped to avoid falling in holes. It was really quite hot. We had no water. Surely the island wasn't this big.
>
> (Cherny 2006)

They continue to climb the hills in the heat until the weather changes suddenly. 'By the time we got around that mountain 10 minutes later, a dense fog swallowed everything. It was better than a hot death march, but I got worried. Just how close to the edge of the cliff were we?' She continues explaining that her worry was justified; 'A few years ago a visiting twitcher[1] kid did fall off the edge. He died. They've now got a scholarship fund set up to bring other young birdwatchers his age to the island, to encourage them to kill themselves too' (Cherny 2006).

Interestingly both Charlton and Cherny deal with weather and death. In Charlton's case, it is a matter of over one hundred locals dying in a storm, while in Cherny's case her experiences with the intense fog remind her of a story of a visitor dying in an accident. Charlton is very close to danger himself, as at the time of the storm he is stuck in a quarantine boat with his fellow travellers. However, he finds the gale-force storm an enjoyable experience. Afterwards he describes the effect of the losses to the communities he meets as well as his encounters with the mourners. Cherny instead, while she is not really in danger, is worried for her personal safety in the fog. Also her approach is different. Her relation to the death that had occurred on the island is more distant, making it possible for her to comment on it sarcastically.

Encounters with locals and other tourists

The previous section showed the narrative tool of contrasting scenery and the place to familiar environment. Another tool in tourist narratives is encounters with people. By comparing the people of the destination and their habits to those with which one is familiar, one can bring out the distinctions between 'here' and 'home'. Similarly, contrasting oneself with other tourists can contribute to the self-definition process. Both Charlton and Cherny make a clear distinction between themselves and two groups of people: locals and other travellers. In Charlton's case the distinction from locals is the stronger, clearer one, while with Cherny the distinction from a group of travellers, the birdwatchers, is more evident.

Charlton creates a clear distinction between himself and the other travellers, as shown previously: many of the others were seasick, and he could not understand why they were not as interested in the scenery as he was. However, he can relate to them, though his first description of Shetlanders places them into quite a separate group of people. Charlton's trip to Shetland is guided by romantic notions of discovery and travels to exotic lands. This also guides his observations of the locals. He describes the first time he saw Shetlanders when a fishing boat passed their ship. While looking over the bows of the boat, he saw how 'two yawls full of, to me, strange looking mortals broke through the mist, pulled astern of the ship without hailing and disappeared in the driving fog' (Charlton 2007: 5). Charlton describes how their clothing, skin coats, breeches and huge boots, reminded him of the pictures he had seen of the 'Esquimaux tribes'. He also notices how the island yawls vanishing into the fog 'imparted an air of romance exceedingly in accordance with my feelings of enterprise' (2007: 5). This type of writing was typical of the nineteenth-century representations of all the Scottish islands, as the writers framed their experiences in a similar vein to the imperialist travellers (Abrams 2005: 3).

Cherny also has some comments on the local population, but more on their behaviour than looks. The island is so small that 'everyone on the island knows everyone and knows everyone's news'. She tells of stories she heard while she was staying. She takes particular interest in the friendliness of the locals, and implies that much of this is towards people of whom she, or many of her compatriots, would not be so tolerant. One example of this is the attitude towards birdwatchers: 'I find it a little surprising how friendly they are, given the bird watchers trampling over their land day and night. Perhaps they are just happy for new social contacts' (Cherny 2006).

The group of people she feels estranged from most are the birdwatchers. Rare birds are one of the key attractions of Fair Isle; there has been a Bird Observatory since the 1940s providing accommodation for visitors. Cherny describes the visitors as follows: 'If Fair Isle is a crossroads for strange birds, the same could be said about the tourists who come to visit them.' These included birdwatchers, or 'twitchers', as well as other types of travellers. While Charlton was observing the local people who appeared to him as a relic of an earlier time, Cherny finds herself observing birdwatchers, whose obsessive behaviour is unfamiliar to her. She finds it odd, how much interest these people are putting in to spotting a particular bird: 'When someone announced they'd seen a citrine wagtail, everyone else rushed to the spot right after the next meal'. Also, the extent to which this is accommodated in the Observatory is amusing for her: 'There was even a whiteboard in the dining room with regular updates to make sure no one missed the news. For a day or so, "the ditch" was reported to be a real hot spot.'

Cherny's unfortunate puffin search described in the previous section took an interesting turn on the way back, as the girls find a rare bird. Next to a normal crossbill, Violet spots a double-barred crossbill, or as she explains; 'an incredibly rare bird' (Cherny 2006). Through difficulty and crawling 'G.I. Joe-style through the dried sheep shit', Cherny manages to take a few photographs where the bird is recognisable. After getting back to the Observatory, she describes how these photographs 'made me a temporary celebrity' among the birdwatcher boys who wanted to see the images of the rare bird. She is even told that bird magazines would 'pay money for these grainy shots', something which she thinks quite amusing. She posts the photographs in her blog with the caption: 'Would YOU pay for these?' These events provide a chance for her to feel equal with the twitcher boys whose professional telescopes and expensive cameras before made her feel inferior.

Cherny (2006) describes the Bird Observatory as 'a strange microculture of its own in the tiny island community'. This observation explains the difference between her and Charlton's comments on the people they meet. While Charlton is interested in the everyday reality of the locals, Cherny's visit focuses on the micro-cosmos of the Bird Observatory where she finds herself in contact with this different breed of people whom she can't quite understand.

Discussion: Heroic travellers

The two travel stories are different in many ways, as are the experiences they describe. Travelling in the 1800s was a pursuit limited to only the privileged, while in the 2000s travelling has become a pursuit followed by large numbers of the population in the western world. While travel to Shetland has become a much easier task, the islands are relatively remote and difficult to get to. The stories bring out these changes as well as others in tourism practices over the centuries. While Charlton stayed in Shetland for a whole summer, Cherny only stayed on Fair Isle for three days. The writing styles are quite different; Charlton's text, as was typical for the Victorian traveller, contains detailed information on various natural history topics varying from the ships to local attire, nature and references to the history and literature about Shetland. These issues are nearly completely missing from the twenty-first-century blog narrative which instead has observations of the daily life of the local community in the style of travel journalism.

Nevertheless, despite their differences, these two stories have significant underlying similarities. While these narratives describe events that have occurred in a distant unfamiliar place, they are more about the tourists. Everything in the place is measured against things that are familiar to them. These narratives also explore the writers' perception of themselves. Through travel to a distant destination on a trip that few will take, both these writers present themselves as 'heroic travellers'. They have to overcome obstacles, such as the slow and difficult travel, but they manage this better than the 'normal' person would – unlike others they tell about, neither of them suffer from seasickness. Charlton even underlines this, 'I was never better in my whole life' (2007: 2).

The dangers and the possibility of death create a sense of validity for the image of a heroic traveller. This sets the writer in a different category from those who stay at home, or only travel to a destination that is more easily accessible. This is especially clear in the old travel diary. Conversely, in the blog narrative the image of the heroic traveller is balanced with the image of an anti-hero. This comes out especially in Cherny's experience of getting lost on a tiny island and her inferior knowledge and equipment compared to the birdwatchers. However, with finding a rare bird she becomes a momentary hero even in their world, providing her with satisfaction in a social reality where she feels she does not belong – nor 'normal' people do as she points out in asking about the pictures: 'Would YOU pay for these?' Even in finding a momentary place in this community, she cheerfully notices at the end of her writing: 'I'll never be a real twitcher, just like I'll never be a boy, thank goodness' (Cherny 2006).

Both Charlton and Cherny represent themselves based on values that are attributed significance in their community (Goffman 1990: 44): independence, exploration and courage. However, while Charlton immerses himself in the role of an independent explorer, Cherny at times clearly reveals her cynicism. She takes a step back; it is as if she does not have full confidence in the role she has chosen for herself (Goffman 1990: 28). However much tourism as a phenomenon and tourism in Shetland has changed, both these stories build a picture of Shetland's otherness in relation to the places they come from. The physical and social reality they encounter has a central place in the narratives and, as others have noted (for example, Abrams 2005; Blaikie 2001), the creation of the 'otherness' of Shetland is dominant.

Conclusions

Through the analysis of two travel narratives located in Shetland, the chapter has shown how the Social Construction of Reality can be utilised in analysing tourist experiences. Tourist narratives are typically constructed in the form of opposing realities, with the events in the tourist destination contrasting the everyday reality of the writers'. The same opposition is clear in the presentation of the differences between the writer and the people they encounter, whether the local population or other tourists. The chapter has shown how these stories of travel experiences are used for presenting oneself. The remoteness of Shetland and the extreme weather are key factors in both stories and, despite the centuries between them, both narratives construct an image of a 'heroic traveller' battling the dangerous elements. While tourist narratives describe a travel destination, the reality they are reconstructing is that of the authors themselves.

Note

1 Birdwatcher; see the following section.

11 Narrating travel experiences: the role of new media

Ulrike Gretzel, Daniel R. Fesenmaier, Yoon Jung Lee and Iis Tussyadiah

Introduction

A significant part of the travel experience is now being shaped by information obtained online in the form of new media, such as consumer-generated videos, reviews and blogs. Gretzel *et al.* (2006) argue that travellers use the Internet for a wide variety of tasks depending upon the stage of the trip (Figure 11.1). During the pre-trip phase, for example, travellers may use the Internet, and specifically consumer-generated media (CGM), to learn about potential travel destinations, create expectations, inform the purchase of airline or hotel reservations, and to dream about and anticipate upcoming vacations. Mobile computing applications supported through such technologies as laptop computers, netbooks and phones, on the other hand, shape en route touristic experiences as people use mobile technologies to address a variety of immediate travel tasks, such as finding a particular restaurant, taking photographs of places visited, or calling someone such as a friend or relative to tell him/her about a particular experience. Finally, the post-travel stage typically involves using technologies for the purpose of documentation, recollection, restructuring and sharing of real and imagined trip experiences (Gretzel *et al.* 2006).

Narration is a key aspect of this consumption process. In the pre-trip phase, stories written and published by other travellers are read to inform decisions and to spark one's imagination. Having access to the personal experience accounts of other travellers is an important way for tourists who have yet to embark on their trip to receive first-hand knowledge as well as highly relevant information from others who they like and/or perceive as similar. Such experience-based information is critical in the context of tourism (Litvin *et al.* 2008) where high-involvement decisions have to be made regarding products and services that lack in standardisation, are difficult to describe, typically cannot be inspected before purchase, are high in emotional content, and can have serious consequences if they lack in quality. During the trip and after the trip, stories are used to encode experiences for the purpose of sharing and documentation. New media increasingly allow travellers to easily narrate and share their experiences when they occur rather than having to recount

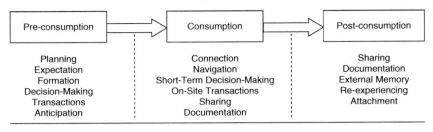

Figure 11.1 Communication and information needs in the three stages of
tourism consumption.

them in the form of stories after the trip is completed. Importantly, story-telling enables tourists to organise their experiences and add meaning to them, and, therefore, it can be considered a very powerful reflective tool (Pudliner 2007). In addition, the recounting of tourism experience plays a significant role in individual and social identity formation processes (Lee *et al.* 2009; McCabe and Foster 2006). Travel narratives are expressions of identity and the telling of these narratives is an essential component of social interactions (O'Reilly 2005; Desforges 2000; Shaffer 2001).

Product and experience evaluations are a fundamental part of the narration of tourism experiences (Tussyadiah and Fesenmaier 2008). Thus, the recounting of tourism experiences is also instrumental in forming attachments to tourism products, brands and destinations (Escalas 2004). From a tourism product provider perspective, tourism experience narratives that involve a specific offering or destination simultaneously provide one of the greatest opportunities and one of the most significant challenges (Gretzel 2006). Being easily shared with millions of other consumers, a single narrative can have a tremendous impact on a business, both in positive and negative ways. Thus, the tourism industry increasingly sees a need to actively manage or at least monitor the conversations about their products that happen through new media (Gretzel *et al.* 2006).

While the narrating of tourism experiences can occur in many ways, written accounts play a particularly important role. Robinson (2004) notes that writing about travel experiences is as old as travel itself. It became particularly important during the times of the European Grand Tour when aristocratic travellers tried to mimic earlier travel narratives by chronicling journeys in diaries and letters (Towner 1985). Shaffer (2001: 266) states that 'travel diaries both codified the tour as a singular experience and served to memorialize one's journey'. Pudliner (2007) also mentions the long tradition of travel journals and the wide-reaching publication of travel narratives in the form of monographs, novels, newspaper stories, and so on. Visual media, such as postcards and photographs, are also instrumental in helping tourists represent, reproduce and recreate tourist moments (Cary 2004). Scrapbooks often represent tourism experiences through a mixture of text, images and artefacts. Shaffer (2001) notes a shift from textual to visual representations with the development of new technologies, such as the first Kodak amateur camera, and the increasing commercialisation of tourism experiences, therefore illustrating the important role of media in shaping the form of travel narratives. In whatever form they appear, personal accounts of travellers contribute significantly to the 'language' of tourism (Dann 1996). The conversations that contribute to the language of tourism are increasingly represented online; in fact, travel narratives and accounts generated by consumers in the form of consumer-generated media (CGM) now constitute a substantial part of the online tourism domain (Xiang *et al.* 2008; Xiang and Gretzel 2010).

Web 2.0 applications, such as blogs and travel review sites, provide travellers with potentially unlimited opportunities for recounting and sharing what they experienced during a trip and, if accessed through mobile technologies or Internet connections at destinations, they also offer opportunities for narrating experiences while they occur. These online representations of trips do not only mediate one's own actual or remembered experience but also the experiences of those who view them, well beyond one's social circle. Thus, their potential for shaping tourism experiences is tremendous (Tussyadiah and Fesenmaier 2009). However, active online content creation in this phase of the tourism experience might not be as widespread as the number and availability of travel reviews, videos and photos implies. Existing research indicates that a majority of user-generated content that is available online is created by a small fraction of online users (Preece *et al.* 2004; Daugherty *et al.* 2008) and writers of online travel reviews differ significantly from those who only read reviews in terms of personal characteristics and travel planning behaviours (Yoo and Gretzel 2008a). The goal of this chapter is to report the results of a study that investigated the extent to which American travellers with Internet access use Web 2.0 applications as part of their pre-trip planning, en route consumption and post-consumption experiences. In addition, this study sought to identify the motivations for content creation, barriers to content creation, and whether those who create content online differ significantly from those who do not.

Background

CGM *use by travellers*

There is a growing literature on consumer-generated media in tourism, identifying CGM as an important form of communication among travellers (Litvin *et al.* 2008). One prominent stream evolves around the analysis of online travel communities and discussion forums (Wang *et al.* 2001; Arsal *et al.* 2008; Chung and Buhalis 2008; Wang and Fesenmaier 2004a; Kim *et al.* 2004), suggesting that these online platforms provide important venues for travellers to engage in travel storytelling and to find information and support for travel planning. Most of the recent papers in this area have particularly focused on travel blogs (Wenger 2008; Pudliner 2007; Lin and Huang 2006; Karlsson 2006; Schmallegger and Carson 2008; Pan *et al.* 2007; Thevenot 2007; Douglas and Mills 2006; Mack *et al.* 2008; Tussyadiah and Fesenmaier 2008; Lee *et al.* 2009). Travel blogs are a type of CGM that most closely resemble traditional travel journals. They have been identified as important opportunities to communicate information outside of the dominant narratives of tourism marketers (Pudliner 2007). Another form of CGM increasingly discussed by tourism researchers are online travel reviews (Yoo and Gretzel 2008b; Vermeulen and Seegers 2009; O'Connor 2008). These reviews include product ratings and short descriptions, and their creation is often directly encouraged by travel marketers. In contrast to other forms of CGM, travel reviews tend to be very structured and do not serve the purpose of documenting an experience for oneself but rather are directed at others. Videos have so far received very little attention in the literature as a medium to portray tourism experiences (Tussyadiah and Fesenmaier 2009). Podcasting has also not been discussed extensively in academic papers, with the exception being Xie and Liew (2008). Most of the existing literature focuses on content analysis of these online consumer-generated travel narratives and discusses marketing opportunities and challenges. However, very little is known about actual use of travel CGM in the context of trip planning, especially beyond the use and impact of travel reviews, as reported by Vermeulen and Seegers (2009) and Yoo and Gretzel (2008b).

CGM *creation – motivations and barriers*

Content creation is another issue related to CGM that is discussed in the literature (Bishop 2007). eMarketer (2007) reports that CGM users outnumber CGM creators by far. The phenomenon of lurkers (i.e. those who use content but do not actively contribute) is well researched (Preece *et al.* 2004), leaving many to wonder what the motivations are of those who actively contribute content. Motivations to contribute content online have been studied by Hennig-Thurau *et al.* (2004) and Kim and Schrier (2007). Hennig-Thurau *et al.* (2004) suggest eight motivations for online content creation: 1) venting negative feelings; 2) platform assistance; 3) concern for other consumers; 4) extraversion/positive self-enhancement; 5) social benefits; 6) economic incentives; 7) helping the company; and 8) seeking advice. Some research exists also regarding the barriers to content creation (Preece *et al.* 2004; Nonnecke and Preece 1999), with feeling no need to post being the top reason reported. Daugherty *et al.* (2008) identified ego-defensive and social motivations as important for content creation, and also found significant differences between active CGM contributors and mere users in terms of what types of CGM they use.

In the context of travel CGM, Wang and Fesenmaier (2004a; 2004b) studied motivations for participation in travel communities, including general participation as well as active contributions, and found a diverse array of motivations, ranging from psychological to social factors. Yoo and Gretzel (2009) studied a sample of TripAdvisor members who actively contribute travel reviews and report that TripAdvisor contributors were mostly driven by altruistic motives rather than vengeance or the need to vent. Both studies used samples of community members rather than a general traveller sample and, thus, provide insights for a rather committed population. Yoo and Gretzel (2008a) found significant differences between online travel review writers and non-writers in terms of demographic characteristics, travel planning, general Internet use and use of online travel reviews for travel decision-making.

While the above-mentioned literature provides some insights regarding CGM use and CGM creation, the studies have been either conducted for consumer products rather than travel, or for very specific types of CGM (e.g. postings in virtual travel communities and online travel reviews). The study reported in this chapter investigated whether findings regarding use and impacts as well as motivations for content creation hold true for travel CGM in general and for a general population of online travellers.

Methodology

An online survey was conducted in July 2008 to investigate the extent of new media use and motivations and barriers to recounting tourism experiences online. The survey invitation was sent to 59,186 members of a commercial online research panel. Only those residing in the United States were considered. A total of 3,109 panelists responded to the survey invitation but only 2,671 indicated they were active Internet users. Furthermore, of those Internet users, 1,682 had travelled for pleasure within 12 months prior to the study. These online travellers form the actual sample for the study.

The questionnaire included questions related to Internet skills and online activities, CGM use and perceptions in the context of travel, questions related to the creation of travel-related CGM, motivations and barriers to CGM creation (adapted from Hennig-Thurau *et al.* 2004; Wang and Fesenmaier 2004b; Preece *et al.* 2004; Nonnecke and Preece 1999), as well as questions about the socio-demographic characteristics of the respondents. Descriptive analyses as well as chi-square statistics were used to investigate various aspects of CGM creation and use by American travellers.

Findings

Although largely descriptive, the findings derived from the analyses provide important insights regarding the prominence of online travel narration activities and differences between online travellers who engage in travel content creation and those who do not.

Travel CGM use – learning from others' travel experiences

The results of the survey show that 50 per cent of online travel planners view other consumers' postings in the course of planning trips. Most of these CGM users look at travel reviews (80.5 per cent) and photos (50.6 per cent). Blogs (21.8 per cent), comments posted on blogs (23.6 per cent) and postings on discussion forums (22.4 per cent) are used by less than a quarter of the CGM users included in the study. Multimedia representations of travel experiences in the form of videos (14.2 per cent) and audio files/podcasts (3.8 per cent) are only used by a small portion of these CGM users. The most commonly used websites to find travel CGM are Yahoo! Travel (40.8 per cent), online travel agency websites (36.1 per cent) and TripAdvisor (29.0 per cent).

A large majority of online travellers (81.6 per cent) at least somewhat trust the information that is posted by other travellers. This percentage is significantly higher (91.5 per cent) for those who actually use CGM in their trip planning, suggesting that trust perceptions influence individual use decisions. Almost 40 per cent of online travellers indicated that they trust CGM more than travel guidebooks and travel articles (49.9 per cent for those who use CGM). Only 18.1 per cent are suspicious about marketers posting content under the disguise of being a consumer (no significant difference between users and non-users). However, 58.7 per cent would still rather place their travel decision on one review from a person they know than 100 reviews written by strangers (55.4 per cent for those who are CGM users). These findings indicate that CGM play an important role in the trip planning of at least half of online travellers in the US. They also show a clear preference for certain media over others and a rather high level of trust in the content produced by other travellers. While many still prefer to receive personal recommendations through traditional word-of-mouth, over 40 per cent believe in the 'collective wisdom of the crowds'. Indeed, most CGM users indicated being influenced by CGM regarding a multitude of travel decisions. The greatest influence was perceived with respect to accommodation decisions, with 81 per cent of CGM users reporting that CGM had at least some influence on their decision, followed by activities (75.2 per cent) and dining (68.3 per cent). Only about half of the CGM users perceived at least some influence on their destination choice (57.2 per cent), shopping (56.2 per cent), how they travelled to the destination (52.5 per cent) and the time the trip was taken (51.5 per cent).

Travel CGM creation – narrating one's own experiences

While half of the surveyed online travellers use travel-related CGM, the online creation of travel-related content is low with only 17 per cent having ever posted travel materials online. Of those who have posted content, most (74 per cent) have posted content in the form of travel reviews, 56 per cent have posted photos on online photo-sharing sites, and 54 per cent have contributed to a travel discussion board or forum. Almost half (47 per cent) have posted a comment to somebody else's travel blog. About

37 per cent have written their own blog and 21 per cent have posted a video (Table 11.1).

Most bloggers started fairly recently, with 35.8 per cent having started within 6 months prior to the survey, 38.8 per cent between 6 months and 2 years, and only 25.4 per cent have blogged for 2 years or more. This finding suggests that blogging is growing quite quickly as a travel narration activity. The majority (72 per cent) write travel blogs to inform people they know, but a considerable number (52 per cent) also write for a general audience. Most (84 per cent) include written text in their blogs and 69 per cent include photos, while only 30 per cent include videos, 24 per cent audio files, 22 per cent graphics and also 22 per cent links to other sites/blogs. Most (81 per cent) write about personal experiences, practical travel information about the destination (63 per cent), local people, food and culture (54 per cent), general facts about the destination (51 per cent), people they met while travelling (49 per cent), warnings and tips for others (48 per cent), and evaluations of travel-related services (43 per cent) (Table 11.2).

The survey also included a number of questions regarding different motivations to create content online. The top three reasons for creating travel-related content online were: 1) to share experiences with others; 2) to help other people; and 3) to share practical information with others. However, these altruistic motivations were closely followed by enjoyment and to document

Table 11.1 Types of content created

CGM type	% of content creators
Travel reviews	74.2
Photos	56.0
Postings on discussion boards/forums	54.4
Comments to an existing travel blog	47.3
Travel blog	36.8
Video	21.4
Contribution to travel-related wiki	19.2
Micro-blog (Twitter)	18.1

Table 11.2 Types of content included in travel blogs

Travel Blog Content	% of travel bloggers
Personal experience	80.6
Practical information about the destination	62.7
Local people/food/culture	53.7
General facts about the destination (geography, etc.)	50.7
People met while travelling	49.3
Warnings to others/security tips	47.8
Evaluation of travel-related services (tour guides, etc.)	43.3

personal experiences. Table 11.3 shows the results grouped by different motivational factors. Again, altruism items generally emerge as very prominent drivers of travel CGM creation. Enjoyment items as a group score highly, as do reciprocity items, concerns for travel providers and documentation of experience. The social interaction and communication aspects of CGM

Table 11.3 Motivation to create content

Motivation		% of content creators who agree/strongly agree
Enjoyment	Because I enjoy it	71.0
	Because it is a fun thing to do	64.2
	To entertain myself	48.8
Social Interaction	To stay in touch with family and friends	53.7
	To express yourself creatively	46.9
	To get feedback from others	46.3
	To entertain others	39.1
	To influence the way others think	34.1
	To network or to meet other people	32.4
	To improve my communication skills	31.3
	To be recognised by others	29.1
Documentation of Experience	To document my personal experience	68.8
	To reflect on my trip experiences after returning home	58.5
	To store information that is important to me	44.7
	To relive my trip experiences	43.7
Incentives	Because I can get rewards for it	26.2
	Because incentives are offered for posting	22.1
	To make money	17.0
Venting	To express my anger about a negative experience I had	43.5
	To vent negative feelings	39.2
	Because it helps me overcome negative feelings	30.8
Reciprocity	Because I benefited and want others to benefit	67.6
	Information posted by other travellers helped me and I want to return the favour	67.0
	Because I want to contribute to a pool of information that assisted me in planning previous trips	63.7
Altruism	To share experiences with others	83.8
	To help other people	77.3
	To share practical information with others	74.8
	To warn others	60.8
Concern for Company	Because good travel providers should be supported	64.8
	To leave feedback for a travel service provider	60.8
	To help a travel service provider	43.2

creation are important for some content creators, as is the opportunity to vent negative feelings. Receiving rewards for posting is not a motivating factor for most of the respondents who engage in CGM creation.

The survey asked CGM users (but not creators) to identify the factors that prevented them from creating travel content online; the survey also asked CGM creators to identify the most important barriers that kept them from doing it more often. The top three reasons for not creating travel-related content online or not doing it more frequently were 1) no interest; 2) not enough time; and, 3) requires too much effort (Table 11.4).

Chi-square analyses were then conducted to distinguish between those who do and those who do not create travel CGM. The results of these analyses indicate that CGM creators are significantly ($p < 0.05$) more likely to indicate that they do not have enough time, while those who do not create CGM are significantly more likely to indicate that they have no interest, that it requires too much effort, that there are not enough monetary incentives, that they do not travel enough, that it is too cumbersome to collect the information while travelling, that they have privacy concerns, they lack confidence, that they do not have the necessary skills, and that they see no need for doing it since others do it anyway.

Characteristics of travel CGM creators

The results of the chi-square analyses also indicate that travel content creators differ significantly from non-creators as far as a number of other

Table 11.4 Barriers to content creation

Barrier	% of CGM users who agree/strongly agree
No interest	57.4
Not enough time	50.9
Requires too much effort	41.5
Privacy concerns	36.6
Forget to do it	35.1
Not enough monetary incentives offered to entice me	34.8
Don't travel enough	30.5
No need for me to do it since others do it anyway	29.3
Not aware of opportunities to post	28.7
Worried that the information will be misused	28.6
Too cumbersome to collect information while travelling	25.3
Lack skills/do not know how	20.7
Lack confidence	16.3
Have Internet access problems	8.1

characteristics are concerned. Specifically, content creators travel more frequently ($\chi^2 = 36.7$; p = .000); they are more involved in travel planning, with 77.1 per cent having planned all or most of their most recent pleasure trip in contrast to 66.5 per cent for non-creators ($\chi^2 = 10.3$; p = .036); and, are more likely to plan trips entirely online (36.1 per cent compared to 26.1 per cent; $\chi^2 = 21.7$; p = .001). No significant difference was found regarding the extent to which trips are planned in advance and regarding how far these trips are planned in advance.

Not surprisingly, most content creators (80.7 per cent) used CGM when planning their most recent pleasure trip while less than half (44.4 per cent) of non-creators used CGM ($\chi^2 = 79.2$; p = .000). While both groups use travel reviews, content creators are more likely to use photos (58.9 per cent vs 48.4 per cent; $\chi^2 = 4.7$; p = .029), videos (26.0 per cent vs 9.6 per cent; $\chi^2 = 27.8$; p = .000), blogs (33.6 per cent vs 18.7 per cent; $\chi^2 = 13.3$; p = .000), comments posted on blogs (32.9 per cent vs 21.8 per cent; $\chi^2 = 7.1$; p = .008), postings in discussion forums (31.5 per cent vs 20.5 per cent; $\chi^2 = 7.2$; p = .007), and audio files/podcasts (8.2 per cent vs 2.5 per cent; $\chi^2 = 8.8$; p = .003). While both groups are equally likely to use online travel agency websites to find travel-related CGM, content creators are more likely to use social sites such as TripAdvisor, YouTube and MySpace as well as local search sites such as Yelp and Citysearch (p < .05).

Content-creators trust user-generated travel content more: while 45.3 per cent of content creators trust or very much trust CGM, only 21.9 per cent of non-creators exhibit such high trust levels ($\chi^2 = 58.9$; p = .000). Over half of content creators (56.3 per cent) trust CGM more than expert reviews compared to only 37.3 per cent of non-creators ($\chi^2 = 38.5$; p = .000). While most non-creators (60.2 per cent) prefer a recommendation from someone they know over 100 reviews from strangers, only 49.2 per cent of content creators have this preference ($\chi^2 = 13.1$; p = .011). In addition, while almost 40 per cent (39.4 per cent) of content creators are not suspicious regarding marketers posting as consumers, only 28.5 per cent of non-creators do not have such suspicions ($\chi^2 = 18.7$; p = .001). Most importantly, content creators were more influenced by CGM in terms of where they ate on their last pleasure trip, where they shopped, how they travelled to the destination, when they travelled, what they did while there and where they stayed overnight (p < .05). Interestingly, no difference was found for destination choice.

In general, content creators are more active Internet users. They read and write more blogs, post comments to blogs, use social networking sites, listen to or download audio podcasts, watch or download videos, post/share audio files and videos, look at photos posted by others, post/share photos, read reviews, rate products or post reviews, read wiki entries, contribute to wikis significantly (p < .05) more often than non-creators. Last, they are also more likely to be Asian American or African American in ethnic origin, single and younger than 45 years. No significant differences were found for gender, household income, level of education and whether children were living in the household.

Conclusion

Online content created by other travellers currently mediates the experience of about half of the American travellers who plan their trips online. Most of the CGM use is focused on travel reviews and, thus, has the greatest influence on accommodation decisions. In terms of narrating one's travel experiences, travel reviews are rather limited as they are typically short and expected to emphasise the experience at a certain accommodation (or dining) establishment. CGM that are able to portray tourism experiences in richer ways are used only by a small portion of American online travellers. Therefore, the role of CGM in the travel planning process is greater for some aspects of travel planning, like accommodation decisions, and for some American travellers. Nevertheless, the findings suggest that accessing information online about the travel experiences of others is a common phenomenon that influences the decisions of travellers beyond the immediate social circle of the narrator. Trust that others will recount their experiences truthfully seems to be an important catalyst of CGM use because of this lack of a personal relationship with the individual who publishes a personal account of a trip online. However, questions concerning why certain types of CGM are more popular than others cannot be answered with the current study and should be the subject of future research in this area.

The results of this study indicate that content creators are different from those travellers who do not engage in online travel content creation, not only with respect to some demographic characteristics, but also in terms of their travel experience and involvement in travel planning. Importantly, online travel content creators tend to use very basic media such as reviews, photo sharing and discussion boards while blogs and videos are less likely to be used. This online travel content creation is directed mostly at known others, but in many instances also at a general online audience. An array of reasons why individuals engage in travel content creation online was identified, with altruistic sharing being the main motivation. Yet, personal enjoyment and the documentation of personal experiences also play an important role, which suggests that content creation allows these travellers to extend their tourism experience far beyond the point of consumption. Social motives, such as being part of a community, were less of a motivational factor than suggested by previous studies which had primarily used samples of online community members.

These findings confirm earlier work by Yoo and Gretzel (2008) as well as Daugherty *et al.* (2008). Content creators seem to be an especially attractive target group for travel marketers. The higher number of online content creators among younger travellers suggests that online travel content creation will become a much more important part of post-consumption in tourism as this new media generation replaces traditional travel consumers. However, one limitation of the study is its exclusive focus on American travellers. There is evidence that CGM adoption and use differs by country (Gretzel *et al.* 2008).

What these differences mean for travel narration by different nationalities has yet to be investigated empirically.

CGM may never replace the many offline conversations about travel experiences, but it seems that as Web 2.0 technologies become more commonly used for everyday tasks, they will be used extensively as one means that supports travel experience narration. Interestingly, just like other forms of published travel narratives, however, it appears that travel CGM is created by few but used by many. However, as social network systems such as Facebook and YouTube and mobile computing systems, including the 100,000+ applications available on iPhones and BlackBerrys, evolve and become fully integrated into society, it is expected that they will become the foundation for communication and interpretation of the tourist experience. Indeed, one might expect that as these new forms of travel narration become open to a much broader group of individuals they will lead to narratives that are widely available for use by others in the process of planning trips. It will be interesting to see whether CGM in the long run will have the same impact on travel as the accounts by Hemingway, Theroux, Kerouac and Krakauer, guidebooks provided by Frommer, Fodor and Lonely Planet, or magazines such as *National Geographic* or *Condé Nast Traveller*.

The tourism industry has yet to fully embrace the role new media play in the narration of travel experiences. While some destinations and providers are currently trying to engage in CGM-based communication with travellers, it is unclear what role tourism marketers and managers can or should play in mediating online travel narration. While they were quick to supply the postcards and Kodak moments that filled travel scrapbooks in the past (Shaffer 2001), current developments of online and mobile tourism applications seem to be largely focused on the functional aspects of travel planning and booking support. More research like the study presented in this chapter is needed to illustrate the importance of narration in the tourism consumption process and the great impact on the narrators as well as the consumers of CGM-mediated travel narratives.

12 Learning from travel experiences: a system for analysing reflective learning in journals

Sarah Quinlan Cutler and
Barbara A. Carmichael

Introduction

Travel experiences are argued to have the ability to improve psychological well-being, promote international understanding, act as a force for peace and friendship, encourage environmental conservation and facilitate learning (Higgins-Desboilles 2006; WTO 1999). The development of generic skills important to educators and businesses – such as problem solving, time management, leadership, effective communication and the management of financial resources – are also linked to the experience of travel (see Gmelch 1997; Pearce and Foster 2007). However, there have been few studies which focus on learning experiences in tourism, investigating reflection on travel.

This chapter will consider travel experience as a catalyst for learning, examining experiential and reflective learning as part of long-haul field trips. Research on learning processes, learning outcomes of travel, reflective thinking and assessment of journal content will be synthesised to provide a basis for the creation of a reflection coding scheme for evaluating journals written on long-haul educational trips. The aim of this coding scheme is to provide a system for evaluating reflective thinking levels of individuals involved in educational tourism or educational field trips and to determine relationships between reflective thinking and other experiential variables.

The learning process in fieldwork

How we learn in our environment has been well researched in the academic literature. Learning involves experiences and perceptions which are stored in memory, contributing to an individual's understanding of the world (Boud 2001; Davidson-Hunt and Berkes 2003). Memory is then drawn upon through the daily practice of life which affects perceptions and attitudes, allowing individuals to understand events and respond to problems.

Cognitive learning, which has become the most supported view of learning and knowledge accumulation, relates to how people make decisions using memories and environmental information (Orams 1994). Cognitive theory involves concepts of dissonance and consonance, where information is processed; that which disagrees with a person's current belief or behaviour causes psychological discomfort and can motivate change to reduce the dissonance, thereby achieving consonance (Luck 2003; Orams 1994). Therefore, cognitive dissonance is seen as a catalyst to learning. Placing individuals in unfamiliar environments can provide new experiences which challenge the learner. This can be termed experiential learning.

Experiential learning theory emphasises the significance of experiencing activities such as fieldwork (Healey and Jenkins 2000). This is often used as a basis to argue for the inclusion of educational field trips in academic disciplines which are considered to be highly beneficial for student learning (Fuller *et al.* 2003; Kent *et al.* 1997; McGuinness and Simm 2005; Mooney and Edwards 2001; Robson 2002; Timmer 2004). McGuinness and Simm (2005) demonstrate this idea of learning in their discussion on fieldwork, stating that it brings students into unfamiliar places and cultures which then offer a rich opportunity for dissonance and disruption, stimulating learning and reflection on geographical understanding. This exposure to new environments can be achieved by taking students on long-haul field trips and incorporating travel and tourism into the overall experience.

Learning in travel and tourism

The notion of travel as education is not new. The Grand Tour, which began during the end of the seventeenth century, was a practice of sending privileged young men to travel in various areas of Europe to extend their education (Brodsky-Porges 1981; Urry 2002). This connection between education and tourism continues today as there are a number of studies which link travel experiences to learning and skill development. Table 12.1 provides a summary of learning and skill development categories and related research.

Gmelch (1997) theorises that most learning does not come from places visited but from the act of travelling itself, as it forces individuals to make decisions on difficult issues in unfamiliar settings. A traveller has to decide what to do, where to go, how to get there, where to change money, where to eat, what to buy, and so on. Solving these problems requires some understanding about the local culture and customs, communication, transportation systems and social systems. These experiences in a strange culture are significant as individuals have to learn new skills to achieve their travel goals safely. This is reiterated by Byrnes (2001) who discusses how exposure to differences in transport, language, food, architectures, culture, dress and money can broaden an individual's world view and provide opportunities to develop life skills.

Some researchers suggest that the development of self is a significant outcome of travel. For example, Noy (2004) finds powerful communications on self-change in the narratives of Israeli backpackers, while research participants in Kuh's (1995) study link travel to increases in self-awareness.

Table 12.1 Learning and skill development linked to travel experiences

Cognitive development involving knowledge and psychological learning such as communication, critical thinking, cultural awareness, environmental learning, global understanding, linguistic skills, mapping, problem solving, research and time management	(Berwick and Whalley 2000; Byrnes 2001; Gmelch 1997; Guy *et al.* 1990; Hunt 2000; Li 2000; Litvin 2003; Pearce and Foster 2007; RoperASW 2002; Walmsley and Jenkins 1992; Wilson 1988)
Affective development involving emotional learning such as stress management, relationship management, patience, responsibility and tolerance	(Byrnes 2001; Gmelch 1997; Noy 2004; Pearce and Foster 2007)
Psychomotor development involving manual or physical skills such as information literacy	(Pearce and Foster 2007)
Personal development involving growth related to self-discovery such as adaptability, independence, self-awareness, leadership, maturity, self confidence, motivation and self-transition	(Byrnes 2001; Gmelch 1997; Hunt 2000; Kuh 1995; Noy 2004; Pearce and Foster 2007; White and White 2004)

However, skills and personal development are not uniform amongst travellers. In reviewing studies on travel experiences, there are several variables that are linked to differences in experiential learning and development.

Motivation for travel is linked to different levels of skill development and learning as research finds that individuals motivated by learning and linguistics tend to develop more skills than individuals motivated by thrill seeking (Pearce and Foster 2007). Studies on specific travel attributes indicate that life stages are also important in allowing for more meaningful travel experiences. Hunt (2000) argues that the learning done through travel is important for youth (those under 29 years of age) as this group may not yet be fully engaged in employment and a structured work environment. White and White (2004) also argue that transitional life phases allow for more meaningful travel experiences as these experiences place people into an environment where they can test their abilities and become more aware of their sense of self.

Studies of cognitive mapping and geographic awareness demonstrate that travel to novel environments can allow for more opportunities to encounter differences and dissonance which challenge preconceived perspectives leading to growth and adaptation (Berwick and Whalley 2000; Hunt 2000). Environmental learning is also heightened through direct and independent experiences with the destination rather than passive experiences, such as travelling in organised tours where individuals are not involved in decision-making

(Guy *et al.* 1990; Walmsley and Jenkins 1992). The amount and quality of interactions with host nationals is also related to learning and skill development with research demonstrating that personal development and cultural learning is enhanced when individuals engage with other cultures (Berwick and Whalley 2000; Hunt 2000).

These variables (motivation, life stage, novelty, direct experience and host–guest interactions) indicate that learning takes places at different levels and can be linked to characteristics of the trip or the individual traveller. However, not all research agrees that travel is a source of learning. In Litvin's (2003) study of attitude change in students who went overseas, the author finds that the study experience does have a significant impact on the students' attitude towards the destination. However, he remains sceptical as to whether or not this impacted cultural understanding. Other authors argue that claims made regarding travel as transformation of self are exaggerated as travel only serves to validate or confirm preconceived ideas (Bruner 1991; Elwood 2004). The experience of other places and cultures is not necessarily effective in skill development and learning unless preconceived ideas are addressed and the experience itself considered (Elwood 2004; Nairn 2005). Therefore, the presence of individuals in other destinations does not automatically mean that learning is taking place. They must be able to assess the experience. To develop skills and learning outcomes, the traveller must move beyond experiential learning into reflective learning.

Reflective thinking and learning

The act of reflection is 'an important human activity in which people recapture their experience, think about it, mull it over and evaluate it' (Boud *et al.* 1985b: 19). Reflection is addressed by many different authors within education literature and other subfields including the medical and nursing literature and the geography literature (see Atkins and Murphy 1993; Baker El-Dib 2007; Boud 2001; Boud *et al.* 1985c; Bourner 2003; Boyd and Fales 1983; Cuppernull *et al.* 2004; Fisher 2003; Harrison *et al.* 2003; Leppa and Terry 2004; Linder and Marshall 2003; Plack *et al.* 2005; Plack *et al.* 2007; Simpson and Courtney 2007; Spalding and Wilson 2002; Williams *et al.* 2002; Wong *et al.* 1995). In the review on individual reflection done by Atkins and Murphy (1993), they summarise the process of reflection with the outcome being a change in perspective. Boyd and Fales (1983) discuss reflection as a key element in experiential learning, defining reflection as a process of creating meaning from experiences in terms of self – both self in relation to oneself and self in relation to the outer world. This process then leads to a change in conceptual perspective. Linder and Marshall (2003) define reflective learning as the exploration of an experience while being mindful of the act of learning. Bourner (2003) describes reflection as an emergent event when experience is turned into learning. In simpler terms, it is not what has happened that matters; it is what one does with what has happened. Plack *et al.* (2005) argue that reflection is what brings meaning to an experience, turning it into practice by linking past, present and future experiences, while Boud (2001) sees the reflection process as one which takes raw experiences and explores them through thought and emotion, to make sense of what has happened. Reflection is seen as a processed response to experiences occurring after the event and this reflecting on experiences is the important part of learning (Boud *et al.* 1985b). This evaluation of experiences can only occur when ideas are brought into consciousness, then the individual is able to make choices about what she or he will and will not do. This, Boud *et al.* (1985b) argue, is why the facilitation of the reflection process is essential.

In reviewing these definitions, there are three common elements. Reflection involves an individual, an event and an evaluation of the event (or outcome). If there is merely an individual and an event and this event is not evaluated, then there is no reflection. Therefore, it is not the experience which is important in learning; it is the individual interpretation of the experience which can then lead to evaluations of emotions, ideas, thoughts, attitudes and behaviours. This interpretation allows for learning to occur whereby events are processed and understood, and can be called upon using memory to inform an individual in future events. In relating this to cognitive learning theory, it is not the dissonance which allows us to learn, it is how we process this dissonance to create consonance in our understanding which can then be used to make decisions.

The process of reflection is known to be highly beneficial in educational settings. Plack *et al.* (2007) argue that reflection allows students to capture the wisdom and lessons from their experiences, encouraging the evaluation of situations from differing perspectives. Furthermore, Platzer *et al.* (2000) find that there are significant changes in perspectives and significant developments in student critical thinking abilities. The students themselves identify positive outcomes of the reflective practice, such as more self-confidence, increased professionalism and greater autonomy in decision-making. Harrison *et al.* (2003) summarise results of other studies, demonstrating how reflection helps students improve the quality of learning, arguing that reflection should be actively promoted in higher education.

Therefore, in fieldwork or in travel experiences, placing people in new environments and subjecting them to new experiences may not in itself lead to learning. An evaluation of those experiences must be encouraged if learning is to take place. Harrison *et al.* (2003) contend that reflection is not automatic and will not occur by chance; it needs to be promoted and supported. This is reiterated by Boud *et al.* (1985a) who argue that brief field trips do not allow students to come to terms with their experiences. Students need to be persuaded to reflect on the experience through the use of assignments. This can be done through various methods, one of which being diaries or journaling. The use of reflective diaries or journals is seen as an important tool in encouraging the assessment of ideas, learning, thought and debate (McGuinness and Simm 2005).

Assessing reflection through journal writing

Journaling is one tool which has been shown to encourage reflection on experiences (Blake 2005; Boud 2001; Connell 2006; Gmelch 1997; Harrison *et al.* 2003; Mayo 2003a, 2003b; McGuinness and Simm 2005; Plack *et al.* 2007; Williams *et al.* 2002) by encouraging students to think out loud and evaluate their observations (Simpson and Courtney 2007). Mayo (2003b), in a study of the observational diaries of psychology students, finds that the students demonstrated higher levels of learning and applicability of knowledge compared to students who are not assigned the diary task. The author argues that journal writing is an excellent teaching tool allowing students to connect theory and practice in the experiences surrounding their daily lives. In keeping a diary of experiences, students take on the role of problem solvers, searching for explanations and relationships regarding real world events.

Blake (2005) outlines several advantages of journaling in developing reflective thinking:

- discovering meaning
- making connections between experiences and the classroom
- instilling values of the profession
- gaining perspectives of others
- reflecting on professional roles
- improving writing skills through student–teacher interactions
- developing critical thinking and problem solving skills
- developing affective skills
- caring for self.

However, Blake (2005) notes that there are few studies which test these benefits. In one such study, Connell (2006) evaluates journals kept by students during a field course in Pacific island states and finds that the students were questioning notions of discovery, cultural sensitivity and autonomy whilst also developing valuable social skills.

Journals are not only advocated as a tool for reflective thinking, but also as a means of assessing reflection, as the individual will have a physical record of their thoughts and emotions based on their experiences. McGuinness and Simm (2005) argue that the use of diaries provides educators and researchers with an opportunity to assess a student's understanding of complex issues. In their discussion on fieldwork, they contend that the initial hostilities of students towards 'deep' forms of learning subsided as students started to engage with more highly developed questions. They attribute this not just to the use of diaries but to the use of diaries in long-haul fieldwork. Therefore, journals can provide evidence of reflection. However, Plack *et al.* (2005) argue that without a means of assessment, educators cannot fully understand how journal writing can facilitate reflective thinking.

Some authors have developed methods to assess the level or type of reflection present in journals (see Plack *et al.* 2005; Plack *et al.* 2007; Williams *et al.* 2002; Wong *et al.* 1995). The reason to assess reflective journals is to provide a benchmark for the reflective process (Plack *et al.* 2007). Berwick and Whalley (2000) contend that journal entries provide a record of experience that can be used as research data. In their study on the learning of Japanese culture by Canadian high school students, they find that students experience personal growth owing to the ability to reflect on social encounters in journals. However, there are concerns about how to judge reflection because it is such a personal process.

Bourner (2003) argues that assessment is difficult because of the subjective nature of learning. However, the author suggests that we can assess reflection in the same way we can assess critical thinking, by looking for searching questions. Bourner (2003) relates this idea to surface learning versus deeper learning, where surface learning is the uncritical discussion of facts and opinions and deeper learning is the questioning of those facts and opinions. Bourner (2003) composed a list of questions which characterise reflective thinking and which can be used to demonstrate the presence of reflection (see Table 12.2). The author argues that these questions can allow for an objective process as they let researchers identify searching questions which are independent from the content of the experience. The questions proposed by Bourner (2003) allow researchers to determine the presence of reflective thinking independent from the content of the experience. Therefore, these questions can be applied to geography field trip journals just as easily as to the nursing practicum journals used in the research by Blake (2005) and Simpson and Courtney (2007).

Table 12.2 Questions for assessing reflective thinking in student writing (adapted from Bourner 2003)

1. What has most surprised you about your experience?
2. What patterns can you recognize within the experience?
3. What was the most fulfilling and least fulfilling part? And what does that suggest to you about your values?
4. What happened that contradicted and/or confirmed any prior beliefs?
5. Compare how you feel about the experience now with how you felt about it at the time.
6. What does the experience suggest to you about your strengths, weaknesses, and opportunities for development?
7. How else could you view your experience?
8. What did you learn from that experience about how you react to various situations?
9. What other options did you have at the time regarding your experience?
10. Was there anything familiar to you about the experience?
11. What might you do differently as a result of the experience and your reflections on it?
12. What actions do your reflections lead you to?

However, these questions evaluate presence/absence of reflective thinking. They do not allow for a more in-depth assessment of the level of reflection on the experience. Several other researchers have proposed criteria for assessing the level of reflective thinking and learning, three of which are outlined in Table 12.3. These assessment criteria involve the evaluation of reflection levels where journal entries can be graded from shallow or low levels of reflection to deeper or higher levels of reflection.

Boud *et al.* (1985b) argue that there are three elements in the Reflective Process: returning to experience, attending to feelings, and re-evaluating experience (see Table 12.3). Plack *et al.* (2005) use the Reflective Process developed by Boud *et al.* (1985b) as three elements in a nine-element system to assess inter-rater reliability of the categorisation of journals. The authors found that this method of assessing reflection in journals was reliable for determining competence in reflective thinking for educational purposes. Wong *et al.* (1995) also used a modification of the Reflective Process to code journals; however, these authors extended the model to include six sub-categories: attending to feelings, association, integration, validation, appropriation and outcome of reflection. The authors found that this method allowed them to distinguish between reflectors and non-reflectors and to then separate reflectors in the first three levels (attending to feelings, association, integration) from the final three levels (validation, appropriation, outcome of reflection). Wong *et al.* (1995) also used broad categories derived from the Model of Reflection (see Mezirow *et al.* 1990 cited in Wong *et al.* 1995). This model categorises individuals as non-reflectors, reflectors and critical reflectors (see Table 12.3). Wong *et al.* (1995) suggest that journal writing can be evaluated for the presence or absence of reflection. This assessment process classifies individual students into categories rather than categorising statements in journals.

In his seminal work on learning domains, Bloom differentiates between orders of cognitive ability (see Bloom 1956). There are six levels of cognitive processing which have become the basis in developing learning objectives within higher education: Knowledge, Comprehension, Application, Analysis, Synthesis and Evaluation. These levels were incorporated into a Coding Schema for Reflective Essays by Cuppernull *et al.* (2004) to evaluate reflective thinking. Bloom's Taxonomy was modified to allow for three levels of assessment (see Table 12.3). This schema was tested by Plack *et al.* (2007), assessed for inter-rater reliability, and applied to journal entries of medical students. The assessment criteria were deemed reliable as a method of determining higher order thinking in student journals. Plack *et al.* (2007) stress the need to provide an assessment procedure which can evaluate competence in reflection without the need to judge topics or themes. Therefore, though an assessment procedure was developed for reflection on paediatric clerkship, it could also be transferred to other areas such as field trip or travel experiences.

All three methods outlined in Table 12.3 have been tested for reliability. However, assessing journals focuses on the qualitative analysis of whole

Table 12.3 Comparison of levels of reflection in three assessment methods

Reflective Process[a]	*Model of Reflection*[b]	*Coding Schema for Reflective Essays using Levels of Bloom's Taxonomy*[c]
Returning to Experience: Evidence of a recollection of events, replaying initial experience, description of significant aspects of the experience.	*Non Reflection:* Evidence of the description of experiences with no questioning or evaluation of events.	*Data Gathering:* Based on Bloom's Taxonomy levels of knowledge and comprehension. A description of experiences which can include explanations of events and descriptions of thoughts, feelings or actions. Recognition of gaps in knowledge (surprise or confusion) or recognition of interesting, different or confusing things related to experience.
Attending to Feelings: Evidence of the consideration of the event and acknowledgement of feelings related to or resulting from the experience.	*Reflection:* Evidence of reflection through the exploration of experiences in order to understand the situation or to make decisions about the situation. Evidence of moving beyond describing events to attempting to question, analyse or understand the experience.	*Data Analysis:* Based on Bloom's Taxonomy level of analysis. Evidence of deconstructing the experience through the analysis of what happened. Evidence of differentiation of perceptions, feelings, thoughts and facts. Evidence of the examination of alternative explanations, the raising of questions, and the exploration of why a particular experience stands out as interesting, different, confusing, unique, etc.
Re-evaluating Experience: Evidence of re-examination of the experience with regard to intent. There may	*Critical Reflection:* Evidence of exploring the existence of problems related	*Conclusion Drawing:* Based on Bloom's Taxonomy levels of synthesis and

Continued

Table 12.3 Continued

Reflective Process[a]	Model of Reflection[b]	Coding Schema for Reflective Essays using Levels of Bloom's Taxonomy[c]
be a reappraisal of current or future events based on past experiences. There may be evidence of association (relating new knowledge with previous knowledge), integration (new relationships amongst experiences), validation (explore the truth of new insights, thoughts and perceptions), or appropriation (incorporation of new meaning/knowledge into personal knowledge, behaviour or attitude).	to an experience, probing how the problem exists or underlying assumptions related to the experience. There may be a criticism of personal assumptions or evidence of modification of biases or preconceived understandings of events.	evaluation. Evidence of attempts to draw conclusions based on the analysis of experiences, the discussion of different strategies for the future, the recognition of what has been learned from the event or experience.

Notes

a Developed by Boud *et al.* (1985b); tested by Plack *et al.* (2005).
b Developed by Mezirow *et al.* (1990) in Wong *et al.* (1995); tested by Wong *et al.* (1995).
c Developed by Cuppernull *et al.* (2004); coding schema provided by L. Cuppernull, personal communication, 15 November 2007; tested by Plack *et al.* (2007).

journals through discussions between two or more coders. Though this method may be reliable for the assessment of journals as educational assignments, it is difficult for other researchers to then apply these models to journals if the goal is to explore reflective content and not to assign grades. Therefore, in order to allow for journal entries to be used as research data in studies on travel learning a new coding system has been designed by the authors of this chapter (see Table 12.4).

Common elements of the Reflective Process, the Model of Reflection, and the Coding Schema for Reflective Essays were used to create the Reflective Content Coding Categories, a three category system that will allow researchers to code statements based on the level of reflection present for the purpose of understanding and evaluating reflective thinking and content.

In the first level, which is the Recollection of experience phase, experiences are remembered and described in the students' writing. This phase is similar to the first level of the Reflective Process and the Model of Reflection as there is no further reflection associated with the experience. Recollection becomes the 'what happened' stage where students recall and describe events, identifying important experiences.

The second level is the Recognition phase, where there is evidence of surface reflection. The importance of the event and the reaction to the event are

Table 12.4 Reflective content coding categories

Category	Coding description	Evidence
Recollection of experience	Description of experiences based on recollection.	• Description • Recollection • *What happened?*
Recognition (surface reflection)	Important or interesting aspects of experiences are recognised and considered through the use of questions, the discussion of feelings, perceptions and thoughts. There is an indication of the results of an experience without further analysis.	• Use of questions • Recognition of emotions, perceptions, thoughts and notable elements • Pointing out multiple factors related to experience • Recognition of the importance of this experience • Reaction to the experience • *What do I think about what happened?*
Reflection (deeper reflection)	Experiences are explored and analysed and information about experience is synthesised and used to draw conclusions. Past and future experiences may be assessed based on the current experience. New understanding, meaning and/or insights are discussed. There may be recognition of patterns, an integration of prior knowledge, judgement, justification, criticism or conclusions.	• Evaluation of assumptions • Comparing or contrasting experiences and/or ideas • Discussion of change in emotions, perceptions, attitude or behaviour • Discussion of lessons learned, new insights or conclusions • *Why did this happen?* • *Why is this experience important?*

considered. This phase is similar to the results section of a paper, where elements of experiences are presented but not analysed in any depth. In the Reflective Process, emotional responses to experiences are recognised while the Model of Reflection and the Coding Schema for Reflective Essays consider this stage to involve the use of questions and the recognition of perceptions and thoughts related to the initial experience.

The third and final level is the Reflection phase which involves deeper reflective thinking on experiences. This is similar to the final level for each previous coding method (see Table 12.3) as it involves a more in-depth evaluation of experiences where information is synthesised and used to draw conclusions. This is the 'why' phase of reflection where experiences are analysed in some detail and is similar to the discussion section of a paper.

Reflection may involve the consideration of past or future experiences based on a current event, or may indicate new understandings, meanings or insights based on the assessment of an experience. This phase could also involve the discussion of changes in thoughts, feelings, attitudes or behaviours based on the outcome of the experience analysis. This three-phase system can allow for individual statement assessment, creating a richer data set which can be used in evaluating reflective learning in travel.

Assessing reflective learning experiences in travel

The goal of reflective learning assessment needs to be determined before data are collected and analysed. Providing individuals with journaling instructions is a question that must be addressed by the educator or researcher before journaling starts. If the goal of research is to determine whether or not individuals are reflecting, then limited instructions should be given so as not to bias student interpretation of experience. However, if the goal is to encourage reflection, then more specific instructions need to be given relating to the reflection process so that individuals are made aware of the expectations of how to evaluate their experience in journals.

In assessing learning experiences in long-haul field trips, it is not only important to identify presence or absence of reflection on travel experiences, but also to determine if individuals are reflecting at a surface level or a deeper level. Therefore, statements need to be qualified in terms of the level of reflection that is occurring (if any). The three-level system presented in Table 12.4 can help researchers determine if there are deeper level reflections regarding field trip or travel experiences.

Determining reflective thinking levels can lead researchers to better understand the travel experience as part of experiential learning. This can also lead to the exploration of numerous other variables of interest which could be addressed using the journal content data. Some of these areas include:

- Student reflection: Are all students reflecting in the same way or are some students reflecting at a deeper level than other students?
- Reflective thinking and sex: Do both males and females reflect in the same way or are there sex differences in the level of reflection?
- Reflective content: Is there a relationship between the content of experiences and the reflection process? Are there certain experiences that are considered more deeply than other experiences?
- Context of reflection: Is there a relationship between the place or context of the experience and the process of reflection? For example, do individuals find themselves reflecting more on experiences which occur within tourist areas, during meals or while on transportation?
- Trip Timeline and Reflection: Do individuals show similar reflection patterns on experiences throughout the trip or do reflection patterns vary during certain times (the beginning, middle or end of the trip)?

In assessing these areas of interest, important reflective thinking variables can be isolated to further explore the relationship between reflection and experience. Therefore, along with qualifying the statement in terms of its reflection level, other data should be extracted (see Table 12.5).

Content findings can be quantified to identify major areas of thought in student travel experiences. In assessing the content of journals, categories could be linked to Table 12.1 to determine if students are demonstrating or reporting on learning outcomes and skill development in cognitive, affective, psychomotor or personal domains. Williams *et al.* (2002) evaluated reflection by physical therapy students during placements and identified the major themes which were being reflected upon:

- process of decision making
- complexity of social interaction
- effects of the environment on learning
- acquisition of organisational skills (flexibility and adaptation)
- integrating previous learning
- evaluation of learning.

These themes could help inform subject-based coding processes as many of these themes can cross over into travel and geographic experiences. For example, the complexity of social interactions could be discussed by students who are learning about social rules in other nations, such as greetings.

Conclusion

Pearce and Foster (2007) argue that learning developed through travel creates a more functional, globally aware and skilled individual who will then return home and benefit their home culture. This is repeated by Noy (2004) who argues that travellers return to their home society in a much more advantageous position. According to these findings, travel – both independent and on field trips – should be actively encouraged and even financially supported as it does not benefit just the individual but also the society into which the individual will contribute. Researching reflective thinking on travel experiences may confirm or refute these findings, but the results should be analysed carefully as there are several limitations to this type of research.

First, findings of reflective thinking in journals are based on situations where participants were asked to record their experiences. This assignment may act as a catalyst for reflective thinking, meaning that individuals might not necessarily reflect on experiences if not given the means to do so through journaling. Second, how can we be sure that the reflective recognition or judgements are related to the travel or field trip experience and were not a result of previous education or experiences before the trip itself? Third, are these journals capturing true individual thoughts? True reflections on sensitive issues might not be written if the individual is aware that

Table 12.5 Example of content analysis categorisation of student journal entries for a field studies course in Morocco

Name	Sex	Statement	Reflective Content Code	Content	Context	Trip Day
Lisa	F	We were able to observe the inside of a local bakery, and were able to sample the bread first hand. Since a lot of homes do not have electricity, individuals are thus unable to bake bread. Therefore, in the mornings poor Moroccan women would bring dough into the bakery and for a couple of Dirhams their dough would be baked and be ready to be picked up within the afternoon.	Recollection	Customs and practices – bread baking	Shop – Bakery	3
Susan	F	We arrived during 'siesta' time – it was astonishing to see the number of men sitting at cafes and bars. That was a culture shock episode for me. I understand and respect Islamic religion – but I couldn't help to think about where the women were? – the wives, mothers, sisters etc. of these men who enjoyed a cup of tea with their male friends. I am so used to enjoying and experiencing my surrounding environment alone or unaccompanied by a male – when I travel. I don't think this will be a good idea here in Morocco.	Recognition	Customs and practices – male and female differences	Cafes & Bars	1
Ryan	M	The desert people have a low quality of life. Most live for less than one dollar a day. Many of the children kept asking us for water. This made me feel like a giant jerk, holding my giant bottle of water. I was questioning the ethics of us walking through such a poor place, I felt as though we created unattainable wants for the children that resided there by showing off our wealth.	Reflection	Socio-economic concern	Desert village	5

a researcher will assess their insights. Nairn (2005) argues that biases and perspectives related to racial or sexist thoughts might not be included in journals as the writer is not given anonymity. Fourth, reflections by individuals on an educational trip may have a more educational focus compared to travel for leisure purposes. The average tourist does not have an instructor or researcher sharing knowledge or encouraging him or her to assess experiences. Therefore, research on reflective thinking and learning in educational tourism or field trip situations may not be applicable to other travel experiences.

Despite these limitations, if it is found that there is considerable reflective thinking and experiential learning during travel experiences then this may further validate the use of field trips in educational curriculum in all areas and encourage research into the educational value of travel in determining how learning can be addressed and improved.

Section 5

Researching tourist experiences: methodological approaches

As observed in the introduction to this book, the tourist experience, or the ways in which tourists interact with and make sense of the places and people they encounter, is complex and diverse; there are, in a sense, as many tourist experiences as there are tourists. Thus, researching the tourist experience may appear to be a difficult, if not impossible, task. Nevertheless, an understanding of the tourist experience is fundamental not only to an understanding of tourism in particular, for tourism itself may be seen as a lens through which societies may themselves be studied and understood. Thus, enhancing our knowledge and understanding of the tourist experience may also, in turn, enhance our understanding of contemporary societies, both those which generate and those that receive tourists. The question that then arises is: what is the most appropriate means of researching the tourist experience, particularly if we are to reveal the depth and richness of knowledge that such research may potentially provide?

Of course, significant attention has been paid in the tourism literature to studying and researching tourism, with debates surrounding such issues as disciplinary foundations of tourism, the appropriateness of different approaches to its study, from the 'practical' to the 'philosophical' (Tribe 2002). The research path towards revealing the 'truth' about tourism (Tribe 2006) still remains complex and controversial and the lack of consensus suggests no particular methodology nor, indeed, any specific philosophy is the 'right one'. Indeed, as the chapters in the final thematic section of the book demonstrate, not only is there evidence of a continuing healthy debate with respect to the study of tourism, but also that innovative approaches can be adopted towards researching the tourist experience. In Chapter 13, Mary Beth Gouthro, suggesting that advances in qualitative approaches in tourism research may help to reveal a deeper meaning within society, explores how an anthropologically informed interpretivist approach to researching the consumption of industrial heritage may shed significant light on tourists' experience of such sites. She goes on to consider the future of qualitative study in tourism, a theme that is continued by Martine Middleton in Chapter 14, who pursues two distinctive themes: first, the role of the senses in differentiating tourist experiences, and the extent to which the senses may be culturally patterned and hierarchically organised and, second, the potential contribution of Q methodology as a means of revealing the richness of (sense-related) views and values. Finally, and with specific reference to the issue of responsible tourist behaviour, Davina Stanford considers in Chapter 15 the use of Kohlberg's Stages of Moral Development concept as a theoretical framework for exploring tourists' reactions to different informative messages designed to influence their behaviour. She concludes that this represents an innovative and, according to her research, successful means of developing communication strategies for visitor management, with implications for both environmental sustainability and the quality of tourist experience.

13 Qualitative method research and the 'tourism experience': a methodological perspective applied in a heritage setting

Mary Beth Gouthro

Introduction: tourism experience and heritage

The experience of tourism has been explored and discussed theoretically by Cohen (1979a), Uriely (2005) and Wang (1999). In places of heritage more specifically, the tourism experience has been discussed by Beeho and Prentice (1995, 1997), Chronis (2005), McIntosh and Prentice (1999), Nuryanti (1996) and Prentice *et al.* (1998). The focus of this chapter is on industrial heritage sites and, in particular, how meaningful experiences are encountered at these sites. In some accounts of tourism research, explicit links have been made between post-industrial mining sites and heritage tourism (for example, Cole 2004; Edwards and Llurdés i Coit 1996; Light and Prentice 1994; Prentice *et al.* 1998; Pretes 2002; Rudd and Davis 1998; Wanhill 2000). However, the majority of these accounts are concerned primarily with the feasibility of transitioning former industrial sites into places of tourism rather than their consumption by visitors. Thus, how and why industrial sites allow for meaningful experiences of tourism remains under-researched.

As Beeho and Prentice (1997) have asserted, theoretical discussions of experience remain fragmented in the context of heritage tourism, and have 'tended at best to be summary'. The evolution of the literature that discusses experience in tourism in general, and in the case of experiencing heritage tourism in particular, has therefore been limited. Indeed, for Chronis, in the heritage context there lacks 'a theoretical viewpoint that will assist in better understanding and facilitating the experience of the past' (Chronis 2005: 213). Thus, with the exception of Cohen's modes of experience and Uriely's postmodernist perspective on the tourist experience, broad theoretical concepts underpinning the tourism experience have not been developed to any great extent in the tourism literature.

There are inherent complexities in attempting to theorise the multifaceted nature of experiencing tourism. In particular, there remains a plethora of variables to consider in conceptualising *experience* as a broad, all encompassing phenomenon. Nuryanti (1996) makes this evident in his analysis of the postmodern heritage tourist, pointing out that the tourist experience is multifaceted because tourists use their own intellect and imagination to construct meaning. This is of interest to advances in tourism research as a fuller range of influences is considered in experiencing tourism and, more specifically, in settings of heritage. Similarly, Meethan (1996) and Ryan (2002a) observe that consuming tourism is part of a much broader process of experiencing our surroundings. For Meethan (1996), the consumption of tourism should not be viewed as a 'distinct activity', but rather as part of wider local and global influences whilst, according to Ryan (2002a), the tourism experience involves a multisensory process that includes sight, sound and smell. Tourists use all of their senses and not simply limit themselves to visual engagement, or a 'gaze'. As noted shortly, the qualitative research into industrial heritage sites described in this chapter adopts a similarly broad perspective by aligning theoretical concepts surrounding religious tourism to meaningful tourism experiences in heritage settings.

The discussion in this chapter is twofold. First, it presents and discusses the theoretical perspective applied to the methodological approach in uncovering how meaningful tourism experiences are constructed at industrial heritage sites. That is, the study discussed in this chapter applies an inquiry paradigm that adopts an interpretivist perspective (Geertz 1973, Lévi-Strauss 1966, Schwandt 1998) to the social phenomenon of tourism under study at these heritage sites. In so doing, interpretivism is used to unpack how meaning is made in meaningful tourism experiences at industrial heritage museums. Second, the chapter also acknowledges issues related to the evolution of qualitative accounts in tourism research more widely. Before doing so, however, the methodological foundation of the qualitative research undertaken at two industrial heritage sites is first introduced below.

The methodological foundation

The interpretivist perspective adopted in the study differentiates itself from other methodological perspectives in that it seeks to generate knowledge and understanding within the social context in which it functions. This is in contrast to objective or naturalistic perspectives in research, which seek to uncover causal relationships between phenomena (Denzin and Lincoln 2000b) and are, thus, associated with variations of the positivist paradigm.

In undertaking an ethnographic approach to the method of data collection in this qualitative study (Denzin 1994; Hammersley and Atkinson 1995; Tedlock 2000; Wolcott 1999), tourists visiting each of two industrial heritage museums were interviewed and observed onsite. They were studied in relation to how they interact both amongst each other and with the museum as part of their tourist experiences. The two industrial heritage museums selected for this study – the Cape Breton Miners' Museum in Glace Bay, Nova Scotia and the Big Pit Museum in South Wales – each tell the story of their respective regions' industrial past. An ethnographic approach to the data collection enhanced the potential for uncovering thick description (Geertz 1973) of the subject matter under investigation.

Interpretivism, then, as the theoretical perspective informing the qualitative inquiry of the study, is embedded in its methodological foundation. The concept of *bricoleur* (Lévi-Strauss 1966) is applied to the interpretive analysis of constructions of meaningful tourism experiences at these sites. When applied as an interpretive analytical tool, the *bricoleur* concept helps to unpack the social phenomenon of making meaning in tourism experiences. This theoretical perspective is, therefore, applied to findings presented further on in this chapter. However, before doing so, the state of qualitative research in tourism is now reviewed, the purpose being to contextualise the challenges associated with evolving perspectives of qualitative inquiry in tourism research. This is of particular relevance to this study of industrial heritage as it frames the gap in knowledge that the research discussed here set out to address.

Qualitative inquiry and its presence in tourism research

This section addresses some of the debates inherent to the nature of qualitative inquiry found in tourism research. However, before looking at qualitative research in the field of tourism in particular, developments in qualitative inquiry in social science more generally are first acknowledged, the purpose being to contextualise the state of qualitative inquiry across traditional academic disciplines, some of which inform tourism scholarship.

As Denzin and Lincoln (1998b) have commented, the state of qualitative research is the subject of ongoing debate across academic disciplines. This applies to how qualitative research is approached and executed and what makes for credible accounts of such research. Qualitative research has evolved over time through five 'moments' (Denzin and Lincoln 1998b), with categories such as 'traditionalist' and 'modernist' approaches to research evolving and then giving way to other categories of paradigmatic inquiry, such as 'blurred genres' and the 'crisis of representation'. These categories have, therefore, evolved through a positivist approach (traditionalist); to a move away from natural science measurement (modernist); then to indistinct boundaries between disciplines (blurred genres); on to a place where the generalising of social research starts to be questioned (crisis in representation); and lastly, to a growing fifth moment of qualitative research which accepts an end to grand narratives.

A splintering of perspectives in the philosophical and practical terms underpinning the above categories of qualitative inquiry has, therefore, evolved in approaches to research over time. Within these 'moments' of qualitative research, Denzin and Lincoln have in later work contended that they 'all circulate in the present, competing with and defining one another' (Denzin and Lincoln 2000a: xiv). This evolution of varying perspectives in qualitative inquiry continues to unfold, making the relatively recent nature of their impact on inquiry paradigms applied to research cause for reflection. For example, according to Denzin and Lincoln (2000b), the third moment of qualitative inquiry, namely 'blurred genres', emerged only relatively recently, around 1970, with subsequent moments following on since that time. Taking into consideration the mainstay of the positivist and deductive approaches to research since the Period of Enlightenment, the evolution of these five moments of qualitative research is evidence of significant ideological transformations to methodological perspectives in the recent past. The corresponding paradigmatic approaches applied to more recent forms of qualitative inquiry have, therefore, developed swiftly in the last half-century.

Alternative approaches to qualitative inquiry have since continued to evolve and grow (Denzin and Lincoln 2000a, 2000b). Since the beginning of the new millennium, the nature of various inquiry paradigms has developed further, with Denzin and Lincoln (2000b) proposing sixth and seventh moments in qualitative inquiry. The former possesses qualities that are post-experimental in nature, whereas the latter posits perspectives for the future and 'is concerned with moral discourse, the development of sacred textualities' (Denzin and Lincoln 2000b: 3). The seventh and last moment is, therefore, concerned with furthering critical debates in the social sciences and humanities, addressing such issues as race, gender and class.

Nevertheless, credible forms of qualitative inquiry remain questioned by those who 'marginalize and politicize the postmodern, poststructural versions of qualitative research, equating them with radical relativism, narratives of self, and armchair commentary' (Denzin and Lincoln 2000a: xiv). Comparatively, a positivist approach to inquiry affirms that truth is found in reliable and valid research accounts, encouraging positivists to question the credibility of alternate forms of qualitative inquiry, such as an interpretivist approach, to produce truths (Tribe 2006). However, interpretivism is not in pursuit of truths; rather, it underpins the credibility of its approach 'by creating different truth-criteria … such as conformability, trustworthiness and transparency' (Tribe 2006: 369). Nevertheless, there continues to be a struggle for certain types of qualitative research to be accepted more broadly in the field of social science and, inevitably, the field of tourism research is neither immune nor excluded from the debate.

Therefore, the status of qualitative tourism research and where it fits in such perspectives deserves consideration. It is the contention of some commentators in tourism scholarship (for example, Franklin and Crang 2001; Hall 2004; Phillimore and Goodson 2004; Rojek and Urry 1997) that research in tourism has been overly influenced by a preoccupation with economic impact perspectives. Accordingly, Franklin and Crang argue that studies of tourism have also been dominated by 'policy led and industry sponsored work so the analysis tends to internalize industry led priorities and perspectives' (Franklin and Crang 2001: 5). For them, the debate surrounding tourism scholarship reveals a need for diversification and expansion from this type of set criteria, so that research inquiry develops beyond long-favoured economic discussions in tourism. Nevertheless, paradigmatic shifts in the area of tourism research have not been as forthcoming as some in the tourism academy would wish or contend they should (Coles *et al.* 2006; Morgan and Pritchard 2005; Tribe 2006), as revealed by analyses of trends in qualitative tourism research.

For example, a study of tourism research journals conducted by Riley and Love (2000) uncovered certain methodological themes in the types of research accounts published. In their analyses of four tourism research journals,[1] the number of qualitative and quantitative based studies published in these journals up to 1996 was reviewed. They found that the majority of studies published in these journals were quantitative in nature; that is, they mostly adopted a positivism paradigm in the presentation and contribution to the body of knowledge in tourism. In a follow-on study of a separate selection of tourism journals,[2] Phillimore and Goodson (2004) took Riley and Love's analyses further to consider the state of qualitative research in tourism between 1996 and 2003. Adopting a more holistic approach to their analysis, Phillimore and Goodson (2004) explored beyond specific types of methods used in studies to include factors such as whether or not methodological reflexivity was employed in reporting the findings as opposed to 'research as expert' perspective. Nevertheless, their study revealed that tourism research continues to be associated with Denzin and Lincoln's 'traditional' period, reflecting the fact that objective, depersonalised accounts remain common in the tourism literature (2004).

The focus of this chapter is, therefore, on research undertaken in a qualitative study of tourism at places of heritage, which embraced an alternative approach in its methodological foundation. As previously noted, this study adopted an interpretivist perspective in investigating how tourists experience meaning at heritage sites, the purpose being not only to enhance knowledge and understanding of the experience of tourism encounters in places of industrial heritage, but also to explore the potential contribution of interpretivist approach to tourism research more generally. In the section that follows, contemporary perspectives on heritage experiences are considered as a contextual framework for this qualitative study of tourism at industrial heritage museums.

Perspectives of the heritage tourism experience

In his widely cited paper, 'A Phenomenology of Tourist Experiences', Cohen (1979a) categorises tourist experiences along a continuum, ranging from the recreational at one end, through diversionary, experiential, experimental, to the existential at the other end. Within these categories, the tourist whose spiritual centre is located firmly 'at home' is in pursuit of mere pleasure (the recreational), whilst the tourist whose spiritual centre is 'out there' takes on the characteristics of a modern pilgrim (the existential). A more recent account by Uriely (2005) provides an analysis of wider conceptual developments in the tourism literature with respect to experience. Acknowledging the influence of seminal tourism works (Boorstin 1964; Cohen 1979a;

MacCannell 1973), Uriely underscores the subjective nature of the tourist experience, supporting this stance by grounding the theoretical complexities of experience in the postmodern arguments of Lash and Urry (1987), Rojek (1995) and Urry (1990a). It is Uriely's (2005: 210) view that subsequent theoretical conceptualisations of the tourist experience should be 'complementary extensions to the earlier theories' as opposed to the results of attempts to contest them.

More specifically to the domain of heritage and tourism experience, Prentice *et al.* (1998) attempted to make strides in the experiential dimensions of tourism by analysing, through the identification of common themes of experience, the benefits of visiting industrial heritage. This was achieved by asking visitors about their range of experiences within an attraction and how these experiences may be facilitated (Prentice *et al.* 1998). In their study, labels were affixed to categories of heritage consumption (i.e. benefits and experience) which were then developed into market segments. Research studies such as this are of undoubted value in terms of their practical applications, the results potentially informing management practice at heritage sites as well as enhancing knowledge and understanding about the types of experiences visitors have at these sites.

Moreover, both quantitative and qualitative methods of research have been used in exploring aspects of consumption and experience of heritage. For example, studies by Beeho and Prentice (1995, 1997) apply models borrowed from leisure and outdoor recreation theory (Haas *et al.* 1980; Manning 1986) to measure the benefits associated with the heritage experience of visitors at two different heritage sites: the Blists Hill museum (1995) and New Lanark World Heritage Village (1997). The findings of each study apply an ASEB[3] Grid Analysis that incorporates the Manning-Haas Demand Hierarchy to conclude that this theoretical framework provides 'a more effective consumer-orientated approach to museum marketing research' (Beeho and Prentice 1995: 249). Beeho and Prentice have, therefore, suggested that such theoretical applications grounded in management sciences do well to inform what more can be known about experiencing heritage. The outcomes of their research then offer practical management applications of heritage experiences in order to benefit heritage attractions in the form of product development initiatives and customer-centric management.

The types of visitors that heritage sites attract has been another common and related area of inquiry of studies into the consumption of heritage sites. Various research perspectives have been adopted and applied in the tourism literature. Light and Prentice (1994) studied the socio-demographic characteristics of visitors to reveal that the majority were of middle class and well educated. A later study by Prentice *et al.* (1998) of a Welsh heritage site also captured the socio-demographic characteristics of visitors, thus grouping them into experience market segments based on their motivation to visit. Pretes' (2002) study of mining tourists offers an in-depth narrative taken from tours of existing silver mines in operation in Bolivia. Rudd and Davis

(1998) explored how a Utah corporation promotes copper mine tourism to alleviate public concern for the environment.

However, the manner in which visitors experience tourism in a meaning-ful way at industrial heritage sites still remains relatively under-researched with, in particular, a limited variety of qualitative perspectives in evidence. That is, the theoretical context between tourism and heritage remains less developed in the literature. As Uriely has pointed out, experiencing heritage is an 'emerging research area of heritage tourism' (Uriely 2005: 206) and, as a contribution to this emergent research, the literature informing meaning-ful accounts in religious tourism is now reviewed as a basis for interpreting visitors' consumption of heritage.

Religious interpretations of experiencing heritage tourism

A unique aspect of the nature of qualitative inquiry in this study is that it aims to address how meaningful experiences are constructed by visiting places of industrial heritage. The study is, furthermore, aligned and interpreted through a religious tourism perspective. This approach is taken in the study's inquiry paradigm to help reveal deeper meanings inherent in the heritage tourism experience and its synergies with religious tourism pursuits. In other words, religious activities in tourism are considered for their parallels in the mani-festation of experiencing heritage tourism in meaningful ways.

The industrial heritage site is not, by nature, a religious site. Yet, where pilgrimage and related practice is interpreted to be meaningful in the reli-gious context, links may be made to the tourism experience in a heritage setting. Visitors make a pilgrimage to a heritage site because the site is mean-ingful to them. The pilgrimage context applied to the heritage site here then adopts the notion that pilgrimage need not be religious (sacred) in nature (Digance 2003; Frey 2004). Rather, as Eade and Sallnow (1991a) assert, the motivation behind pilgrimage is historically and culturally specific. The phys-ical features of industrial heritage are also unique to pilgrimage. As Coleman states, 'pilgrimage does not merely involve an intensified form of prayer' (Coleman 2004: 53), but rather involves varying forms of engagement with the physical assets, thus providing for meaning in pilgrimage. The physical assets engaged in the likeness of pilgrimage here are made up of the remnants of industrial heritage. The ethnographic excerpts below that are drawn from the study are, therefore, interpreted in terms of how visitors made meaning of their tourist experience.

In the following passage, a direct link is made between having family working in the area of the Big Pit Museum in South Wales and also identi-fying with being Welsh:

> *Young Welsh couple*: We are both Welsh, proud of our heritage. My grandfather was a miner. It is really interesting to be underground. I am proud to be Welsh [lifts up shirt sleeve to display tattoo of red dragon].

In essence, meaning is made because the group are experiencing something together, in this case a pilgrimage to an industrial heritage site together.

For some visitors to industrial heritage sites, it is not necessarily the coal mining industry per se that brings them to these areas. Rather, it is a link to the industrial past more generally and, in this case, the exploitation of the earth – mining – being at one time a major employer in Wales. For example, for the following visitors the death of their father in the North Wales slate quarry and the relationship between him and heavy industry resonates at the Big Pit Museum:

> *Couple (brother 70 years old and sister 61 years old) from Scotland*: Our father died in a quarry, he was the quarry man, the manager ... he had two accidents, he said that if there was ever a third, he wouldn't get out. There was a blast, he was hit from behind, suffered a fractured skull and punctured lung ... he didn't make it. He couldn't get away quick enough ... children need to see this, to see how hard it was ... our grandfather was a miner. And our dad a quarry man ... I don't think men would go down the mines today ... would they? Not that they shouldn't, mind you. Would be good for them. But they had no choice then ... did they ... ?

This brother and sister are undertaking a 'pilgrimage' to the Big Pit Museum to remember the untimely death of their father in an industrial accident. These accounts were shared when these siblings were asked about their experience of the site and what made it meaningful to them. Through a pilgrimage, then, to an industrial site, they are remembering a family member and also building a sense of meaning of the site for themselves.

Although reference to pilgrimage has traditionally been associated with religious connotations, Graburn (1977) reminds us that tourism itself has ancient roots in the act of pilgrimage. In the accounts described above, visitors to places of heritage sites are experiencing tourist pursuits, yet they come to these sites for particular reasons. As Frey (2004) has noted, tourists who engage in pilgrimage do so for any number of reasons, including the cultural, spiritual or personal. It is argued then that the history associated with industrial heritage sites resonates with some of its visitors, making the account of the experience meaningful *because* it is shared with family and friends.

In another case at the Cape Breton Miners' Museum, an elderly lady makes a point of bringing her family to the museum to share in the industrial history of the region with those important to her – family members. Although it has been 50 years since she lived in the area, she brings children and grandchildren here to show them *her* past and, in essence, they make pilgrimage to the area *with* her:

> *Elderly lady*: I brought my family here today. My family originally came [to Canada] from the Ukraine, at the foot of the Carpathian Mountains ... in 1909, my father came here from Russia. I left Glace Bay in 1943, and

remember making my brothers their lunch when they started working in the mines. I was 13 years old. I tell my kids these stories, and they always tell me 'g'way ma ... you're telling tales. That is not true ... ' they don't believe me!

In the above excerpt, this lady is making a point of visiting the Cape Breton region and the coal mining museum with her family a priority. In so doing, she is sharing in the meaning and representations of the area's industrial remnants by making pilgrimage to the museum. The experience of being there is made more meaningful because it is indeed shared with loved ones.

Reflecting on the above examples of pilgrimage in heritage, these visitors are furthermore making personal connections to the site, the history, and in effect, also sharing a meaningful tourism experience with other family members. Not unlike pilgrimage to Australia's Uluru Rock to connect with its spiritual and emotional significance (McGrath 1991), pilgrimage to heritage tourism settings may hold similar appeal to visitors.

Pilgrimage, then, is a useful theoretical concept in terms of its applicability to postmodern manifestations of experiencing tourism in meaningful ways. The concept of pilgrimage and its diverse practices show how it has evolved over time, thus reflecting more secular examples in practice. If a site gives a meaningful experience to a visitor, it can also demonstrate its ability to make a spiritual connection for the visitor. Thus, in taking religious tourism pursuits into consideration, the tourism experiences at these heritage sites are interpreted to uncover the similar meaningful pursuits for its visitors often associated with religious contexts of tourism.

From a methodological perspective, it is thus the notion of the *bricoleur* that binds together the interpretive analyses applied to the above. For Lévi-Strauss' (1966), the *bricoleur* is a person who constructs something new from a range of separate functioning materials so as to perform a newly specialist function. This concept is integrated into the inquiry paradigm of the qualitative study so that notions inherent to social practice may be unpacked to uncover meaning in tourism experiences.

The *bricoleur* lends well to the interpretivist perspective of the study. As a theoretical concept, the *bricoleur* performs tasks with tools and materials that are at hand, and acquired from 'odds and ends' (Lévi-Strauss 1966). The *bricoleur*, then, appreciates the holistic view in the practices contributing to social phenomena: '[t]he scientist creating events (changing the world) by means of structures and the "bricoleur" creating structures by means of events' (Lévi-Strauss 1966: 22). Thus, what can be taken from this conceptual approach is the 'blending together of whatever is available into a complete story' that frames the inquiry into the social evidence under study at these places of industrial heritage. The social evidence considered in this study is that which encompasses visiting, talking, reflection, and contemplation with and among other visitors at the sites. It is then considered for its parallels with other theoretical concepts and applications in tourism (e.g. pilgrimage) so as to interpret meaningful experiences in tourism. In the process, the visitors of heritage are creating meaning in an industrial past through their experiences of the site and because it is done with others.

Accordingly, for Geertz, social activity and its manifestations in society (e.g. experiencing tourism) is not something that can be 'causally attributed; it is a context, something within which they can be intelligibly – that is *thickly* – described' (Geertz 1973: 14). In effect, the research findings are first interpreted then described in relation to theoretical 'odds and ends', that is, pilgrimage, in unpacking how tourism experience is made meaningful at these heritage sites. This supports an interpretivist stance to the findings above for their ability to contribute to the created knowledge in accounts of 'tourism research'. By adopting an interpretivist perspective to the methodological foundation of the study, deeper meaning inherent in the complex ways in which the heritage is experienced in tourism is uncovered. As a qualitative study that is both inductive and interpretive, a deeper level of analysis is enabled for the social practices underpinning meaningful experiences that are made in places of heritage tourism. It is infrequent that the minutia of social practice has been examined in the context of tourism experience. The interpretivist theoretical perspective allows for knowledge into the making of meaning of visitation to places of industrial heritage to be constructed as a result.

As the previous discussion on the status of qualitative accounts of tourism research uncovered, there is a gap in the methods employed in heritage tourism literature (quantitative vs qualitative) in which another level of understanding in the consumption of heritage experience is obtained. Although the findings above capture and conceptualise a study taken into tourism experience of heritage, gaps remain in the body of knowledge supporting perspectives of tourism experience. The section that follows acknowledges some of the challenges discussed in relation to the domain of qualitative accounts in tourism research.

Qualitative inquiry and the future of tourism research

While evolutions of research inquiry serve to expand the boundaries of 'accepted' approaches in research more generally, tourism as a field remains currently at the mercy of accepted practice in tourism scholarship. This impacts upon what tourism research is published and why. Hall (2004) has pointed out that specific approaches to qualitative research in tourism are not embraced by the editorial boards of some tourism journals, reflecting a hesitancy of these editorial boards to publish certain types of research. Some of these approaches include those that engage a reflexive point of view in the research, those written in the first person (Hall 2004). Such perspectives, however, do not set out to devalue quantitative studies in tourism. Indeed, quantitative research serves the field in building a knowledge base. As Phillimore and Goodson (2004: 4) acknowledge, quantitative approaches used in tourism research demonstrate that 'there is an ongoing need for statistical insights into aspects such as market and migration trends, income generation, and so forth'. Nevertheless, other commentators see an opportunity for the field of tourism research to diversify in its methodological perspectives. As Franklin and Crang (2001: 78) argue, 'what is lacking in tourism research and academic settings is discussion and debate on the diverse qualitative research approaches that can be employed to do justice to the inter-disciplinary domain of tourism studies – and hence to facilitate legitimation of the area of tourism scholarship'.

As with Hall, Franklin and Crang contend that this may be done by adding more reflexive accounts in tourism research, because tourism is itself a reflection of broader social phenomena in contemporary life. Advances in qualitative approaches in tourism research help us understand 'the human dimensions of society, which in tourism include its social and cultural implications' (Phillimore and Goodson 2004: 4). Similarly, first person accounts in tourism research are still largely absent in published accounts of qualitative tourism research. An exception to this is the work of Morgan and Pritchard, an auto-ethnographic account of meanings found in souvenirs of tourism. In their own commentary, they acknowledge the hesitancy of the tourism academy to embrace their adopted method of qualitative inquiry. They comment '"blind" reviewing makes a fully auto-ethnographic narrative difficult to achieve' (Morgan and Pritchard 2005: 48) rendering this type of research not easily presentable for publication, which in turn makes it subject to a high degree of rejection (Phillimore and Goodson 2004). Indeed, there has been a continued preference in the tourism academy for specific ways of reporting tourism research, those that convey 'an impression of objectivity and scientific rationality which is almost the antithesis of the realisations of reflexive modernity' (Hall 2004: 142).

Tribe's (2006) 'knowledge force-field of tourism' further reflects that the trends mentioned above continue to influence how knowledge is created in the tourism academy. The force-field model reveals that accounts captured from the objective and distanced researcher continue to be encouraged in their inquiry approaches to tourism research: 'A deeply entrenched mind/body dichotomy has prevailed in research where an objective mind has been cultivated as if it was detached and immune from bodily impressions' (Tribe 2006: 362–63). By taking an objective approach to tourism research, it offers 'reliable' accounts of new knowledge making for valid contributions to the field. This could act as a hindrance for other forms of research in being able to inform the tourism academy. Tribe (2006) has, therefore, argued that new knowledge is attainable by incorporating the contextual nature of the researcher's mind and body to inform *credible* and *trustworthy* accounts of research. This would include research written from a reflexive standpoint, that is, first person accounts.

Current barriers to publication in tourism research in which authors are required to write in the third person was first acknowledged in Riley and

Love's (2000) study. This again reflects an engrained practice across tourism academy where classic scientific methods of reporting research are often standard. The accepted criteria for certain types of research to be published often means many are not considered unless major modifications are made to the work. The editorial policy of many tourism journals reinforces this mindset, as Hall contends further:

> Under the rubric of convention and style, academic institutions and the culture of academia have therefore greatly influenced what is acceptable or unacceptable in being represented as tourism knowledge.
>
> (Hall 2004: 142)

Moreover, there are *other* issues in the tourism academy that hitherto further impact the way in which tourism research is reported. For example, it is argued that tourism research to date has primarily used qualitative methods as 'a set of methods rather than a set of thinking tools' (Phillimore and Goodson 2004: 5). To engage a *different set of thinking tools* is to equip researchers with an alternative way of executing a certain approach to research. To do so means to develop new ways in which things come to be known ontologically. This would then make a contribution to alternate perspectives in qualitative research and its ability to inform the creation of new knowledge in tourism research. In particular to doctoral studies in tourism, rarely is training for the philosophy and practice of qualitative inquiry incorporated into the curriculum, even though it remains common in sociological and anthropological study environments (Riley and Love 2000). Therefore, such a practice further inhibits the development of research in the field of tourism. Other fields of study in the social sciences have embraced advances of qualitative inquiry, leaving the field of tourism with still some catching up to do:

> ... tourism scholars have generally been more hesitant in their adoption and acceptance of qualitative research, and more specifically in their understanding of the philosophical and theoretical process that underpins knowledge production and practice.
>
> (Phillimore and Goodson 2004: 4)

This insight is set against a study conducted by Botterill *et al.* (2002) of doctoral dissertations of tourism in the UK and Ireland. Their study revealed that there was little sign of in-depth engagement 'with epistemological debate as evidenced by the use of the term itself or its principle form of expression in the Social Sciences, that is, the terms "Constructivism" and "Realism"' (Botterill *et al.* 2002: 293) in doctoral level research in tourism. It is quite conceivable, then, that developments in qualitative inquiry continue to be exercised in the social sciences more broadly, yet the field of tourism lags behind. On another level, the diversity of evolving criteria for alternate approaches to qualitative inquiry feed animosity within scholarship and thereby stoke further debate across conflicting camps of 'academic tribes' (Tribe 2006).

Nonetheless, as Jamal and Hollinshead (2001) point out, scholarship need not accept that 'anything goes' as far as qualitative research is concerned. On the contrary, in their considered discussion addressing the 'underserved power of qualitative research' in tourism (Jamal and Hollinshead 2001), debates in scholarship are cause for further reflection. One way of gauging the credible accounts in qualitative research is to see if certain objectives are accomplished. For example, 'did the multiple points of view, narratives and emotions described in the text offer the reader an in-depth, substantive understanding of the topic of the research?' (Jamal and Hollinshead 2001: 76). Conversely, for Geertz, explanations offered in research should be measured 'not against a body of uninterpreted data, radically thinned descriptions', but against the 'power of the scientific imagination to bring us in touch with the lives of strangers' (Geertz 1973: 16).

If the domain of tourism research is to progress the field's body of knowledge, then '[q]ualitative researchers in tourism must resist attempts to discredit qualitative inquiry methods just at the time when the field is coming of age methodologically and theoretically' (Morgan and Pritchard 2005: 48). This means taking into consideration those research approaches that adopt participatory and situated accounts that use 'novel forms of expressing lived experience (including auto-biographical, multi-voiced and visual representations' in approaching tourism research (2005).

In the study of experience at industrial heritage discussed in this chapter, alternate perspectives on qualitative inquiry were taken into consideration. The inquiry paradigm has allowed for the voices of the subjects to inform the interpretation of the research findings. This is a step away from a traditionalist application of qualitative inquiry in which researcher is positioned as sole expert in interpreting the accounts as part of the research process (Denzin and Lincoln 2000b).

Some of the views surrounding the current state of qualitative tourism research are discussed here to acknowledge some of the issues and ideological debates currently impacting the academy of tourism and, thus, influencing the approach adopted in the study of experience at industrial heritage. Yet, even though for some the domain of tourism research is itself new (Franklin and Crang 2001), for others the positivist approach has dominated how tourism research is done, reported and subsequently published (Ateljevic 2000; Jamal and Hollinshead 2001; Riley and Love 2000). In terms of the impact this has on tourism publications, the extent to which the underlying nuances of meaningful experiences are understood and theoretically underpinned in research accounts of tourism remain limited.

Nevertheless, recent accounts of tourism research have shown that intellectual ruptures and challenges are becoming more commonplace in the field, particularly since the inception of tourism as an academic field of inquiry.

That is, in academic contexts tourism has not been considered as a discipline but rather a field of study (Tribe 1997). Casting a broader view of methodological perspectives onto the field of tourism can only serve to expand on the current breadth and depth of knowledge it produces. This chapter has sought to expand perspectives upon tourism's current reach in theoretical and methodological contexts in qualitative research. This is not only in reference to tourism experience that is studied in places of industrial heritage, but also to consider the possibilities of alternative research perspectives into the future.

Notes

1 Riley and Love (2000) examined publications in: *Journal of Travel Research*, *Annals of Tourism Research*, *Tourism Management* and the *Journal of Travel & Tourism Marketing*. The justification for these choices was '[t]hese journals were chosen to represent the broad range of disciplines that publish tourism research' (2000: 171).
2 Phillimore and Goodson's (2004) review of tourism journals included two used in Riley and Love's (2000) study: *Annals of Tourism Research* and *Tourism Management*. However, in Phillimore and Goodson's analyses, they added *Tourism Geographies*, *Journal of Sustainable Tourism*, *International Journal of Tourism Research*, *Progress in Tourism and Hospitality Research* and *Leisure Studies*.
3 ASEB (Activities, Settings, Experiences and Benefits) is a grid analysis modified from Manning (1986) by the authors (Beeho and Prentice 1995: 232) and is based on the elements of SWOT analysis.

14 Exploring space, the senses and sensitivities: spatial knowing

Martine C. Middleton

Introduction

Tourists and travel serve to symbolise generic concepts within tourism studies. The places tourists travel to, and the activities they offer, form the very receptacle wherein experience is construed; one that is often particularly intense when far away from home. By travelling to different places and exploring different cultures, an evocation of the familiar and the unknown becomes compared and contrasted. In this sense, the tourist experience is a socially constructed term whereby cognition can denote meaning, derived from the multiple interpretations from social, environmental and behavioural facets that create the overall encounter (Tussyadiah and Fesenmaier 2009).

Yet there is no unanimously accepted definition or clearly defined method for operationalising intrinsic experience. As such, considerable scholarly attention has focused upon 'place' as either a physical destination or, alternatively, sought to consider the social dimension of the tourist experience, with few attempts ever made to assimilate the two. As might be expected, destinations continue to quantify tourists and travel through the measurement of determinable factors, such as visitor numbers, origin, motive of visit and length of stay. Yet, many authors know that far from being a homogenous group, individuals are able to share the same surroundings, yet experience new and unfamiliar settings in a multitude of different ways (Crouch 2000). Indeed, Hollinshead (1999) argues that it is such multiplicity that leads the tourist to be perceived as an agent of seeing, being, experience, cultural invention and knowing. Each individual creates his/her own experience based on backgrounds, values, attitudes and beliefs determined by internal means, not external. Such determinants of self, especially when elsewhere, detract from the external prominent quantification of 'doing' and instead highlight the intrinsic and inconspicuous consumption of 'being'. Lagerkvist (2007: 155) expands upon this assertion further to point out that places present multisensuous and highly engaging environments that particularly entwine the sensory practices performed by tourists. Howes (2005) refers to these as the intersensorial experiences of sight, taste and touch. Lagerkvist urges for a deeper and more critical evaluation of how visitors actually make sense of, and contribute to, the transformation of places.

There is a need to probe further and enquire how sensory response, senti-ment, memory and mediation may work together to create an 'intersenso-rium' through the multisensuous immersion of the body. Such an assertion combines both the spatial and social world of every tourist to embody his or her temporal surroundings through the fluid yet judicious approach of expe-riential learning. In this sense, a spatial world can represent any specific site or type of tourist place so as to form a tangible resource within which expe-rience may be accrued and possibly determined. This notion has led 'place', with its identifiable form and function, to act as the central tenet within assessing experiential learning through an emphasis upon the surrounding physical characteristics. However, a more complex and ethereal part of this enquiry is the independent cultural composition and social disposition of every tourist as a distinct and discerning individual. Thus, cultural interplay between spatial and social interaction forms a central tenet towards under-standing any dichotomy that may emerge between understanding place and people today. On balance, the role of emotion within geography deserves to receive increased acknowledgement. Crouch and Desforges (2003) and other theorists advocate the immediate and intimate notion of embodiment as a profound sensual act. Davidson and Milligan express a similar view-point stating that 'Emotions, to be sure, *take place* within and around the closest of spatial scales' (2004: 523). They argue that through an exploration of diverse senses of space, we would become better placed to appreciate the emotionally dynamic spatiality of contemporary life, aptly signified through tourism today.

It is well accepted that the continuing impact of globalisation, deregula-tion of travel and the abject incessant commercialisation of place act as evident catalysts towards facilitating unprecedented levels of growing tourist mobility. As a result, considerable academic attention remains directed towards tourist behaviour and the type of experience that results from spatial interaction (Carr 2006; Cary 2004; MacCannell 1976; Ryan 2002a). All recognise that the same activity is able to have 'differing social meanings and role relations at different times' (Kelly 1974: 192). Yet some academics argue that nothing can ever be more fundamental to tourist knowledge about the spatial character of an unfamiliar environment than sensory distinctions (Dann and Jacobsen 2003; Golledge and Stimson 1997; Rodaway 1994). One con-stant and determinable socio-demographic factor applicable to the spatial and social world of the tourist in determining experience is the tourist point of geographical origin. Perhaps, from this fixed starting point, not only geo-graphical travel may be assessed but also the spatial knowing and experience that is a natural concomitant to 'being a tourist'. It is to what extent the tourist and his or her place of origin and the chosen destination is able to 'cultur-ally connect' and engage within that experience becomes established.

The purpose of this conceptual and exploratory account is to query the role of the human senses within understanding tourism experience and thereby propose a suitable manner whereby distinctions, that may be cultural, can become illuminated. One such approach is Q methodology (Brown 1995; Stephenson 1953), which represents an established technique that allows any research text to be collated and described 'through the eyes of people' as individuals. Subsequent correlations then reveal any emergent similarities as definable groups united by their shared meanings and interpretations. Indeed, the study of subjectivity and the possible ways within which distinctions may be revealed remains crucial throughout the social sciences and, arguably, beyond. Seminal work that recognises a differentiation of the senses by Classen (1993) and others (David and Luke 2003; Howes 2003) collectively argue that different cultures present different ways of 'making sense' of the same world, a world in which the human senses actively absorb new spatial knowledge to wield into the assimilation of accrued intrinsic experience. Yet analysis of such a shared and sensory involvement remains often ignored within the construction of tourist experience, especially in any structural way. Such a contention is shared by many (Classen 1993; Howes 2003; Tuan 1998) who all believe that individuals may differ in their perceptions, yet there is nevertheless an identity or similarity of those sensed worlds shared (Rodaway 1994: 22).

Exploring the senses

Any unification between the fundamental constructs of place and space remains implicit in the assimilation of social knowledge. A social-phenomenological approach to spatial knowing seeks to build upon tourist cognition and their appreciation of a temporary environment to focus upon the 'scapes' of each individual towards their new surroundings. Many geographers agree that such man–environment relations reflect complex and dynamic problems that pose significant challenges within applied research (Amadeo 1993; Golledge 1991; Hall and Page 2009; Tuan 1974). Indeed, the tourist symbolises a motivated social/cultural being whose decisions and actions become mediated through the personal cognition of space (Gold 1992). Landscape itself carries numerous interpretations yet Cosgrove (1984: 57) sought to emphasise landscape 'as not merely the world we see, it is a construction, a composition of the world'. Such concepts are perpetuated by Tuan (1998) who raises connections between landscape explorations that deliberately include cultural values and spatial attitudes as agents of more profound emotional and spiritual forms of spatial knowing. Adaptations of landscape include 'cityscapes' (Lynch 1981), 'knowledgescapes' (Nonaka and Konno 1998) and, significantly, 'sensoryscapes' (Crang 1999; Rodaway 1994) with the construction of social knowledge to be as much a process of interpretation as understanding. As Shariq (1999: 224) suggests, spatial learning acts as interplay between the internal and external forces that combine to form a 'knowledgescape' for each individual. This forms a temporal 'knowedgescape' created in a form comparable to the Japanese concept of 'Ba', which is equivalent to 'place' in English. The concept represents the shared physical, virtual and mental spaces for knowledge interchange, with knowledge being insep-arable from context. Nonaka and Konno (1998) maintain that, to support the process of knowledge creation, a foundation of 'Ba' is essential. While the desire for spatial knowledge is attainable, it might well be said that the pri-mary goal of any tourist is experiential, yet the experiential dimension of tourism visits has not been extensively studied. Typically, any attempt to 'get inside the head' of the tourist attracts considerable conceptual, theoretical and empirical contest.

   Some academics argue that any physical landscape that is unfamiliar must impart some 'culturally derived meaning', particularly wherein people actively strive to make sense of somewhere new (Crouch 2000; Howes 2003; Middleton 2003; Suvantola 2002; Tuan 1998). Urry (1999) extends this fur-ther to propose that diverse societies place a different emphasis on the senses, with the city in particular able to ignite new meanings. Such sensuous awak-enings constructed within the dense and unfamiliar environment of a city become heightened by the intense unfamiliarity wherein tourist experience is said to be at its most intense (Urry 1999). Perhaps, a shift towards gaining spatial understandings that treat cultures as ways of sensing the world is really becoming increasingly applicable (Howes 2003). Classen (1993: 136) agrees and refers to sensory models as conceptual models, with sensory values as cultural values so as to infer the way a society senses is the way it understands. Often, insight into sensual perception and practice is approached from the habitual and known space of one social group alone, and is some-times contrasted with the practice of another. Less understood is the sensory deployment and interpretation of individuals within unfamiliar space and any practical assessment that may exist. The most probable reason for such a time-honoured omission is either our inability to extrapolate objectivity from our increasingly subjective assumptions, or possibly the belief that such an act could be a contradiction in terms.

A sensitivity to place

Traditionally, the visual sense alone remains the customary way in which a tourist is said to come to know a place, with the remaining senses receiving scant attention (Classen 1993; Crouch and Lubbren 2003). Arguably, in focusing all attention on visual symbolism, the figurative functions of the other senses remain ignored. Yet Rojek contends the differentiation between everyday experiences and the extraordinary are not removed from one another (1997). The tourist acts as a keen 'sensory filter' seeking to actively gather a range of new environmental information. Sight is perceived as the 'noblest' of senses, with all others able to capture the composite extent of spatial information to include sound, taste, smell and touch (Classen 1993). In experiential terms, visual consumption becomes enhanced and comple-mented by the evocation of sounds, smell, touch and even taste that differ from the norm; a distinction aptly cited as 'Place may smell and sound, space never does' (Nielson 1999: 278). Accordingly, it is the range of affective responses that influences the individual's experience of different physical environments. Cognitive responses include thinking, information processing and representation of the environment, whereas affective responses encompass those that influence verbal and non-verbal relationships within environmental settings (Golledge and Stimson 1997; Rapoport 1976). In doing so, individuals maintain mental terms of reference that act as a catalyst to experiential learning. According to Rojek (1997), such a mental process involves the 'indexing' and 'dragging' of responses from the habitual and familiar into the unknown. Similarly, indexing ascribes a set of visual, textual and symbolic representations to the original object, remembering that tourist activity and the assimilation of the tourist experience are susceptible and emotive human processes. Dragging, as identified by Rojek, is the means by which certain elements can be pulled out of the 'files' of representation and associated with each other. Thus, dragging refers to the combination of elements from separate files of representation to create a new value. What is particularly pertinent to experiential learning is that dragging operates on both conscious and unconscious levels and, indeed, Tuan (1998) notes visual perception to remain only the initial part of the fuller conscious awareness afforded by tourists.

Golledge (1991), Rojek (1997) and others (Carmen and Hernández 2001; Crouch 2000) agree that all of the human senses emanate from knowledge base that already exists, and thereby control the rules for attaching new meaning to an experience. While knowledge must be individual in nature and personally constructed, some components of knowledge are commonly agreed upon. In this context, consensus can be symbolised as culture through the sharing of meanings, images and habits of a recognisable group. Ethnicity has long been used to sort and categorise people, with culture symbolising a 'way of life' (Hottola 2004; Winchester *et al.* 2003). Sensory and exploratory interpretations offer insight in a distinct and specialised way that may then inform others. The dissemination of culture within sensory appraisal yet between people and place can only ever be an approximation of the truth, yet the truth as perceived by the cultural and sensory receptors themselves, urban tourists. Howes (2003) agrees and refers to the idea of McLuhan who coins a sensorium as a 'combinatory', with cultures consisting of contrasting 'ratios of sense perception' (1962: 55). Notions of ratio within sensory and cultural interplay signify a sharing between people yet denote differences within relations too. It is to what extent such contrasts exist that tends to remain heuristic and difficult to explicate.

The senses and subjectivity

As discussed above, the capability to determine human subjectivity remains a complex and perennial problem. Still, any desire to combine quantitative rigour within forms of qualitative analysis appears contrary to some, and unthinkable to others. As a result, a mixed methodological design has been referred to as 'incompatible' (Smith and Heshusios 1986), a 'forbidden zone' (Jamal and Hollinshead 2001) and, more recently, coined as 'qualiquantological' (Stenner and Stainton-Rogers 2004). However, one mixed methodological approach more commonly found in psychology and political science is Q methodology. Such a method affords a deep and critical insight into the realm of human subjectivity, one that is both defined and differentiated by statistical scientific means. Simply put, numbers are used to cluster people through their shared subjective sensitivities to any given topic. In this way, 'difference' is rendered real by what it thematically is and where it statistically actually lies.

Q methodology represents an established, yet underrated, research technique within the social sciences. Invented by William Stephenson (1935), a British physicist-psychologist, the method has become most frequently associated with quantitative analysis owing to its involvement with factor analysis. Stephenson's work was later continued by Brown (1996) and developed in the United States based upon seeking understandings from the standpoint of the lived experience of the person. However, the central tenet of research focus seeks to get to the very core of subjectivity to reveal how people 'think' about a specific topic. For example, within questionnaire surveys, the more familiar R factor analysis applies a systematic measure of related 'items', that is, those stated and written variables within the survey. In contrast, Q analysis differs in that it deploys factor analysis in order to identify 'groups of participants' who make sense of items in comparable ways (Watts and Stenner 2005). They note a clear turn towards 'subjective experience within social science research' and with the ongoing development of social constructionist viewpoints providing a more receptive audience. A recent study conducted by ten Klooster *et al.* (2008) compared the Q-sort method and Likert attitude questionnaire. Their findings reveal a similarity in themes yet offers a different prominence upon the research process. For Q, the emphasis relates to the unique opportunity to distinguish salient groupings through similarly structured attitudes focused solely upon the directed topic. Alternatively, a Likert analysis provides the opportunity to broaden the scope of enquiry to encompass other aspects such as services, brands and organisations. They do, however, note the practical advantage of the Q-sort ranking activity as an attractive form of data collection in the eyes of participants, particularly in a time when people's willingness to be involved in questionnaire-based research appears to be decreasing. With the Q-sorting technique, a distinctive set of psychometric and operational principles are encompassed that, applied with specialised statistical analysis, provide a systematic and rigorously quantitative means for examining human subjectivity (McKeown and Thomas 1988). Such an unfolding of meaning serves to reveal the separate group types that exist and the emergent differences between them, in a defined and critical way. In sum, the method combines the diversity and depth of a qualitative approach with the numerical testing and interpretation of quantitative analysis. Notably, any subjective issue can be approached in 'virtually any form of text'. Written, visual, oral or audio items, or a combination of any, can be utilised (Brown 1993).

Thus, the Q-sorting task, described below, serves as a projective device (Kerlinger 1986) through which participants are able to express the *relative importance* of various factors, something impossible with a standard measurement scale. The Q technique further seeks to achieve greater social relevance by introducing the idea of *social validity* (Wolf 1978), enabling social values to be numerically assigned and assessed. Participants are allowed to reveal combinations of items that most accurately describe their own personal attitude or meaning towards the object of study in a unique and insightful manner.

The Q-sort technique

As already stated, it is the quantitative measurement of individual opinions and attitudes that gets to the heart of subjectivity, and it is in this sense that Q methodology has a critical role to play. Developed by William Stephenson (1935; 1953) it has become increasingly utilised as a means within which to examine subjective behaviour. It now forms an established research technique of over 60 years' standing, especially within psychology and political science. Although central to qualitative understanding, it is often associated solely with quantitative approaches owing to its involvement with factor analysis, of which it is a variant. As such, the method provides a numerical perspective on subjectivity, providing a means of ranking quantitative and qualitative understandings. The unique and distinctive characteristic of Q is the ability to statistically measure the responses of the individual. Yet, through its use of numerical data and statistical analysis, the technique can appear at odds within the qualitative field of enquiry that Q seeks to determine – subjectivity. It is the 'communicability' in Q that refers to the flows of ideas, statements, commentaries, beliefs, etc. of respondents that surround any topic or text (Brown 1980).

Q-sort methods have a substantial validity, as Stephenson (1978) remarks, 'Q sorts don't just put ideas into empty heads. The factors are vectors of existence.' The Q-sorting technique encompasses a distinctive set of psychometric and operational principles that, applied with specialised statistical analysis, provide a systematic and rigorously quantitative means for examining human subjectivity (McKeown and Thomas 1988). The individual's level of comprehension and subjective interpretation is retained and assessed within the analysis, including the person's point of view, opinion or attitude towards any matter of personal or social significance. Central to this proposition is that any subjective viewpoint has the ability to be communicated and is personally determined from a stance of 'self-reference' (Golledge 1991). Thus, an intrinsic insight that exceeds the boundaries of how we think, to interpret why we think the way we do must take the debate further in a substantive way.

As a methodology, Q sort allows a distinctive orientation towards the systematic study of human behaviour, and applications of the Q method are considered to have a number of advantages. Firstly, there is the significant amount of quantitative data that can be gathered, while secondly, there is the potential to substitute written forms for visual forms of text. These include the ability to encompass a wide variety of settings, to focus on subjects (Amadeo *et al.* 1989), and to do so in ways that allow sensitivity to individual responses and, in so doing, give richness to the data (Palmer 1997; Pitt and Zube 1979). Brown (1993) states that any subjective issue can be approached in 'virtually any form of text'. Written, visual, oral or audio items, or a combination of any, can be utilised. In the widest sense, written statements on cards form the most common set of items. Instead of words, the visual text of photographs sustains a universal means of communication and assessment. Subsequently, the scaled photographic items then provide the means to stimulate discussion during the interview, to further add language with narrative and context, and to further elucidate and enrich the data sets. Q methodology typically uses relatively small numbers of respondents and assumes that a relatively limited number of viewpoints upon any one given topic exist; thus studies are replicable (Thomas and Baas 1992).

An application of Q

The Q-sort procedure operates by taking the ranked data related to each of the item (written statement/photographic) 'sorts' carried out by respondents. These data are correlated and rotated using Q-Principal Component Analysis (QPCA). Factors based on variables and/or groups of variables are then extracted. Each person in the study is associated with the resultant factors through factor loadings that reflect their position in the multidimensional space constructed by the factor solution. The correlation matrix, factor loadings and factor scores are numerically presented for interpretation.

In processing the data deriving from the Q-sort process, significant issues concern the reliability of the factor structure and the choice of model for the rotation and extraction of factors. Reliability is a natural and primary concern for any numerical calculation. In this regard, the application of Kaiser's criterion is implicit within Q analysis and selects only those factors that have an eigenvalue greater than one, as is normal with the more familiar R modes of factor and principal components analysis. For Q sorts with 30 items, the standard error of a factor loading is $1./n = 0.18$, and at the 0.01 probability level a loading has to be at least $0.18 \times 2.58 = 0.47$. Only loadings that are 'pure', that is, for which there is a significant loading on **only one factor**, are used to define the factors. What is equally significant is that the number of factors is purely empirical and wholly dependent upon how the Q sorters actually perform. Brown (1993) refers to this as a rigorous yet naturalistic approach to defining operant factors within subjective study. The mechanical phase of Q methodology thus combines scientific judgement with statistical analysis. The former includes the proper framing of the problem, the collection and theoretical structuring of the Q sample and participant set, the specification of condition of instruction and the completion of the post-sort interview, and the subsequent rotation of factors and their interpretation. The instrumental component includes the scoring, coding and data entry, and both correlation and factor analysis, including the computation of factor scores.

Any form of text, whether written (statements), visual (images) or audio (sounds), can act as items to be distributed by the respondent. For example, photography remains a widely used tool within environmental research. It is colloquially expressed that 'a photograph says more than a thousand words' and thus represents a well-tested visual medium for analysis. Recent studies to utilise Q methodology using photographs within tourism research include (Dewar *et al.* 2007; Fairweather and Swaffield 2001; Middleton 2003; Swaffield and Fairweather 1996). In each instance, visitors were required to sort environmental images by preference. It is always recommended that the technique should include a subsequent data collection. This often takes the form of an interview whereby participants are able to elaborate and justify their own selection process. Other forms include the completion of a questionnaire, often to generate socio-demographic data of an extensive form. This might include gender, nationality and age and extend into the motivation and determinants of the tourist. Such data frames the analysis further within the objective-subjective dichotomy and continuum.

The way in which the Q-sort method was operationalised in one empirical study required each respondent to complete a 'Q sort' of a set of 30 photographs (Middleton 2003). Respondents were given a set of 30 photographs and were asked to sort them literally into physical piles of 'dislike', 'like' and 'indifferent'. In this exercise, a typical Q-sort distribution consisted of nine piles of photographs with the number of photographs in each pile running in the following sequence, which approximates a normal distribution.

The pattern presents participants with a forced sorting procedure that limits the number of items that may be placed at the extremes and requires a specified number of items to be placed in each column. This is a requirement of the mode of analysis so that the participant is forced to make explicit choices about the ranking of each item, relative to other items, along the entire continuum. The right-hand of the distribution contained photographs that people liked, and these were allocated a positive score. The left-hand contained photographs that people disliked and, therefore, allocated a negative score. The piles in the middle contained photographs that had not evoked any strength of feeling. Respondents were asked to take their time and look at all of the photographs prior to starting the selection procedure. When each respondent had completed their Q sort, individuals were asked to justify and discuss their reasons for selecting the six top and the six

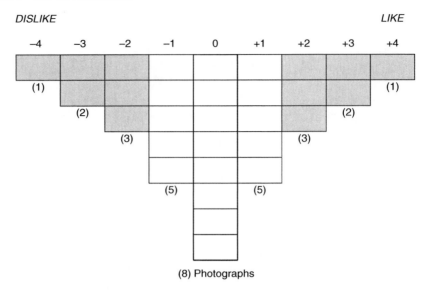

Figure 14.1 A typical Q-sort distribution (*N* = 30).

bottom-ranked photographs. In this way, the utilisation of a qualitative approach contributes statistical rigour to any interpretive research study.

Statistical analysis reveals factors categorised along a bipolar, negative to positive scale. It is important to reiterate that Q factor analysis correlates 'people and not items' thereby clustering individuals into groups. Alternatively, R factor analysis, as commonly used with questionnaire analysis, simply correlates the written items offered for selection. 'The variables are no longer tests or hypothesised traits, but the persons who take part in the study' (Watts and Stenner 2005: 72). In this sense, Q serves to overcome the traditional constraint of researcher bias of semantics and intervention. Instead, the technique serves to 'get into the head of the tourist' and the very heart of social science, subjectivity. The results of a Q methodology study can be used to categorise a population of viewpoints. In this way, Q can be extremely helpful in exploring the views, values, preferences, motives and sensitivities of people across the social science spectrum. In this study, the sample consisted of 30 participants of diverse geographical origin from across five continents. All completed the Q-sort task of ranking the photographic images and statistical analysis revealed four distinct emergent types. These same respondents concluded each interview with a sensory association reminiscent of 'home' and then their current 'tourist destination'. Interestingly, a clear taxonomy sensory similarity emerged determined by cultural distinctions. This extended beyond vision alone, as determined by the Q-sort exercise of photographic analysis, to reveal a consensus of sensory viewpoints shared from a cultural background of viewing the world around us.

Conclusion

This chapter has presented two themes for further research consideration. The initial debate focused upon the role of the senses within differentiating tourism experience, especially within a cultural context. It is argued that space does become 'place' as the senses combine together to actively gather a range of environmental information even in a subliminal way. As cultural beings, we see the world through a frame of reference structured from our known and familiar, the notion of home. However, this raises questions as to whether there is a hierarchy of the senses, and if so does it differ between cultures? Ethnographic and phenomenological studies suggest that a taxonomy of difference very probably exists and, for many, this celebrates the distinct diversity of tourism behaviour with experience. Spatial exposure towards, and the ability to participate within, distinctive places and their activities are important. It's what memories are made of.

Second, it is indisputable that any research activity into the realm of human subjectivity remains a rich and complex challenge, particularly if any degree of a transferability of results is to be made. Discussion here sought to introduce and illustrate the technique of Q and not to progress onto the emergent qualitative themes that result from such statistical analysis. The technique is particularly suitable for thematic identification within which the strength of views and values of respondents become visible through shared commonality as factor groups and their degree of intensity. At this juncture, the ability to compare/contrast any difference in views towards the same topic is able to illuminate subjective values in a very real and manageable way. In sum, difference and similarity are exposed and positioned where such distinctions actually rest. The necessary software application and support tutorials are freely available from http://www.qmethod.org. What is argued is that any progression in our ability to measure 'the subjective' must form a valuable and versatile asset within which academic research can advance. All too frequently, the observer is invariably implicated in what is being observed. Both of these obstacles are overcome by the use of Q methodology. Using the same mathematics as quantum theory, the apparent contradiction between the objective and subjective becomes, instead, a question of what is being measured. Judgement, whether conscious or otherwise, lies within the human psyche and its sensory deployment, appreciation and differentiation. Considerations between what we like or dislike, become attached to yet disconnected from, communicate the very basis upon which tourist experience and personal satisfaction becomes real. Yet, subjectivity as a science offers as many interpretations as it does explanations and remains infinitely harder to determine. This chapter has considered for some an inconceivable mixed methodology that aspires to extrapolate the finite greyness (constraints) of objectivity from the infinite florescence of subjectivity; a study method that is socially determined, constructed and assessed through a scientific and meaningful technique. However, if academic reticence does exist to extend beyond the conceptual and acknowledged theories to the empirical deconstruction of experience, then advancement will be hindered. In the end, all social research studies at best present an approximation of the truth as we see it, at that moment in time. To this extent, Q methodology removes the intervention of the researcher and relies on the views of the participants as expressed by themselves. Through the use of Q methodology it is possible to construct a unique configuration of each participant's engagement with a topic through a ranking device and simultaneously contributes to correlations between people and their diversity of viewpoints. By correlating people, as opposed to questionnaire items, Q factor analysis exposes the similarities and differences of viewpoints to reveal clusters of consensus. For those researchers receptive to a scientific study of subjectivity through a mixed methodological approach, the possibilities are endless.

15 Kohlberg's Stages: informing responsible tourist behaviour

Davina Stanford

Introduction

The negative impacts of tourism are well documented, calling increasingly for action which encourages a more sustainable, more responsible tourism. Communication, in one form or another, has consistently been cited as an important visitor management tool capable of influencing appropriate tourist behaviour (Broadhurst 2001; Eber 1992; Forsyth 1996; France 1997; Gunn 1988; Krippendorf 1984; Prosser 1992; Reisinger 1997) yet, in practice, attempts to develop persuasive messages are often made with little theoretical basis. This research uses a theoretical framework to explore tourists' reactions to different informative messages in three comparative scenarios, each with a different context: economic, environmental and cultural.

The messages presented in these hypothetical scenarios are adapted from Kohlberg's Stages of Moral Development. The results will be particularly useful for management purposes, as well as theoretically, to establish if there are any obvious consistencies or differences according to both the type of message and to the context in which it is presented. The scenarios used were based on realistic challenges for visitor management in two case study sites in New Zealand: Rotorua and Kaikoura. Rotorua is a large and mature resort with a wide range of activities, including geothermal and adventure tourism, and it is a major centre for the presentation of Maori culture. Kaikoura is a smaller and more recently established destination. With a rich marine habitat close to shore, its tourism product focuses mainly on ecotourism, such as whale and dolphin watching. Both sites have sensitive environments which require careful visitor management to encourage tourists to demonstrate certain behaviours, from appropriate behaviour viewing a seal colony to observing Maori protocol when experiencing Maori culture.

In a broader context, this destination-specific research has implications for visitor management in New Zealand as a whole. New Zealand's diverse landscape offers tourists a range of attractions and experiences, many of which are nature-based and rely heavily on the use of the country's natural resources. Furthermore, the itinerant nature of the tourist in New Zealand frequently takes them into fragile areas, which requires careful visitor management. It is important for tourists to have an understanding of how to act responsibly in these settings.

The aim of this chapter is twofold: first, to identify which types of communication based on Kohlberg's Stages of Moral Development are most influential, which are least influential and why; second, to identify similarities and differences in the effectiveness of the communications across three different scenarios. New Zealand, of course, is not alone in needing to address such issues for the management of visitor impacts is a universal concern. Thus, while the specific scenarios which are dealt with here are drawn from the New Zealand context, the broader issues that they represent are commonly experienced elsewhere. Consequently, the approach adopted and the findings obtained are likely to have a much wider applicability.

Encouraging responsible tourist behaviour through effective communication

This chapter concentrates on information and how it is presented. There are many modes by which information may be imparted, such as interpretation, codes of conduct and guidebooks, and there is a vast literature on the study of information. Despite this, there has been little synthesis within this field across subject matter, with studies tending to have a very specific subject focus. Interpretation studies, for example, focus either on environmental and outdoor recreational situations (for example, Aiello 1998; Ballantyne et al. 1998) or on cultural situations (for example, Howard et al. 2001; Keelan 1993; Moscardo 1998).

What this previous research does show is that certain types of behaviour are more easily managed by information than others, for example unskilled, or uninformed actions will be more receptive to information than illegal or careless actions (Roggenbuck 1992). It has also been established that different recipients will be affected differently by messages depending on their attention to the message (Petty et al. 1992), their travel style and motivation (Ballantyne et al. 1998) and their values. Communication should attempt to identify common values held by the recipients of the message and align the messages accordingly (Scottish Natural Heritage 2004). This chapter attempts to take a more conceptual approach to the study of communication to establish whether certain types of information may be more appealing and successful in driving responsible behaviour, regardless of the context or medium, based on the recipients' values or level of moral development.

Kohlberg's Stages of Moral Development

The issue of responsible tourist behaviour is, to some extent, involved with informing the tourist of desired behaviour and encouraging them to choose that behaviour over less appropriate actions. As with everyday life, it is useful to apply a set of guidelines or principles which can help to lead the tourist towards the required action. Morality and the understanding of moral reasoning is a field which has been dominated by the work of Lawrence Kohlberg and his Stages of Moral Development. Originally intended to understand the progressive development of morals in children, the stages were developed using a hypothetical moral dilemma, based on whether or not a man should steal drugs for his dying wife (Kohlberg 1980). Kohlberg observed 50 males from the ages of 10 to 28. He noted that, given the same scenario, the reasoning which the respondents offered in response to the scenario became increasingly more sophisticated as they grew older. These differences gave Kohlberg a framework of six stages of reasoning to account for moral judgements or actions, split into three broad categories: pre-conventional morality, understood in the hedonistic consequences of action (punishment or reward); conventional morality, relating to social order, peers, wider society and demonstrating good citizenship; and post-conventional morality, relating to defined moral values and principles.

Kohlberg's stages are a seminal work in understanding moral development and reasoning. They provide a clear and easily understandable framework and a flexibility that has been successfully applied in a broader range of situations relating to adult behaviour. In particular, Christenson and Dustin (1989) found in their analysis of existing interpretative messages in a national park that the interpretative messages did relate to Kohlberg's Stages of Moral Development. For example, Stage 1 interpretation would relate to punishment, Stage 2 to communicating benefits and gains, Stage 3 to what others think, Stage 4 emphasising good citizenship, Stage 5 outlining consequences of behaviour and Stage 6 applying universal ethical principles. They suggest several areas for further research: to investigate when a message aimed at individual Stages of Moral Development may be effective, in what kind of settings and to influence what kinds of behaviour, and when a certain stage may not be effective.

Despite its usefulness, Kohlberg's theory has been criticised for a number of reasons. Firstly, it is based only on a sample of 50 males. Gilligan (1982) suggests that female moral development is different and will diverge from that of males at the post-conventional level, with women having greater emphasis on caring as the highest value. Second, Kohlberg's assumption that all cultures will follow the same Stages of Moral Development and that there are universal truths, morals and values has also been challenged, suggesting that there may be some cultural differences (Snarey 1985). Snarey suggests that one should expect there to be some cultural nuances and that Kohlberg's existing stages cannot accommodate such differences as, with particular regard to the post-conventional morality, these stages are based primarily on Western philosophy. Finally, although Kohlberg posits that there is consistency of moral reasoning from one context to another, this has been found not to be the case (Carpendale 2000). This research uses the stages as a framework to develop information for tourists which guides appropriate behaviour and to test which is most effective.

Study methods

A visitor survey, to be undertaken face to face, was developed with respondents stating their reactions to signage or an announcement based on Kohlberg's Stages of Moral Development for three different scenarios. The research was part of a larger project which was conducted over two phases: the first phase to identify appropriate scenarios and the second to develop and implement the survey. At each of the two case study sites, in-depth, semi-structured interviews were held with tourism industry representatives to identify key issues in visitor management for each of the sites on which the scenarios could be based.

Following discussions with key stakeholders, three realistic scenarios were developed. These scenarios were intended to represent situations where responsible behaviour could be encouraged through information in different contexts. Different contexts were chosen to reflect the complex nature of responsible tourism and to test if the effectiveness of messages was consistent or if the context of the message had any influence. The three scenarios (Table 15.1) related to different experiences that the visitor might encounter at Rotorua or Kaikoura, specifically voluntary payments for a geothermal walk, behaviour at a seal colony, where tourists were requested to approach no closer than 10 metres, and behaviour at a Maori cultural performance, requesting that tourists remained seated until the end of the performance. In each case six different messages based on the different stages were presented. For each of the scenarios, six different rationales were given for displaying the desired behaviour (Table 15.1). These different messages were based on Kohlberg's Stages of Moral Development.

The second phase of the research involved a face-to-face visitor survey based on the three scenarios. The survey was undertaken over two months in the summer of 2004: in Kaikoura in February 2004 and in Rotorua in March 2004. The survey was held throughout the week, including weekends. In Kaikoura, two sites were chosen for the collection of data, the Visitor Information Centre and the seal colony, and in Rotorua the sites chosen for the collection of data were the Visitor Information Centre, the lake front and the Government Gardens. In total, questionnaires were completed by 372 respondents. All the respondents were presented with the same set of three scenarios.

The survey sample was limited primarily to independent tourists as it was difficult to intercept package tourists; some respondents had to be filtered on the basis of their level of English language ability; and domestic tourists were also under-represented owing to the time of year. Domestic vacations typically peak in January, and only 11 per cent of the sample were from New Zealand, the rest were international tourists. There were also problems with the scenarios used. Some respondents found this kind of question very difficult to answer as they found it hard to imagine themselves in the situation which was described for them. For example, the scenario based at

Table 15.1 Tourism scenarios used to examine Kohlberg's Stages of Moral Development

	Economic	Environmental	Cultural
	Voluntary payment	Appropriate wildlife viewing	Appropriate cultural behaviour
	Geothermal walk in Rotorua	The Kaikoura Seal Colony	A Maori cultural performance
	You are about to walk in a geothermal reserve in Rotorua. The managers of the land want tourists to pay $5.00 for the cost of the walk. You are supposed to put the money into a ticket machine at the start of the walk and the machine issues you with a ticket. However, in this scenario, you are travelling on a budget and are reluctant to spend too much money, so you are thinking of entering the reserve without paying. Which of the following signs are likely to influence you to pay the $5.00?	You have just arrived at the seal colony at Kaikoura. The Department of Conservation is trying to stop too many tourists getting too close to the seals. However, in this scenario, you want to get really close to a seal to get a good photograph. Which of the following signs are likely to influence you to stay the required distance?	You have paid to watch a Maori cultural performance. The Maori cultural performers want the audience to stay seated for the duration of the performance. However, in this scenario, it is a very hot day and you want to leave for five minutes to get an ice cream. Which of the following are likely to make you remain seated?
	A sign saying…	A sign saying…	A performer tells you…
Stage of moral development Stage 1 Fear of punishment	Please pay $5.00. $50 fine for non-compliance.	Please stay 10 metres from the seals. Seals can bite.	Please do not leave before the performance ends. You may not be readmitted to the auditorium if you leave.

Continued

Table 15.1 Continued

Stage 2 Maximising pleasure/minimising pain	Please pay $5.00. If you are found without a ticket you will be asked to leave the reserve.	Please stay 10 metres from the seals. Approaching closer will make them retreat to the water.	Please do not leave before the performance ends. Leaving the auditorium before the end of a performance may affect the quality of the performance.
Stage 3 What significant others think	Please pay $5.00. Don't spoil this experience for other visitors.	Please stay 10 metres from the seals. Don't spoil this experience for other visitors.	Please do not leave before the performance ends. Don't spoil this experience for other visitors.
Stage 4 What society thinks, emphasising good citizenship	Please pay $5.00. Contribute towards New Zealand's beautiful environment.	Please stay 10 metres from the seals. Respect New Zealand's beautiful environment.	Please do not leave before the performance ends. Please respect Maori culture.
Stage 5 Social contract or utility based on reasoning	Please pay $5.00. Walking the path causes erosion and is costly to repair, your money will help pay for essential maintenance.	Please stay 10 metres from the seals. Approaching the seals can frighten them and their young.	Please do not leave before the performance ends. This is a sign of disrespect and may cause offence.
Stage 6 Universal ethical principles	Please pay $5.00. It's up to you to do the right thing.	Please stay 10 metres from the seals. It's up to you to do the right thing.	Please do not leave before the performance ends. It's up to you to do the right thing.

the Kaikoura seal colony evoked responses such as 'but I don't like seals so I wouldn't go to see them ... can I pretend it's a bird colony?'

Survey respondents were asked to score each of the messages on a scale of 1 to 5 with 1 being 'unlikely' and 5 being 'very likely' to influence behaviour. For the actual survey, the stages were presented in random order, these were then reordered from Stages 1 through to 6 for the analysis. The data were analysed throughout comparing the three scenarios together, first using the mode and mean responses based on the scores of 1 to 5. The mode shows the overall effectiveness of Kohlberg's stages as a way of influencing behaviour through information and the means give an overview of any differences or similarities between the three scenarios.

Focusing in greater depth on Kohlberg's stages, respondents were then asked which single message would be the most and least likely to influence them. The identification of messages most or least likely to influence behaviour is particularly important as for the initial part of the question rating each message on a scale of 1 to 5, many respondents chose '5' (very likely to influence) for all the messages with little distinction between the scenarios. Finally, respondents were asked to explain in their own words why a specific message was most or least likely to influence them. These responses were then regrouped according to the stages they related to as understood by the recipient rather than how they were intended by the researcher. New groupings were used where the respondents' reasons did not relate to Kohlberg's stages, and these new groupings along with the existing stages were analysed according to scenario shown as a percentage of the total. This latter step gave a greater depth to the data, and also allowed the research to be cross-checked, to ascertain whether the reasons given by the respondents for choosing a certain reason corresponded with the suggested stage of moral development. It also provided insights into why certain types of message might be successful, and why they might not be.

Results

Looking first at the mode response from Figure 15.1, it can be seen that the mode for all three of the scenarios for Stages 1 (punishment), 4 (good citizenship) and 5 (reasoned argument) messages is 5 (very likely to influence). Indeed, many of the respondents ticked 5 (very likely to influence) for all the stages and all the scenarios, explaining that all the messages would be likely to influence them. However, there are some exceptions; the mode for the Stage 2 (reward) message drops to 3 for the cultural performance scenario, as does the Stage 3 message (considering peers) for the geothermal walk and seal colony scenarios. For all three scenarios, the mode for the Stage 6 message (universal ethical principles) is 3, indicating that for all three scenarios, this might be the least likely stage/message to influence.

From Figure 15.2, which presents the means, a clearer picture of preference starts to emerge. Overall, the messages based on the fourth and fifth stages

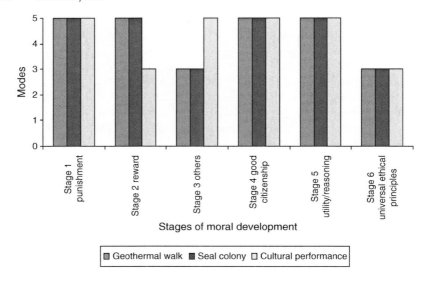

Figure 15.1 Mode for all three scenarios.

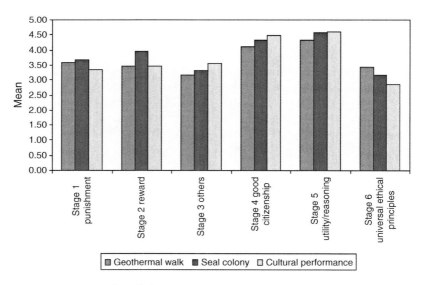

Figure 15.2 Mean for all three scenarios.

of development (good citizenship and reasoned argument respectively) appear to have the most influence for all three scenarios. Messages based on Stages 1 and 2 of moral development (punishment and reward respectively) have a slightly lower mean for the cultural performance scenario, with the messages based on Stage 3 of moral development (considering peers) having a slightly lower mean for the geothermal walk and seal colony scenarios. Again, the message based on the sixth stage of moral development (universal ethical principles) has a relatively low mean for all three scenarios, although slightly less so for the scenario of the geothermal walk.

From Figure 15.1, then, it is possible to see that overall the mode of response was high, and from Figure 15.2 it can be seen that Stages 4 and 5 (good citizenship and reasoned argument respectively) were rated as more likely to influence behaviour for all three scenarios, although there are specific differences for the other stages depending on the scenario.

The following sections look at respondents' messages which are singled out as the overall most or least likely message to influence behaviour. Figure 15.3 demonstrates that the messages stated as most likely to influence behaviour for all three of the scenarios are based on Stages 4 and 5 of moral development (good citizenship and reasoned argument). In particular, the Stage 5 message, which for all scenarios provides a reason for the requested behaviour, is highly likely to influence behaviour for the seal colony and, to a lesser extent, Maori cultural performance scenarios. Stage 4 messages (good citizenship) are also influential, while messages based on Stages 2 and 3 of moral development (reward and considering peers) are not particularly influential for any of the scenarios. The messages based on Stage 1 (punishment) have little more influence. The messages 'to do the right thing' based on Stage 6 (universal ethical principles) have little influence for the seal colony and Maori cultural performance scenarios, with some respondents answering that this would be the most likely to influence them for the geothermal walk scenario. A small number of respondents did not choose any message as

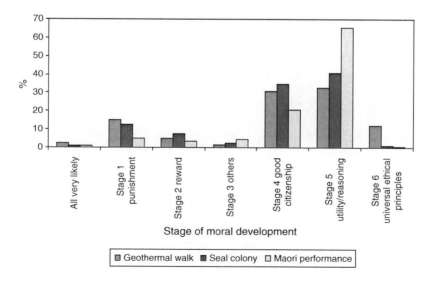

Figure 15.3 Stage most likely to influence behaviour.

being overall most likely to influence them stating that they would all be very likely to influence their behaviour.

As far as the least likely messages to influence behaviour are concerned (see Figure 15.4), this is something of a mirror image of the most likely responses. The messages based on Stage 6 (universal ethical principles) seem overall to be the least likely to influence behaviour, in particular for the seal colony and Maori cultural performance scenarios. Messages based on Stage 1 (punishment) are particularly unlikely to influence behaviour for the geothermal walk and the Maori cultural performance scenario. Finally, the messages based on Stage 3 of moral development (considering peers) are unlikely to influence behaviour in the geothermal walk and seal colony scenarios.

The analysis also looked at respondents' given reasons why they have or have not been influenced by a certain message. This allows the key reasons why the messages are influential to be established, based not on how the message was intended by the researcher, but on how the message was interpreted by the recipient. The reasons tourists gave for choosing certain messages as most likely did relate to Kohlberg's Stages of Moral Development. For example, with regards to the Maori cultural performance scenario, the response, 'I've paid, I don't want to lose my money', relates to Stage 1 (punishment) as does the response to the seal colony scenario as 'I don't want to be bitten'. The stage of the original message, however, did not always correspond with the interpretation of the respondents. For example, many respondents chose the Stage 5 message (reasoned argument) but explained their choice in terms of Stage 4 (good citizenship; for example, at the seal

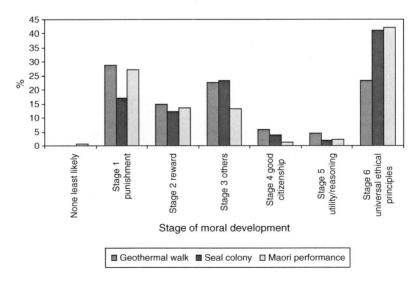

Figure 15.4 Stage least likely to influence behaviour.

colony the respondents stated they chose this message as most likely to influence because they wanted to respect wildlife). The category of 'positive/ fair' was added based on tourists' reasoning.

Figure 15.5 summarises the reasons given by respondents, grouped to correspond with the stages. This shows that typically, regardless of context, messages which are understood by the respondent as an appeal to good citizenship or to respect the wider community are the most influential. This is followed by messages which are interpreted as providing a reason and by messages which are understood as appeals to one's conscience or values.

By scenario it can be seen that certain influences may be more relevant depending on the situation. The influences for the voluntary payment at a geothermal walk are the most dispersed, but with the greatest number of responses for this scenario indicating that the main influence is based on broader ethical principles 'conscience/justice/values'. Messages which have been understood in terms of 'respect for wider community', 'punishment' or 'reasoned' have a fairly equal influence for this scenario. With regard to the seal colony, the most frequent influence is 'respect for wider community', in this case, the wildlife of New Zealand. Responses which were grouped in this category included answers such as 'I want to respect the environment', 'I don't want to disturb/frighten/harm the seals', 'to respect the seals and nature'. 'Reasoned' and 'punishment' messages are of a lesser influence. For the Maori cultural performance, 'respect for wider community', in this case respect for someone's culture, was the most influential reasoning (e.g. 'to respect the performers', 'to respect someone's culture', 'I don't want to cause

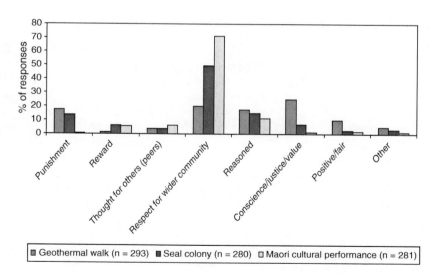

Figure 15.5 Respondents' views on why a message is most likely to influence their behaviour.

offence'). Being given a reasoned argument was also, to some extent, influential. It is interesting to note the hierarchy within the category of 'respect for wider community', rising in significance from respect for the environment, to respect for wildlife and, finally, respect for people and culture. A further point to note is that, again concerning the category of 'respect for wider community', with regard to the voluntary payment at a geothermal walk, respect is understood in terms of the environment, rather than respecting the appeal for a monetary contribution. Indeed, the financial aspect proved unappealing to some respondents and the debate of whether or not one should pay for nature-based experiences was raised.

The stage of the message, however, did not always correspond with the interpretation of the respondents. Taking the example of Maori culture, it can be seen that the most likely message to influence behaviour in Figure 15.5 is one which was interpreted as 'respect for wider community', corresponding with Stage 4 of moral development, whereas, from Figure 15.3 it can be seen that Stage 5 messages (reasoned argument) are chosen as the most likely to influence behaviour for this scenario. In fact, many respondents chose the Stage 5 message (the reasoned argument) but explained their choice in terms of a Stage 4 development (good citizenship): that they wanted to respect Maori culture and did not want to 'cause offence'. It seems that giving an explanation is still useful in evoking a response and creating a greater understanding and respect for culture, even if this is not how the message was intended. The same is true of the seal colony, where it can be seen from Figure 15.3 that respondents choose Stage 5 (reasoned argument) as their most preferred and give the reason that they want to respect the wildlife.

Respondents also gave their reasoning as to why they chose a certain message as the least likely to influence them. To some extent their responses are the opposite to those most likely to influence, for example, 'reasoned/not reasoned'. Other reasons, however, do not correspond to any of Kohlberg's. For instance, Stage 1, 2 and 3 messages (punishment, reward and considering peers respectively) were seen by some as 'patronizing', 'harsh', 'threatening' or 'greedy'. These replies were grouped as 'negative'. Stages 1 and 2 messages (punishment and reward respectively) are frequently mentioned as being the least likely to influence behaviour as the respondent negotiates with the content of message arguing that the consequences of a $50.00 fine are not that bad, or that they could outrun a seal, or sneak out of an auditorium without being noticed. Some respondents stated that messages were unlikely to influence behaviour because they felt that the message was untrue or they could discredit it. This reasoning is found particularly for Stages 2, 3 and 5 (reward, considering others and reasoned argument respectively). Stage 3 messages, which appeal to the respondent to think of others, frequently evoked a response 'would other people think of me?' Overall, however, the main reason given to explain why a message was unlikely to influence behaviour was because it was 'not reasoned'. This response was given for the messages at all stages, but is most noticeable at Stage 6 (universal principles); respondents simply do not know what 'the right thing is'. Though, not particularly influential, other categories were created such as 'reverse psychology', where respondents stated that certain message would encourage them to participate in the undesired behaviour, a lack of reward in so much as there was little incentive for them to comply, that it was their right to do as they pleased, that the information did not make them feel sufficiently guilty, that other people wouldn't comply with the signs, that the wording was not appealing and that they would not undertake the incorrect action anyway, so therefore the information had little impact upon them.

Figure 15.6 is a breakdown of why messages are unlikely to influence behaviour according to scenarios. It can be seen from this that there is a fairly consistent pattern for all three scenarios, 'not reasoned', 'negotiable' and 'disbelief/discredit' indicating three distinct clusters with 'not reasoned' appearing overall the most common response. There are, however, some exceptions. For example, for voluntary payment at a geothermal walk, messages which are interpreted as being negative are unlikely to influence behaviour. There is also a definite hierarchy for the 'not reasoned' responses, rising from the geothermal walk scenario, to the seal colony scenario and being the most common response for a message to lack influence at the Maori cultural performance. For these last two in particular, respondents commented that they require reasoned messages, as the context is unfamiliar and they require some guidance as to what is deemed to be appropriate behaviour. Tourists want to be told what to do and not to do when visiting a seal colony or experiencing a Maori cultural performance and they want to know why.

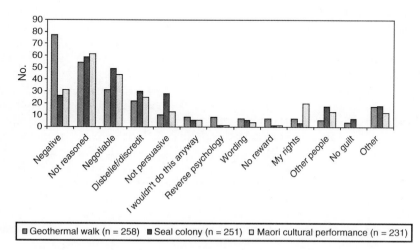

Figure 15.6 Respondents' views on why a message is unlikely to influence their behaviour.

The results for why messages are the 'least likely' to influence are interesting when they are compared with the 'most likely' answers as they do not always correspond. Figure 15.6 shows that the main reason why a message may not be influential is because it is not reasoned. This is particularly relevant to the Maori cultural performance. However, from Figure 15.5 reasoning was not given as the main choice of why a message might be influential, yet here it is shown that reasoning is important to ensure that the recipient of the message does not dismiss it. Messages which have negative implications were the second most frequent response in Figure 15.6 as to why a message is unlikely to influence. Again, this is not reflected in Figure 15.5 for which only a few respondents give the response of positive or fair.

By comparing the patterns of responses in all the figures it can be seen that it is important to know not only which messages are influential, but why. An effective type of communication would combine this knowledge. From the examples used here, effective communication may be based not only on the most common type of influential message, that which appeals to good citizenship, but may also include some elements to avoid a negative response to the communication, such as providing a reason and being positive. Providing a reason is particularly important to avoid the recipient negotiating with the meaning or discrediting it.

Conclusions

Kohlberg's Stages of Moral Development have proven to be a useful theoretical framework with which to examine the question of identifying effective means of communication for visitor management. The scenarios developed in the New Zealand context have provided new insights into messages that are likely to influence visitor behaviour and promote responsible tourism while at the same time demonstrating the utility and potential of the innovative methodology employed. This final section discusses the findings and their implications and outlines avenues for future research based on the methodology used.

Application of Kohlberg's Stages of Moral Development to the three scenarios developed in Rotorua and Kaikoura has shown that it is possible to measure and explain the different influences that various types of messages may have on recipients in different scenarios. Certain messages were found to be more or less influential than others, and the reasons underlying their effectiveness were identified. Significantly, there appears to be much commonality between the different scenarios and clear conclusions can be drawn regarding which messages are most likely and least likely to influence behaviour regardless of context.

The most influential messages will be based on Stages 4 and 5 of moral development (good citizenship and reasoned argument respectively). The least likely are messages based on Stages 1, 3 and 6 (punishment, considering peers and universal ethical principles respectively). These proved unpopular as Stage 1 messages (punishment) are perceived as negative, Stage 3 messages (considering peers) are disbelieved and discredited, and Stage 6 messages (universal principles) do not provide enough information or a rationale. Effective communication should, therefore, take into account both the reasons why a message is influential and why it is not. Based on this, effective communication would include an appeal to good citizenship, combined with a reasoned and positive argument. This is consistent with research in the area of management ethics based on rule-utilitarian approaches whereby the individual can learn through an understanding of the consequences of their actions (Malloy and Fennell 1998).

Despite the strong commonalities across the three scenarios (economic, environmental and cultural), some subtle differences do occur between them. Of particular note is the Maori cultural performance scenarios, for which messages based on Stage 5 of moral development (utility/reasoned argument) are more frequently chosen. This appears to be a function of not knowing what behaviour is appropriate in this situation as many respondents explained their answers by saying they are not familiar with Maori culture. From the respondents' own interpretation of the messages it can be seen that messages interpreted as appealing to good citizenship are influential in this context. Also of note is the voluntary payment for a geothermal walk scenario. For this scenario, preference for certain messages is split across the Stages of Moral Development, with both Stage 1 (punishment) and Stage 6 (universal ethical principles) proving effective. In the respondents' own interpretation of how the messages are understood, appeals to be a good citizen appear to be the most influential overall.

As far as messages which are least likely to influence are concerned there are also differences by scenarios. Stage 6 (universal ethical principles) messages lack influence in the seal colony and Maori cultural performance scenarios, probably as insufficient information is provided and respondents do not know what the right thing is in these contexts. Stage 1 (punishment) messages are less influential for the geothermal walk scenario and the seal colony scenario, typically because of the negative nature of the message. Stage 3 (considering peers) messages are also less influential for the geothermal walk and the seal colony scenario, with many respondents indicating that they did not understand how the inappropriate action would affect others, although they are more able to understand this with regard to disturbing an audience at a Maori cultural performance.

This enhanced understanding of what influences tourists' responses to soft visitor management practices will enable tourists to be incorporated more effectively into responsible tourism strategies. The results provide clear practical guidelines as to which types of message are likely to prove most effective in encouraging responsible tourist behaviour. This in turn demonstrates the value of underpinning visitor management practices with theoretically informed research grounded in a sound understanding of relevant local issues.

It is, therefore, also appropriate to reflect upon the framework used and the methodology developed. This study has shown that Kohlberg's Stages of Moral Development, if a little simplified, are a useful concept for establishing effective types of communication designed to influence responsible behaviour. Although creating scenarios and messages which truly reflect the Stages of Moral Development can be challenging, the framework allows for variations to be established with regard to both the context and the recipient of the message. It also allows an overall picture of the most effective Stage of Moral Development for influential communication. The scenarios themselves, while not substituting experimental research, attempt to take the research and the researched nearer to realistic experiences.

Inconsistencies with Kohlberg's findings were also apparent from this research. Kohlberg states that people are unlikely to demonstrate reasoning at stages removed from one another. However, these scenarios demonstrate that preference for a different stage of reasoning can be evoked depending on the situation. Kohlberg's scenarios use imposing life and death moral scenarios such as stealing food or drugs to save one's dying wife, or civil disobedience to help slaves escape before the Civil War. Maybe these grand dilemmas are more likely to produce consistent reasoning compared with the more mundane scenarios (avoiding a $5.00 payment, getting close to a seal to take a photograph and leaving a cultural performance before it finishes) used here. This is a position supported by Carpendale (2000) who states that people may fail to use their highest stage of moral judgement when reasoning about the moral dilemmas encountered in everyday life.

Clear avenues for further research arise from this research. First, these scenarios are hypothetical, and the respondents of this survey were a somewhat captive audience – once they had agreed to the questionnaire they were guaranteed to read the messages. There is, of course, no such guarantee in the real world, and ensuring that the recipients read the message is as important as providing the most effective message. Therefore, establishing the optimum positioning and mode of the communication may be as important as the message itself. Second, the method could be refined by allowing groups of tourists to negotiate their answers and arrive at a joint decision (as may more often happen in reality) thereby eliminating the problems identified earlier as 'partner interference'.

These findings, and the method used to arrive at them, also have implications for visitor management beyond the three scenarios presented here and could also be applied to a variety of different types of communication be it interpretation or code of conduct, oral or written. While there is commonality between the scenarios, using a value-based framework shows that tourists' values are not necessarily consistent from one scenario to another and it would be worthwhile for those involved in visitor management and guiding appropriate visitor behaviour to consider the subtle contextual differences which might influence the effectiveness of persuasive communication. Furthermore, the method explored here in simplified version may prove useful to identify effective communication or a combination of effective messages tailored specifically to the demographics of tourists to that particular site, according perhaps to the cultural or gender preferences. Communication intended to influence visitor behaviour could be first trialled before expensive (and potentially ineffective) signage is produced.

Further research along these lines will add greatly to the debate on responsible tourism and the role that tourists and visitor management may play.

Bibliography

Abercrombie, N., Hill, S. and Turner, B. (eds) (1994) *The Penguin Dictionary of Sociology*. London: Penguin Books.

Abrams, L. (2005) *Myth and Materiality in a Woman's World: Shetland, 1800–2000*. Manchester: Manchester University Press.

African Burial Ground (n.d.) *Memorial*. Online. Available at: http://www.africanburialground.gov/Memorial/ABG_MemorialDesign_RodneyLeon.htm (Accessed 22 December 2008).

African Burial Ground (n.d.) *Reinternment*. Online. Available at: http://www.africanburialground.gov/ABG_Reinterment.htm (Accessed 11 February 2009).

African Burial Ground National Monument (n.d.) Online. Available at: http://www.nps.gov/afbg (Accessed 11 February 2009).

Ahmed, Z., Krohn, F. and Heller, V. (1994) International tourism ethics as a way to world understanding. *Journal of Tourism Studies* 5(2), 36–44.

Aiello, R. (1998) Interpretation and the marine tourism industry, who needs it? A case study of great adventures, Australia. *The Journal of Tourism Studies* 9(1), 51–61.

Aitchison, C., MacLeod, N. and Shaw, S. (2000) *Leisure and Tourism Landscapes: Social and Cultural Geographies*. London: Routledge.

Allport, G. W. (1937) *Personality: A Psychological Interpretation*. New York: Holt.

Allport, G. W. (1955) *Becoming: Basic Considerations for a Psychology of Personality*. New Haven: Yale University Press.

Allport, G. W. (1961) *Pattern and Growth in Personality*. New York: Holt, Rinehart and Winston.

Amadeo, D. (1993) Emotions in person-environment-behaviour episodes. In T. Garling and R. G Golledge (eds) *Behaviour and Environment*, pp. 83–116. Amsterdam: Elsevier.

Amadeo, P. K., Pitt, D. G. and Zube, E. M. (1989) Landscape feature classification as a determinant of perceived scenic value. *Landscape Journal* 8(1), 36–50.

Amanpour, C. (1996) Balkans war leaves devastation behind. *CNN*, http://www.cnn.com/WORLD/Bosnia/updates/9606/11/rebuilding.sarajevo/, 11 June 1996.

Amir, Y. and Ben-Ari, R. (1985) International tourism, ethnic contact and attitude change. *Journal of Social Issues* 41(3), 105–15.

Andrade, R. de (2002) *Fotografia e antropologia: olhares fora-dentro*. São Paulo: EDUC.

Ap, J. (1990) Resident perception research of the social impacts of tourism. *Annals of Tourism Research* 17(4), 610–16.

Ap, J. (1992) Residents' perceptions on tourism impacts. *Annals of Tourism Research* 19(4), 665–90.

AP (2007) Township tourism booming as visitors want to see 'real' South Africa. *International Herald Tribune*. Africa & Middle East. 3 January 2007.

Aries, P. (1981 [2008]) *The Hour of Our Death: The Classic History of Attitudes Toward Death Over the Last One Thousand Years*, 2nd edn. London: Vintage Books.

Arsal, I., Backman, S. and Baldwin, E. (2008) Influence of an online travel community on travel decisions. In P. O'Connor, W. Höpken and U. Gretzel (eds) *Information and Communication Technologies in Tourism 2008*, pp. 82–93. Vienna, Austria: Springer Verlag.

Ashworth, G. and Hartmann, R. (eds) (2005) *Horror and Human Tragedy Revisited: The Management of Sites of Atrocities for Tourism*. New York, NY: Cognizant Communication.

Ateljevic, I. (2000) Circuits of tourism: stepping beyond the 'production/consumption' dichotomy. *Tourism Geographies* 2(4), 369–88.

Atkins, S. and Murphy, K. (1993) Reflection: a review of the literature. *Journal of Advanced Nursing* 18(8), 1188–92.

Atkinson, M. (2000) Brother, can you spare a seat? Developing recipes of knowledge in the ticket scalping subculture. *Sociology of Sport Journal* 17(2), 151–70.

Atkinson, P. and Hammersley, M. (1994) Ethnography and participant observation. In N. Denzin and Y. Lincoln (eds) *Handbook of Qualitative Research*, pp. 248–61. London: Sage.

Auschwitz-Birkenau Memorial and Museum (2002) *Information Bulletin July–December 2000*. Online. Available at: http://www.auschwitzmuzeum.oswiecim.pl/html/eng/aktualnosci/biuletyn_2_2000.html (Accessed 29 January 2002).

Badgett, L. (1997) Beyond biased samples: challenging the myths on the economic status of lesbians and gay men. In A. Gluckman and B. Reed (eds) *Homo Economics: Capitalism, Communism and Lesbian and Gay Life*. Cited in H. Hughes (2004) A gay tourism market: reality or illusion, benefit or burden? *Journal of Quality Assurance in Hospitality and Tourism* 5(2/3/4), 57–74.

Baker El-Dib, M. (2007) Levels of reflection in action. An overview and an assessment tool. *Teaching and Teacher Education* 23, 24–35.

Bakhtin, M. M. (1984) *Rabelais and his World*. Translated by Hélène Iswolsky. Foreword by Krystyna Pomorska. Bloomington, Indiana: Indiana University Press.

Bakhtin, M. M. (1986) *Speech Genres and Other Late Essays*. C. Emerson and M. Holquist (eds). Translated by V. W. McGee. Austin, Texas: University of Texas Press.

Bale, J. (1994) *Landscapes of Modern Sport*. Leicester: Leicester University Press.

Balkan Insight (Author unknown) (2008) Take a Tour in Karadzic's Footsteps. Available online at: *Balkan Insight*, http://www.balkaninsight.com/en/main/life_and_style/12196/ (Accessed 31 July 2008).

Ball, M. (1992) *Analyzing Visual Data*. Newbury Park: Sage Publications.

Ballantyne, R., Packer, J. and Beckmann, E (1998) Targeted interpretation: exploring relationships among visitors' motivations, activities, attitudes, information needs and preferences. *Journal of Tourism Studies* 9(2), 14–25.

Banducci Jr, A. and Barretto, M. (eds) (2001) *Turismo e Identidade Local: uma visão antropológica*. Campinas: Papirus.

Banta, M. (1986) *From Site to Sight: Anthropology, Photography, and the Power of Imagery.* Cambridge: Peabody Museum Press.

Barkan, S., Cohn, S. and Whitaker, W. (1995) Beyond recruitment: predictors of differential participation in a national antihunger organisation. *Sociological Forum* 10, 113–32.

Barrer, P. (2007) Satan is God! Reimaging contemporary Slovak national identity through sport. *Sport in Society* 10(2), 223–38.

Barretto, M. (2003) O imprescindível aporte das ciências sociais para o planejamento e a compreensão do turismo. *Horizontes Antropológicos*, Porto Alegre, 20, 15–30.

Basin, A. (1982) The ontology of the photographic image. In A. Trachtenberg (ed.) *Classic Essays on Photography.* pp. 237–44. New Haven: Leete's Islands Books.

Baudrillard, J. (1975) *The Mirror of Production.* Translated by Mark Poster. St Louis, Mo.: Telos Press.

Baudrillard, J. (1981) *For a Critique of the Political Economy of the Sign.* St Louis, Mo.: Telos Press.

Baudrillard, J. (1983) *Simulations.* New York: Semiotext Inc.

Beeho, A. and Prentice, R. (1995) Evaluating the experiences and benefits gained by tourists visiting a socio-industrial heritage museum: An application of the ASEB grid analysis to Blists Hill Open-Air Museum, The Ironbridge Museum, United Kingdom. *Museum Management and Curatorship* 14(3), 229–51.

Beeho, A. and Prentice, R. (1997) Conceptualizing the experiences of heritage tourists: A case study of New Lanark World Heritage Site. *Tourism Management* 18(2), 75–87.

Beerli, A. and Martin, J. D. (2004) Factors influencing destination image. *Annals of Tourism Research* 31(3), 657–81.

Bell, C. (2002) The big 'OE': young New Zealand travellers as secular pilgrims. *Tourist Studies* 2(2), 143–58.

Benjamin, W. (1994) Pequena história da fotografia In W. Benjamin (ed.) *Magia e técnica, arte e política.* São Paulo: Brasiliense.

Berger, J. (1982) Understanding photography. In A. Trachtenberg (ed.) *Classic Essays on Photography.* pp. 291–94. New Haven: Leete's Island Books.

Berger, P. and Luckmann, T. (1971 [1966]) *The Social Construction of Reality: A Treatise in the Sociology of Knowledge.* Harmondsworth: Penguin.

Berlin, I. (2003) *Generations of Captivity.* Cambridge, MA: Harvard University Press.

Berwick, R. and Whalley, T. (2000) The experiential bases of culture learning: a case study of Canadian high schoolers in Japan. *International Journal of Intercultural Relations* 24(3), 325–40.

Bhattacharya, C. B., Rao, H. and Glynn, M. (1995) Understanding the bond of identification: An investigation of its correlates among art museum members. *Journal of Marketing* 59(October), 46–57.

Bishop, J. (2007) Increasing participation in online communities: A framework for human-computer interaction. *Computers in Human Behavior* 23, 1881–93.

Bitner, M. J., Booms, B. H. and Tetreault, M. (1990) The service encounter: diagnosing favorable and unfavorable incidents, *Journal of Marketing* January, 71–84.

Blaikie, A. (2001) Photographs in the cultural account: contested narratives and collective memory in the Scottish Islands. *Sociological Review* 49(3), 345–67.

Blake, T. (2005) Journaling; An active learning technique [Electronic Version]. *International Journal of Nursing Education Scholarship* 2. Retrieved 30 October 2007, from http://www.bepress.com/ijnes/vol2/iss1/art7.

Blom, T. (2000) Morbid tourism – a postmodern market niche with an example from Althorp. *Norsk Geografisk Tidsskrift – Norwegian Journal of Geography* 54, 29–36.

Bloom, B. (1956) *Taxonomy of Educational Objectives: the Classification of Educational Goals*. New York: David McKay Co.

Boissevain, J. (1996) *Coping with Tourists. European Reactions to Mass Tourism.* Providence: Berghahn Books.

Bonnes, M. and Secchiaroli, G. (1995) *Environmental Psychology: A Psycho-social Introduction*. London: Sage Publications.

Boorstin, D. (1964) *The Image: A Guide to Pseudo-Events in America*. New York: Harper and Row.

Botterill, D., Gale, T. and Haven, C. (2002) A survey of doctoral theses accepted by universities in the UK and Ireland for studies related to tourism 1990–99. *Tourist Studies* 2, 283–311.

Boud, D. (2001) Using journal writing to enhance reflective practice. *New Directions for Adult and Continuing Education* 90, 9–18.

Boud, D., Keogh, R. and Walker, D. (1985a) Introduction: What is reflection in learning? In D. Boud, R. Keogh and D. Walker (eds), *Reflection: Turning Experience into Learning*, pp. 7–17. London: Kogan Page Ltd.

Boud, D., Keogh, R. and Walker, D. (1985b) Promoting reflection in learning: a model. In D. Boud, R. Keogh and D. Walker (eds), *Reflection: Turning Experience into Learning*, pp. 18–40. London: Kogan Page Ltd.

Boud, D., Keogh, R. and Walker, D. (eds) (1985c) *Reflection: Turning Experience into Learning*. London: Kogan Page Ltd.

Bourner, T. (2003) Assessing reflective learning. *Education and Training* 45(5), 267–72.

Boyd, E. and Fales, A. (1983) Reflective learning: Key to learning from experience. *Journal of Humanistic Psychology* 23(2), 99–117.

Boyte, H. (1980) *The Backyard Revolution: Understanding the New Citizen Movement.* Philadelphia: Temple University Press.

Brewer, J. (2000) *Ethnography*. Buckingham: Open University Press.

Briggs, C. (1986) *Learning How to Ask. A Sociolinguistic Appraisal of the Role of the Interview in Social Science Research*. Cambridge: Cambridge University Press.

Broadhurst, R. (2001) *Managing Environments for Leisure and Recreation*. London and New York: Routledge.

Brodsky-Porges, E. (1981) The grand tour travel as an educational device 1600–1800. *Annals of Tourism Research* 8(2), 171–86.

Brown, C. G. (1998) *Up-helly-aa. Custom, Culture and Community in Shetland.* Manchester: Manchester University Press.

Brown, S. R. (1980) *Political subjectivity: Applications of Q methodology in Political Science*. New Haven: Yale University Press.

Brown, S. R. (1993) A primer on Q methodology. *Operant Subjectivity* 16(3/4), 91–138.

Brown, S. R. (1995) Q methodology as the foundation for a science of subjectivity. *Operant Subjectivity* 18(1/2), 1–16.

Brown, S. R. (1996) Q methodology and qualitative research. *Qualitative Health Research* 6(4), 561.

Bruner, E. (1991) Transformation of self in tourism. *Annals of Tourism Research* 18(2), 238–50.

Bruner, E. (1996). Tourism in Ghana. *American Anthropologist* 98(2), 290–304.

Buckley, P. and Witt, S. F. (1987) The international tourism market in Eastern Europe. *The Service Industries Journal* 7, 91.

Burns, P. (1999) *An Introduction to Tourism and Anthropology*. London: Routledge.

Butcher, J. (2003) *The Moralisation of Tourism: Sun, Sand ... And Saving the World?*. London: Routledge.

Butler, D. L. (2001) Whitewashing plantations: the commodification of a slave-free Antebellum South. *International Journal of Hospitality and Tourism Administration* 2(3/4), 159–71.

Butler, D. L., Carter, P. L. and Dwyer, O. J. (2008) Imagining plantations: slavery, dominant narratives, and the foreign born. *Southeastern Geographer* 48(3), 288–302.

Butler, R. W. (1980) The concept of a tourist area cycle of evolution: Implications for management of resources. *The Canadian Geographer* 24(1), 5–12.

Butler, R. W. (1998) Tartan mythology. The traditional tourist image of Scotland. In G. Ringer (ed.) *Destinations. Cultural Landscapes of Tourism*, pp. 121–39. London: Routledge.

Butler, R. W. (2006a) *The Tourism Area Life Cycle Vol. 1: Applications and Modifications*. Clevedon: Channel View Press.

Butler, R. W. (2006b) *The Tourism Area Life Cycle Vol. 2: Conceptual and Theoretical Issues*. Clevedon: Channel View Press.

Butler, R. W. and Fennell, D. (1994) The effects of North Sea oil development on the development of tourism. The case of the Shetland Isles. *Tourism Management* 14(5), 347–57.

Buzinde, C. (2007) Representational politics of plantation heritage tourism: the contemporary plantation as a social imaginary. In C. McCarthy, A. Durham, L. Engel, M. Giardina, A. Filmer and M. Malagreca (eds) *Globalizing Cultural Studies: Ethnographic Interventions in Theory, Method, and Policy*, pp. 229–51. New York: Peter Lang Pub Inc.

Byrnes, D. (2001) Travel schooling: helping children learn through travel. *Childhood Education* 77(6), 345–50.

Campbell, C. (1987) *The Romantic Ethic and the Spirit of Modern Consumerism*. Oxford: Blackwell.

Cane River Creole National Historical Park, (n.d.) Online. Available at: http://www.nps.gov/cari (Accessed 11 February 2009)

Carmen, H. M. and Hernández, B. (2001) Place attachment: conceptual and empirical questions. *Journal of Environmental Psychology* 21(3), 273–81.

Carneiro, S. de Sa and Freire-Medeiros, B. (2005) Antropologia e 'novas' modalidades de turismo: múltiplas interfaces. *Religião e Sociedade*, Rio de Janeiro 24(2), 100–125.

Carpendale, J. (2000) Kohlberg and Piaget on Stages and Moral Reasoning. *Developmental Review* 20, 181–205.

Carr, N. (2006) Tourist behaviour: themes and conceptual schemes. *Journal of Sustainable Tourism* 14(5), 523–25.

Carroll, J. (1998) *Ego and Soul: The Modern West in Search of Meaning*. Sydney: HarperCollins.

Cary, S. H. (2004) The tourist moment. *Annals of Tourism Research* 31(1), 61–77.

Casais, J. (1940) *Un turista en el Brasil*. Rio de Janeiro: Livraria Kosmos.

Cass, V. C. (1979) Homosexual identity formation: A theoretical model. *Journal of Homosexuality* 4(3), 219–35.

Castro, C. (2001) A natureza turística do Rio de Janeiro. In Á. Banducci Jr and M. Barretto (eds) *Turismo e Identidade Local: uma visão antropológica*, pp. 117–26. Campinas: Papirus.

Cater, C. (2005) Looking the part: The relationship between adventure tourism and the outdoor fashion industry. In Ryan, C., Page, S. J. and Aicken, M. (eds) *Taking Tourism to the Limits*, pp. 183–206. Oxford: Pergamon.

Chagas, V. (2006) *O venhevai do turismo e o sobidesce da 'favela'*. Online. Available at: http://www.overmundo.com.br/overblog/o-venhevai-do-turismo-e-o-sobidesce-da-favela (Accessed 16 November 2009).

Charlton, E. (2007) *Travels in Shetland 1832–52*. Edited by William Charlton. Lerwick: Shetland Times Ltd.

Cherny, L. (2006) The Twitchers and Tweeters of Fair Isle. *Ghostwater.com – web essays*. Online. Available at: http://www.ghostweather.com/essays/fair-isle.html (Accessed November 2008).

Christenson, H. and Dustin, D. (1989) Reaching recreationists at different levels of Moral Development. *Journal of Park and Recreation Administration* 7, 72–80.

Chronis, A. (2005) Our Byzantine heritage: consumption of the past and its experiential benefits. *Journal of Consumer Marketing* 22(4), 213–22.

Chung, J. Y. and Buhalis, D. (2008) Web 2.0: A study of online travel community. In P. O'Connor, W. Höpken and U. Gretzel, (eds) *Information and Communication Technologies in Tourism 2008*, pp. 70–81. Vienna, Austria: Springer Verlag.

Clark, T. and Salaman, G. (1998) Telling tales: management gurus' narratives and the construction of managerial identity. *Journal of Management Studies* 35(2), 137–61.

Classen, C. (1993) *Worlds of Sense*. London: Routledge.

Cleverdon, R. (2005) *Tourism 2020 Vision: Global Forecasts and Profiles of Market Segments*. Madrid: United Nations World Tourism Organisation.

Clift, S. and Forrest, S. (1999) Gay Men and Tourism: Destinations and Holiday Motivations, *Tourism Management* 20(5), 615–25. Cited in H. Hughes (2004) A gay tourism market: reality or illusion, benefit or burden? *Journal of Quality Assurance in Hospitality and Tourism* 5 (2/3/4), 57–74.

Coakley, J. J. (2009) *Sport in Society: Issues and Controversies*. New York: Mcgraw-Hill.

Cohen, A. (1987) *Whalsay: Symbol, Segment and Boundary in a Shetland Island Community*. Manchester: Manchester University Press.

Cohen, E. (1972) Towards a sociology of international tourism. *Social Research* 39(1), 64–82.

Cohen, E. (1974) Who is a tourist? A conceptual clarification. *Sociological Review* 22(4), 527–55.

Cohen, E. (1979a) A phenomenology of tourist experiences. *Sociology* 13,179–201.

Cohen, E. (1979b) Rethinking the sociology of tourism, *Annals of Tourism Research* 6(1), 18–35.

Cohen, E. (1982a) Marginal paradises: Bungalow tourism on the islands of Southern Thailand. *Annals of Tourism Research* 9(2), 189–228.

Cohen, E. (1982b) Thai girls and farang men: The edge of ambiguity. *Annals of Tourism Research* 9, 403–28.

Cohen, E. (1988a) Authenticity and commoditization in tourism. *Annals of Tourism Research* 15 (3), 371–86.

Cohen, E. (1988b) The social psychology of tourist behaviour. *Annals of Tourism Research* 15(1), 29–46.

Cohen, E. (1992) Pilgrimage centres: concentric and excentric. *Annals of Tourism Research* 19(1), 33–50.

Cole, D. (2004) Exploring the sustainability of mining heritage tourism. *Journal of Sustainable Tourism* 12(6), 480–94.

Cole, T. (1999) *Selling the Holocaust, From Auschwitz to Schindler, How History is Bought, Packaged and Sold*. New York: Routledge.

Coleman, S. (2004) Pilgrimage to 'England's Nazareth': Landscapes of myth and memory at Walsingham. In E. Badone and S. Roseman (eds) *Intersecting Journeys: The Anthropology of Pilgrimage and Tourism*, pp. 52–67. Chicago: University of Illinois Press.

Coles, T., Hall, M. and Duval, D. (2006) Tourism and post-disciplinary enquiry. *Current Issues in Tourism* 9(4 & 5), 293–319.

Collins, D. (2007) When sex work isn't 'work': Hospitality, gay life, and the production of desiring labour. *Tourist Studies* 7(2), 115–39.

Connell, J. (2006) 'I can't eat that, it's purple': a geography field course in Vanuatu and Fiji. *Geographical Research* 44(1), 17–27.

Cornwall, A. and Nyamu-Musembi, C. (2004) Putting the 'rights-based approach' to development into perspective. *Third World Quarterly* 25(8), 1415–37.

Correia, A. and Esteves, S. (2007) An exploratory study of spectators' motivation in football. *International Journal of Sport Marketing and Management* 2 (5/6), 572–90.

Cosgrove, D. E. (1984) *Social Formulation and Symbolic Landscape*. London: Croom Helm Ltd.

Crang, M. (1999) Knowing tourism and practice of vision. In D. Crouch (ed.) *Leisure/Tourism Geographies: Practices and Geographical Knowledge*, pp. 238–76. London: Routledge.

Crawford, G. (2004) *Consuming Sport: Fans, Sport and Culture*. London: Routledge.

Crawshaw, C. and Urry, J. (1997) Tourism and the photographic eye. In J. Urry and C. Rojek (eds) *Touring Cultures: Transformations of Travel and Theory*, pp. 176–95. London: Routledge.

Crespi, M. (2004) *A Brief Ethnography of Magnolia Plantation: Planning for Cane River Creole National Historical Park*. Online. Available at: http://www.cr.nps.gov/aad/pubs/studies/study04a.htm (Accessed 23 February 2009).

Cresswell, T. (2004) *Place: A Short Introduction*. Oxford: Blackwell Publishing.

Creswell, J. W. and Tashakkori, A. (2007) Editorial: Differing perspectives on mixed methods research. *Journal of Mixed Methods Research* 1(4), 303–8.

Crick, M. (1988) Sun, sex, sights, savings and servility: representations of international tourism in the social sciences. *Criticism, Heresy and Interpretation* 1, 37–76.

Crocker, J. and Major, B. (1989) Social stigma and self esteem: The self-protective properties of stigma. *Psychological Review* 96, 608–30.

Crompton, J. (1979) Motivations for pleasure vacation. *Annals of Tourism Research* 6(4), 408–24.

Crouch, D. (2000) Places around us: embodied lay geographies in leisure and tourism. *Leisure Studies* 19(2), 63–76.

Crouch, D. and Desforges, L. (2003) The sensuous in the tourist encounter: Introduction: the power of the body in tourist studies. *Tourist Studies* 3(1), 5–22.

Crouch, D. and Lubbren, N. (2003) *Visual Culture and Tourism*. Oxford: Berg.

Csikszentimihalyi, M. (1975) *Beyond Boredom and Anxiety*. San Francisco: Jossey-Bass.

Csikszentimihalyi, M. and Csikszentimihalyi, I. S. (eds) (1988) *Optimal Experience: Psychological Studies of Flow in Consciousness*. Cambridge, NY: University of Cambridge Press.

Cuppernull, L., Marquez, M., Confessore, S. and Greenberg, L. (2004) *Teaching Medical Students the Lifelong Skill of Reflection Through Journaling: A Pilot Study*. Paper presented at the Pediatric Academic Societies' Annual Meeting, San Francisco, California.

Danielzik, C. and Khan, R. (2006) Fern Weh: Statisten ihres eigenen Alltags. Townshiptouren in Kapstadt als Herausforderung für die Tourismuskritik. *iz3w* 291, 37–39.

Dann, G. (1977) Anomie, ego-enhancement and tourism. *Annals of Tourism Research* 4(4), 184–94.

Dann, G. (1981) Tourist motivation: an appraisal. *Annals of Tourism Research* 8(2), 187–219.

Dann, G. (1996) *The Language of Tourism: A Sociolinguistic Perspective*. Wallingford: CABI.

Dann, G. (1998) *The Dark Side of Tourism*. Etudes et rapports, Série L. Aix-en-Provence: Centre International de Recherches et d'Etudes Touristiques.

Dann, G. (1999) Writing out the tourist in space and time. *Annals of Tourism Research* 26(1), 159–87.

Dann, G. and Jacobsen, J. (2002) Leading the tourist by the nose. In Dann, G. (ed.) *The Tourist as Metaphor of the Social World*, pp. 209–37. Wallingford: CABI.

Dann, G. and Jacobsen, J. (2003) Tourism smellscapes. *Tourism Geographies* 5(1), 3–25.

Dann, G. and Seaton, A. (eds) (2001) *Slavery, Contested Heritage and Thanatourism*. Binghamton, NY: Haworth Hospitality Press.

Daskalaki, M. (2003) *Gay Men's Holiday Choice: Destinations and Holiday Motivations*. Unpublished MA Dissertation, Preston: University of Central Lancashire.

Daugherty, T., Eastin, M. S. and Bright, L. (2008) Exploring consumer motivations for creating user-generated content. *Journal of Interactive Advertising* 8(2). Online. Available at: http://www.jiad.org/article101 (Accessed 13 August 2008).

David, C. and Luke, D. (2003) The sensuous in the tourist encounter: Introduction: The power of the body in tourist studies. *Tourist Studies* 3(1), 5–22.

Davidson, J. (2006) The necessity of queer shame for gay pride. In J. Caudwell (ed.) *Sport, Sexualities and Queer/Theory*, pp. 90–103. London: Routledge.

Davidson, J. and Milligan, C. (2004) Embodying emotion sensing space: Introducing emotional geographies. *Social & Cultural Geography* 5(4), 523–32.

Davidson-Hunt, I. and Berkes, F. (2003) Learning as you journey: Anishinaabe perception of social-ecological environments and adaptive learning. *Conservation Ecology* 8(1), 5. Online. Available at: http://www.consecol.org/vol8/iss1/art5/.

Davis, M. (2006) *Planet of Slums*. London: Verso.

Deane Young, P. (1994) *Lesbians and Gays in Sports*. New York: Chelsea House Publications.

Deeter-Schmelz, D. and Sojka, J. (2004) Wrestling with American values: An exploratory investigation of World Wrestling Entertainment as a product based subculture. *Journal of Consumer Behaviour* 4(2), 132–43.

Deleuze, G. and Guattari, F. (1988) *A Thousand Plateaus: Capitalism and Schizophrenia*. Brian Massumi, Translation. London: Athlone Press.

Denzin, N. (1994) The art and politics of interpretation. In N. Denzin and Y. Lincoln (eds) *Handbook of Qualitative Research*, pp. 500–515. London: Sage.

Denzin, N. and Lincoln, Y. (1998a) *Handbook of Qualitative Research*. London: Sage.

Denzin, N. and Lincoln, Y. (1998b) *The Landscape of Qualitative Research: Theories and Issues*. London: Sage.

Denzin, N. and Lincoln, Y. (2000a) Preface. In N. Denzin and Y. Lincoln *Handbook of Qualitative Research*, 2nd edn, pp. ix–xx. London: Sage.

Denzin, N. and Lincoln, Y. (2000b) Introduction: The discipline and practice of qualitative research. In N. Denzin and Y. Lincoln (eds) *Handbook of Qualitative Research*, 2nd edn, pp. 1–29. London: Sage.

Department of Conservation (1996) *Visitor Strategy*. Wellington: Department of Conservation.

Desforges, L. (2000) Traveling the world: Identity and travel biography. *Annals of Tourism Research* 27(1), 203–24.

Dewar, K., Wen, M. and Davis, C. (2007) Photographic images, culture, and perception in tourism: A Q Methodology study of Canadian and Chinese university students. *Journal of Travel & Tourism Marketing* 22(2), 35–44.

Dias, R. (2003) *Sociologia do Turismo*. São Paulo: Atlas.

Diener, E. (1992) *Assessing Subjective Well Being: Progress and Opportunities*. Unpublished paper, University of Illinois.

Diener, E. and Diener, C. (1996) Most people are happy. *Psychological Science* 7, 181–85.

Diener, E. and Diener, M. (1995) Cross-cultural correlates of life satisfaction and self-esteem. *Journal of Personality and Social Psychology* 68, 653–63.

Digance, J. (2003) Pilgrimage at contested sites. *Annals of Tourism Research* 30 (1), 143–59.

Digance, J. (2006) Religious and secular pilgrimage: journeys redolent with meaning. In D. Timothy and D. Olsen (eds) *Tourism, Religion and Spiritual Journeys*, pp. 36–48. Abingdon: Routledge.

Diller, E. and Scofidio, R. (eds) (1994) *Back to the Front: Tourisms of War*. Basse-Normandie: FRAC.

Donnelly, J. (1989) *Universal Human Rights in Theory and Practice*. New York: Cornell University Press.

Douglas, A. and Mills, J. (2006) Logging brand personality online: content analysis of Middle Eastern and North African destinations. In M. Hitz, M. Sigala and J. Murphy (eds) *Information and Communication Technologies in Tourism 2006*, p. 345. Vienna, Austria: Springer Verlag.

Dowling, R. M. (2007) *Slumming in New York: From the Waterfront to Mythic Harlem*. Urbana and Chicago: University of Illinois Press.

Dzeko, S. (2001) Sarajevo goes out to the world. *Turist*, Sarajevo: Tourism Canton of Sarajevo.

Eade, J. and Sallnow, M. (1991a) *Contesting the Sacred: The Anthropology of Christian Pilgrimage*. London: Routledge.

Eade, J. and Sallnow, M. (1991b) Introduction. In J. Eade and M. Sallnow (eds) *Contesting the Sacred: The Anthropology of Christian Pilgrimage*, pp. 1–29. London: Routledge.

Eber, S. (1992) *Beyond the Green Horizon: A Discussion Paper on Principles for Sustainable Tourism*. Godalming: WWF UK.

Edwards, J. and Llurdés i Coit, J. (1996) Mines and quarries: Industrial heritage tourism. *Annals of Tourism Research* 23(2), 341–63.

Egner, H. (2006) Autopoiesis, Form und Beobachtung. *Mitteilungen der Österreichischen Geographischen Gesellschaft* 148, 92–108.

Eichstedt, J. and Small, S. (2002) *Representations of Slavery: Race and Ideology in Southern Plantation Museums.* Washington, DC: Smithsonian Institute Press.

Elwood, S. A. (2004) Experiential learning, spatial practices and critical urban geographies. *Journal of Geography* 103, 55–63.

eMarketer (2007) UGC users outnumber creators. Online. Available at: http://www. Emarketer.com (Accessed 2 July 2007).

Emery, F. (1981) Alternative futures in tourism. *International Journal of Tourism Management* 2(1), 241–55.

Eriksen, T. (2001 [1995]) *Small Places, Large Issues: An Introduction to Social and Cultural Anthropology.* London: Pluto Press.

Escalas, J. E. (2004) Narrative processing: Building consumer connections to brands. *Journal of Consumer Psychology* 14(1/2), 168–80.

Escobar, A. (1995) *Encountering Development: The Making and Unmaking of the Third World.* Princeton: Princeton University Press.

Escobar, A. (2005) Imagining a post-development era. In M. Edelman and A. Haugerud (eds) *The Anthropology of Development and Globalisation: From Classical Political Economy to Contemporary Neoliberalism*, pp. 341–51. Oxford: Blackwell Publishing.

Esteva, G. (1988) El desastre agrícola: adiós al México imaginario. *Comercio Extrerio* 38(8), 662–72.

Ewart, A. (1989) *Outdoor Adventure Pursuits: Foundations, Models and Theories.* Columbus Ohio: Publishing Horizons.

Fairley, S. (2006) *Sport Fan Tourism: Understanding Those Who Travel to Follow Sport Teams.* Unpublished PhD Thesis, Griffith Business School, Griffith University, Brisbane.

Fairley, S. and Gammon, S. (2005) Something lived, something learned: nostalgia's expanding role in sport tourism. *Sport in Society: Cultures, Commerce, Media, Politics* 8(2), 182–98.

Fairweather, J. and Swaffield, S. (2001) Visitor experiences in Kaikoura, New Zealand. *Tourism Management* 22(3), 219–28.

Featherstone, M. (1990) Perspectives on consumer culture. *Sociology* 24(1), 5–22.

Featherstone, M. and Lash, S. (1999) *Spaces of Culture.* London: Sage Publications.

Fedarko, K. (1993) Monday, Holidays In Hell, *Time Magazine*, 23 August. Online. Available at: http://www.time.com/time/magazine/article/0,9171,979078-2,00.html.

Feifer, M. (1985) *Going Places.* London, Macmillan.

Ferguson, S. and Todd, S. (2005) Acquiring status through the consumption of adventure tourism. In C. Ryan, S. Page and M. Aicken (eds) *Taking Tourism to the Limits*, pp. 149–54. Oxford: Pergamon.

Field, N. (1995) *Over the Rainbow: Money, Class and Homophobia.* London: Pluto. Cited in H. Hughes (2004) A gay tourism market: reality or illusion, benefit or burden? *Journal of Quality Assurance in Hospitality and Tourism* 5 (2/3/4), 57–74.

Fink, J., Trail, G. and Anderson, D. (2002) An examination of team identification: which motives are most salient to its existence? *International Sports Journal* 6 (summer), 195–207.

Fisher, K. (2003) Demystifying critical reflection: defining criteria for assessment. *Higher Education Research and Development*, 22(3), 313–25.

Foley, M. and Lennon, J. (1996) JFK and dark tourism: a fascination with assassination. *International Journal of Heritage Studies* 2(4), 198–211.

Football Association (n.d.) *FA Sports Equity Strategy*. London: Football Association.

Forsyth, T. (1996) *Sustainable Tourism: Moving from Theory to Practice*. Godalming: WWF UK and Tourism Concern.

Foucault, M. (1977) *Discipline and Punish: The Birth of the Prison*. London: Penguin Books.

France, L. (1997) *Sustainable Tourism*. London: Earthscan.

Franklin, A. (2009) The sociology of tourism. In T. Jamal and M. Robinson (eds) *The Sage Handbook of Tourism Studies*, pp. 65–81. London: Sage Publications.

Franklin, A. and Crang, M. (2001) The trouble with travel and tourism theory? *Tourist Studies* 1(1), 5–22.

Freire-Medeiros, B. (2000) *Cultura de Viagem: uma visita à produção acadêmica anglo-americana*. Revista Interseções, Rio de Janeiro.

Freire-Medeiros, B. (2006) *A favela que se vê e que se vende: Reflexões e polêmicas em torno de um destino turístico*. Paper apresentado no XXX Encontro Nacional da Anpocs – Caxambu, Outubro.

Freire-Medeiros, B. (2007) A favela que se vê e que se vende: reflexões e polêmicas em torno de um destino turístico. *Revista Brasileira de Ciências Sociais* 22, 61–72.

Freire-Medeiros, B. (2008) And the favela went global: the invention of a trademark and a tourist destination. In M. Valença, E. Nel and W. Leimgruber (eds) *The Global Challenge and Marginalization*. New York: Nova Science Publishers.

Freire-Medeiros, B. (2009a) The favela and its touristic transits. *Geoforum* 40(4), 580–88.

Freire-Medeiros, B. (2009b) *Gringo na laje – Produção, circulação e consumo da favela turística*. Rio de Janeiro: Editora FGV.

Frey, N. (1998) *Pilgrim Stories: On and Off the Road to Santiago*. University of California Press: USA.

Frey, N. (2004) Stories of the return: pilgrimage and its aftermaths. In E. Badone and S. Roseman (eds) *Intersecting Journeys: The Anthropology of Pilgrimage and Tourism*, pp. 89–109. Chicago: University of Illinois Press.

Friedman, D. and McAdam, D. (1992) Collective identity and activism. In A. D. Morris and C. McClurg Mueller (eds) *Frontiers in Social Movement Theory*, pp. 156–173. New Haven: Yale University Press.

Fugate, D. (1993) Evaluating the US male homosexual and lesbian population as a viable target market segment. *Journal of Consumer Marketing* 10(4), 46–57.

Fuller, I., Gaskin, S. and Scott, I. (2003) Student perceptions of geography and environmental science fieldwork in the light of restricted access to the field, caused by Foot and Mouth Disease in the UK in 2001. *Journal of Geography in Higher Education* 27(1), 79–102.

Funk, D. C., Mahony, D. F., Nakazawa, M. and Hirakawa, S. (2001) Development of the sport interest inventory (SII): Implications for measuring unique consumer motives at team sporting events. *International Journal of Sports Marketing and Sponsorship* 3, 291–316.

Funk, D., Mahony D. and Ridinger, L. (2002) Characterising consumer motivation as individual difference factors: augmenting the sport interest inventory (SII) to explain level of sport. *Sport Marketing Quarterly* 11, 33–43.

Gaffney, C. and Bale, J. (2004) Sensing the stadium. In P. Vertinsky and J. Bale (eds) *Sites of Sport: Space, Place, Experience*, pp. 25–39. London: Routledge.

Galani-Moutafi, V. (2000) The Self and the Other. Traveller, ethnographer, the tourist. *Annals of Tourism Research* 27(1), 204–24.

Gammon, S. (2004) Secular pilgrimage and sport tourism. In B. Ritchie and D. Adair (eds) *Sport Tourism: Interrelationships, Impacts and Issues*, pp. 1–28. Clevedon: Channel View Publications.

Gammon, S. (2007) Introduction: sport, heritage and the English. An opportunity missed? In S. Gammon and G. Ramshaw (eds) *Heritage, Sport and Tourism: Sporting Pasts – Tourist Futures*, pp. 1–8. London: Routledge.

Gammon, S. and Fear, V. (2007) Stadia tours and the power of backstage. In S. Gammon and G. Ramshaw (eds) *Heritage, Sport and Tourism: Sporting Pasts – Tourist Futures*, pp. 23–32. London: Routledge.

Gardner, K. and Lewis, D. (1996) *Anthropology, Development and the Post-modern Challenge*. London: Pluto Press.

Geertz, C. (1973) *The Interpretation of Cultures*. New York: Basic Books.

Gentleman, A. (2006) Slum tours: a day trip too far? *The Observer*, 7 May.

Gibson, H. (1998) Sport tourism: a critical analysis of research. *Sport Management Review* 1 (1), 45–76.

Gibson, H. (2004) Moving beyond the 'what is and who' of sport tourism to understanding 'why'. *Journal of Sport Tourism* 9(3), 247–65.

Gibson, H. (2005a) Towards an understanding of 'why sport tourists do what they do'. *Sport in Society Special Issue: Sport Tourism: Concepts and Theories* 8(2), 198–217.

Gibson, H. (2005b) Understanding sport tourism experiences. In J. Higham (ed.) *Sport Tourism Destinations: Issues, Opportunities and Analysis*. Oxford: Butterworth Heinemann.

Gibson, H. and Yiannakis, A. (2002) Tourist roles, needs and the life course. *Annals of Tourism Research* 29(2), 358–83.

Gilligan, C. (1982) *In a Different Voice*. Cambridge, MA: Harvard University Press.

Giulianotti, R. (2005) *Sport: a Critical Sociology*. Cambridge: Polity Press.

Gmelch, G. (1997) Crossing cultures: Student travel and personal development. *International Journal of Intercultural Relations* 21(4), 475–90.

Goffman, E. (1990 [1959]) *Presentation of Self in Everyday Life*. London: Penguin Books.

Gold, J. R. (1992) Image and environment: the decline of cognitive-behaviouralism in human geography and grounds for regeneration. *Geoforum* 23(2), 239–47.

Golledge, R. G. (1991) Cognition of physical and built environments. In T. Garling and G. Evans (eds) *Environment, Cognition and Action: An Integrated Approach*, pp. 35–62. New York: Oxford University Press.

Golledge, R. G. and Stimson, R. J. (1997) *Spatial Behavior: A Geographic Perspective*. New York: Guildford.

Graburn, N. (1983) The anthropology of tourism, *Annals of Tourism Research* 10 (1), 9–33.

Graburn, N. (1977) Tourism: the sacred journey. In V. Smith (ed.) *Hosts and Guests: The Anthropology of Tourism*, pp. 33–47. Oxford: Basil Blackwell.

Graburn, N. (1989) Tourism: the sacred journey. In V. Smith, (ed.) *Hosts and guests: the anthropology of tourism*, pp. 17–32. Philadelphia: University of Pennsylvania Press.

Graburn, N. (2001) Secular ritual: a general theory of tourism. In V. Smith and M. Brent (eds) *Hosts and Guests Revisited: Tourism Issues in the 21st Century*, pp. 42–50. New York: Cognizant Communication Corporation.

Graburn, N. (2002) The ethnographic tourist. In G. Dann (ed.) *The Tourist as a Metaphor of the Social World*, pp. 19–40. Wallingford: CABI.

Graham, B. J., Ashworth, G. J. and Tunbridge, J. E. (2000) *A Geography of Heritage: Power, Culture, and Economy*. London: Arnold.

Green, C. and Jones, I. (2005) Serious leisure, social identity and sport tourism. *Sport in Society* 8(2), 198–217.

Greenwood, D. J. (1989) Culture by the pound: An anthropological perspective on tourism and cultural commodification. In V. Smith (ed.) *Hosts and Guests: The Anthropology of Tourism*, pp. 17–31. Philadelphia: University of Pennsylvania Press.

Gretzel, U. (2006) Consumer generated content – trends and implications for branding', *E-Review of Tourism Research* 4(3). Online. Available at: http://ertr.tamu.edu/attachments/199_c-4-3-1.pdf (Accessed 20 June 2006).

Gretzel, U., Fesenmaier, D. R. and O'Leary, J. T. (2006) The transformation of consumer behaviour. In D. D. Buhalis and C. Costa (eds) *Tourism Business Frontiers*, pp. 9–18. Burlington, MA: Elsevier/Butterworth-Heinemann.

Gretzel, U., Fesenmaier, D. R., Formica, S. and O'Leary, J. T. (2006) Searching for the future: challenges faced by destination marketing organizations. *Journal of Travel Research* 45(2), 116–26.

Gretzel, U., Kang, M. and Lee, W. (2008) Differences in consumer-generated media adoption and use: A cross-national perspective. *Journal of Hospitality Marketing and Management* 17(1/2), 99–120.

Gross, M. J. and Brown, G. (2006) Tourism experiences in a lifestyle destination setting: the roles of involvement and place attachment. *Journal of Business Research* 59(6), 696–700.

Gross, M. J. and Brown, G. (2008) An empirical structure model of tourists and places: Progressing involvement and place attachment into tourism. *Tourism Management* 29(6), 1141–51.

Grunert, K. and Grunert, S. (1995) Measuring subjective meaning structures by the laddering method: theoretical considerations and methodological problems. *International Journal of Research in Marketing* 12(3), 209–25.

Gu, H. and Ryan, C. (2008) Chinese clientele at Chinese hotels – Preferences and satisfaction. *International Journal of Hospitality Management* 27(3), 337–45.

Guaracino, J. (2007) *Gay and Lesbian Tourism: The Essential Guide for Marketing*. Oxford: Butterworth Heinemann.

Guba, E. (1990) *The Paradigm Dialog*. Newbury Park, CA: Sage.

Guha, R. (1983) The prose of counter-insurgency. In R. Guha, *Subaltern Studies* 11. New Delhi: Oxford University Press.

Guha, R. (1988) Preface. In R. Guha and G. Spivak, *Selected Subaltern Studies*. New York: Oxford University Press.

Guha, R. (1996) The small voice of history. In R. Guha, *Subaltern Studies* 9. New Delhi: Oxford University Press.

Gunn, C. (1988) *Tourism Planning*. New York: Taylor and Francis.

Guran, M. (2002) *Linguagem fotográfica e informação*. Rio de Janeiro: Editora Gama Filho.

Guy, B., Curtis, W. and Crotts, J. (1990) Environmental learning of first-time travelers. *Annals of Tourism Research* 17(3), 419–31.

Haas, G., Driver, B. and Brown, P. (1980) *Measuring Wilderness Experiences*. In *Proceedings in the Wilderness Psychology Group*, pp. 20–40. New Hampshire: Durham.

Hadley, C. and Hall, D. (2004) *Representations of Slavery: Race and Ideology in Southern Plantation Museums*, by Jennifer L. Eichstedt and Stephen Small. Reviewed in: *The Public Historian* 26(3), 69–71.

Halberstam, J. (2003) What's that smell? Queer temporalities and sub-cultural lives. *International Journal of Cultural Studies* 6, 313–33.

Hall, C. M. (1994) *Tourism and Politics: Power, Policy and Place*. Chichester: John Wiley & Sons.

Hall, C. M. (2004) Reflexivity and tourism research: situating myself and/with others. In J. Phillimore and L. Goodson (eds) *Qualitative Research in Tourism: Ontologies, Epistemologies, Methodologies*, pp. 137–55. London: Routledge.

Hall, C. M. (2006) Travel and journeying on the Sea of Faith. In D. Timothy and D. Olsen (eds) *Tourism, Religion and Spiritual Journeys*, pp. 64–77. Abingdon: Routledge.

Hall, C. M. and Page, S. (2009) Progress in Tourism Management: From the geography of tourism to geographies of tourism – A review. *Tourism Management* 30(1), 3–16.

Hall, S. (1997) *Representation: Cultural Representations and Signifying Practices*. London: Sage/Open University.

Hall, S. (2002) The West and the Rest: discourse and power'. In S. Scheh and J. Haggis (eds) *Development: A Cultural Studies Reader*, pp. 56–64. Oxford: Blackwell Publishers.

Hall, S. C. (1853) *Pilgrimages to English Shrines*. London: Hall, Virtue & Co.

Hamm, B. (2001) A human rights approach to development. *Human Rights Quarterly* 23, 1005–31.

Hammer, J. (2008) Landscape after battle. *Condé Nast Traveller*. Online. Available at: http://www.concierge.com/cntraveler/articles/11854?pageNumber = 7 (Accessed March 2008).

Hammersley, M. and Atkinson, P. (1995) *Ethnography: Principles in Practice*, 2nd edn. London: Routledge.

Harrison, M., Short, C. and Roberts, C. (2003) Reflecting on reflective learning: the case of geography, earth and environmental sciences. *Journal of Geography in Higher Education* 27(3), 133–52.

Harrison, R. P. (2003) *The Dominion of the Dead*. Chicago: Chicago University Press.

Havitz, M. and Dimanche, F. (1990) Propositions for testing the involvement construct in recreation tourism contexts. *Leisure Sciences* 12,179–95.

Healey, M. and Jenkins, A. (2000) Kolb's experiential learning theory and its application in geography in higher education. *Journal of Geography* 99(5), 185–95.

Heath, E. and Wall, G. (1992) *Marketing Tourism Destinations*. Toronto: John Wiley & Sons.

Hekma, G. (1994) *As Long As They Don't Provoke*. Amsterdam: Het Spinhuis. Cited in De Knop, P. and Knoppers, A. (2003) Gay/lesbian sports clubs and events: Places of homo-social bonding and cultural resistance? *International Review of Sociology of Sport* 38, 441–56.

Hennig-Thurau, T., Gwinner, K. P., Walsh, G. and Gremler, D. D. (2004) Electronic word-of-mouth via consumer-opinion platforms: What motivates consumers to articulate themselves on the Internet? *Journal of Interactive Marketing* 18(1), 38–52.

Higgins-Desboilles, F. (2006) More than an 'industry': The forgotten power of tourism as a social force. *Tourism Management* 27, 1192–208.

Higham, J. and Hinch, T. (2009) *Sport and Tourism: Globalization, Mobility and Identity*. Oxford: Butterworth-Heinemann.

Hinch, T. and Higham, J. (2001) Sport tourism: a framework for research. *The International Journal of Tourism Research* 3(1), 45–58.

Hinch, T. and Higham. J. (2004) *Sport Tourism Development*. Clevedon: Channel View Publications.

Hinch, T. and Higham, J. (2005) Sport Tourism and Authenticity. *European Sport Management Quarterly* 5, 243–56.

Hodge, P. (2004) *Development Issues. Volunteer Work Overseas: for Australians and New Zealanders*. Newcastle: Global Exchange.

Hollander, P. (1981) *Political Pilgrims: Travels of Western Intellectuals to the Soviet Union, China, and Cuba 1928–1978*. Oxford: Oxford University Press.

Hollinshead, K. (1998a) Tourism, hybridity, and ambiguity: The relevance of Bhabha's 'Third Space' cultures. *Journal of Leisure Research* 30(1), 121–56.

Hollinshead, K. (1998b) Tourism and the restless peoples: A dialectical inspection of Bhabha's Halfway Populations. *Tourism, Culture and Communication* 1(1), 49–77.

Hollinshead, K. (1998c) Disney and commodity aesthetics: a critique of Fjellman's analysis of 'Distory' and the 'Historicide' of the past. *Current Issues in Tourism* 1(1), 58–119.

Hollinshead, K. (1999) Surveillance of the worlds of tourism: Foucault and the eye-of-power, *Tourism Management* 20(1), 7–24.

Holloway, I. and Todres L. (2003) The status of method: flexibility, consistency and coherence. *Qualitative Research* 3(3), 345–57.

Hottola, P. (2004) Culture confusion: intercultural adaptation in tourism. *Annals of Tourism Research* 31(2), 447–66.

Hötzl, M. (2006) Reading histories and telling stories, time and time again … . *Kontakt*. Online. Available at: http://www.kontakt.erstebankgroup.net/report/stories/issue15_Lesen+in+den+Geschichten+und+erzaehlen_dt+en/en (Accessed September 2008).

Howard, J., Thwaites, R. and Smith, B. (2001) Investigating the roles of the indigenous tour guide. *The Journal of Tourism Studies* 12(2), 32–39.

Howes, D. (2003) *Sensual Relations: Engaging the Senses in Culture and Social Theory*. Michigan: University of Michigan Press.

Howes, D. (2005) *Introduction to Empire of the Senses: The Sensual Cultural Reader*. Oxford: Berg.

Howitt, W. (1840) *Visits to Remarkable Places: Old Halls, Battlefields, and Scenes Illustrative of Striking Passages in English History* (2 Vols). London: Longman.

Hsu, C. H. C., Cai, L. A and Wong, K. K. F. (2007) A model of senior tourism motivations: Anecdotes from Beijing and Shanghai. *Tourism Management* 28(5), 1262–73.

Hughes, G. (1995) Authenticity in tourism. *Annals of Tourism Research* 22(4), 781–203.

Hughes, G. (1998) Tourism and the Semiological Realization of Place. In G. Ringer (ed.) *Destinations: Cultural Landscapes of Tourism*, 17–32. London: Routledge.

Hughes, H. (1993) Olympic tourism and urban regeneration; 1996 Summer Olympics. *Festival Management and Event Tourism* 1(4), 137–84.

Hughes, H. (1997) Holidays and homosexual identity. *Tourism Management* 18(1), 3–7.

Hughes, H. (2004) A gay tourism market: reality or illusion, benefit or burden? *Journal of Quality Assurance in Hospitality and Tourism* 5 (2/3/4), 57–74.

Hunt, J. (2000) Travel experience in the formation of leadership: John Quincy Adams, Frederick Douglass and Jane Addams. *Journal of Leadership and Organizational Studies* 7(1), 92–106.

Hutnyk, J. (1996) *The Rumour of Calcutta: Tourism, Charity and the Poverty of Representation.* London: Zed Books.

Hymes, D. (1962) The ethnography of speaking. In T. Gladwin and W. Sturtevant (eds) *Anthropology and Human Behavior.* Washington DC: Anthropological Society of Washington.

Illich, I. (2001a) Development as planned poverty. In M. Rahnema and V. Bawtree (eds) *The Post-Development Reader*, pp. 94–102. London: Zed Books.

Illich, I. (2001b) Needs. In W. Sachs (ed.) *The Development Dictionary: A Guide to Knowledge as Power*, pp. 88–101. London: Zed Books.

International Olympic Committee (2008) *Olympic Marketing Factfile.* Online. Available at: http://multimedia.olympic.org/pdf/en_report_344.pdf (Accessed on 23 November 2009).

Iso-Ahola, S. E. (1982) Towards a social psychological theory of tourism motivation: a rejoinder. *Annals of Tourism Research* 9(2), 256–62.

Ittelson, W. H. (1973) Environment perceptions and contemporary perceptual theory. In W. H. Ittelson (ed.) *Environment and Cognition*, New York: Seminar Press.

Iwashita, C. (2003) Media construction of Britain as a destination for Japanese tourists: Social construction and tourism. *Tourism and Hospitality Research* 4(4), 331–40.

Jackson, P. and Sullivan, G. (eds) (1999) *Lady Boys, Tom Boys, Rent Boys: Male and Female Homosexualities in Contemporary Thailand.* Oxford: Haworth Press.

Jaguaribe, B. and Hetherington, K. (2004) Favela Tours: indistinct and mapless representations of the real in Rio de Janeiro. In M. Sheller and J. Urry (eds) *Tourism Mobilities. Places to Play, Places in Play*, pp. 155–66. London, New York: Routledge.

Jalland, P. (1996) *Death in the Victorian Family.* Oxford: Oxford University Press.

Jamal, T. (2007) *Bridging the production-consumption divide: towards a framework for conceptualizing dark tourism.* Paper presented on 29 November 2007, at the Colloquium of the Melbern G. Glasscock Center for the Humanities, Texas A&M University, College Station, Texas.

Jamal, T. and Hill, S. (2002) The home and the world; (post) touristic spaces of (in) authenticity? In G. Dann (ed.) *The Tourist as a Metaphor of the Social World*, pp. 77–107. Wallingford: CABI.

Jamal, T. and Hollinshead, K. (2001) Tourism and the forbidden zone: the underserved power of qualitative enquiry. *Tourism Management* 22(1), 63–82.

Jamal, T. and Kim, H. (2005) Bridging the interdisciplinary divide: Towards an integrated framework for heritage tourism research. *Tourist Studies* 5(1), 55–83.

James, J. and Ross, S. (2004) Comparing sport consumer motivations across multiple sports. *Sport Marketing Quarterly* 13, 17–25.

Jarvie, G. (2006) *Sport, Culture and Society: An Introduction.* London: Routledge.

John, G. (2002) Stadia and tourism. In S. Gammon and J. Kurtzman (eds) *Sport Tourism: Principles and Practice*, pp. 53–61. Eastbourne: LSA Publications.

Johnston, H. and Klandermans, B. (1995) (eds) *Social Movements and Culture.* Minneapolis: University of Minnesota Press.

Jones, I. (2006) Examining the characteristics of serious leisure from a social identity perspective. In S. Elkington, I. Jones and L. Lawrence (eds) *Serious Leisure: Extensions and Applications*, pp. 47–60. Eastbourne: LSA.

Jones, L. and McCarthy, M. (2010) Mapping the landscape of gay men's football. *Leisure Studies* 29(2), 161–173.

Karlsson, L. (2006) The diary weblog and the travelling tales of diasporic tourists. *Journal of Intercultural Studies* 27(3), 299–312.

Kasimati, E. (2003) Economic aspects and the Summer Olympics: a review of related research. *International Journal of Tourism Research* 5(6), 433–44.

Kaufman, J. (2002) *NATO and the Former Yugoslavia: Crisis, Conflict, and the Atlantic Alliance*. Maryland: Rowman and Littlefield Publishers.

Keelan, N. (1993) Maori heritage, visitor management and interpretation. In M. Hall and S. McArthur (eds) *Heritage Management in New Zealand and Australia*. Oxford: Oxford University Press.

Keil, C. (2005) Sightseeing in the mansions of the dead. *Social & Cultural Geography* 6(4), 479–94.

Kell, J. R. (1974) Socialization towards leisure: a developmental approach. *Journal of Leisure Research* 6(3), 181–93.

Kellehear, A. (2007) *A Social History of Dying*. Cambridge: Cambridge University Press.

Kelly, G. A. (1955) *The Psychology of Personal Constructs*. Norton: New York.

Kelly, R. (1974) Socialization toward leisure: a developmental approach. *Journal of Leisure Research* 6, 181–93.

Kendle, A. (2008) Poverty tourism: exploring the slums of India, Brazil and South Africa. *Vagabondish: The Travelzine for Today's Vagabond*, 7 February 20. Online. Available at: http://www.vagabondish.com/poverty-tourism-touring-the-slums-of-india-brazil-and-south-africa (Accessed 16 November 2008).

Kent, M., Gilbertson, D. and Hunt, C. O. (1997) Fieldwork in geography teaching: a critical review of the literature and approaches. *Journal of Geography in Higher Education* 21(3), 313–32.

Kerlinger, F. N. (1986) *Foundations of Behavior Research*, 3rd edn. New York: Holt, Rinehart and Winston.

Kim, W. G., Lee, C. and Hiemstra, S. J. (2004) Effects of an online virtual community on customer loyalty and travel product purchases. *Tourism Management* 25, 343–55.

Kim, E. K. and Schrier, T. R. (2007) eWOM: what motivates consumers to write hotel reviews on the Internet. Proceedings of the 12th Annual Graduate Education & Graduate Student Research Conference in Hospitality & Tourism, Houston, Texas, January 4–6, 2007.

Kirshenblatt-Gimblett, B. (1998) *Destination Culture: Tourism, Museums and Heritage*. Berkeley: University of California Press.

Klandermans, B. and Oegema, D. (1987) Potentials, networks, motivations and barriers: steps towards participation in social movements. *American Sociological Review* 52, 519–31.

Klein, N. (2004) Reclaiming the commons. In T. Mertes (ed.) *A Movement of Movements: Is Another World Really Possible?* London: Verso.

Klenosky, D. (2002) The 'pull' of tourism destinations: A means-end investigation. *Journal of Travel Research* 40 (May), 385–95.

Knoke, D. (1988) Incentives in collective action organisations. *American Sociological Review*, 53, 311–29.

Knox, D. (2006) The sacralised landscapes of Glencoe: from massacre to mass tourism, and back again. *International Journal of Tourism Research* 8(3), 185–97.

Kohlberg, L. (1976) Moral Stages and moralization: the Cognitive-Developmental Approach. In T. Lickona (ed.) *Moral Development and Behavior: Theory, Research and Social Issues*. New York: Holt, Rinehart and Winston.

Kohlberg, L. (1980) Stages of Moral Development as a basis for moral education. In B. Munsey (ed.) *Moral Development, Moral Education and Kohlberg: Basic Issues in Philosophy, Psychology, Religion and Education*. Birmingham, Alabama: Religious Education Press.

Koivunen, E.-R. (2006) 'Ulan Bator – Doncaster, what's the difference!' Meaning creation and the internet in an island community. Unpublished thesis, University of Helsinki.

Kossoy, B. (1999) *Realidades e Ficções na Trama Fotográfica*. São Paulo: Ateliê Editorial.

Kotler, P., Haider, D. and Rein, I. (1993) *Marketing Places: Attracting Investment, Industry and Tourism to Cities, States and Nations*. New York: Free Press.

Koumelis, T. (2007) Bosnia and Herzegovina makes WTM debut. *World Travel Market*. Online. Available at: http://www.traveldailynews.com (Accessed October 2007).

Koven, S. (2006) *Slumming: Sexual and Social Politics in Victorian London*. Princeton: University Press.

Krane, V., Barber, H. and McClung, L. (2002) Social psychological benefits of Gay Games participation: a social identify theory explanation. *Journal of Applied Sport Psychology* 14, 27–42.

Kretchmarr, A. S. (1994) *Practical Philosophy of Sport*. Champaign, Il: Human Kinetics. Cited in Weed, M. and Bull, C. (2004) *Sports Tourism: Participants, Policy and Providers*. Oxford: Elsevier Butterworth Heinemann.

Krippendorf, J. (1984) *The Holiday Makers: Understanding the Impact of Leisure and Travel*. Oxford: Butterworth Heinemann.

Krippendorf, J. (1986) Tourism in the system of industrial society. *Annals of Tourism Research* 13(4), 517–32.

Kuh, G. (1995) The other curriculum: Out-of-class experiences associated with student learning and personal development. *The Journal of Higher Education* 66(2), 123–55.

Kuhn, T. (1970) *The Structure of Scientific Revolutions*. Chicago: University of Chicago Press.

Kurtzman, J. (2005) Sports tourism categories. *Journal of Sports Tourism* 10(1), 15–20.

Lagerkvist, A. (2007) Gazing at Pudong – 'With a Drink in Your Hand': Time travel, mediation, and multisensuous immersion in the future city of Shanghai. *The Senses & Society* 2(2), 155–72.

Lash, S. and Urry, J. (1987) *The End of Organized Capitalism*. Cambridge: Polity Press.

Lash, S. and Urry, J. (1994) *Economies of Signs and Space*. London: Sage Publications.

Laxson, J. (1991) How 'we' see 'them': tourism and Native Americans. *Annals of Tourism Research* 18(3), 365–91.

Lee, Y., Yoo, K.-H. and Gretzel, U. (2009) Social identity formation through blogging: Comparison of U.S. and Korean travel blogs', Paper presented at the 14th Annual Graduate Student Research Conference in Hospitality and Tourism, Las Vegas, January 4–6, 2009.

Leiper, N. (1983) Why people travel: a causal approach to tourism. Working Paper. Sydney, Australia. Sydney Technical College.

Leiper, N. (2008) Why the 'Tourism Industry' is misleading as a generic expression: The case for the plural variation, 'tourism industries'. *Tourism Management* 29(2), 237–51.

Lennon, J. and Foley, M. (2000.) *Dark Tourism: The Attraction of Death and Disaster.* London: Continuum.

Lennon, J. J. and Mitchell, M. (2007) The role of sites of death in tourism. In M. Mitchell (ed.) *Remember me: constructing immortality, beliefs on immortality, life and death*, pp. 167–78. New York: Routledge.

Leppa, C. and Terry, L. (2004) Reflective practice in nursing ethics education: international collaboration. *Journal of Advanced Nursing* 48(2), 195–202.

Lévi-Strauss, C. (1966) *The savage mind (La pensée sauvage).* London: Weidenfeld and Nicolson. (Published in French by Librairie Plon 1962.)

Li, Y. (2000) Geographical consciousness and tourism experience. *Annals of Tourism Research* 27(4), 863–883.

Lichterman, P. (1996) *The Search for Political Community: American Activists Reinventing Commitment.* Cambridge: Cambridge University Press.

Light, D. (2000) Gazing on communism: Heritage tourism and post-communist identities in Germany, Hungary and Romania. *Tourism Geographies* 2(2), 157–176.

Light, D. and Prentice, R. (1994) Who consumes the heritage product? Implications for European heritage tourism. In G. Ashworth and P. Larkham (eds) *Building a New Heritage: Tourism, Culture and Identity in the New Europe*, pp. 90–116. London: Routledge.

Lin, Y-S. and Huang, J-Y. (2006) Internet blogs as a tourism marketing medium: A case study. *Journal of Business Research* 59, 1201–5.

Linder, C. and Marshall, D. (2003) Reflection and phenomenography: towards theoretical and educational development possibilities. *Learning and Instruction* 13(3), 271–84.

Litvin, S. W. (2003) Tourism and understanding: The MBA Study Mission. *Annals of Tourism Research* 30(1), 77–93.

Litvin, S. W., Goldsmith, R. E. and Pan, B. (2008) Electronic word-of-mouth in hospitality and tourism management. *Tourism Management* 29(3), 458–68.

Ljumgman, C. (2005) A rights based approach to development. In B. Mikkelsen (ed.) *Methods for Development Work and Research – A New Guide for Practitioners.* New Delhi: Sage.

Löfgren, O. (1999) *On Holiday: A History of Vacationing.* Berkeley: University of California Press. Cited in Franklin, A. and Crang, M. (2001) The trouble with tourism and travel theory? *Tourist Studies* 1(1), 5–22.

Lonely Planet (2006) *Lonely Planet Bluelist 2007.* London: Lonely Planet Publications.

Luck, M. (2003) Education on marine mammal tours as agent for conservation – but do tourists want to be educated? *Ocean & Coastal Management* 46, 943–56.

Ludvigsen, A. (2002) *Langa is not an island. Township tourism in South Africa.* Unpublished Masters Thesis. Copenhagen: University of Copenhagen.

Lury, C. (1996) *Consumer Culture.* Cambridge: Polity Press.

Lynch, K. (1981) *The Theory of Good City Form.* Cambridge, Mass.: MIT Press.

McAdam, D. and Rucht, D. (1993) The cross-national diffusion of movement ideas. *AAPSS Annals* 528, 56–74.

McCabe, S. and Foster, C. (2006) The role and function of narrative in tourist interaction. *Journal of Tourism and Cultural Change* 4(3), 194–215.

MacCannell, D. (1973) Staged authenticity: arrangements of social space in tourist settings. *The American Journal of Sociology* 79(3), 589–603.

MacCannell, D. (1976) *The Tourist: A New Theory of the Leisure Class.* New York: Schocken Books.

MacCannell, D. (1989) *The Tourist: A New Theory of the Leisure Class,* 2nd edn. New York: Schocken Books.

MacCannell, D. (1992) *Empty Meeting Grounds: The Tourist Papers.* London: Routledge.

MacCannell, D. (1999) *The Tourist: A New Theory of the Leisure Class,* 3rd edn. London: University of California Press.

McGehee, N. (2002) Alternative tourism and social movements. *Annals of Tourism Research,* 29(1), 124–43.

MacGonagle, E. (2006) From dungeons to dance parties: contested histories of Ghana's slave forts. *Journal of Contemporary African Studies* 24(2), 249–60.

McGrath, A. (1991) Travels to a distant past: the mythology of the outback. *Australian Cultural History* 10, 1113–24.

McGregor, E. and Boorman, C. (2005) *Long Way Round: Chasing Shadows Across the World.* London: Sphere.

McGuinness, M. and Simm, D. (2005) Going global? Long-haul fieldwork in undergraduate geography. *Journal of Geography in Higher Education* 29(2), 241–53.

McIntosh, A. and Prentice, R. (1999) Affirming authenticity: consuming cultural heritage. *Annals of Tourism Research* 26(3), 589–612.

McIntosh, A. and Thyne, M. (2005) Understanding tourist behaviour using means-end chain theory. *Annals of Tourism Research* 32 (1), 259–62.

McKeown, B. and Thomas, D. (1988) *Q Method.* Newbury Park: Sage.

McLuhan, M. (1962) *The Gutenberg Galaxy.* Toronto: University of Toronto Press.

McMichael, P. (2004) *Development and Social Change: A Global Perspective,* 3rd edn. California: Sage.

Machado, D. S. (2007) *Turismo de Favela e Desenvolvimento Sustentável Um estudo do Turismo de Favela no bairro de Vila Canoa, zona sul do Rio de Janeiro.* Rio de Janiero: PUC–Rio, Departamento de Servico Social.

Machado da Silva, L. (1994) Violência e sociabilidade: tendências da atual conjuntura urbana no Brasil. In L. Queiroz Ribeiro and O. A. Santos Jr (eds) *Globalização, Fragmentação e Reforma Urbana.* Rio de Janeiro, Ed. Civilização Brasileira.

Mack, R. W., Blose, J. E. and Pan, B. (2008) Believe it or not: Credibility of blogs in tourism. *Journal of Vacation Marketing* 14(2), 133–44.

Maguire, J. (1993) Globalization, sport and national identities: 'The Empire Strikes Back'? *Loisir et société/Society and Leisure* 16(2), 293–322.

Malloy, D. and Fennell, D. (1998) Codes of ethics and tourism: an exploratory content analysis. *Tourism Management* 19, 453–61.

Mangan, J. A. (2006) A personal perspective: twenty-five years, IJHS. *The International Journal of the History of Sport* 23(1), 1–2.

Manning, R. E. (1986) *Studies in Outdoor Recreation. A Review and Synthesis of the Social Science Literature in Outdoor Recreation.* Corvallis, Oregon: Oregon State University Press.

Margraf, M. (2006) *Community Based Tourism: Ein Instrument nachhaltiger Entwicklung ehemals benachteiligter Bevölkerungsgruppen am Beispiel Kaymandi, Südafrika.* Saarbrücken: VDM-Verlag.

Marín, K. (1993) Estas vacaciones, a la Guerra, El 'turismo bélico' es la última oferta de tiempo libre ideada por un empresario milanés, *El País*, 30 January 1993. Online. Available at: http://www.elpais.com/articulo/ultima/ITALIA/vacaciones/guerra/elpepiult/19930130elpepiult_1/Tes.

Mariovet, S. (2006) UEFA Euro 2004 Portugal: The social construction of a sports mega-event and spectacle. *The Sociological Review* 54(2), 125–43.

Marsh, P. (2007) *Backcountry adventure as a spiritual experience: A means-end study*. Unpublished PhD thesis, Indiana University.

Masberg, B. and Silverman, L. (1996) Visitor experiences at heritage sites: a phenom-enological approach. *Journal of Travel Research*, 34(4), 20–25.

Masters, K. and Ogles, B. (1995) An investigation of the different motivations of marathon runners with varying degrees of experience. *Journal of Sport Behavior* 18, 69–79.

Masters, K., Ogles, B. and Jolton, J. (1993) The development of an instrument to measure motivation for marathon running: The Motivations of Marathoners Scales (MOMS). *Research Quarterly for Exercise and Sport* 64, 134–43.

May, T. (2004) *Pesquisa social : questões, métodos e processos*. Porto Alegre: Artmed.

Mayo, J. A. (2003a) Journal writing revisited: Using life-adjustment narratives as an autobiographical approach to learning in psychology of adjustment. *Journal of Constructivist Psychology* 16(1), 37–47.

Mayo, J. A. (2003b) Observational diary: The merits of journal writing as case-based instruction in introductory psychology. *Journal of Constructivist Psychology* 16(3), 233–47.

Meethan, K. (1996) Consuming (in) the civilized city. *Annals of Tourism Research* 23(2), 322–40.

Mehmetoglu, M. and Olsen, K. (2003) Talking authenticity: what kind of experiences do solitary travelers in the Norwegian Lofoten Islands regard as authentic? *Tourism, Culture & Communication* 4(3), 137–52.

Mellor, P. (1993) Death in high modernity: the contemporary presence and absence of death. In D. Clarke (ed.) *The Sociology of Death*, pp. 11–30. Oxford: Blackwell.

Mellor, P. and Shilling, C. (1993) Modernity, self-identity and the sequestration of death. *Sociology* 27, 411–31.

Melucci, A. (1996) *Challenging Codes: Collective Action in the Information Age*. Cambridge, UK: Cambridge University Press.

Menezes, P. (2007a) Turismo e favela: reflexões sobre ética e fotografia. *Dialogando no Turismo* 1(3), 10–30.

Menezes, P. (2007b) *Gringos e câmeras na favela da Rocinha*. Monografia (Bacharelado) – Departamento de Ciências Sociais da Universidade do Estado do Rio de Janeiro.

Menezes, P. (2007c) *Objeto e sujeito da fotografia: gringos e câmeras na favela da Rocinha*. Cadernos de Antropologia e Imagem, n. 25. Rio de Janeiro: Contra Capa/UERJ, NAI.

Meschkank, J. (2009) *Untersuchungen zu Raum und Kulturkonstruktionen anhand des Slumtourismus in Mumbai, Indien*. Unpublished Masters Thesis. Potsdam: University of Potsdam.

Miceli, S. (2001) Artifício e Autenticidade: O turismo como experiência antropológica. In Alvaro Banducci jr e Margarita Baretto. *Turismo e identidade local: uma visão antropológica*. Campinas: Papirus.

Middleton, M. C. (2003) City settings, structures and sensitivities: The case of Manchester. *Tourism* 51(2), 171–92.

Middleton, M. C. (2007) Framing urban heritage and the international tourist. *Journal of Heritage Tourism* 2(1), 1–13.

Miles, W. (2002) Auschwitz: museum interpretation and darker tourism. *Annals of Tourism Research* 29(4), 1175–78.

Milne, G. and McDonald, M. (1999) *Sport Marketing: Managing the Exchange Process*. Sudbury, MA: Jones and Bartlett Publishers.

Mitchell, M. (2007) *Remember me: constructing immortality, beliefs on immortality, life and death*. New York: Routledge.

Modlin, E. A. (2008) Tales told on the tour: mythic representations of slavery by docents at North Carolina plantation museums. *Southeastern Geographer* 48(3), 265–87.

Montes, J. and Butler, D. L. (2008) Debating race through the tourist plantation: analyzing a New York Times conversation. *Southeastern Geographer* 48(3), 303–15.

Mooney, L. and Edwards, B. (2001) Experiential learning in sociology: service learning and other community-based learning initiatives. *Teaching Sociology* 29(2), 181–94.

Morgan, M. (2007) 'We're not the Barmy Army!': Reflections on the sports tourist experience. *International Journal of Tourism Research* 9, 361–72.

Morgan, N. and Pritchard, A. (2005) On souvenirs and metonymy: Narratives of memory, metaphor and materiality. *Tourist Studies* 5(1), 29–53.

Morinis, E. (1992) Introduction: the territory of the anthropology of pilgrimage. In E. Morinis (ed.) *Sacred Journeys: The Anthropology of Pilgrimage*, pp. 1–27. Westport, Conn.: Greenwood Press.

Moscardo, G. (1998) Interpretation and sustainable tourism: functions, examples and principles. *The Journal of Tourism Studies* 9(1), 2–13.

Mosher, S. (1991) Fielding our dreams: rounding third in Dyersville. *Sociology of Sport Journal* 8, 272–80.

Nairn, K. (2005) The problems of utilizing 'direct experience' in geography education. *Journal of Geography in Higher Education* 29(2), 293–309.

Nash, D. (1996) *Anthropology of Tourism*. Oxford: Pergamon.

National Park Service (n.d.) *Celebrate African American Heritage in America's National Parks*. Online. Available at: http://www.nps.gov/pub_aff/african_am/celebrate.htm (Accessed 22 December 2008).

National Park Service (n.d.) *The Significance of Magnolia Plantation*. Online. Available at: http://www.nps.gov/cari/historyculture/upload/significanceofmagnoliaplantation wpictures.pdf (Accessed 22 December 2008).

National Park Service (2008). *A Broader View: Exploring the African Presence in Early New York* Online. Available at: http://www.nps.gov/afbg/upload/African%20Presence%20walking%20tour_2008-2.pdf (Accessed 10 February 2009).

Nauright, J. (1996) 'A Besieged Tribe'?: Nostalgia, white cultural identity and the role of rugby in a changing South Africa. *International Review for the Sociology of Sport* 31(1), 69–85.

Nielsen, N., Bech-Larsen, T. and Grunert, K. (1998) Consumer purchase motives and product perceptions: A laddering study on vegetable oil in 3 Countries. *Food Quality and Preference* 6, 455–66.

Nielson, P. (1999) Knowledge by doing. *Journal of Tourism Research* 14, 278–301.

Nixon, H. L. and Frey, J. H. (1995) *A Sociology of Sport.* London: Wadsworth. Cited in Weed, M. and Bull, C (2004) *Sports Tourism: Participants, Policy and Providers.* Oxford: Elsevier Butterworth Heinemann.

Nonaka, I. and Konno, N. (1998) The concept of 'ba': building a foundation of knowledge creation. *California Management Review* 40(3), 40–54.

Nonnecke, B. and Preece, J. (1999) Shedding light on lurkers in online communities. In K. Buckner (ed.) *Ethnographic Studies in Real and Virtual Environments: Inhabited Information Spaces and Connected Communities*, pp. 123–28. January, 24–26. Edinburgh.

Noy, C. (2004) This trip really changed me: Backpackers' narratives of self-change. *Annals of Tourism Research* 31(1), 78–102.

Nuryanti, W. (1996) Heritage and postmodern tourism. *Annals of Tourism Research* 23(2), 249–60.

O'Connor, P. (2008) User-generated content and travel: A case study on TripAdvisor.com. In P. O'Connor, W. Höpken and U. Gretzel (eds) *Information and Communication Technologies in Tourism 2008*, pp. 47–58. Vienna, Austria: Springer Verlag.

Ogles, B. and Masters, K. (2000) Older versus younger adult male marathon runners: Participative motives and training habits. *Journal of Sport Behavior* 23(3),1–14.

Ogles, B. and Masters, K. (2003) A typology of marathon runners based on cluster analysis of motivations. *Journal of Sport Behavior* 26(1), 69–85.

Oh, H. (2001) Revisiting importance-performance analysis. *Tourism Management* 22(6), 617–27.

Oldenburg, R. (1989) *The Great Good Place – Cafes, Coffee Shops, Community Centers, Beauty Parlors, General Stores, Hangouts and How They Get Through the Day.* New York: Paragon House.

Oldenburg, R. and Brissett, D. (1982) The Third Place. *Qualitative Sociology* 5(4), 265–84.

Orams, M. (1994) Creating effective interpretation for managing interaction between tourist and wildlife. *Australian Journal of Environmental Education* 10, 21–31.

O'Reilly, C. C. (2005) Tourist or traveller? Narrating backpacker identity. In A. Jaworski and A. Pritchard (eds) *Discourse, Communication and Tourism*, pp. 150–72. Tonawanda, NY: Channel View Publications.

Osterreith, A. (1997) Pilgrimage, travel and existential quest. In R. Stoddard and A. Morinis (eds) *Sacred Places, Sacred Spaces: The Geography of Pilgrimages, Geoscience and Man*, pp. 25–39. Baton Rouge: Dept of Geography and Anthropology, Louisiana State University.

Palmer, J. F. (1997) Stability of landscape preferences in the face of change. *Landscape and Urban Planning* 37(1–2), 109–13.

Pan, B., MacLaurin, T. and Crotts, J. C. (2007) Travel blogs and the implication for destination marketing. *Journal of Travel Research* 46, 35–45.

Parajuli, P. (2001) Power and knowledge in development discourse: new social movements and the State of India. In G. Jayal (ed.) *Democracy in India*, pp. 258–88. New Delhi: Oxford University Press.

Parasuraman, A., Zeithaml, V. A. and Berry, L. L. (1994) Alternative scales for measuring service quality: a comparative assessment based on psychometric and diagnostic criteria. *Journal of Retailing* 70(3), 201–30.

Parrinello G. (1993) Motivation and anticipation in post-industrial tourism. *Annals of Tourism Research* 20(2), 233–49.

Pearce, P. (1982) *The Social Psychology of Tourist Behaviour*. Oxford: Pergamon Press.

Pearce, P. (1988) *The Ulysses Factor: Evaluating Visitors in Tourist Settings*, New York: Springer Verlag.

Pearce, P. (2005) *Tourist Behaviour: Themes and Conceptual Schemes*. Clevedon: Channel View Publications.

Pearce, P. and Foster, F. (2007) A 'University of Travel': backpacker learning. *Tourism Management* 28, 1285–98.

Pearce, P. and Moscardo, G. (1986) The concept of authenticity in tourist experience. *Australian and New Zealand Journal of Sociology* 22, 121–32.

Petty, R., McMichael, S. and Brannon, L. (1992) The Elaboration Likelihood Model of Persuasion: applications in recreation and tourism. In M. Manfredo (ed.) *Influencing Human Behavior: Theory and Application in Recreation, Tourism and Natural Resource Management*. Champaign, Illinois: Sagamore.

Phillimore, J. and Goodson, L. (2004) Progress in qualitative research in tourism: epistemology, ontology and methodology. In J. Phillimore and L. Goodson (eds) *Qualitative Research in Tourism: Ontologies, Epistemologies, Methodologies*, pp. 3–29. London: Routledge.

Phillips, W. and Jang, S. (2007) Destination image and visit intention: examining the moderating role of motivation. *Tourism Analysis* 12(4), 319–26.

Pickard, P. (2007) Dark Tourism, in *Lonely Planet Bluelist*, Melbourne: Lonely Planet.

Pitt, D. G. and Zube, E. H. (1979) *The Q sort method: Use in landscape assessment research and landscape planning*. Beverley, Calif.: Pacific SW Forestry and Range Experimental Station.

Pizam, A., Uriely, N. and Reichel, A. (2000) The intensity of tourist-host social relationships and its effects on satisfaction and change of attitudes: the case of working tourists in Israel. *Tourism Management* 21(4), 395–406.

Plack, M., Driscoll, M., Blissett, S., McKenna, R. and Plack, T. (2005) A method for assessing reflective journal writing. *Journal of Allied Health* 34, 199–208.

Plack, M., Driscoll, M., Marquez, M., Cuppernull, L., Maring, J. and Greenberg, L. (2007) Assessing reflective writing on a pediatric clerkship by using a modified Bloom's taxonomy. *Ambulatory Pediatrics* 7(4), 285–91.

Platzer, H., Blake, D. and Ashford, D. (2000) An evaluation of process and outcomes from learning through reflective practice groups on a post-registration nursing course. *Journal of Advanced Nursing* 31(3), 689–95.

Poon, A. (1989) Competitive strategies for a 'new tourism'. In C. Cooper (ed.) *Progress in Tourism, Recreation and Hospitality Management*, pp. 91–102. London: Belhaven Press.

Poon, A. (1993) *Tourism, Technology and Competitive Strategies*. Wallingford: CABI.

Poria, Y. Butler, R. and Airey, D. (2003) The core of heritage tourism. *Annals of Tourism Research* 30(1), 238–54.

Poria, Y., Reichel, A. and Biran, A. (2006) Heritage site perceptions and motivations to visit. *Journal of Travel Research* 44(3), 318–26.

Porter, R. (1999a) Classics revisited: The hour of Philippe Aries. *Mortality* 4(1), 83–90.

Porter, R. (1999b) *The Greatest Benefit to Mankind. A Medical History of Humanity from Antiquity to the Present*. London: Fontana.

Poster, M. (ed.) (1988) *Jean Baudrillard: Selected Writings – Simulacra and Simulations*. Stanford: Stanford University Press.

Pott, A. (2005) Kulturgeographie beobachtet. Probleme und Potentiale der geographischen Beobachtung von Kultur. *Erdkunde* 2, 89–101.

Pott, A. (2007) *Orte des Tourismus. Eine raum und gesellschaftstheoretische Untersuchung*, Bielefeld: Transcript.

Pott, A. and Steinbrink, M. (2010) Die Kultur des Slum(ming)s. Zur historischen Rekonstruktion eines globalen Phänomens. In H. Wöhler, A. Pott and V. Denzer (eds) *Tourismusräume. Zur soziokulturellen Konstruktion eines globalen Phänomens*. Bielefeld: Transcript (in press).

Prayag, G. and Ryan, C. (2009) From motivations to perceptions of place: the influence of nationality and ethnicity. Paper submitted to *Current Issues in Tourism*.

Preece, J., Nonnecke, B. and Andrews, D. (2004) The top 5 reasons for lurking: Improving community experiences for everyone. *Computers in Human Behavior* 20(2), 201–23.

Prentice, R. and Light, D. (1994) Current issues in interpretive provision at heritage sites. In A. V. Seaton (ed.) *Tourism: The State of the Art*. Chichester: John Wiley & Sons Ltd.

Prentice, R., Witt, S. and Hamer, C. (1998) Tourism as experience: the case of heritage parks. *Annals of Tourism Research* 25(1), 1–24.

Pretes, M. (2002) Touring mines and mining tourists. *Annals of Tourism Research* 29(2), 439–56.

Priest, S. and Bunting, C. (1993) Changes in perceived risk and competence during whitewater canoeing. *Journal of Applied Recreation Research* 18(4), 265–80.

Pronger, B. (1990) *The Arena of Masculinity: Sports, Homosexuality, and the Meaning of Sex*. New York: St. Martin's Press.

Prosser, R. (1992) The ethics of tourism. In D. Cooper and J. Palmer (eds) *The Environment in Question: Ethics and Global Issues*. London: Routledge.

Prstojević, M. (1993) *Sarajevo Survival Guide*. Srajevo: FAMA.

Pruess, H. (2005) The economic impact of visitors at major events multi-sport-events. *European Sport Management Quarterly* 5(3), 283–304.

Pudliner, B. A. (2007) Alternative literature and tourist experience: Travel and tourist weblogs. *Journal of Tourism and Cultural Change* 5(1), 46–59.

Rahnema, M. (1997) Introduction. In M. Rahnema and V. Bawtree (eds) *The Post-Development Reader*, pp. ix–xix. London: Zed Books.

Ramamurthy, A. (2004) Spectacles and illusions: photography and commodity culture. In L. Wells (ed.) *Photography: A Critical Introduction*. New York: Routledge.

Ramchander, P. (2004) *Towards the Responsible Management of the Socio-Cultural Impact of Township Tourism*. Pretoria: University of Pretoria, Department of Tourism Management. Online. Available at: http://upetd.up.ac.za/thesis/available/etd-0826200-30507 (Accessed 16 November 2009).

Ramchander, P. (2007) Township tourism: blessing or blight? The case of Soweto in South Africa. In G. Richards (ed.) *Cultural Tourism: Global and Local Perspectives*, pp. 39–67. New York: Haworth Press.

Ramsay, H. (2005) *Reclaiming Leisure: Art, Sport and Philosophy*. Houndmills: Palgrave Macmillan.

Ramshaw, G. and Gammon, S. (2010) On home ground? Twickenham Stadium tours and the construction of sport heritage. *Journal of Heritage Tourism* 5(2), 87–102.

Rapoport, A. (1976) Environmental cognition in cross-cultural perspectives. In R. G. Golledge and G. T. Moore (eds) *Environmental Knowing: Theories, Research, and Methods*. Pennsylvania: Dowden, Hutchinson and Ross Inc.

Rapoport, A. (1982) *The Meaning of the Built Environment*. Beverley Hills, Calif.: Sage.

Rath, J. (ed.) (2007) *Tourism, Ethnic Diversity and the City*. New York, London: Routledge.

Reed, A. (2004) Sankofa Site: Cape Coast Castle and its museum as markers of memory. *Museum Anthropology* 27(1), 13–24.

Reisinger, Y. (1997) Social contact between tourists and hosts of different cultural backgrounds. In L. France (ed.) *Sustainable Tourism*. London: Earthscan.

Relph, E. (1976) *Place and Placelessness*. London: Pion.

Riley, R. and Love, L. (2000) The state of qualitative tourism research. *Annals of Tourism Research* 27(1), 164–87.

Ritchie, J. R. (1984) Assessing the impact of hallmark events: conceptual and research issues. *Journal of Travel Research* 23(1), 2–11.

Robinson, M. (2004) Narratives of being elsewhere: Tourism and travel writing. In A. Lew, C. M. Hall and A. Williams (eds) *A Companion to Tourism*, pp. 303–15. London: Blackwell.

Robinson, M. and Andersen, H. C. (2002) *Literature and Tourism*. London: Continuum.

Robson, E. (2002) 'An Unbelievable Academic and Personal Experience': issues around teaching undergraduate field courses in Africa. *Journal of Geography in Higher Education* 26(3), 327–44.

Rodaway, P. (1994) *Sensuous Geographies*. London: Routledge.

Rogerson, C. M. (2003) Tourism and transformation. Small enterprise development in South Africa. *Africa Insight* 33(2), 108–14.

Rogerson, C. M. (2004) Urban tourism and small tourism enterprise development in Johannesburg: The case of township tourism. *Geojournal* 60(3), 249–57.

Roggenbuck, J. (1992) Use of persuasion to reduce resource impacts and visitor conflicts. In M. J. Manfredo (ed.) *Influencing Human Behavior: Theory and Application in Recreation, Tourism and Natural Resource Management*. Champaign, Illinois: Sagamore.

Rojek, C. (1993) *Ways of Escape: Modern Transformations in Leisure and Travel*. Basingstoke: Macmillan.

Rojek, C. (1995) *Decentering Leisure Theory*. London: Sage.

Rojek, C. (1997) Indexing, dragging and the social construction of tourist sites. In C. Rojek and J. Urry (eds) *Touring Cultures – Transformations of Travel and Theory*, London: Routledge.

Rojek, C. and Urry, J. (eds) (1997) *Touring Cultures*. London: Routledge.

Rolfes, M. (2009) Poverty tourism: theoretical reflections and empirical findings regarding an extraordinary form of tourism. *GeoJournal*, DOI 10.1007/s10708-009-9311-8.

Rolfes, M., Steinbrink, M. and Uhl, C. (2009) *Township as Attraction. An Empirical Study of Township Tourism in Cape Town*. Potsdam: Universitätsverlag.

RoperASW (2002) 2002 *Global Geographic Literacy Survey*. Online. Available at: http://www.nationalgeographic.com/geosurvey2002/download/RoperSurvey.pdf (Accessed 5 November 2007).

Ross, S. and Wall, G. (1999) Evaluating ecotourism: the case of North Sulawesi, Indonesia. *Tourism Management* 20(6), 673–82.

Rudd, M. and Davis, J. (1998) Industrial heritage tourism at the Bingham Canyon Copper Mine. *Journal of Travel Research* 36, 85–89.

Ryan, C. (1991) *Recreational Tourism – A Social Science Perspective*. London and New York: Routledge.

Ryan, C. (1995) Tourism and leisure: the application of leisure concepts to tourist behavior: a proposed model. In A. V. Seaton, C. Jenkins, R. Wood, P. Dieke, M. Bennett, L. R. MacLellan and R. Smith (eds) *Tourism, The State of the Art*, pp. 294–307. London: John Wiley & Sons.

Ryan, C. (1997a) *The Tourist Experience: A New Introduction*, 1st edn. London: Cassell.

Ryan, C. (1997b) Rafting in the Rangitikei, New Zealand: an example of adventure holidays. In D. Getz and S. Page (eds) *The Business of Rural Tourism: International Perspectives*, pp. 162–90. London: International Thomson Business Press.

Ryan, C. (2001) Holidays, sex and identity: a history of social development. In C. Ryan and C. M. Hall. *Sex Tourism: Marginal People and Liminalities*. London: Routledge.

Ryan, C. (2002a) *The Tourist Experience*, 2nd edn. London: Continuum.

Ryan, C. (2002b) Equity, management, power sharing and sustainability – issues of the 'new tourism'. *Tourism Management* 23(1), 17–26.

Ryan, C. (2003) Risk acceptance in adventure tourism: paradox and context. In J. Wilks and S. Page (eds) *Managing Tourist Health and Safety in the New Millennium*, pp. 55–66. Oxford: Pergamon.

Ryan, C. (2007a) Re-enacting the Battle of Aiken: Honour Redeemed. In C. Ryan (ed.) *Battlefield Tourism: History, Place and Interpretation*, pp. 195–206. Oxford: Pergamon.

Ryan, C. (2007b) Yorktown and Patriot's Point, Charleston, South Carolina: Interpretation and Personal Perspectives. In C. Ryan (ed.) *Battlefield Tourism: History, Place and Interpretation*, pp. 211–20. Oxford: Pergamon.

Ryan, C. and Aicken, M. (2005) *Indigenous Tourism: The Commodification and Management of Culture*. Oxford: Pergamon.

Ryan, C. and Gu, H. (2008) Destination branding and marketing: The role of marketing organizations. In H. Oh (ed.) *Handbook of Hospitality Marketing Management*, pp. 383–411. Oxford: Butterworth Heinemann.

Ryan, C. and Gu, H. (2010) *Tourism at a Taoist Site*. Paper submitted for the Asia Pacific Tourism Conference, 2010.

Ryan, C. and Huyton, J. (2000) Who is interested in Aboriginal tourism in the Northern Territory, Australia? A cluster analysis. *Journal of Sustainable Tourism* 8(1), 53–88.

Ryan, C. and Trauer, B. (2005) Adventure tourism and sport: an introduction. In C. Ryan, S. Page and M. Aicken (eds) *Taking Tourism to the Limits*, pp. 143–48. Oxford: Pergamon.

Ryan, C. and Wang, L. (2010) *Tourism Places, Planning and Residing*. Nanking: Nanking University Press (in Mandarin).

Saarinen, J. (1998) The social construction of tourist destinations. The process of transformation of the Saariselkä tourism region in Finnish Lapland. In G. Ringer (ed.) *Destinations. Cultural Landscapes of Tourism*. London: Routledge.

Sachs, W. (1992) One world. In W. Sachs (ed.) *The Development Dictionary*, pp. 102–15. London: Zed Books.

Sanderson, T. (1999) *How to be a Happy Homosexual*. London: The Other Way Press.

Sands, R. (2000) *Sport Ethnography*. Champaign, Ill.: Human Kinetics.

Savage, J. (2005) *England's Dreaming: Sex Pistols and Punk Rock*. London: Faber.

Schmallegger, D. and Carson, D. (2008) Blogs in tourism: Changing approaches to information exchange. *Journal of Vacation Marketing* 14(2), 99–110.

Schröder, H. (2007) Armut live. *Südwind Magazin*, Wien, 2: 24.

Schwandt, T. (1998) Constructivist, interpretivist approaches to human inquiry. In N. Denzin and Y. Lincoln (eds) *The Landscape of Qualitative Research: Theories and Issues*. London: Sage.

Schwandt, T. (2000) Three epistemological stances for qualitative inquiry: interpretivism, hermeneutics, and social constructionism. In N. Denzin and Y. Lincoln (eds) *Handbook of Qualitative Research*, 2nd edn, pp. 189–214. London: Sage.

Scottish Natural Heritage (2004) *Communication, Not Conflict: Using Communication to Encourage Considerate Shared Recreational Use of the Outdoors*. Perth: Scottish Natural Heritage Publications.

Seaton, A. (1996) Guided by the dark: from thanatopsis to thanatourism. *International Journal of Heritage Studies* 2(4), 234–44.

Seaton, A. (1999) War and thanatourism: Waterloo 1815–1914. *Annals of Tourism Research* 26(1), 130–58.

Seaton, T. (2009) Thanatourism and its discontents: An appraisal of a decade's work with some future issues and directions. In T. Jamal and M. Robinson. (eds) *The Sage Handbook of Tourism Studies*, pp. 521–42. London: Sage.

Selby, M. (2004) Consuming the city: conceptualising and researching urban tourist knowledge. *Tourism Geographies* 6(2), 186–207.

Sex Pistols (1977) Holidays in the Sun. *Never Mind the Bollocks – Here are the Sex Pistols*. Wessex Sound Studios, London: Virgin Records (Track One), http://www.sexpistolsofficial.com.

Shaffer, M. S. (2001) *See America First: Tourism and National Identity, 1880–1940*. Washington, DC: Smithsonian.

Shamir, B. (1992) Some correlates of leisure identity salience: three exploratory studies. *Leisure Studies* 24(4), 301–23.

Shandley, R., Jamal, T. and Tanase, A. (2006) Location shooting and the filmic destination: Transylvanian myths and the post-colonial tourism enterprise. *Journal of Tourism and Cultural Change* 4(3), 137–58.

Shariq, S. (1999) How does knowledge transform as it is transferred? Speculations on the possibility of a cognitive theory of knowledgescapes. *Journal of Knowledge Management* 3(4), 243–51.

Sharpley, R. (2005) Travel to the edge of darkness: towards a typology of dark tourism. In C. Ryan, S. Page, and M. Aicken (eds) *Taking Tourism to the Limit: Issues, Concepts and Managerial Perspectives*, pp. 217–28. London: Elsevier.

Sharpley, R. (2009) Tourism, religion and spirituality. In T. Jamal and M. Robinson (eds) *The Sage Handbook of Tourism Studies*, pp. 237–53. London: Sage Publications.

Sharpley, R. and Stone, P. R. (eds) (2009) *The Darker Side of Travel: The Theory and Practice of Dark Tourism*. Clevedon: Channel View Publications.

Shipler, D. K. (1997) *A Country of Strangers: Blacks and Whites in America*. New York: Alfred A. Knopf.

Shipway, R. and Jones, I. (2007) Running away from home: Understanding visitor experiences in sport tourism. *International Journal of Tourism Research* 9, 373–83.

Shipway, R. and Jones, I. (2008) The great suburban Everest: An 'insiders' perspective on experiences at the 2007 Flora London Marathon. *Journal of Sport and Tourism* 13(1), 61–77.

Siegal, S. and Lowe Jr, E. (1995) *Uncharted Lives – Understanding the Life Passages of Gay Men*. New York: Plume/Penguin.

Siegenthaler, P. (2002) Hiroshima and Nagasaki in Japanese guidebooks. *Annals of Tourism Research* 29(4), 1111–37.

Silk, M. (2005) Sporting Ethnography: Philosophy, Methodology and Reflection. In D. Andrews, D. Mason and M. Silk (eds) *Qualitative Methods in Sports Studies*, pp. 65–103. Oxford: Berg.

Simon, T. (1979) *Jupiter's Travels*. Harmondsworth: Penguin Books Ltd.

Simon, T. (2007) *Dreaming of Jupiter*. London: Little, Brown.

Simpson, B. (1993) Tourism and tradition: from healing to heritage. *Annals of Tourism Research* 20(2),164–81.

Simpson, E. and Courtney, M. (2007) A framework guiding critical thinking through reflective journal documentation: A Middle Eastern experience. *International Journal of Nursing Practice* 13, 203–8.

Skeggs, B. (1999) Matter out of place: visibility and sexualities in leisure spaces. *Leisure Studies* 18, 213–32.

Slim, H. (2002) Making moral ground. Rights as the struggle for justice and the abolition of development. In *PRAXIS, The Fletcher Journal of Development Studies* Vol. XVII. As posted on http://fletcher.tufts.edu/praxis/xvii/Slim.pdf, December 2003.

Smith, A. and Stewart, B. (2007) The travelling fan: understanding the mechanisms of sport fan consumption in a sport tourism setting. *Journal of Sport and Tourism* 12 (3/4), 155–81.

Smith, J. K. and Heshusios, L. (1986) Closing down the conversation: the end of the quantitative-qualitative debate amongst educational researchers. *Educational Research* 15, 4–12.

Smith, M. and Duffy, R. (2003) *The Ethics of Tourism Development*. London: Routledge.

Smith, V. (1989) *Hosts and Guests: The Anthropology of Tourism*, 2nd edn. Philadelphia, Pa.: University of Pennsylvania Press.

Smith, V. (1998) War and tourism: an American ethnography. *Annals of Tourism Research* 25(1), 202–27.

Snarey, J. (1985) Cross-cultural universality of social-moral development: a critical review of Kohlbergian research. *Psychological Bulletin* 97, 202–32.

Sontag, S. (1981 [1973]) *Sobre Fotografia*. São Paulo: Companhia das Letras.

Sontag, S. (2003) *Diante da dor dos outros*. São Paulo: Companhia das Letras.

Spalding, E. and Wilson, A. (2002) Demystifying reflection: a study of pedagogical strategies that encourage reflective journal writing. *The Teachers College Record* 104, 1393–1421.

Spivak, G. (1988) Can the subaltern speak? In C. Nelson and L. Grossberg (eds) *Marxism and the Interpretation of Culture*, pp. 271–314. Urbana: University of Illinois Press.

Spivak, G. (1996) Subaltern Talk: Interview with the Editors 1993–94. In D. Landry and G. Maclean (eds) *The Spivak Reader*, pp. 287–308. New York: Routledge.

Springwood, C. F. (1996) *Cooperstown to Dyersville: A Geography of Baseball*. Oxford: Westview Press.

Standeven, J. and De Knop, P. (1999) *Sports Tourism*. Champaign, Ill.: Human Kinetics.

Stebbins, R. (2001) *New Directions in the Theory and Research of Serious Leisure*. Lewiston: Edwin Mellor.

Stebbins, R. (2007) *Serious Leisure: A Perspective For Our Time*. New Brunswick: Transaction.

Stenner, P. and Stainton-Rogers, R. (2004) Q methodology and qualiquantology: the example of discriminating between emotions. In Tod, Z., Nerlich, B., McKeown, S. and Clarke, D. (eds) *Mixing Methods in Psychology*, pp. 101–20. London: Routledge.

Stephenson, W. (1935) Correlating persons instead of tests. *Character and Personality* 4, 17–24.

Stephenson, W. (1953) *The Study of Behavior: Q technique and its Methodology*. Chicago: The University of Chicago Press.

Stephenson, W. (1978) Concourse theory of communication. *Communication* 3, 21–40.

Stevens, T. (2005) Sport and urban tourism destinations: the evolving sport, tourism and leisure functions of the modern stadium. In Higham, J. (ed.) *Sport Tourism Destinations. Issues, Opportunities and Analysis*, pp. 205–21. London: Elsevier.

Stewart, J. J. (1987) The commodification of sport. *International Review for the Sociology of Sport* 22(3), 171–90.

Stone, P. (2006) A dark tourism spectrum: towards a typology of death and macabre related tourist sites, attractions and exhibitions. *Tourism* 54(2), 145–60.

Stone, P. (2009a) Making absent death present: consuming dark tourism in contemporary society. In R. Sharpley and P. Stone (eds) *The Darker Side of Travel: The Theory and Practice of Dark Tourism*, pp. 23–38. Clevedon: Channel View Publications.

Stone, P. (2009b) Dark tourism: morality and new moral spaces. In R. Sharpley and P. Stone (eds) *The Darker Side of Travel: The Theory and Practice of Dark Tourism*, pp. 56–72. Clevedon: Channel View Publications.

Stone, P. (2010) *Death, Dying and Dark Tourism in Contemporary Society: A Theoretical and Empirical Analysis*. Unpublished PhD, University of Central Lancashire (UCLan), UK.

Stone, P. and Sharpley, R. (2008) Consuming dark tourism: a thanatological perspective. *Annals of Tourism Research* 35(2), 574–95.

Strange, C. and Kempa, M. (2003) Shades of dark tourism: Alcatraz and Robben Island. *Annals of Tourism Research* 30(2), 386–403.

Strom Thurmond Institute of Government and Public Affairs (1998) *African-American traveler*. Online. Clemson, SC: Clemson University. Available at: http://www.strom.clemson.edu/publications.html (Accessed 11 February 2009).

Stynes, D. J. and Sun, Y. (2004) *Cane River National Heritage Area: Visitor Characteristics and Economic Impacts*. East Lansing, Mich.: Department of Community, Agriculture, Recreation and Resource Studies, Michigan State University.

Suvantola, J. (2002) *Tourist's Experience of Place*. Aldershot: Ashgate Publishing Ltd.

Swaffield, S. R. and Fairweather, J. R. (1996) Investigation of attitudes towards effects of land use change using image editing and q sort method. *Landscape and Urban Planning* 35(4), 213–30.

Swarbrooke, J. and Horner, S. (1999) *Consumer Behaviour in Tourism*. Oxford: Butterworth Heinemann.

Tagg, J. (1988) *The Burden of Representation: Essays on Photographies and Histories*. London: Macmillan and Amherst, Mass.: University of Massachusetts Press.

Tanner, A. (2008) Sarajevo may rebuild wartime tunnel. *Reuters*, Fri Aug 15. Online. Available at: http://www.reuters.com/article/worldNews/idUSLE71457020080815 (Accessed 15 August 2008).

Taylor, J. (1994) *A Dream of England: Landscape, Photography and the Tourist's Imagination*. Manchester: Manchester University Press.

Tedlock, B. (2000) Ethnography and ethnographic representation. In N. Denzin and Y. Lincoln (eds) *Handbook of Qualitative Research*, 2nd edn, pp. 455–85. London: Sage.

ten Klooster, P. M., Visser, M. and de Jong, M. D. T. (2008) Comparing two image research instruments: The Q-sort method versus the Likert attitude questionnaire. *Food Quality and Preference* 19 (5), 511–18.

Tercier, J. (2005) *The Contemporary Deathbed: The Ultimate Rush*. Basingstoke: Palgrave MacMillian.

Thevenot, G. (2007) Blogging as social media. *Tourism and Hospitality Research* 7, 287–89.

Thoits, P. and Virshup, L. (1997) Me's and we's: forms and functions of social identities. In R. Ashmore and L. Jussim (eds) *Self and Identity*, pp. 106–36. Oxford: Oxford University Press.

Thomas, D. and Baas, L. (1992) The issue of generalization in Q methodology: 'Reliable schematics' revisited. *Operant Subjectivity* 16(1), 18–36.

Thompson, G. (2000) Reaping what was sown on the old plantation. *New York Times*, 22 June. Online. Available at: http://www.nytimes.com/library/national/race/062200thompson-plantation.html (Accessed 11 February 2009).

Thornton, A. (2004) Anyone can play this game: ultimate frisbee, identity and difference. In B. Wheaton *Understanding Lifestyle Sports: Consumption, Identity and Difference*, pp. 175–96. London: Routledge.

Thornton, S. (1995) *Club Cultures: Music, Media and Subcultural Capital*. Cambridge: Polity.

Timmer, A. (2004) Learning through doing: The importance of fieldwork in the education of the undergraduate. *National Association for the Practice of Anthropology Bulletin* 22(1), 106–12.

Towner, J. (1985) The Grand Tour: A key phase in the history of tourism. *Annals of Tourism Research* 15(1), 47–62.

Trail, G. and James, J. (2001) The motivation scale for sport consumption: Assessment of the scale's psychometric properties. *Journal of Sport Behavior* 24(1), 108–27.

Trauer, B. and Ryan, C. (2005) Destination image, romance and place experience: an application of intimacy theory in tourism. *Tourism Management* 26(4), 481–92.

Tribe, J. (1997) The indiscipline of tourism. *Annals of Tourism Research* 24(3), 638–57.

Tribe, J. (2002) The philosophic practitioner. *Annals of Tourism Research* 29(2), 338–57.

Tribe, J. (2006) The truth about tourism. *Annals of Tourism Research* 33(2), 360–81.

Tsang, T. (2000) Let me tell you a story: A narrative exploration of identity in high-performance sport, *Sociology of Sport Journal* 17(1), 44–59.

Tsing, A. (2000) The global situation. *Cultural Anthropology* 15(3), 327–60.

Tuan, Y. F. (1974) *Topophilia*. Englewood Cliffs, NJ.: Prentice Hall.

Tuan, Y. F. (1998) *Escapism*. London: John Hopkins University Press.

Tunbridge, J. and Ashworth, G. (1996) *Dissonant Heritage: The Management of the Past as a Resource of Conflict*. New York: John Wiley & Sons.

Turner, L. and Ash, J. (1975) *The Golden Hordes: Tourism and the Pleasure Periphery*. London: Constable.

Turner, V. (1969, 1977) *The Ritual Process: Structure and Anti-Structure*. London: Routledge and Kegan Paul.

Turner, V. (1974) *Dramas, Fields and Metaphors: Symbolic Action in Human Society*. Ithica, NY and London: Cornell University Press.

Turner, V. (1982) *From Ritual to Theater: The Human Seriousness of Play*. New York: PAJ Publications.

Turner, V. and Turner, E. (1978) *Image and Pilgrimage in Christian Culture*. New York: Columbia University Press.

Tussyadiah, I. P. and Fesenmaier, D. R. (2008) Marketing places through first-person stories: An analysis of Pennsylvania Roadtripper blog. *Journal of Travel and Tourism Marketing* 25(3–4), 299–311.

Tussyadiah, I. P. and Fesenmaier, D. R. (2009) Mediating tourists experiences: Access to places via shared videos. *Annals of Tourism Research* 36(1), 24–40.

Tylor, E. (1920 [1871]) *Primitive Culture*. New York: J.P. Putnam's Sons. 1.

UNWTO (2009) *World Tourism Barometer* Vol. 7, Issue 3. Madrid: United Nations World Tourism Organisation.

Urban, G. (1996) *Metaphysical Community. The Interplay of the Senses and the Intellect*. Austin: University of Texas Press.

Uriely, N. (2005) The tourist experience: Conceptual developments. *Annals of Tourism Research* 32(1), 199–216.

Urry, J. (1990a) *The Tourist Gaze*, 1st edn. London: Sage Publications.

Urry, J. (1990b) The consumption of 'tourism'. *Sociology* 24(1), 23–35.

Urry, J. (1990c) *O Olhar do Turista: lazer e viagens nas sociedades contemporâneas*. São Paulo: Nobel.

Urry, J. (1994) Cultural change and contemporary tourism. *Leisure Studies* 13(4), 233–38.

Urry, J. (1995) *Consuming Places*. London: Routledge.

Urry, J. (1999) Sensing the city. In D. Judd and S. Fanstein (eds) *The Tourist City*, pp. 71–86. Yale University Press.

Urry, J. (2002) *The Tourist Gaze*, 2nd edn. London: Sage Publications.

U.S. Census Bureau (2000) *Overview of Race and Hispanic Origin*. Online. Available at: http://www.census.gov/prod/2001pubs/c2kbr01-1.pdf (Accessed 11 February 2009).

Valladares, L. (2000) *A Gênese da Favela Carioca*. Revista Brasileira de Ciências Sociais 15 No. 44.

Valladares, L. (2005) *A invenção da favela: do mito de origem a favela.com*. Rio de Janeiro: FGV Editora.

Vannoppen, J., Verbeke, W., Huylenbroek, G. V. and Viaene, J. (2001) Consumer valuation of short market channels for fresh food through laddering. *Journal of International Food and Agribusiness Marketing* 12(1), 41–69.

Van Tuijl, P. (2000) Entering the global dealing room: reflections on a rights-based framework for NGOs in international development. *Third World Quarterly* 21(4), 617–26.

Veijola, S. and Jokinen, E. (1994) The body in tourism. *Theory, Culture and Society* 11, 125–51.

Ventura, Z. (1994) *Cidade Partida*. São Paulo: Companhia das Letras.

Vermeulen, I. E. and Seegers, D. (2009) Tried and tested: The impact of online hotel reviews on consumer considerations. *Tourism Management* 30(1), 123–27.

Viggiano, B. (2008) Dharavi through a peephole. *The Times of India*, 18 May.

Virilio, P. (2006) The Museum of Accidents. *The International Journal of Baudrillard Studies* 3 (Republished and translated for journal from earlier edition).

Visit Bosnia-Herzegovina (2009) Online. Available at: http://www.visit-bosniaherzegovina.com/Sarajevo1984XIVOlympicWinterGames.aspx (Accessed 23 November 2009)

Walmsley, D. and Jenkins, J. (1992) Tourism cognitive mapping of unfamiliar environments. *Annals of Tourism Research* 19(2), 268–86.

Walter, T. (2008) *The Presence of the Dead in Society*. Death and Dying in 18–21 Century Europe Conference, Alba Iulia, Romania, September.

Walter, T. (2009) Dark tourism: mediating between the dead and the living. In R. Sharpley and P. R. Stone (eds) *The Darker Side of Travel: The Theory and Practice of Dark Tourism*, pp. 390–55. Clevedon: Channel View Publications.

Wang, N. (1999) Rethinking authenticity in tourism experience. *Annals of Tourism Research* 26(2), 349–70.

Wang, N. (2000) *Tourism and Modernity: A Sociological Analysis*, Oxford: Pergamon Press.

Wang, Y. and Fesenmaier, D. R. (2004a) Modeling participation in an online travel community. *Journal of Travel Research* 42(3), 261–70.

Wang, Y. and Fesenmaier, D. R. (2004b) Towards understanding members' general participation in and active contribution to an online travel community. *Tourism Management* 25, 709–22.

Wang, Y., Yu, Q. and Fesenmaier, D. R. (2001) Defining virtual tourism community. In P. Sheldon, K. Wöber and D. Fesenmaier (eds) *Information and Communication Technologies in Tourism 2001*, pp. 262–71. Vienna, Austria: Springer Verlag.

Wanhill, S. (2000) Mines – A tourist attraction: Coal mining in industrial South Wales. *Journal of Travel Research* 39, 60–69.

Wann, D. (1995) Preliminary validation of the sport fan motivation scale. *Journal of Sport and Social Issues*, 19, 377–96.

Wann, D. and Dolan, T. (1994) Attributions of highly identified sports spectators. *The Journal of Social Psychology* 134(6),783–92.

Wann, D., Tucker, K. and Schrader, M. (1996) An exploratory examination of the factors influencing the origination, continuation and cessation of identification with sports teams. *Perceptual and Motor Skills* 82, 995–1001.

Wansink, B. (2003) Using laddering to understand and leverage a brand's equity. *Qualitative Market Research: An International Journal* 6(2), 111–18.

Watts, S. and Stenner, P. (2005) Doing Q methodology: Theory, method and interpretation. *Qualitative Research in Psychology* 2(1), 67–91.

Weed, M. (1999) Sports tourism and identity: developing a 'Sports Tourism Participation Model'. *Journal of Sports Tourism*, conference abstract, 191–93.

Weed, M. (2005) Sports tourism theory and method – concepts, issues and epistemologies. Guest Editorial, *European Sport Management Quarterly* (3), 229–42.

Weed, M. (2006) Sports tourism research 2000–2004: A systematic review of knowledge and a meta-evaluation of methods. *Journal of Sport and Tourism* 11(1), 5–30

Weed, M. (2008) *Olympic Tourism*. Oxford: Butterworth-Heinemann.

Weed, M. and Bull, C. (2004) *Sports Tourism: Participants, Policy and Providers.* Oxford: Elsevier Butterworth Heinemann.

Weiler, B. (1991) Learning or leisure? The growth of travel-study opportunities in Australia. *Australian Journal of Leisure and Recreation* 1(1), 19–22.

Weiner, E. (2008) Slum visits: tourism or voyeurism, *New York Times – Travel*, 9 March.

Wellard, I. (2002) Men, sport, body performance and the maintenance of 'exclusive masculinity'. *Leisure Studies* 21, 235–47.

Welz, G. (1993) Slum als Sehenswürdigkeit. Negative Sightseeing im Städtetourismus. In D. Kramer and R. Lutz (eds) *Tourismus-Kultur, Kultur-Tourismus*, pp. 39–53. Münster: Lit-Verlag.

Wenger, A. (2008) Analysis of travel bloggers' characteristics and their communication about Austria as a tourism destination. *Journal of Vacation Marketing* 14(2), 169–76.

Wheaton, B. (2000) Just do it: Consumption, commitment and identity in the windsurfing culture. *Sociology of Sport* 17, 254–74.

White, N. and White, P. (2004) Travel as transition: Identity and place. *Annals of Tourism Research* 31(1), 200–18.

Wickens, E. (1994) Consumption of the authentic: The hedonistic tourist in Greece. In A. V. Seaton, C. Jenkins, R. Wood, P. Dieke, M. Bennett, L. R. MacLellan and R. Smith (eds) *Tourism, the State of the Art*, pp. 818–25. Chichester: John Wiley & Sons.

Wight, C. (2006) Philosophical and methodological praxes in dark tourism: Controversy, contention and the evolving paradigm. *Journal of Vacation Marketing* 12(2), 119–29.

Williams, C. (1994) Exercise and well-being. Unpublished paper to the Sports Science Group, Loughborough University.

Williams, R. M., Wessel, J., Gemus, M. and Foster-Seargeant, E. (2002) Journal writing to promote reflection by physical therapy students during clinical placements. *Physiotherapy Theory and Practice* 18, 5–15.

Willmott, H. (2000) Death. So what? Sociology, sequestration and emancipation. *The Sociological Review* 4, 649–65.

Wilson, A. H. (1988) Reentry: Toward becoming an international person. *Education And Urban Society* 20(2), 197–210.

Winchester, H., Kong, L. and Dunn, K. (2003) *Landscapes: Ways of Imagining the World.* Harlow: Pearson Education Ltd.

Wolcott, H. (1999) *Ethnography: A Way of Seeing.* London: Altamira Press.

Wolf, M. M. (1978) Social validity: The case for subjective measurement, or how applied behavior analysis is finding its heart. *Journal of Applied Behavior* 11, 203–14.

Wong, F. K. Y., Kember, D., Chung, L. Y. F. and Yan, L. (1995) Assessing the level of student reflection from reflective journals. *Journal of Advanced Nursing* 22(1), 48–57.

Wood, L. (1999) Think Pink! Attracting the Pink Pound, *Insights* (January), A107-A110. Cited in H. Hughes (2004) A gay tourism market: Reality or illusion, benefit or burden? *Journal of Quality Assurance in Hospitality and Tourism* 5(2/3/4), 57–74.

Woodside, A. G., Crouch, G. I., Mazanec, J. A., Oppermann, M. and Sakai, M. Y. (2000) *Consumer Psychology of Tourism, Hospitality and Leisure.* Wallingford: CABI.

World Tourism Organisation (WTO) (1999) *Global Code of Ethics for Tourism*. Retrieved 15 September 2009, from http://www.world-tourism.org/code_ethics/eng/brochure.htm.

Xiang, Z. and Gretzel, U. (2010) Role of social media in online travel information search. *Tourism Management* 31(2), 179–88.

Xiang, Z., Wöber, K. and Fesenmaier, D. R. (2008) Representation of the online tourism domain in search engines. *Journal of Travel Research* 47(2), 137–50.

Xie, F. and Liew, A. A. (2008) Podcasting and tourism: An exploratory study of types, approaches and content. *Journal of Information Technology & Tourism* 10(2), 173–80.

Yerkes, R. N. and Dodson, J. D. (1908) The relation of strength of stimulus to rapidity of habit formation. *Journal of Comparative Neurological Psychology* 18, 459–82.

Yiannakis, A. and Gibson, H. (1992) Roles Tourists Play. *Annals of Tourism Research* 19(2), 287–303.

Yoo, K.-H. and Gretzel, U. (2008a) Understanding differences between travel review writers and non-writers. Working Paper. College Station, Tex.: Laboratory for Intelligent Systems in Tourism.

Yoo, K.-H. and Gretzel, U. (2008b) Use and impact of online travel reviews. In P. O'Connor, W. Höpken and U. Gretzel (eds) *Information and Communication Technologies in Tourism 2008*, pp. 35–46. Vienna, Austria: Springer Verlag.

Yoo, K.-H. and Gretzel, U. (2009) What motivates consumers to write online travel reviews? *Journal of Information Technology & Tourism* 10(4), 283–96.

Yoo, K.-H., Lee, Y. J., Gretzel, U. and Fesenmaier, D. R. (2009) Trust in travel-related consumer generated media. In W. Höpken, U. Gretzel and R. Law (eds) *Information and Communication Technologies in Tourism 2009*, pp. 49–60. Vienna, Austria: Springer Verlag.

Young, J. E. (1993) *The Texture of Memory: Holocaust Memorials and Meaning*. New Haven, Conn.: Yale University Press.

Yuill, S. M. (2003) *Dark tourism: understanding visitor motivation at sites of death and disaster*. Master's thesis, Texas A&M University. Online. Available at: http://handle.tamu.edu/1969.1/89 (Accessed 1 November 2008).

Yurchyshyn, A. (2008) *A Dose of Reality. Poverty-tour guides explain the relatively new concept – and show how to find an excursion that's right for you*. Online. Available at: http://www.budgettravel.com/bt-dyn/content/article/2008/01/07/AR2008010701680.html.

Zaluar, A. (2000) *A Máquina e a Revolta*. São Paulo, Brasiliense.

Zaluar, A. and Alvito, M. (2004) *Um século de favela*, 4th edn. Rio de Janeiro: FGV Editora.

Zuvela, M. (2007) Bosnia sells new image as tourist haven, *Reuters Online*, 24 July. Online. Available at: http://uk.reuters.com/article/idUKL1267712220070724 (Accessed 10 December 2009).

Index